TREASURY

of

Baseball

A CELEBRATION OF AMERICA'S PASTIME

CONTRIBUTING WRITERS

PAUL ADOMITES

DICK JOHNSON

LUKE SALISBURY

GLENN STOUT

SAUL WISNIA

PUBLICATIONS INTRNATIONAL, LTD.

CONTRIBUTING WRITERS
....

Paul Adomites is the author of *October's Game* and was a contributing writer to *Total Baseball* and *Encyclopedia of Baseball Team Histories.* He has edited *The Cooperstown Review, The SABR Review of Books,* and *Cooperstown Corner,* and is a frequent sports contributor to *Pirates Magazine* and *In Pittsburgh.* (Chapters 4 and 7)

Dick Johnson serves as curator of the Sports Museum of New England in Cambridge, where he has mounted exhibits celebrating the achievements of the Boston Braves, Women in Sports, and the Boston Bruins. He is book review editor of *New England Sport Magazine* and is co-author of *Ted Williams: A Portrait in Words and Pictures* with Glenn Stout and of *Young At Heart, the Story of Johnny Kelly* with Frederick Lewis. Johnson is a member of the Society of American Baseball Research and is also a founder of the Universal Baseball Association. (Chapter 10)

Luke Salisbury is the author of *The Answer is Baseball* and a freelance baseball writer, lecturer, and sports expert. He is an American sports correspondent for the Japanese newsweekly *AERA.* He once appeared on the Tom Snyder Show following an unsuccessful attempt to take over the Boston Red Sox on behalf of local fans. Salisbury is Associate Professor of Communications at Bunker Hill Community College. (Chapter 9)

Glenn Stout is senior editor of *The Best American Sports Writing* and co-author of *Ted Williams: A Portrait in Words and Pictures* with Dick Johnson. Stout is a freelance sports contributor to many publications, including *New England Sport, The Sporting News, The Official Red Sox Yearbook,* and *The Boston Herald.* He is a member of the Society of American Baseball Research and the Sports Museum of New England. (Chapters 1 and 6)

Saul Wisnia is a sportswriter for *The Washington Post* and a freelance sportswriter. He has written for *The Boston Globe* and the *Boston Red Sox Program Magazine,* and he was editor of the Boston Bruins fan magazine. He has also served as archivist for the Sports Museum of New England and co-hosted a weekly Boston sports radio talk show. (Chapter 2)

_____

Cover illustration: Rene Milot
Chapter opener photo tinting: Sheryl Winser

_____

Contents

·····················

Beginnings of Baseball

THE BIRTH OF AMERICA'S PASTIME

No one person invented baseball, not Abner Doubleday, not Alexander Cartwright. The game's evolution from a number of similar bat-and-ball games—such as cricket and rounders—is a distinctly American story; the development of baseball echoes the transformation of the culture. Beginning as a diversion played by gentlemen, the game's lofty ideals emulated those of cricket. Spread by the Civil War, baseball lost its amateurism in 1869 when the all-professional Cincinnati Red Stockings toured the country. By 1920 it was more business than sport. Baseball changed because America changed, yet it remains truly the National Pastime.

Abner Doubleday did not invent baseball. In fact, there is no evidence that suggests he ever played the game. He may have watched baseball during the Civil War, in which he served as a general in the Union Army, but if he did, the experience apparently left no lasting impression.

Yet the myth that Abner Doubleday invented baseball survives. The Baseball Hall of Fame is located in Cooperstown, New York, precisely because of the spurious belief that Doubleday invented baseball. No single person "invented" baseball. The game evolved from a number of similar ball games of English origin.

The evolution of baseball is a distinctly American story. In tracing the game's development, one also traces the growth and transformation of American culture. The game began as a disorganized diversion played by gentlemen and soon was recognized as the National Pastime. Played by many and enjoyed by all, baseball eventually evolved into a large and complicated business, equal part both sport and entertainment. Baseball changed because America changed. The game is not so much a mirror of America as it is a part of America. The history of the game of baseball is a treasured part of the American story. So why did Abner Doubleday receive all the credit?

In 1907, Abraham Mills, the fourth president of the National League, headed a commission to unearth the genesis of the game. The commission concluded that the game of baseball was of solely American origin and, "according to the best evidence

A West Point cadet in 1839, Abner Doubleday was supposedly a schoolboy chum with Abner Graves; Graves in 1907 convinced the Mills Commission that Doubleday did indeed map out a baseball diamond.

obtainable to date," was created by Abner Doubleday at Cooperstown in 1839.

The committee based its decision on the testimony of an elderly former resident of Cooperstown named Abner Graves. He stated that on one day in 1839, during a game of town ball between the Otsego Academy and Green's Select School, Doubleday divided the players into two sides to play a game he called "Base Ball." From within a six-foot ring, a pitcher threw a ball to a batter, who in turn struck the ball with a bat. Runners scurried around four bases, hence the name "base ball."

This is the first baseball club of Great Britain. It was probably a converted cricket club. A developed sport in Great Britain in the early 19th century, cricket lent early baseball much of its organization.

It was a nice story but entirely untrue. Doubleday was attending the Military Academy in West Point at the time. The commission, in a flush of Anglophobia, simply selected a story that best preserved its desire to "prove" that the American Pastime was, indeed, American in origin. While credible historians knew the commission was wrong, their conclusion passed into the realm of American folklore, and the falsehood has been repeated many times since. But while it is true that the game was not conceived in America, as the nation itself matured, so, too, did baseball grow to adulthood.

Baseball actually evolved from a number of English bat-and-ball games, such as cricket, rounders, one-cat, and town ball. Roughly speaking, in each of these games a batter struck some kind of object with a bat, then raced between two or more points before being put out, either when the object was caught or when it was touched to the runner. Over time, the games blended with one another, changed and evolved. Late in the 18th century, some Americans were already playing a game they called "base ball."

Cricket, the more established of these early games, retained its own identity, and eventually lent baseball much of its structure and terminology. As baseball continued to take shape, two distinct strands emerged. The "Massachusetts Game" featured an irregular, four-sided field of play with four bases. The "striker," or batter, was located some distance from the home base. But the "New York Game" soon supplanted its New England cousin. In 1845, at the suggestion of Alexander J. Cartwright, a bank teller, a number of sporting gentlemen organized the "New York Knickerbocker Club." Many members had belonged to a similar group, "The New York Base Ball Club." The dual activities of the clubs provided the dynamic that led to organized baseball.

Over the next decade, the Knickerbockers and similar clubs slowly but surely adopted a common set of rules. While Cartwright is often incorrectly credited as the rules' sole creator, the clubs developed a basic set of rules to govern the play of the game, eventually resulting in a diamond-shaped infield with four bases set 90 feet apart. The game featured a pitcher who tossed the ball underhanded from 45 feet to a batsman at the home base. A batter was put out when the ball was caught on the fly or one bounce. Each team had nine players, and each inning three outs.

On June 19, 1846, the Knickerbockers played their first official match versus the New York Base Ball Club at the Elysian Fields in Hoboken, New Jersey, with Cartwright the umpire. The Knickerbockers lost, 23-1, in four innings. Yet, for perhaps the

Alexander Joy Cartwright by all accounts had two passions in his life: baseball and fire fighting. Cartwright and others in the Knickerbockers club increased the distance between bases from a more or less 50 feet stretch to a standard 90 feet.

first time, the game that was played was clearly, albeit crudely, recognizable as the game of "baseball."

The game spread quickly among other clubs in and around New York. Within a decade it was being played throughout the Northeast and the Midwest. In 1858, 25 clubs organized to form the National Association of Base Ball Players. The National Association codified the rules, established the nine-inning game, and approved of charging admission for spectators. By 1860 the Association included more than 60 clubs.

Soldiers in the Civil War spread baseball across the country. As it grew in popularity, the game became increasingly commercial. Many players were paid "under the table," and in 1863 the Association grudgingly was forced to accept openly "professional" players. Baseball's "Age of Innocence" was over.

The Cincinnati Red Stockings, created by Cincinnati businessman Aaron Chapman and player-manager Harry Wright, were the first openly professional team. Harry's brother, George, virtually invented the shortstop position and was the game's first star. In 1869, the Red Stockings toured the country and went undefeated in some 60 games, often winning by such scores as 56-12 or 47-4. Within a year, the Red Stockings spawned a host of imitators. The National Association tried to stem the tide of professionalism but failed. The National Association of Professional Baseball Players was formed in March of 1871.

The Association was the first professional baseball league. While poorly organized, the league still worked to further the development of the game. Teams built crude wooden ballparks and paid some players as much as several thousand dollars per year. The Red Stockings moved to Boston and dominated play. The National Association lasted four years before collapsing

Harry Wright is considered by many the first strategic genius in baseball. One of his best strategies was paying his players, especially his brother, George, baseball's first great shortstop.

after the 1875 season when seven of the league's 13 teams failed to finish the schedule.

William Hulbert, owner of the Association's Chicago club, was the driving force behind the creation of the National League in 1876. He raided other Association clubs of their players. Fearing reprisals, he talked a number of investors and several other Association clubs into forming the eight-team National League of Professional Base Ball Clubs. The new National League was a business, and its organization improved markedly on the old Association. The league settled disputes between clubs and cut down on contract-jumping by insisting on tightly written contracts for players. Pitcher and manager Albert Spalding led Hulbert's White Stockings to the first National League pennant in 1876 with a 52-14 record.

The National League initially struggled to survive. On the brink of financial failure in 1879, the league slashed salaries and instituted the "reserve clause" in player contracts, effectively binding a player to a team and keeping salaries low. With the advent of the reserve clause, NL teams started making money.

The league flourished in the 1880s. Pressed by the growth of the rival American Association, in 1883 the NL accepted the AA under the National Agreement as a rival major league. The two circuits agreed to protect each other's territories and respect each other's contracts for their mutual benefit, a relationship put to good use in 1884 when the two leagues combined forces to crush the fledgling Union Association.

William Hulbert was not only involved in the first professional sports league in the United States, the National Association, but he created the most enduring pro sports organization in the country's history, the National League.

Until this time, a handful of black players appeared on the rosters of some clubs, occasionally even playing in exhibition games against National League teams. Moses Fleetwood Walker, a catcher, was a member of the Toledo team when the club joined the American Association in 1884. He appeared in 42 games for Toledo that year, but when Toledo dropped from the Association in 1885, Walker's major-league career ended. While neither the National League nor any other "major" league specifically banned African Americans from playing at any time thereafter, there was a tacit agreement that organized baseball was for whites only. On rare occasions, a few blacks played in the minor leagues, but the vast majority were relegated to all-black "barnstorming" teams or teams in the Negro Leagues that operated outside the reach of organized baseball. Not until 1947, when Jackie Robinson appeared in a Brooklyn uniform, was the color barrier finally lifted.

Rules changed and evolved rapidly. In the 1880s, the pitching distance was increased from 45 to 50 feet, overhand pitching was allowed, and the three-strike, four-ball rule was formally adopted. The result was a faster, quicker, more entertaining game that was increasingly popular.

In an attempt to cash in on America's growing enthusiasm for the game, from 1884 through 1890 the National League and American Association champions met in a postseason series to determine the "Champions of the World." In 1884, the NL Providence Grays beat the New York Mets of the American Association to win the first such championship. The National League dominated early postseason play, winning five of the six series.

Pitchers such as John Clarkson of Chicago and Tim Keefe of New York became stars, pitching 400 to 500 innings each season and often winning 40 games or more. Swaggering outfielder Mike

John McGraw was a top-notch player as well as a great manager during the early part of the century. His ferocious style of play for the 1890s Baltimore Orioles lived on throughout the dead-ball era.

"King" Kelly of Chicago became baseball's first "superstar" and a nationwide celebrity, making off-season theatrical appearances and endorsing a host of commercial products. He was purchased by Boston in 1888 for the then-unbelievable sum of $10,000.

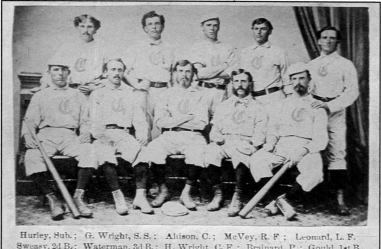

Hurley, Sub.; G. Wright, S.S.; Allison, C.; McVey, R.F.; Leonard, L.F. Sweasy, 2d B.; Waterman, 3d B.; H. Wright, C.F.; Brainard, P.; Gould 1st B.

RED STOCKING B. B. CLUB OF CINCINNATI.

The 1869 Cincinnati Red Stockings, pictured on this trading card, were the first openly all-professional team. There were other teams before this who paid their players, but these transactions were mostly done in secret.

Not all players were as fortunate as Kelly. In 1885, frustrated by the increasing power of the men who owned baseball, star player and lawyer John Montgomery Ward helped organize the Brotherhood of Professional Base Ball Players. Originally a benevolent society, by 1887 the Brotherhood was representing players in labor negotiations. The National League tried to institute a rating system whereby players would be paid up to $2,500 according to rank. The Brotherhood resisted the plan and broke off negotiations with the owners. In 1890, the Brotherhood formed the Players' League, which planned to share profits between players. Most of the game's stars joined the new league.

The two leagues went head-to-head. The National League pulled out all stops to put the Players' League out of business. NL owners bribed players to return, filed lawsuits, lowered ticket prices, and took other measures to undermine the new league. While the NL lost money in 1890, most club owners retained money in reserve. Most PL teams did not, and the loop collapsed after one season. Players had no choice but to return to the NL gaining only self-respect for challenging the status quo.

The American Association collapsed after the 1890 season due to fall-out from the Players' League war. The National League expanded from eight to 12 teams and, despite a decade-long national recession, was able to turn a profit (though it dwindled during the 1890s). In 1893, the pitching distance was pushed back to the now familiar 60 feet 6 inches. League batting averages jumped 35 points.

The game became even more exciting. Represented best by teams in Boston and Baltimore, most clubs featured so-called "scientific" baseball, a hard-fought, aggressive, offensive game. Teams scratched and battled for every run by way of bunts, stolen bases, sacrifices, and the hit and run. While run-scoring and batting averages skyrocketed, the so-called "dead" ball didn't carry particularly well. There was a brief spurt in home runs, but after pitchers adapted to the new pitching distance, the home run became relatively rare.

Teams from Boston, Brooklyn, and Baltimore won every NL pennant between 1892 and 1899. Beginning in 1893, the first-place and second-place clubs met in the Temple Cup series at the end of the season to determine the world championship. The players didn't take the series very seriously, however, and it was discontinued after 1896.

The National League was still struggling for financial survival when the Spanish-American War broke out in 1898. Then the integrity of the league was undermined by the creation of syndicates, whereby one man owned two teams, stripping one club of its best players to supply the other. Fans scoffed at such shenanigans. After the 1899 season, the National League dropped four clubs and again became an eight-team league. The war ended, and profits were up in 1900.

Ban Johnson seized the day. In 1900, he changed the name of the Western League, of which he was founder and president, to the American League. Baseball's existing National Agreement expired.

Ban Johnson was able to do what no other person in history was able to: take on the National League and win. His work with the American League took tremendous foresight, good timing, and a little luck.

King Kelly was one of the original gate attractions in baseball. Upset that the White Stockings sold Kelly to Boston in 1887, many Chicago fans boycotted except when Boston was in town.

Opposite page: Did Shoeless Joe Jackson intentionally try to lose the 1919 World Series? It is a question that still haunts fans.

Due to the NL's recent contraction, there were plenty of available players and a number of cities without major-league teams. Johnson took advantage of the situation and declared in 1901 that the American League was a "major" league. He placed franchises in Chicago, Boston, and six other cities and went into head-to-head competition with the National League. American League teams raided the NL of some of their best players. The American League took advantage of disorganized and divided leadership in the National League. After the 1902 season, the National League sued for peace. Under the National Agreement of 1903, the two leagues were separate but equal organizations, governed by the same rules and recognizing each other's contracts. The same basic dynamic has driven the growth of major-league baseball ever since.

Under the 1903 agreement, the two league presidents, Johnson and Harry Pulliam of the National League, were made members of the National Commission. August "Garry" Hermann, president of Cincinnati and an old friend of Johnson's, served as the chairman and third member of the committee. The Commission, representing the men who owned baseball, ruled the game for the next 17 years. Johnson dominated the triumvirate and earned the appellation "Czar of Baseball."

In 1903, the champions of each league met in the first modern "world's series," as it was initially dubbed by the press. Boston's American League team, featuring such former NL stars as pitcher Cy Young and third baseman Jimmie Collins, defeated the Pittsburgh Pirates in nine games to capture the crown.

The two leagues settled into an easy and mutually profitable peace. Pitching dominated the game. They took advantage of the fact that the same ball was often used for an entire game and became masters of scuffing and scarring the ball to make it sail,

blackening it with tobacco juice to make it hard to see, and throwing spitballs and other trick pitches. Christy Mathewson, Walter Johnson, Grover Cleveland Alexander, and even old Cy Young were masters of the art. It was not unusual for a pitcher to throw 350 innings and pitch in 50 or more games. Often, a team's pitching staff included only five or six men.

Bat control, speed, and defense were at a premium. Such players as Ty Cobb, Nap Lajoie, Honus Wagner, and Joe Jackson were the acknowledged stars of the era. They became adept at hitting the ball between fielders, stealing bases, and disrupting the defense with a well-placed bunt.

The Boston Red Sox paced the American League in its first few seasons before Connie Mack's A's, the White Sox, and then the Detroit Tigers all won pennants. Then the Red Sox took over again. Between 1901 and 1919, Boston won five pennants, Philadelphia six, Chicago four, and Detroit three.

In the National League, John McGraw's New York Giants dominated the league and captured six pennants. Both Pittsburgh and Chicago won four titles, with the Cubs winning a record 116 games in 1906.

American baseball fans responded to the two-league configuration in increasing numbers. Player salaries rose. Stars, such as Cobb, earned as much as $20,000. Nearly every team built new, modern, concrete-and-steel ballparks that seated between 25,000 and 30,000 fans. In the first two decades of the 20th century, baseball became the nation's foremost source of entertainment. Most newspapers featured several pages of baseball news. Fans who couldn't attend games gathered around diamond-shaped scoreboards and followed the players around the bases, as

Because of scouting and business acumen, Jack Dunn built a superb Orioles minor-league team in the early part of the century.

reported by telegraph. Gambling increasingly became an important, although unsanctioned, part of the game.

In 1910, a cork-center baseball was developed that promised an eventual end to the "Dead-Ball Era." In 1914, Jack Dunn, owner and manager of the Baltimore Orioles of the International League, spotted a young incorrigible playing baseball at the St. Mary's Industrial School for Boys. Dunn thought he was the greatest prospect he'd ever seen, had himself named the boy's guardian, and signed him to a contract. His name was George Herman Ruth.

The other Orioles referred to the young Ruth as "Dunn's Babe," and the nickname stuck. After starring as a pitcher for the Orioles, Ruth was purchased by the Boston Red Sox. He became perhaps the best left-hander in the league. Playing with the enthusiasm of a child, Ruth became the most popular player in the game.

Maybe the greatest scout in history, Jack Dunn signed the player many think is the greatest hitter of all time (Babe Ruth) and the player many think is the greatest pitcher of all time (Lefty Grove).

The Federal League was formed in 1914. Taking a lesson from the American League, the new circuit raided rosters of both established leagues. But the Feds lacked the fortuitous timing of Johnson's AL challenge. The Federal League staggered through two seasons, accepted a $5 million buyout from organized baseball, then folded. Teams in both surviving leagues suffered financially but were again able to operate without competition.

In 1918, America entered the Great War and baseball begrudgingly followed. Rosters were decimated as players were either drafted, joined the service on their own, or took exempt jobs in the war industries. The Red Sox were short a few players and Ruth filled in during spring training in the outfield and at first base. He started hitting home runs, and hit them longer, farther, and more often than anyone else in the history of the game. His days as a pitcher were numbered.

Ban Johnson pleaded with the government to let the season continue. Some teams were still struggling to recoup from losses suffered during the clash with the Federal League. In July, the government ruled that the baseball season could continue but cut it short by one month. Fans were distracted by the war, disgusted by Johnson's groveling, and thought many of the players were "slackers" trying to avoid their military obligations. They stayed away from the ballpark in droves, and for the first time in two decades the popularity of baseball seemed to be on the decline.

Rabbit Maranville, left, and Ernie Shore discuss baseball life in the Hub. Shore was a fine pitcher for the Boston Red Sox, while Maranville was a great-fielding shortstop for the Boston Braves.

At the end of the war, all baseball's stars returned. The game was growing again. The Cincinnati Reds surprised everyone by winning the National League pennant. In the American League, Babe Ruth traded his mound duties for a place in the Red Sox outfield and smacked a remarkable 29 home runs, 17 more than any other player. But the Red Sox finished fifth to the Chicago White Sox.

The White Sox were heavy favorites to win the World Series. Several Chicago players performed poorly, however, and Cincinnati won the series five games to three. Rumors abounded that the White Sox had thrown the Series. It was a piece of bad news baseball could ill afford.

As the game entered the third decade of the 20th century, baseball was at a crossroads. From its humble and discrete beginnings on the town greens and open spaces of its cities a century or more before, baseball had slowly evolved into what was truly the

National Pastime. No longer just a game, baseball was increasingly a business—and has become even more so. A fan's relationship to baseball remains essentially personal. Some take pleasure in the game simply by playing, from backyard whiffle ball and Little League to Over-30, Over-40, and Over-50 leagues. Others delve into the game's past and history through its memorabilia and baseball cards, while still more find their pleasure in the stark beauty of baseball's numbers, and rush to the newspaper every morning.

People from all walks of life have discovered the beauty of the game. Poets write baseball poetry, artists paint portraits of players, and baseball is represented in movies, music, and literature. Every evening thousands of fans sit in the ballpark while many more watch the game on television or listen to it on the radio.

The beauty of baseball is that the game played today, while ever-evolving, is still the game played some 150 years ago. Tomorrow's game will share that same history. The treasury of baseball continues to be replenished and renewed.

The 1919 White Sox—known as the "Black Sox" for several members' complicity in throwing the World Series—were originally favored 3-1 and fell to 8-5 underdogs before the Series.

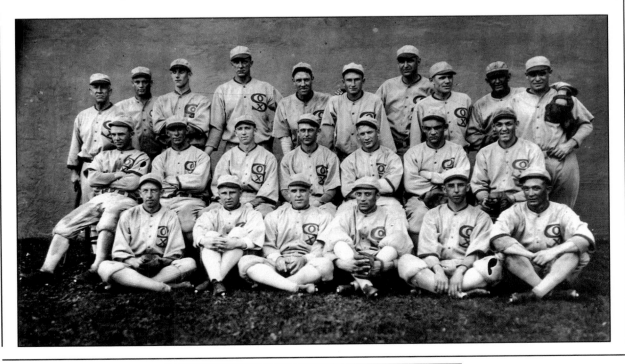

Baseball Headlines

FROM SANDLOTS
TO STADIUMS

Before 1920, "inside baseball"—scoring one run at a time—was the custom, and Ty Cobb was the game's top star. But after Kenesaw Mountain Landis in 1920 banned the "Black Sox" accused of throwing the 1919 Series, baseball looked for a new avenue to attract patrons. Babe Ruth delivered with his bat. In 1920 Ruth demolished his own home run record with 54 homers—no other team hit as many that year—and his Yankees became baseball's first 1 million-drawing team.

Broadcast revenue generated profit, and the 1953 Braves' move to Milwaukee presaged franchise shifts to follow market share. With free agency, players began to receive their share in the business of baseball.

BLACK SOX, BAMBINO, AND BIG BUCKS

For most of its existence before 1920, baseball had been played one run at a time—with bunts, steals, and hit-and-run plays the preferred offense. The tactic was known as "inside baseball," and Ty Cobb—who utilized it with great success—was the game's top star. Cobb never hit more than nine home runs, but routinely notched more than 50 stolen bases (his high of 96 stood as a record for nearly 50 years) and 100 runs a sea- son with an aggressive, surly style, including spike-first slides. He was at once baseball's most respected and hated player, and his lifetime aver- age of .367 and 12 batting titles in 13 years going into 1920 left no doubt he was also deserving of its top salary of $30,000.

But Cobb's popularity and that of baseball itself was challenged that season, when it was proven that members of the Chicago White Sox had conspired to throw the 1919 World Series. Chicago first baseman Chick Gandil and pitch- er Eddie Cicotte had been frustrated by the poor salaries given them by notoriously cheap White Sox owner Charlie Comiskey. Eliciting the aid of both gamblers and teammates, they fixed the

Kenesaw Mountain Landis (left) in 1931 presented gold watches to the Philadelphia A's to observe their second consecutive world title.

best-of-nine Series with the Cincinnati Reds. As baseball's first commissioner, Judge Kenesaw Mountain Landis won strong public support when he banished from baseball for life the eight players accused in the conspiracy.

Another person went even further in restoring the game's image—George Herman Ruth. Ruth was as uproariously loud as Ty Cobb was steely silent, as uncultured and untamed as Cobb was cool and precise. Ruth was, in fact, everything his predecessor was not, but he would wrench the title of baseball's greatest star away from Cobb by taking a new approach to an old sport—an approach a disillusioned fandom could identify with and emulate.

Once the best left-handed pitcher in the game, Ruth was moved to the outfield by the world champion Boston Red Sox in 1919 and promptly set a major-league record with 29 home runs. Even as rumors of the Black Sox scandal were beginning to unfold, most of the baseball news over the winter of 1919 and 1920 had centered on Ruth's sale to the Yankees by Boston owner Harry Frazee for a record $125,000 cash and a $300,000 loan against Fenway Park's mortgage. The move has forever haunted the Red Sox, and most fans agree it was

Chick Gandil, the ringleader of the Black Sox conspiracy, was a line-drive-hitting, good-fielding first baseman.

the biggest mistake in baseball history.

Once in New York, Ruth took advantage of new rules outlawing the spitball and other trick pitches and demolished his old record with 54 homers for the Yankees in 1920. The total was even more astounding considering no other team hit as many, and Ruth showed he was no mere slugger by also notching a .376 average and team-high 14 steals. Matching his powerful stroke with an equally electrifying enthusiasm for life and its pleasures (including a voracious appetite for women, food, and spirits), the Babe packed ballparks throughout the league and enabled the Yankees to become the first 1-million-drawing team in baseball.

Ruth's achievements ushered in a new era of power and offensive play, and league batting averages leaped in 1921 from a 15-year mean of .250 to beyond .285, where they would remain more or less for the next decade. An embittered Cobb would never accept the new style, but fans were obviously ready for a change. The abandonment of inside baseball for the "bam game" accompanied a similar change in moods and tastes occurring throughout the country. Worn out and disgruntled by World

War I, Americans were learning to live for themselves and the moment. A dynamic advertising industry and its newest agent—the radio—set the stage for heroes to emerge, and of those who did only Charles Lindbergh would challenge the Babe for popularity.

Ruth was a complete player who hit .342 lifetime and won 20 games prior to his shift to the outfield, but it was his towering home runs that secured his legend. Big hits meant big crowds, and big crowds meant big money. After Ruth's $20,000 salary was more than doubled to $41,000 the following year, more players began swinging for the fences and bigger contracts. No team before Ruth's 1920 Yankees had ever hit 100 homers, but by 1925 nine had accomplished the feat. The 16 major-league clubs had combined for 338 homers in 1917; in 1925 they would accumulate 1,167. Earned

run averages shot up accordingly (from around 2.85 to over 4.00), but nobody, including the pitchers, was complaining. Seven teams set attendance records in 1920, and that meant more money for all.

In 1924 Yankee owner Jake Ruppert admitted his players had been averaging $12,000 a season since Ruth's first year with the club, and although no other team could match such generosity, other stars were able to gain hefty raises thanks to the Babe. Cobb commanded $70,000 a year as his career wound down, and Cardinals great second baseman and manager Rogers Hornsby collected $42,000 annually after three .400 seasons. Ruth himself reached a high of $80,000 in 1930, and when told he was making more than President Hoover quickly replied, "I had a better year."

In addition to changing the game itself, Ruth helped alter the way ballplayers were viewed and treated off the field. Rising to stardom just as flash photography, movies, and radio were emerging, he became the most photographed and recognizable person in America. The fact he not only accepted his lack of privacy but relished in it while maintaining his uproarious behavior—upon greeting President Calvin Coolidge, he commented, "Hot as hell, ain't it Prez?"—only added to his legend. By consistently capturing headlines, the Babe enabled baseball to hold off threats to its popularity from other sports—such as football, tennis, and golf—while giving all players a chance to bask in his glow.

Above: Babe Ruth (left) signs a $70,000 contract for 1928 with Yankee owner Jacob Ruppert. *Opposite page:* Before the Babe, Ty Cobb was the biggest gate attraction. Cobb started earning $20,000 in 1918, and he made more beginning in 1921. In one season, 1927, Cobb may have outearned Ruth, making $70,000 to $80,000.

Ruth was among the first to "ghost-write" articles and books with the help of sportswriter-agent Christy Walsh, and soon dozens of stars were adding their names to others' work for big profit. Babe's face appeared in endorsements of everything from Wheaties to tobacco to underwear, and in time the faces of Lou Gehrig and Lefty Grove were popping up as well. Ruth went on postseason barnstorming tours, others followed; Ruth appeared on the radio, others did too. Almost every marketing and promotional trend the Babe set was picked up by fellow ballplayers, giving stars and even average performers a chance to consistently pick up extra income.

The stock market crash and subsequent Depression would cut deeply into baseball attendance and profits. Salary levels would flatten out, drop, and not rise significantly again for 10 years or more. While the attendance at the average game in the decade of the 1920s was 7,500, the attendance at the average game in the 1930s was 6,600. But the wheels of progress put in motion by Ruth never really stopped spinning; ballplayers were celebrities no matter what the era, and home runs always meant excitement and a hefty paycheck. Television and expansion only strengthened baseball's image as the National Pastime.

Today, however, that image is in jeopardy. The autographs that Ruth and his contemporaries spent hours giving out free have become a valuable commodity, and players receive five-figure paychecks for a couple of hours spent

signing. Whereas baseball once dominated the sports pages only for its on-the-field activities, there are now as many headlines surrounding salary disputes and court appearances as game-winning homers.

Few players possess major corporate sponsorships, and while television viewers routinely see such basketball superstars as Shaquille O'Neal and David Robinson endorsing everything from sneakers to soda pop, the only major-leaguer who got significant air play in 1993 was 46-year-old Nolan Ryan. White Sox slugger Frank Thomas has an $8 million deal from an athletic shoe company, but where are the endorsements for Barry Bonds and Ken Griffey Jr.?

Baseball is at a crossroads. There are many young superstars of all nationalities playing today. The marketability of these players is not being utilized, and as pro basketball, football, and hockey continue to make promotional strides, a solution needs to be found to the exposure problem the same way David Stern cleaned up the moribund NBA 15 years ago.

The game doesn't need another George Herman Ruth. It just needs to get its current crop of players some of the attention the Babe used to get just for eating a hot dog.

Opposite page: Babe Ruth, left, and Lou Gehrig had incongruous salaries. Gehrig's largest salary topped out at about $44,000, while for many years Ruth made twice that. After asking the frugal Yankee GM Ed Barrow for a raise, Joe DiMaggio was told that although he was young he was making only $1,000 less than Gehrig, who had been a Yankee for years. DiMaggio replied, "Mr. Barrow, there is only one answer to that—Mr. Gehrig is terribly underpaid."

SIGHTS AND SOUNDS OF THE NATIONAL PASTIME

◆

Before Aug. 5, 1921, the only way to follow a major-league baseball team besides going to the ballpark was through the game accounts, columns, and sacred boxscores found in the daily newspapers. On that afternoon, however, the way fans viewed the sport and how it viewed itself as a commercial venture would be forever altered. Harold Arlin broadcast the first major-league baseball game—from Forbes Field in Pittsburgh between the Pirates and the Phillies—over radio station KDKA.

Today, baseball is being sent around the world on radio and television. Cable superstations have become a huge portion of team revenue, and players heard and seen on a regular basis have become more visible and rich than ever before. Broadcasters have even become celebrities themselves, and the game a means of entertainment as well as sport.

The original baseball broadcaster, Harold Arlin (right), joins Bob Prince on KDKA. Arlin also called the first football broadcast, in 1921, between Pitt and West Virginia.

In the beginning, of course, there were glitches. Radio transmitters often didn't work, and Arlin was once forced to imitate Babe Ruth for an entire broadcast when the Babe himself was rendered speechless by the microphone. Still, the medium began to catch on, and by the next autumn 5 million fans listened over a three-station "network" as legendary *New York Herald* sportswriter Grantland Rice broadcast the World Series from the Polo Grounds. More than 3 million American homes now possessed a radio, but many fans caught the action in storefronts, cafes, and street corners, listening to receivers through open windows. A love affair was born, a connection between fans, players, and announcers bringing them together.

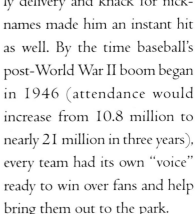

Harold Arlin

Mesmerized, folks continued to tune in. By the early 1930s there were 18 million radios in American homes plus many more in cars, and in 1933 owners finally became enlightened and began charging for World Series broadcast rights. Ford paid $100,000 for rights to the 1934 Tigers-Cardinals Series, and baseball's overall radio revenue skyrocketed from less than $20,000 in 1933 to $830,000 six years later. Sponsors ranged from gasoline and cigarette companies to cereal manufacturers and drug-stores, and everybody profited.

When 50,000-watt WOR signed up cultured, straight-talking Southerner Red Barber to do every home and away Dodger game in 1939, the Brooklyn club received $77,000 in sponsorship rights. Broadcasting was still only a tiny portion of a baseball team's total revenue, but the numbers of listeners (over 25 million for the 1942 World Series) made it apparent the money was only going to get better. Following Brooklyn's lead, the Yankees responded with excitable, admittedly partisan Mel Allen—whose friendly delivery and knack for nicknames made him an instant hit as well. By the time baseball's post-World War II boom began in 1946 (attendance would increase from 10.8 million to nearly 21 million in three years), every team had its own "voice" ready to win over fans and help bring them out to the park.

But as local and national stations battled for control of America's 56 million radios, a new medium was emerging. Few people owned TV sets when Ivy League foes Princeton and Columbia battled in baseball's first telecast of May 17, 1939, but that would change quickly. By the time RCA introduced the first postwar sets in 1946, televisions were being bought at an increasingly rapid rate by Americans who viewed them as a piece of the good life as vital as a house in the suburbs.

Once again there was money to made, and this time most baseball owners would not take quite so long to catch on. When the Yankees signed a $75,000 deal with DuMont that year,

Grantland Rice (right) and Yankee catcher Bill Dickey hit the links. Rice was America's most treasured and respected sportswriter when he went on the air in 1922. He coined the phrase, "It's not whether you win or lose, it's how you play the game."

Red Barber was the first baseball broadcaster on television, as well as being New York City's first baseball broadcaster on radio.

they became the first professional sports team to sell their own television rights. NBC began broadcasting major-league games in 1947, and a revolution was underway. When the Boston Braves and Cleveland Indians squared off in the 1948 World Series, more than 50,000 ticketless fans gathered outdoors a few miles from Braves Field to watch the action on 100 television sets assembled on the Boston Common. Overall, 7.1 million watched the Series on TV—more than 20 times the number that saw it in person.

Radio and television had combined for only 3 percent of baseball's total revenue in 1946, but within 10 years that figure had risen to 16.8 percent. All-Star Game and World Series rights netted the majors $1.2 million annually from 1951 to '56, and 15 of the major's 16 teams had local television contracts netting them an average of $200,000 per club by 1953. Yet while broadcast revenue skyrocketed in the first half of the 1950s, overall baseball revenue dropped from $65 million to $60 million.

The attendance boom of the late 1940s had been followed by a severe decline—from 21.3 million in 1948 to 14.4 million five years later—and TV was seen as the culprit. The November 1952 *Baseball* magazine addressed the issue under a headline reading "TV Must Go . . . Or Baseball Will." The dwindling crowds likely had more to do with decaying ballparks, night games, the move to suburbia, and an increase in urban crime than with television, however. New stadiums and expansion would help cure the ills, and by 1962 major-league baseball was again setting attendance marks.

The pot kept growing. Baseball's annual network television revenues reached $3.25 million in 1960, $16.6 million in 1970, and $47.5 million in 1980. Radio and television combined for 28 percent of baseball's total income by 1970, and by 1990 fully one-half the game's profit was broadcast-generated. When it appeared baseball was in danger of dropping below pro football (and, most notably, Howard Cosell and *Monday Night Football*) in popularity, along came the fabulous 1975 World Series between the Red Sox and Reds (its seventh game alone was seen by over 61 million viewers) to cause another leap in attendance.

The newest broadcast trend began that same year, when Ted Turner bought the Atlanta Braves to provide programming for his national cable network, WTBS. Within a few years Braves games were being telecast for free by cable companies from Hawaii to Alaska, and as his audience grew to over 20 million so did Turner's wealth. Other owners took note, and today cable and superstations are some of the game's biggest sources of revenue. But while teams like the Yankees can make $50 million from cable contracts, the $3 million deals given small-market clubs threaten their survival in the free-agent era.

Network telecasts have also encountered problems. In December 1988, outgoing commissioner Peter Ueberroth signed a four-year contract with CBS guaranteeing $1.1 billion over four years for exclusive broadcast rights to the All-Star Game, playoffs, World Series, and 12 regular-season games from 1990 through 1993—37 percent more than ABC and NBC had paid under their prior baseball contracts combined. Struggling behind the other two major networks, CBS was confident the game's popularity would bring it back in the ratings. Hoping for a boost of its own, ABC subsidiary

Ted Turner managed the Braves to one loss in 1977 before the NL forced him out. Turner is the first former manager to be named *Time* Man of the Year.

ESPN—cable's all-sports network—signed a more modest $100 million deal for broadcast rights during the regular season.

Things didn't go as planned. A four-game sweep of the Athletics by the Reds in the 1990 World Series cost the network hundreds of millions, and losses mounted as fans finally grew disillusioned with baseball's increasingly dollar-driven image and began turning toward pro basketball and football. When CBS signed off in October 1993 after Joe Carter's dramatic World Series-winning home run, they had lost $500 million in four years.

Many of baseball's recent exposure problems can be directly linked to moves made to increase broadcast revenue. Added commercial time between innings has helped cause the average length of a nine-inning game to grow from an efficient two hours to a dragging three-hours-plus, and doubleheaders are largely a thing of the past. The addition of two "wild-card" teams, two more divisions, and a third playoff round dilutes the importance of sport's longest regular season just for the chance at more postseason broadcast money.

To pick up prime-time audiences and higher advertising rates, an ever-increasing number of games are played at night—including nearly every playoff and World Series contest. Games often don't start until 8:30 P.M. or later on the East Coast, and Carter's Series-winning home run was struck at well past midnight—long after many fans were asleep. Children who used to sneak radios to school to listen to Series

Ted Turner in 1977 skippered *Courageous* to the America's Cup, a year after he bought the Atlanta Braves to provide programming for superstation TBS.

games are now tuning in to the NBA, which broadcasts playoff games well before their bedtime. Warns broadcasting expert Curt Smith: "What they've done is write off an entire generation of Americans. . . . If you don't learn to love baseball as a kid, you never will."

The current television contract provides that baseball will receive money only as advertising time is sold. Dealing with severe cutbacks, owners reacted by releasing high-priced players. Local revenue sharing and a salary cap might finally become a reality, if only for the survival of the league. The days of no free broadcasts and pay-per-view games—including the playoffs—may not be far off.

EXPLORING NEW MARKETPLACES: DOMES TO PARKS

◆

From 1903 to 1952, baseball was played by the same 16 teams in the same 10 cities. The game's stability in an ever-changing world was a symbol of its strength—the stock market may rise and fall, the world may go to war, but the Dodgers would always be in Brooklyn. From the Wright Brothers to fighter jets, Teddy Roosevelt to Dwight Eisenhower, the structure of the major leagues remained the same.

In 1953, all that changed. Frustrated by a dramatic drop in attendance that had seen his Boston Braves go from drawing 1,455,000 fans when they won the National League pennant in 1948 to a major-league low of 281,000 just four years later, owner Lou Perini announced on March 18 that he was cutting his mounting losses of $1.2 million and heading west for Milwaukee, Wisconsin. The move would prove a tremendous success, and over the next five years, four more teams would pull up roots in pursuit of greener pastures and rosier finances.

Braves Field, it seemed, was not the only place attracting fewer fans. The postwar boom that saw major-league attendance rise from 7.7 million in 1943 to 21.3 million five years later had leveled off and begun to drop—to 17.2 million in 1950 and just over 15 million two years later.

However proud and historic its past, the basic fact was baseball needed change.

The last great ballpark boom had occurred between 1909 and 1915, when fireproof steel-and-concrete stadiums replaced the wooden ball grounds of the previous century. Now these "modern" parks had grown old, and in many cases the cities around them were crumbling as well—their inhabitants fleeing for the affordable single-family homes of the suburbs that personified the American dream. Baseball no longer held its fans captive during the summer, and the hassles of night games, traffic jams, and increasing crime didn't seem worth a long drive to the park—especially when a family could watch a game at home for free.

In breaking new ground, Perini reversed his fortunes. Milwaukee fans turned out 12,000

Lou Perini (right) moved the Braves from Boston to Milwaukee in 1953, and that year his ballclub drew a National League-record 1.8 million fans.

strong to greet the Braves when their train arrived from spring training, and filled brand-new County Stadium to capacity throughout the summer. By year's end the young team had improved by 28 games to a 92-62 second-place finish, and had drawn 1,826,397 rabid fans—a National League record. Perini was a happy man, and other struggling owners got to thinking. If they couldn't get fans to come to their games, why not bring their games to fans who would appreciate them?

Over the next dozen years, that's just what happened. The St. Louis Browns, winners of only one pennant in their 51-year history, were next to go. The Brownies had averaged just over 325,000 fans a season at Sportsman's Park from 1947 to 1953, but in 1954 they opened the season in Maryland as the Baltimore Orioles and

drew nearly 1.1 million to brand-new Memorial Stadium. The Philadelphia Athletics watched their 1954 attendance fall to 304,666—lowest since the Depression—but the next year as the Kansas City Athletics they played before 1,393,054 in their new park, double-decked Municipal Stadium.

The one city fans expected to survive this era of change was America's largest—New York. But the same problems were happening there. The Dodgers had fielded top-notch teams since the arrival of Jackie Robinson and a pennant in 1947, but after drawing 1.8 million fans that season had dropped off considerably in attendance despite five more World Series appearances. Owner Walter O'Malley complained that ancient Ebbets Field (capacity 31,902) was too small and lacked parking, but when only

The 1944 St. Louis Browns won the franchise's first pennant but lost to the Cardinals in the only all-St. Louis World Series. It was the high point for the franchise, as they lost games and customers. Bill Veeck bought the Browns in 1951 but, unable to compete as the second club in a medium-sized market, by 1953 sold them to a business concern that moved them to Baltimore.

Walter O'Malley (left), with Walt Alston, joined the Dodgers in 1933 as a lawyer and shortly thereafter became a minority stockholder. O'Malley outmaneuvered Branch Rickey in 1950 to become the majority stockholder and president of the club. By 1958 he moved the Dodgers to Los Angeles—just two years after the Dodgers finally beat the Yankees in the World Series.

1,028,258 came out in 1957 it was hard to put the blame solely on a lack of space. The same seats had been filled 10 years earlier.

Giants owner Horace Stoneham faced a similar dilemma. After winning a World Series in 1954, his team had failed to draw even 900,000 fans to the Polo Grounds in four years since. When commercial airlines introduced the Boeing 707 jet transport in 1957—a plane that could cross the continent in six hours—it was a clear case of new technology enabling a new start. The West Coast was calling, and over the winter of 1958 both O'Malley and Stoneham moved their teams to California. Their old boroughs would never forgive them, but neither would regret the move. Within five years the Los Angeles Dodgers and San Francisco Giants had set team attendance records in new parks, and their rivalry was stronger than ever.

Despite the shifts, many large cities were still without teams. This and the gap left in New

Horace Stoneham (right), with San Francisco Mayor George Christopher, surveyed a site for a new stadium; the shovel was used for adding fill in the Bay for parking.

York got 78-year-old Branch Rickey thinking there was money to be made from a third major league. Gathering support and making a few initial scouting and player hirings, the venerable, shrewd baseball guru planned to get the "Continental League" playing by 1961. Major-league owners wanted no such competition and reacted quickly with a new measure—granting expansion franchises to New York (the Mets), Los Angeles (the Angels), and Houston (the Colt .45s).

When financially strapped Washington Senators owner Calvin Griffith sought permission to move to Minneapolis around the same time, it too was quickly granted—leading to two more clubs: the Minnesota Twins (really the old Sen-

Horace Stoneham, right, with Willie Mays, was honored in 1955 for meritorious service by the New York Baseball Writer's Association of America.

Calvin Griffith took over the Washington Senators from his father, Clark, in 1955.

Mets challenged the Dodgers for the majors' top crowds while fielding the worst team in the majors.

Even one move wasn't enough for some teams. Baseball's best-drawing franchise just a few years before, the Milwaukee Braves departed for Atlanta in 1966 after attendance fell from 2.2 million in their world championship season of 1957 to under 560,000 nine seasons later. The first major-league team to play in the deep South, the Braves would draw 1,539,801 fans their first year in brand-new Atlanta (now Fulton County) Stadium. They had spent just 13 seasons in Milwaukee, their previous home. The Athletics also spent 13 short but dismal years in Kansas City, during which they never finished above .500 and drew less than a million fans their last 11 seasons, then left for the West Coast and Oakland.

The moves left two major cities without teams, and in 1969 Kansas City got another chance with the AL expansion Royals—who from their onset combined competitive clubs and outstanding public relations to become one of baseball's most successful franchises. The same could not be said of the Seattle Pilots, who drew just 677,944 their lone season before the AL took over their $1 million debt and gave Milwaukee its second team of the decade—the Brewers—in 1970. These shifts, combined with two more NL expansion outfits in San Diego (the Padres) and Montreal (the Expos), meant there were 24 clubs playing in two countries by decade's end.

ators) and the "new" Washington Senators (like all expansion teams, a motley crew of second-rate players drafted from other clubs). The Twins, expansion Senators, and Angels all started American League play in 1961, with the Mets and Colts joining the National League the following spring. With three of his proposal cities already eliminated, Rickey soon abandoned his Continental League plans.

To compensate for its new teams, the AL and NL had to expand their schedules from 154 to 162 games in 1961 and 1962. Although some critics argued that expansion was diluting baseball's overall talent level, fans didn't seem to mind. All four new clubs soon drew a million spectators despite sub-.500 records, and the

To accommodate for the growth, a new alignment was devised in 1969 splitting each league into an Eastern and Western division. Divisional winners now met in a best-of-five playoff, the winner advancing to the World Series. It took a while for the "Championship Series" to catch on, but eventually it boosted attendance and became a strong source of extra revenue for the league.

Complementing baseball's changing makeup, 10 new parks opened during the 1960s—seven in the National League alone. Built primarily in suburban areas near major highways and complete with cookie-cutter configurations (a 1958 edict had set standards for future outfield dimensions), immense parking lots, and colorful plastic seats far from the playing field, the new arenas were much more all-purpose stadiums than ballparks. Although a few (especially Dodger Stadium) were aesthetically pleasing, they lacked the quirks and unique qualities that had set places like Ebbets Field and the Polo Grounds apart.

There was, of course, one notable exception to the cookie-cutter format—the Houston Astrodome. Opened in 1965 to house the Colt .45s (who subsequently became the Astros), baseball's first domed stadium was instantly dubbed one of the eight wonders of the modern world. The surging crowds (Astros attendance tripled to 2,151,470) had no trouble distinguishing it from other parks, and from its first

Oriole Park at Camden Yards, opened in 1992, was baseball's return to a classic asymmetric ballpark of the early 1910s.

Wrigley Field was built by Charles Weeghman in 1914 to house the Chicago Whales of the Federal League and was originally named "Weeghman Field." When Weeghman acquired the Cubs in 1916, he moved them to Weeghman Field. William Wrigley bought the Cubs in 1921 and renamed the ballpark in 1927.

air-conditioned days when the grass refused to grow and players continuously lost fly balls in the roof it was destined to be different. Domes were later added in Seattle, Minnesota, and Toronto (the impressive SkyDome, featuring baseball's first retractable roof). Rising costs, however, have kept the trend to a minimum.

As America's population and family income rate continued rising during the 1970s, more expansion became a necessity. The Seattle Mariners and Toronto Blue Jays joined the American League in 1977, giving it 14 teams to the NL's 12. Six more stadiums also sprang up during the decade, and by 1980 only four pre-expansion parks—Tiger Stadium, Fenway, Comiskey, and Wrigley Field—remained standing as shrines to a bygone era.

Expansion continues, and the additions of National League teams in Denver (the Colorado Rockies) and Miami (the Florida Marlins) in 1993 rated as baseball's most successful yet. Both clubs drew outstandingly well in their maiden seasons, the Marlins playing before 3,064,847 fans and the Rockies a major-league record 4,483,350—including 80,227 on Opening Day. Sport's latest craze—logo and apparel merchandising—enabled the new owners to earn millions in additional revenue, and once again the losses (98 for the Marlins, 95 for the Rockies) didn't seem to make a difference as tens of thousands lined up for season tickets.

Now featuring 28 teams, six divisions, and a three-round playoff format, the major leagues have changed more in the past 40 years than in the previous 50. Yet with all the revisions, baseball's newest ballparks indicate desire on the part of owners and fans to return to the past. The new Comiskey Park opened in 1991 as the first since Royal Stadium in 1973 not also built for football. Baltimore's spectacular Camden Yards unveiled in 1992 was a tribute to the beautifully constructed brick parks built in the early part of the century—complete with ads on the outfield walls. New ballparks in Cleveland and Texas also pay testimony to yesteryear, combining modern convenience with old-fashioned charm and craftsmanship.

In a game that continues growing and expanding, the excitement generated by these newest structures is a reminder that sometimes you *can* go back.

DAYS OF STRUGGLE, FREEDOM, AND REWARDS

◆

*I*n 1876 it cost 50 cents to watch a baseball game in person; in 1993, tickets to a major-league game could be found for as low as $4. While fans can still enjoy an afternoon at the ballpark for a reasonable price, the working conditions of the men playing the game have changed drastically. Players have progressed from a state of near servitude under ownership to the point where today they can to a large degree choose for whom and how long they are going to perform—and for how much.

Chicago's White Stockings of 1876 earned an average of $1,380 for the season, and while they were free to sign with any club they wished the following year, this practice was soon done away with after the 1887 passage of the "reserve clause." Under the clause, owners held complete legal control over a player—even after his contract expired. Players had road expenses and uniform costs deducted from their salary, and pay rose little from year to year despite a large increase in baseball's overall revenue.

The formation of the upstart American League in 1901 and the inter-league bidding for talent that ensued had a phenomenal effect on player salaries, escalating them to the point where stars like Detroit batting king Ty Cobb were able to command $30,000 a season (which would be equivalent to around $400,000 today) for their services. The boom continued after World War I, as the popularity generated by Babe Ruth enabled baseball's gross revenues to grow to 80 times their 1883 level. Attendance soared to nearly 10 million fans a season, and the New York Yankees alone made $3.5 million during the 1920s.

The Depression changed everything. Baseball attendance plummeted to 8.1 million in 1932 and just 6.1 million in 1933, and average salaries dropped from $7,500 in 1929 to $6,000 four years later. Owners tried everything to earn extra cash, including the introduction of night baseball at Cincinnati's Crosley Field on May 24, 1935. Used successfully in the minors the previous three seasons, night ball was an instant attendance-booster for the majors. The Reds routinely drew 15,000-plus at night as opposed to 1,500 during the day. By 1940 11 teams had installed lights. Only war restrictions slowed the trend, and by 1947 every club but the Cubs (who would hold out until 1988) was playing a portion of its home games at night.

National and local radio rights also helped Depression-era clubs earn extra cash, but just when the economy and salaries began to improve, along came World War II. A federal salary freeze in 1942 ignored baseball's standard of paying players in relation to performance, and by 1945 some of the game's top talent was being pitifully compensated. Whereas Hank Greenberg's $55,000 salary had topped the majors in 1941, three years later Bill Dickey was top man at just $22,000.

The end of the war brought prosperity and a sense of security to Americans such as they had never experienced. People had more time and money to spend on leisure than ever before, and overall attendance jumped to 18.1 million in 1946—80 percent above the previous high. Accompanying the trend was an equally powerful sense of pride; people were not only encouraged by the prospect of a better life, they felt entitled to it. Minorities and union groups were demanding better treatment and working conditions, and baseball players joined in the fight.

Headed by former National Labor Relations Board examiner Robert Murphy, the American Baseball Guild in 1946 won for players a $5,000 minimum salary, free medical benefits, a 25 percent limit on salary cuts, and a spring-training allowance in 1946. The Guild's greatest victory, however, was the establishment of a player pension—ensuring $50 a month for life after five years in the majors, and $10 more for each additional year up to 10. Owners grumbled at the new policies but figured they could squash future player mobilization by giving over some mild concessions.

They were wrong. When owners tried to abolish the pension in 1953, players mobilized again as the Major League Baseball Players Association and threatened court action to keep it intact. The Association lacked a strong leader, however, and the minimum salary rose slowly—from $5,000 in 1946 to just $7,000 in

Bill Dickey (above) was the highest-paid player in the mid-1940s, with a salary of $22,000. Ernie Lombardi, another fine catcher, made $10,000 in 1943.

1967. Only when the militant struggle of the 1960s found its way into baseball did its ranks rise up again. More money-conscious than their predecessors, the players of this era realized they were performers whose talents were making others rich and guaranteeing themselves nothing but a short, uncertain career. They wanted the same security and rights as the rest of society, but they needed someone to rally their cause.

In 1966, they got him: 49-year-old labor economist Marvin Miller. A former negotiator for the United Steel Workers of America, Miller overhauled the Association into a proficient labor organization and used federal laws to force owners into negotiating formal contracts in writing. His deep conviction for the fight and his ability to paint baseball's owners and executive management as a beatable foe won over the players, and in four separate agreements over the next decade Miller was able to do more for player conditions than anyone before.

The 1967 "Basic Agreement" raised the minimum salary from its 10-year level of $7,000 to $10,000, while also forcing owners to contribute an additional $4.1 million a year to the pension fund. The second Basic Agreement of 1970 (another three-year pact) won players the right to agent representation in contract negotiations, boosted the minimum salary to $13,500, and forced ownership to accept the Association as baseball's official bargaining agency in all matters but individual salaries. The accord also allowed for outside arbitrators to settle certain disputes between ownership and players, which would come in handy a few years later.

One thing owners refused to negotiate was the reserve clause. When Cardinal outfielder Curt Flood vetoed a 1969 postseason trade that sent himself and three others to the Phillies in a

Marvin Miller helped the players achieve free agency and salary arbitration.

seven-player deal, he posed a legal challenge to that clause. Angry at being uprooted from his personal life and photography store in St. Louis (where he had played since '57), Flood felt he had earned the right to choose his own employer.

Miller warned Flood that a suit might end his playing career, but Flood sued anyway, behind the free legal services of former Supreme Court Justice Arthur Goldberg. Sitting out the 1970 season (in which he could have earned over $90,000) to show his conviction, Flood still lost his case in the Supreme Court in 1972. A jump-start to his career with the Senators also proved futile, but Flood's fight paved the way for future battles against the reserve clause.

When owners stalled 1972 Basic Agreement negotiations by calling for an increase in pension and medical benefits, players voted 663-10 to strike in March and walked out of training camp. Finally settled in mid-April, the strike won players an additional $500,000 in pension money and cost the owners $5 million in lost receipts for the seven to nine regular-season games each team missed. Players also lost a portion of their salaries (the average which had now risen to $32,000), but again they had stood firm.

Curt Flood was with the Cards from 1958 to 1969.

The third Basic Agreement of 1973 further boosted salaries and pension and health benefits, but more importantly won players with two or more years of service the right to seek binding arbitration in salary disputes. Players could now also veto any trade after 10 years of major-league service and five with the same team—a right that came one year too late for Flood.

That fall 29 players exercised the arbitration option, under the stipulation that arbitrators choose either the player's last demand or ownership's best option. Thirteen players won, but the real craziness started the following year, when 40 players filed—including Jim "Catfish" Hunter, ace pitcher for the three-time defending world champion Athletics. Hunter made $100,000 in 1974, but by showing arbiters that stingy A's owner Charlie Finley had not followed certain stipulations in his contract won himself the right to sign with any team as a "free agent." Choosing the Yankees from many bidders, he received a five-year contract worth $3.75 million in salary, deferred payments, and other benefits. Baseball's first instant millionaire, Hunter would be far from its last.

Miller now saw a chance to further challenge the reserve clause, filing a grievance against the one-year "option-to-renew" clause owners put in contracts to allow themselves the option of releasing players. Stipulating that the clause could be interpreted to mean that owners only had one year to sign a player before he could go elsewhere, Miller found two players (star pitchers Dave McNally and Andy Messersmith) willing to refuse to sign their contracts before the option year.

After pitching in 1975 unsigned, McNally and Messersmith appealed to the Association for an arbitration hearing. They won their right to free agency, and although ownership tried to conspire against them by not submitting bids, eventually a few owners realized they needed a 20-game winner more than their pride. McNally retired, but Messersmith signed for $1 million with the Braves, a deal that threatened to destroy the reserve clause altogether.

Dave McNally

Owners saw 1976, when the third Basic Agreement would expire, as their chance to get back. Refusing to open spring training camps (in effect, a strike against the players), owners sought the right to eight years of controlled service before a player could become a free agent. Miller fought for only six years, and, even with commissioner Bowie Kuhn publicly against it, the Association won out with a new four-year Basic Agreement stating that after six years, all

Ray Grebey (left) talks to reporters during the 1981 strike; there were some owners
who made money during the walkout because of the strike insurance.

an owner was entitled to for a player was a draft pick from his new team.

Reggie Jackson topped all 1976 free agents with a five-year Yankee pact worth $2.93 million, and 24 players won a total of $25 million. When such signings multiplied and salary averages crept up and over the $100,000 mark in 1979, Kuhn resorted to blaming the Association for higher ticket prices, a lack of competitive balance, and a rise in complacency and greed among players. The free-agency technique could indeed backfire (after signing a 10-year deal for $2.3 million from the Indians, pitcher Wayne Garland went 28-48 the rest of his career), but teams seemed willing to take the chance and fans (attendance was rising each year) didn't appear

to mind if Nolan Ryan made $1 million, as long as he could strike people out. As for balance, 1980's four divisional winners were all different from the previous season.

Owners continued to warn of potential problems. Players making more than their coaches and manager would be harder to discipline, and the traditional practice of trading for talent was in jeopardy of disappearing. These and other perceived dangers prompted owners to once again challenge the players in 1981, with their biggest demand being higher free-agent compensation. When both sides refused to give in, the result was a 50-day strike and 713 canceled games (an average of 50 a team) starting on June 11. The owners and their negotiator, Ray

Grebey, had covered themselves with $50 million in "strike insurance" from Lloyds of London, but when Miller threatened the formation of a new players' league in 1982, ownership began to get worried.

Fans and media rallied early around the players—a *Sports Illustrated* headline read: "STRIKE! The Walkout The Owners Provoked." Eventually folks grew tired of waiting and minor-league attendance soared. When it became obvious to both sides there could be no winner (and the Lloyds policy was running out), a settlement was reached on July 31. Owners claimed a small victory in that teams losing free agents would now receive a major leaguer or top minor leaguer as compensation, but both groups suffered. The owners lost more than $50 million, despite their insurance, and the players lost about $30 million, and feelings between the two sides were so strong that Miller refused to pose with Grebey for a "peace ceremony" picture after the settlement.

Baseball fans are a forgiving group, and attendance soared to an all-time high of 45 million in 1982. Salaries continued to rise, and by the time the fifth Basic Agreement expired in 1984, the average was $363,000—with 20 players earning $1 million or more. Owners believed arbitration was behind the huge numbers and

Fay Vincent

over the winter of 1985 refused to sign a new contract until the two years of player service needed for arbitration was lengthened or a salary cap decided upon.

Player obstinacy led to another strike on Aug. 6, but thankfully it lasted just two days and resulted in no games lost. Neither side wanted a repeat of 1981, and both emerged under the sixth Basic Agreement with victories. The length of service required for arbitration rights was extended to three years, but no ceiling was set on salaries. Players won another pension hike, and 10-year veterans could now earn $91,000 annually in their retirement— quite a jump from the high of $1,200 agreed upon in 1946.

The agreement did little to stop salary growth, and owners once again attempted to thwart the trend by conspiring to not sign free agents between 1985 and 1987. Miller and the Association countered with successful collusion charges that earned the affected players $100 million in retribution, and fearful of future charges owners began bidding openly during future free-agent periods.

Thanks largely to Miller, salaries have exploded to the point where the average contract well exceeds $1 million a season. Stars sign deals calling for $25 million or more, and even the marginal performer who plays for only a few years can set himself up for life.

Baseball Heroes

Baseball Heroes

PLAYERS WHO DEFINED BASEBALL

The essence of America's relationship with baseball is its love affair with the greatest players to ever step on a diamond.

While they put up great numbers, more than just great statistics elevated Christy Mathewson, Ty Cobb, Joe DiMaggio, Hank Aaron, and George Brett. Everyone remembers Willie, Mickey, and the Duke. It is players like those—and athletes such as Cool Papa Bell, so fast that he could turn out the light and be in bed before the room got dark, and Stan Musial, able to hit a home run in his first at bat after becoming a grandfather—whose gifts raise the level of the game.

HANK AARON

★

On April 23, 1954, Hank Aaron hit his first of 755 major-league home runs, more than any player in major-league history.

Henry Louis Aaron (born in 1934) grew up one of eight children in Mobile, Alabama. He hauled 25-pound blocks of ice as a child, and he learned baseball by hitting bottle caps with a broomstick. He started playing semipro ball in Mobile at age 16. By 1951, the Indianapolis Clowns of the Negro Leagues signed him as a shortstop. He was a cross-handed hitter for awhile, but switched to a conventional grip and hit two home runs in his first game with the new grip.

The Braves signed Aaron in 1952 and sent him to Eau Clair of the Northwest League, where he batted .336. In 1953, he was one of three players to integrate the Sally League. He led the circuit with a .362 batting average, 125 RBI, and 115 runs scored. Braves outfielder Bobby Thomson broke his ankle early in 1954, and Hank had a job in Milwaukee.

Aaron endured the bigotry and segregation of the major leagues at that time with poise and silence. In his early years in the majors, he was an enigma to most players and fans. He let his bat do the talking for many years, and only gradually did his image evolve from that of a hitting machine to an intelligent, forceful man, who could set seemingly impossible goals and achieve them.

Hank had an all-around game that was second to none. He became one of the top outfielders in the game after coming up as an infielder. He was consistent and careful and deadly. His quick wrists were the stuff of legend. He led the NL with a .328 batting average in 1956. In 1957, he won the National League MVP Award with a .328 batting average, 44 home runs, and 132 RBI. The Braves won the pennant that year and then went on to defeat a powerful Yankee team in the World Series.

Hank Aaron is the all-time RBI leader with 2,297.

In 1973, Hank Aaron set a record for the most home runs (40) by a player who collected fewer than 400 at bats. He had 392 at bats that year, and only 12 of his 118 hits were doubles.

Hank hit .393 with three home runs in the seven games. Although the Braves remained a strong team for many years, it was to be Aaron's only world championship.

In 1966 the Braves moved from Milwaukee, with one of the worst parks for hitters in baseball, to Atlanta. Aaron was granted a reprieve; Fulton County Stadium proved to be a great hitters' park. He hit 245 home runs after turning 35 years old, a record. On April 8, 1974, Aaron broke Babe Ruth's lifetime home run record. Racism and fans' misguided reverence for the Babe added to the difficulty of that monumental task. Always a quiet, serious professional, Henry withstood the burden and scrutiny of an all-out media assault with cool and restraint. "Thank God it's over," he said after the record-breaking game.

Aaron won a record eight total-bases titles, en route to the all-time record of 6,856 total bases. He slugged over .500 19 times and batted .300 14 times. He drove in 100 runs in 13 consecutive seasons and 15 times in all, finishing with an all-time best 2,297 RBI. He hit 30 more homers in 15 seasons. Curt Simmons said, "Throwing a fastball by Henry Aaron is like trying to sneak sunrise past a rooster."

GROVER ALEXANDER

★

Grover Cleveland Alexander (1887-1950) paced the New York State League at age 23 with 29 wins in 1910, and Syracuse sold him to the Phillies for $750.

With the acquisition of Alexander, the Phillies almost instantly became a contender. In 1911, "Pete" won 28 games, a modern rookie record, and also set NL rookie marks for strikeouts and shutouts that have since been broken.

Pete's seven years in Philadelphia were the most successful and probably the happiest of his life. In 1915, his 31 wins spearheaded the Phillies to their first pennant. The following season Alexander scored a personal-high 33 victories and notched an all-time record 16 shutouts. When he won 30 again in 1917, he became the last pitcher to be a 30-game winner in two consecutive seasons, let alone three.

With the United States involved in World War I, the Phillies traded Pete to the Cubs, thinking he would soon be drafted. After pitching just three games for the Cubs in 1918, Pete was sent to France with the 89th Infantry Division. Serving on the front lines, he lost the hearing in one ear as a result of a shelling and also began experiencing the first symptoms of epilepsy. Between the illness and the shell shock he had suffered, Alexander came to rely more and more on alcohol for solace.

Upon his return from overseas, Pete rejoined the Cubs and had several outstanding years with Chicago. Waived to the Cardinals in early 1926, now known as "Old Pete," Alexander came to St. Louis with a chronic sore arm and a reputation for no longer being able to keep his drinking under control. In the Mound City his arm revived, however, enabling him to win nine games for the

Grover Alexander turned in an amazing season in 1920, leading the National League in wins, strikeouts, and ERA after returning from World War I deaf in one ear and suffering from epilepsy.

"Old Pete" Alexander notched 27 or more victories in six different seasons.

Cardinals down the stretch.

In the 1926 World Series against the Yankees, Pete won both the second and sixth games as a starter. Then in game seven, when New York loaded the bases in the seventh inning with two out, Alexander was called out of the bullpen to protect a 3-2 St. Louis lead and proceeded to fan Tony Lazzeri, on four pitches. Pete then set down the vaunted New Yorkers in the final two innings without surrendering a hit.

Pete won 21 games in 1927, the ninth time he reached the magic circle. He had a career 373-208 record with 2,199 strikeouts. He was named to the Hall of Fame in 1938.

WALTER ALSTON

★

*W*alter Alston was at the helm of the Dodgers from their mid-1950s battles with the Yankees to their mid-1970s races with the Big Red Machine. Alston managed the Dodgers for 23 years, winning seven pennants and four World Series.

Walter Emmons Alston (1911-1984) was an infielder who played for Miami University in Ohio. He was signed by general manager Branch Rickey's Cardinals in 1935, and Alston got his only major-league at bat at the end of the 1936 season with St. Louis. He started his managerial career in 1940 while still a player, with Portsmouth of the Mid-Atlantic League. Rickey hired Walt into the Dodger organization in 1944. Branch brought Alston along like he did players, allowing him to experience success at higher and higher levels. In 1946, Rickey chose Alston as one of two managers to manage black players by placing Don Newcombe and Roy Campanella on Alston's Nashua, New Hampshire, team. From 1948 to 1953, Walt managed in Triple-A.

After winning two pennants in 1952 and '53 as the Brooklyn manager, Chuck Dressen

Walter Alston, left, signs another contract for Dodger owner Walter O'Malley, while O'Malley seems very pleased that the length of the contract is for one year.

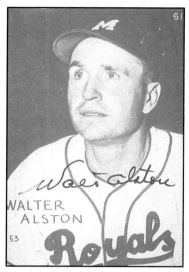

Walter Alston always remained versatile and was able to effectively manage in Brooklyn in the 1950s and LA in the 1970s.

was fired for demanding a multiyear contract. Alston was the surprise choice as Dressen's replacement, and Walt accepted one-year contracts for the next 23 years. Alston was a quiet, businesslike man. As a field general, he was in control. He was a devotee of bunts, the hit-and-run, intentional passes, stolen bases, platooning, and pinch hitters.

The Dodgers finished second in Alston's first season, 1954, and then won the pennant in 1955. For the first time in five tries, the Bums finally beat the Bombers in the Series. The Dodgers also won the NL pennant in 1956. In 1958, the Dodgers' first year in Los An-

geles, the team finished seventh. Walt did his best managing job in '59, driving an insufficiently talented Dodger team to the championship.

Alston helped to rebuild the Dodgers along the lines of a team that he wanted to manage, emphasizing speed, defense, pitching, and more pitching. With Sandy Koufax and Don Drysdale taking the mound, the Dodgers won the world cham-

pionship in 1963 and again in '65, and the NL pennant in 1966. His teams went into a slight decline, rebounded by 1970, and challenged for the NL West crown each year until he retired in 1976. The Dodgers won the NL pennant in 1974. Alston won 2,040 games in his career, had a .558 winning percentage, and was inducted into the Hall of Fame in 1983.

CAP ANSON

★

Born in Marshalltown, Iowa, Adrian Constantine Anson (1852-1922) was one of the very few early stars whose father encouraged him to pursue a career in professional baseball. The elder Anson even wrote a letter to the Chicago team in 1869 recommending his son. The letter was ignored, and Anson instead entered Notre Dame in 1870. A year later he left school to join the Rockford team in the newly formed National Association.

The following year, Anson signed with the Philadelphia Athletics and remained with them through 1875. When the National League was formed in 1876, he deserted Philadelphia along with several other Athletics stars. Anson cast his lot with the Chicago White Stockings seven years after his father had tried to interest a Chicago team in him. For the next 22 seasons he was a fixture there, setting a 19th-century loyalty record for the longest stint by a player with one team.

Still primarily a third baseman when he first came to the White Stockings, Anson moved to first base when he became the club's manager in 1879. Fielding was never Anson's strong point. It was at the plate that he excelled. Only three times in his 27-year career did he bat below .300, and he was the first player to accumulate 3,000 career hits. Although a line-drive hitter, Cap also could hit with power, and he was particularly dangerous with men on base. Anson led the National League in RBI no less than nine times in the 12-year period between 1880 and 1891. Furthermore, he topped the loop twice in batting average and on three occasions in slugging average. As a player-manager, Anson led Chicago to five pennants.

Anson was not without flaws, however. His language on the field was often so vile that it evoked fines from umpires, and rival fans called him "Crybaby" Anson because of the way he whined and moaned when events did not go his way. Moreover, Anson was a racist, believing the major-league game should be the province only of white players. Because of his threat to organize a strike, several black performers were clandestinely barred from the major leagues before the 1885 season, a ban that lingered, albeit unofficially, until 1947.

After the 1897 campaign, White Stockings president James Hart demanded that Cap resign his manager's seat. When Anson refused he was summarily fired. The White Stockings, minus Anson for the first time in their 23-year history, became known as the Orphans. In 1939, Anson was elected to the Hall of Fame.

Cap Anson was the first player in major-league history to retire with 3,000 hits.

LUIS APARICIO

★

While shortstop Luis Aparicio was patrolling American League infields from the mid-1950s to the 1970s, he was widely regarded as one of the best fielders at that position that the game had ever seen. He teamed with Nellie Fox to form for the White Sox one of the best keystone combinations in history.

Luis Ernesto Aparicio y Montiel was born in 1934 in Maracaibo, Venezuela, to one of the most highly regarded baseball players in that country's history. Luis Aparicio Sr. was the best shortstop in Venezuela for 25 years, and he passed on his skill and love of the game to his son. Luis Jr. took over his father's position on the town team in 1953, and was signed by the Chicago White Sox in '54.

"Little Looie" so impressed the White Sox during his two years in the minors that the White Sox traded their starting shortstop, Chico Carrasquel (also a Venezuelan native) to make room for Aparicio in 1956. He made an immediate impact on the league, hitting .266 with a league-best 21 stolen bases and winning the Rookie of the Year Award.

Aparicio was also the catalyst of a "Go-Go Sox" team that challenged the Yankees dominance of the 1950s. After being a runner-up for several years, the Sox finally won the flag in 1959. They finished dead last in home runs but first in steals. All-Star Aparicio teamed with keystone partner Nellie Fox as each led the league at their positions in

Though appreciated primarily for his glove, Luis Aparicio also was valuable at bat, compiling 2,677 hits, 1,335 runs scored, 736 bases on balls, and 506 stolen bases.

putouts, assists, and fielding percentage. Fox won the Most Valuable Player Award, and Luis was second in the voting.

Aparicio's 56 steals in 1959 (his previous best was 29) not only led the league but represented a new level of performance for Luis, a level that left the rest of the league in the dust. He posted totals of 51, 53, 31, 40, and 57 over the next five seasons, but only one rival was able to swipe more than 30 during the same span. He won nine consecutive stolen base titles, a record that has never been broken. Along with Maury Wills of the Dodgers, Aparicio was a vanguard of an emerging generation that relied on speed.

Aparicio was unparalleled as a defensive player. By the time he retired, he had played more games at shortstop (2,581), was involved in more double plays (1,553), and threw out more men than any shortstop in history. He had more assists than any other shortstop and won nine Gold Gloves in three decades. He led AL shortstops in fielding average in eight seasons, assists seven times, and putouts four times. Luis was inducted into the Hall of Fame in 1984.

LUKE APPLING

★

*L*uke Appling was a batsman second to none, hitting over .300 16 times in his 20-year career. He had outstanding command of the strike zone, once fouling off 19 pitches in a single at bat.

Lucius Benjamin Appling (1909-1991) grew up in Atlanta and was an all-city shortstop in high school. He attended Atlanta's Oglethorpe University, where, despite weighing 155 pounds, he was a football player as well as a baseball star. In 1930, after his sophomore year, he was signed by At-

lanta in the Southern Association. After hitting .326, Luke was purchased by the White Sox and debuted that year. He batted .308 in six games and showed the Chicago South Side what he could do at bat.

Defensively, though, Appling didn't adjust to major-league standards. He became the full-time shortstop in 1933 and won the first of his two batting titles in 1936 when he hit .388, his career high. He had 204 hits and 128 RBI that season. He was also named the outstanding major-league shortstop by *The Sporting News,* an honor he was to receive twice more in his career.

Billy Sullivan (from left), Billy Herman, Jimmy Adair, and Luke Appling discuss hitting about 1931. Herman and Appling, both Hall of Famers pictured at the start of their career, went on to comparable success, with Herman the better glove man and Appling the better hitter.

Luke hit .317 in 1937, but in 1938 he broke his leg, robbing him of some speed and range. He still managed to hit over .300 that year. In 1940, he lost the batting crown to Joe DiMaggio by four points, .352 to .348. Appling won another batting title in 1943 with a .328 average, but in 1944 he went to war, missing the entire season and playing in just 18 games in 1945.

Pushing 40, Appling hit over .300 each year from 1946 to 1949. He always seemed to have a knee or back problem, and he always seemed to make sure the whole team under-stood that, so much so that his nickname was "Old Aches and Pains." In 1949, he hit .301 in 142 games, and when his average slipped to just .234 the following year, he retired.

When Luke retired he left behind all-time records for major-league shortstops in games and double plays, as well as American League records for putouts, assists, and total chances. The records lasted 23 years until fellow South-Sider Luis Aparicio broke them. Appling never got the chance to play in a World Series, but he was one of the best-hitting shortstops in history.

RICHIE ASHBURN

★

A consistent leadoff hitter who led the NL in on-base average four times, Richie Ashburn was more impressively one of the best defensive center fielders of all time.

Although Ashburn had only 29 career homers, he was a potent offensive weapon for his teams; his career on-base average was .397, and he scored over 90 runs in nine seasons. A great flycatcher, Don Richard Ashburn (born in 1927) started his pro career surprisingly enough as a catcher. Ashburn signed two contracts—the first from the Indians in 1943 at the age of 16 and the second with the Cubs in 1944—that were both declared invalid. He finally signed with the Philadelphia Phillies' organization in 1945.

In spring training of 1948, Ashburn beat out the defending NL batting champ, Harry Walker, for the starting center field slot. Ashburn hit an impressive .333 during his debut that year. In 117 games, he had 154 hits and a league-leading 32 stolen bases. Immediately,

Luke Appling in 1984 hit a homer in an old-timers game at age 75.

he proved his fielding prowess with a .981 average and a league-best 3.1 chances per game. He followed with another good year in 1949.

Ashburn and his Phillies club enjoyed very fine success in 1950, winning the NL pennant (the Phillies' first since 1915). Ashburn hit .303 and

again paced the National League in fielding putouts and total chances.

On the last day of the season, "The Whiz Kids" won the pennant from the heavily favored Brooklyn Dodgers. Ashburn saved the game and the league title for the Phillies when he threw out Brooklyn's

Cal Abrams trying to score in the ninth inning. Philadelphia won the game in the 10th inning to advance to the World Series. The Phillies, however, were swept in the 1950 World Series by the Yankees; Ashburn batted only .176.

Ashburn was a center-field fixture for the Phillies throughout the 1950s. He compiled a consecutive game streak of 730 and never played in fewer than 109 games in a season. He won two batting crowns--in 1955 with a .338 average and in 1958 with a .350 mark.

Ashburn's average sank to .264 in 1959 as the Phillies continued to finish near the bottom of the NL. The needy Phils traded Ashburn to the Cubs for three players before the 1960 season. Ashburn started for the Cubs in center field and hit a team-leading .291. After a down year in 1961, he was sold to the first-year expansion New York Mets, who went 40-120. Ashburn was one of the team's bright spots, batting .306. He is one of the few players to retire after having a .300 average as a starter in his last season. After his retirement, Ashburn became a long-time member of the Phillies' broadcast team.

Richie Ashburn rivaled Willie Mays as the best-fielding center fielder in the NL during the 1950s, and they remained one-two until Curt Flood and Vada Pinson joined the league and Richie turned 32.

HOME RUN BAKER

★

John Franklin Baker (1886-1963) was born on a farm in Trappe, Maryland, the only home he ever knew. After flunking a brief trial with the Baltimore Orioles of the Eastern League in 1907, Frank in '08 joined Reading of the Tri-State League on the recommendation of Buck Herzog, a fellow Marylander who saw promise in the young third sacker. Herzog was virtually alone, though, in his estimation of Baker's talents. It came as a surprise to most observers when Connie Mack purchased Baker for the Philadelphia Athletics on Aug. 28, 1908.

By the conclusion of the 1909 season, Mack's judgment was more than vindicated. In his rookie season Baker hit .305 and 19 triples, an AL yearling record.

Two years later Baker received his nickname of "Home Run" when he topped the AL in four-baggers and clubbed two more homers in the World Series that fall against the New York Giants. The first came off Rube Marquard, who was chastised the next day in a newspaper column by Christy Math-

Home Run Baker was the top third sacker of his day. A top-notch fielder, he was also a fine power hitter for several years, ranking behind Ty Cobb, surprisingly enough, and few others.

ewson for pitching "carelessly" to Baker. By that evening Mathewson himself had been victimized by the new slugging star, surrendering a game-tying home run in the ninth inning.

Baker comprised part of what for three years, starting in 1912, was known as the "$100,000 infield." The other three members were first baseman Stuffy McInnis, second baseman Eddie Collins, and shortstop Jack Barry. The 1912 season was also Baker's best; he led the AL in both homers and RBI and hit .347, a record for a junior-circuit third baseman that stood until 1980, when George Brett batted .390.

In 1913 Baker notched 12 home runs, a career high, and led the American League for the third straight time (out of four times). Baker's tenure with the A's remained pleasurable and productive until the finish of the 1914 season. After the A's were swept embarrassingly in the World Series by the "Miracle" Braves, Mack opted to break up his team, and he refused to pay Baker what he was worth. Baker sat out the entire 1915 campaign—and the following year, the Yankees purchased Baker from the A's for $35,000. A year away from the game apparently affected Baker, and he was never again an important offensive force in the majors.

When his first wife died in 1920, Baker again chose to retire temporarily. He returned to the Yankees the following spring, just in time to play on the club's first pennant winner. He retired, this time for good, in 1922. He was elected to the Hall of Fame in 1955.

ERNIE BANKS

★

Ernie Banks's reputation as a goodwill ambassador should not obscure his great playing ability. He was a fine fielding shortstop and a power hitter who had an unbridled enthusiasm for the game of baseball.

Born in 1931, Ernest Banks was a four-sport athlete in high school, but it was his play in a church-sponsored softball league that induced a scout for the semipro Amarillo Colts to sign Ernie at age 17, in 1948. Within two years, he made it to the Kansas City Monarchs, one of the strongest teams in the Negro Leagues. He played one season before he was drafted into the Army for a two-year stint.

After his discharge, Ernie played the 1953 season for the Monarchs. The major-league teams were interested in Banks, but Monarchs owner Tom Baird refused to sell Ernie's rights to a minor-league club, insisting that Banks go directly to the bigs. The Cubs relented, and Ernie, the first African American on the Cubs, played in 10 games for Chicago that year.

Banks was the everyday shortstop in 1954, hitting .275 with 19 home runs and 79 RBI. In 1955, he batted .295 and clubbed 44 home runs, with five grand slams. He hit .285 with 43 homers in 1957. He was the first player from a sub-.500 team to be voted the league's Most Valuable Player when he led the league with 47 home runs (the most ever by a shortstop) and 129 RBI in 1958. The following year he became the first player in the NL to win back-to-back MVP Awards. Banks again led the league in RBI (143) and had 45 homers. He led the NL with 41 homers in 1960.

Banks was a fine shortstop for nine seasons, winning a

After his rookie year, Ernie Banks was unquestionably a fine fielder, three times leading loop shortstops in fielding average.

Gold Glove in 1960. His 105 double plays total in 1954 is still a rookie record. He was a nine-time All-Star. His move to first base in 1962 was brought on by knee injuries, not defensive shortcomings. He had 37 homers and 104 RBI that year.

Banks hit over 40 homers five times and had over 100 RBI in eight seasons. He had over 80 RBI and more than 20 homers in 13 seasons. Although the Cubs failed to win a pennant during Ernie's 19-year career, he earned the title "Mr. Cub." He was well known for his love of the game and his credo, "Nice day for baseball. Let's play two." has become part of the language. He remained a hero in Chicago after his retirement as a player, as he took up a new career in the Cubs' front office. Banks was inducted into the Hall of Fame in 1977.

At the close of the 1959 season, his seventh in the majors, Ernie Banks had a .558 career slugging average, the highest of any middle infielder except Rogers Hornsby. Every year thereafter, however, Banks's slugging average declined steadily. He finished with a .500 slugging average, still the highest ever by anyone who played 1,000 or more games at shortstop.

COOL PAPA BELL

★

Cool Papa Bell was a switch-hitter with the speed to beat out ground balls and to score from second on fly-outs. He also owned the power to hit the long ball right-handed. He was widely recognized as the fastest man in baseball, and long-time teammate Satchel Paige said Bell could turn out the light and be in bed before the room got dark.

James Thomas Bell (1903-1991) at age 17 moved from Starkville, Mississippi, to St. Louis, where his mother felt he would get a better education. The St. Louis Stars signed him in 1922 as a left-handed knuckleball pitcher. Before he was switched to the outfield, he earned his nickname when he fell asleep before he was supposed to pitch. He was a "Cool Papa."

Bell was popular in St. Louis, and he remained with the Stars for 10 seasons. He gained his fame with the great Pittsburgh Crawfords team and, later, with the Homestead Grays. He joined the Crawfords in 1933, a team that also raided other ballclubs (including the Steel City rival Grays) for the services of future Hall of Famers Satchel Paige, Oscar Charleston, Judy Johnson, and Josh Gibson. Other very good players—such as Sam Bankhead, Sam Streeter, Rap Dixon, Cy Perkins, Leroy Matlock, and Vic Harris—played for the Crawfords at some time from

Cool Papa Bell may have been the fastest man ever to play baseball. He was once clocked rounding the bases in 12 seconds; the fastest official time was set by Evar Swanson in 1929 at 13.3 seconds.

'33 to 1936. It might have been the greatest concentration of talent in baseball at that time or any other.

Cool Papa joined other Negro League stars and went south, playing in both the Dominican Republic and in Mexico. Bell was in such demand that he played for 29 summers and 21 winters. He was still hitting .300 when he was age 48. In his day they would at times play three games in three towns in a day, play 200 games in a season, and travel everywhere by bus.

Bell's lifetime average, by available records, was .338, and he hit .395 in exhibition games against major leaguers. He once stole over 175 bases in a 200-game season, but as he remembered, "one day I got five hits and stole five bases, but none of that was written down because they didn't bring the scorebook to the game that day." Bell was elected to the Hall of Fame in 1974.

Monte Irvin said, "The only comparison I can give is—suppose Willie Mays had never had a chance to play big league? Then I were to come to you and try to tell you about Willie Mays. Now this is the way it is with Cool Papa Bell."

JOHNNY BENCH

★

*J*ohnny Bench was the best offensive and defensive catcher in baseball for more than a decade. The first player from the draft to be inducted into the Hall of Fame (in 1989), he had the greatest career of any catcher in National League history.

Born in Oklahoma City, Oklahoma, in 1947, Johnny Lee Bench was an outstanding high school athlete, and Cincinnati drafted him in the second round of the 1965 draft. He was named the 1966 Carolina League Player of the Year, hitting 22 homers in 98 games. He had 23 homers at Buffalo in '67.

The Reds promoted Johnny in 1968. He was the National League Rookie of the Year with a .275 average, 15 homers, and 82 RBI, second on the club. He hit 26 homers in 1969. He also laid the foundations for a defensive reputation that was to become legendary. He led the '68 NL in putouts and assists, and popularized a one-handed catching method that gave him greater mobility and allowed him to utilize his cannonlike right arm.

He was so overpowering that baserunners simply didn't challenge him much throughout his prime.

Bench won Most Valuable Player Awards in 1970 and '72, leading the Reds to the playoffs both years. In 1970, at age 22, he was the youngest man to ever win the Award. He led the league with 45 homers and 148 RBI. It capped a meteoric rise to stardom that took even Bench by surprise. His second MVP Award came two years later, in 1972, after batting .270 with 40 home runs and 125 runs batted in.

Bench and the Reds won consecutive World Series in

Johnny Bench as a rookie instantly took over a leadership role behind the plate *(above)*. *Opposite page:* Bench was the first catcher since Roy Campenella to lead his loop in RBI.

A Bench-signed baseball.

1975 and '76, and the Big Red Machine won 210 games during those two seasons. Johnny hit in the middle of a lineup that included Pete Rose, Joe Morgan, George Foster, Tony Perez, and Dave Concepcion. In the fourth and final game of the 1976 World Series, Bench had two homers and five RBI, and hit .533 for the Series, to win the World Series MVP Award.

Bench's 327 homers as a catcher were a record when he retired after the 1983 season, and he rates near the top in many defensive categories. He had 20 or more home runs in 11 seasons, drove in more than 100 runs six times, and won Gold Gloves from 1968 to 1977. During his last three seasons he played more games at first and third to extend his career. Bench drove in more runs in the 1970s (1,013) than any other player and played in 11 All-Star games.

YOGI BERRA

★

Yogi Berra was a mainstay of the most dominating baseball team in history, the New York Yankee team that played from the end of World War II until the early 1960s. Although he never led the league in a single major offensive category, he was just the third man to win three Most Valuable Player Awards, and he played in 14 World Series.

Lawrence Peter Berra (born in 1925) grew up in a largely Italian neighborhood in St. Louis. One of his neighbors was Joe Garagiola, and they played American Legion baseball together. When both went to a Cardinal tryout in 1943, the Redbirds offered Garagiola $500 to sign, and they offered Yogi less. His pride hurt, Berra refused, eventually signing with the Yankees for the $500. He played in the Piedmont League until he joined the Navy. He saw action in the Normandy Invasion of 1944.

In 1946, Berra was discharged and played for Newark, hitting .314 with 15 homers. He was called up to the Yankees that season, where he would star until 1963.

Berra captured the imagination of baseball fans with his malapropisms. "It ain't over till it's over" has become a rallying cry for anyone trailing in a game. He was stocky, short, with a broad face and a well-publicized penchant for comic books and a natural quality that fans found amusing and endearing. He was also one of the most dangerous hitters in the American League.

Yogi didn't become the Bomber's No. 1 catcher until 1949. In 1950 he batted .322 with 28 homers and 124 RBI. Although his 1951 season wasn't as impressive (a .294 batting average, 27 home runs, and 88 RBI), he won his first MVP Award. His 1952 or 1953 seasons weren't much different than his 1954 (a .307 average, 22 homers, 125 RBI) and his 1955 (a .272 average, 27 homers, 108 RBI), but he won consecutive MVPs in 1954 and '55. It was a tribute to his

Opposite page: Yogi Berra was not an accomplished backstopper immediately upon breaking into the big leagues. He worked many hours with Yankee legend Bill Dickey to master the position. Once Berra learned, however, he became one of the better fielding catchers in the league. Berra was a big-league hitter from his first at bat.

consistency that his three MVP seasons were not necessarily his best years. He had 90 RBI in nine seasons, and 20 homers in 11 seasons.

Berra worked to become a fine defensive catcher, and in 1958 fielded a perfect 1.000. He was a wonderful handler of pitchers and a wizard, for a catcher, at the double play. Although he played with Mickey Mantle and Whitey Ford,

Berra's teams were not stocked like the 1927 Yankees, yet they won five consecutive World Series. Berra owns a host of World Series records, he was named an All-Star from 1948 to 1962, and he had perhaps the greatest career of any catcher in baseball history. He also managed the Yankees and the Mets to pennants. He was inducted into the Hall of Fame in 1972.

Yogi Berra celebrates winning his second MVP Award, in 1954, with sons Tim, left, and Larry. It was the first season in five years that the Yanks missed the AL pennant, though. Yogi's son Dale, born in 1956, played shortstop in the big leagues for 11 seasons.

WADE BOGGS

No one in the 1980s or early 1990s got on base with more consistent success than Wade Boggs.

Wade Anthony Boggs, born in 1958 in Omaha, was a seventh-round draft pick by the Boston Red Sox in 1976. He batted .263 for Elmira in the New York-Penn League that year, the only year of his entire career until 1992 in which he hit less than .300. He rebounded the next year to hit .332 at Winston-Salem in the Carolina League. When he won the International League batting title with a .335 effort in 1981, the Red Sox finally gave Boggs his chance, after six years in the minor leagues.

In the minors, he played all the infield positions before narrowing his choices to first and third base in his 1980 and 1981 seasons with Triple-A Pawtucket. When Boggs first made the Red Sox in 1982, he played first and third base and batted .349. He was handed the starting third baseman's job the next season, after the Red Sox jettisoned incumbent third sacker (and 1981 AL batting champ) Carney Lansford.

Boggs's career in the major leagues was one of high averages and record-breaking accomplishments. From his rookie season through 1989, his worst batting average was .325 in 1984. He won five American League batting titles in his first seven years in the majors. For seven consecutive years (1983 to 1989) he produced 200 or more hits. Even more incredible is the fact that he is the first major leaguer to have 200 or more hits and 100 or more walks in the same season since power hitter Stan Musial accomplished that same feat back in 1953. Boggs proved to be a disciplined batter, never swinging at the first pitch and seldom chasing pitches which weren't strikes.

In addition to his offensive prowess, Boggs devoted extra work into perfecting his defense, making him the complete player. He led American League third basemen in the 1986 season with 121 putouts. Twice he has led AL third baseman in making double plays. His

Wade Boggs has led an almost obsessively methodical existence. Each evening he fields exactly 150 grounders in practice, takes batting practice at precisely 5:17 P.M., and does wind sprints at exactly 7:17 P.M.

work habits could be categorized as almost obsessive; he arrives at the ballpark at a certain time, preparing for the game in the same fashion every day with a schedule that is detailed down to the minute.

In the 1986 American League playoffs, he batted only .233, which was quite a slump for Boggs. His hitting improved for the World Series, where he averaged .290. A torn right hamstring, which had kept him on the bench for the last four games of the regular season, undoubtedly accounted for these disappointing postseason statistics. He made up for them in the 1988 and 1990 ALCS, however, by batting .385 and .438, respectively.

LOU BOUDREAU

Many argue that no decade in this century has had more great shortstops than the 1940s. Of the great ones, most analysts rate Lou Boudreau the best.

Louis Boudreau (born in 1917) grew up in Harvey, Illinois, and was a three-time all-state basketball player. He played basketball and baseball for the University of Illinois in 1936 and '37. The Indians signed him to an agreement in 1938, and Big 10 officials ruled Lou ineligible. He joined the Indians' Cedar Rapids farm club that year and also played pro basketball.

In 1939, Boudreau was in Cleveland to stay. In 1940, his initial year as a regular, he hit .295 and drove in 101 runs. The next season he topped the AL in doubles. In 1944, Lou copped the AL bat crown and seemed headed for a repeat win the next season before a broken ankle sidelined him.

Before the 1942 campaign, although just age 24, Lou applied for and was given the Cleveland manager's post, thus becoming the youngest pilot to open the season at the helm of

Wade Boggs's specialty was not just batting but getting on base. He led the AL in on-base average each year from 1985 to 1989. He averaged about 31 points difference between himself and whoever was the No. 2 on-base batter in the league. In '88 he compiled a .480 on-base average, and No. 2 Mike Greenwell had a .420 mark.

Lou Boudreau celebrates after his fall classic triumph in 1948. Despite having several fine batters, the Tribe batted just .199 in the Series.

a major-league team. Known as the "Boy Manager," Boudreau quickly showed he was mature beyond his years. Among his many leadership qualities were remarkable self-confidence and a willingness to experiment.

Boudreau created the famous "Williams Shift" in 1946 to combat lefty pull-hitter Ted Williams. Lou moved to the right side of second base, challenging Ted to hit the other way. Lou also moved the strong-armed Bob Lemon from a third baseman to a pitcher.

When Bill Veeck took over as Cleveland owner in 1946, he at first wanted Boudreau to give up the manager's reins and concentrate solely on playing. The torrential protests of Cleveland fans made Veeck reconsider. His change of mind paid off when the Indians won the world championship in 1948. The 1948 AL MVP, during the regular season Lou hit .355, and in the playoff game he belted two homers.

Owing to weak ankles, Boudreau was one of the slow-est infielders in the game and had a mediocre arm. Lou was so thoroughly schooled, however, that he almost never er-rored on a routine play and had an unerring sense of anticipa-tion. Between 1940 and 1948, Boudreau led the AL in field-ing every year but one.

Released by Cleveland in 1950, Lou signed with the Red Sox as a player, and took over in the Red Sox dugout in 1952. He later managed the A's and the Cubs. Boudreau was elected to the Hall of Fame in 1970.

GEORGE BRETT

★

One of the top players during his era and best third basemen of all time, George Brett led the expansion Royals rise into a championship club on his way to 3,000 hits.

In 1980, George Howard Brett (born in 1953) came closer to batting .400 than any player since Ted Williams in 1941. Brett was hitting .400 into the final weeks of the '80 season, and ended the year with a .390 batting average. While he was considered a very good player before then, Brett became a superstar in 1980, winning the AL MVP by adding 24 homers and 118 RBI. He led KC to the ALCS, where the Royals finally defeated the Yankees. The finale was iced by a clutch three-run homer by Brett off ace reliever Goose Gossage. Although the Royals lost the World Series to Philadelphia in six games, Brett collected nine hits for a .375 average.

Brett is the younger brother of big-league pitcher Ken, who was 83-85 in 14 seasons. George had a less-than-stellar minor-league career, never hitting .300 and experiencing some trouble in the field.

Although he never had more than 118 runs batted in during a season, George Brett retired with 1,595 RBI, tying Mike Schmidt in that category. Brett retired in 1993 fifth on the all-time doubles list with 665.

When he was first called up to Kansas City, late in 1973, he managed only a .125 batting average. After a brief stint for Triple-A Omaha in 1974, he was called up to the big leagues to stay.

The 1975 season gave the first hint of Brett's ability. He led the AL with 195 hits and 13 triples while batting .308. He won his first batting crown in 1976 (at age 23) with a .333 mark. He also tied a major-league record by leading the league in triples for the second straight year. The Royals won the AL West in only their eighth year of existence, only to lose to the Yankees, a fate that Kansas City would suffer the next two years.

The Royals won their first world championship in 1985 against the Cardinals. That season Brett had 30 homers, 112 RBI, and a .335 average. He had three homers, five RBI, and a .348 average as the Royals came back from a three-games-to-one deficit to beat Toronto in the playoffs. The Royals also rallied from a three-games-to-one deficit to win the Series, with George batting .370 with five runs.

Brett made headlines in the famous "Pine Tar Incident" on May 24, 1983, when Yankee manager Billy Martin pressured the umpires to disallow a Brett game-winning, two-out home run because of technicality of pine tar running too far up the bat, calling him out instead. Brett became enraged, KC protested, and the ruling was later overturned. Brett was also the first player to win batting crowns in three different decades by winning the title in 1976, 1980, and in 1990 at age 37.

LOU BROCK

★

*I*n 1964, the Chicago Cubs acquired Ernie Broglio, Bobby Shantz, and Doug Clemens from the Cards for Paul Toth, Jack Spring, and Lou Brock. Hitting .251 for the Cubs at the time of the trade, Brock went on to hit .348 the rest of the season, as the Cardinals overcame a six and one-half game deficit in two weeks to win the NL pennant. He hit .300 with a homer and five RBI in the 1964 World Series as the Cardinals won. Brock ruled left field in St. Louis for 15 more seasons.

Louis Clark Brock (born in 1939) was a left-handed pitcher in high school, but he switched to the outfield when he went to Southern University in 1958. He played there for three seasons, then signed with the Cubs in 1961. He led the Northern League with a .361 batting average and 117 runs in 128 games that year, and was in Chicago to stay in 1962. He batted reasonably well in those two years, hitting .263 and .258 in 1962 and '63, with 73 and 79 runs scored, though he was an inferior outfielder.

In 1965, Lou scored 107 runs and stole 63 bases, while batting .288. He swiped an NL-high 74 bases in 1966, getting his first stolen base crown. Brock was an aggressive player, saying, "Baserunning arrogance is just like pitching arrogance or hitting arrogance. You are a force, and you have to instill that you are a force to

As a leadoff man, Lou Brock's job was to score runs, which he did with great regularity. He scored more than 100 runs in seven seasons and more than 90 in 10 seasons. Not one to walk early in his career, Brock eventually notched more than 70 walks in two seasons.

the opposition. You have to have utter confidence."

Lou led the Cards to two consecutive NL pennants in 1967 and '68. He led the NL with 113 runs in '67 and had a career-high 21 homers. In 1968, he led the circuit with 46 doubles and 14 triples. In each of those World Series, he hit over .400 and stole seven bases.

Brock stole 51 bases in 1970, but he didn't lead the league, losing out to Bobby Tolan. Lou led the NL from 1966 to 1969, and from 1971 to 1974. In 1970 and '71, he had more than 200 base hits and 100 runs scored a season, leading the NL with 126 in 1971. In 1974, a 35-year-old Brock stole 118 bases, break-

ing Maury Wills's 1962 single-season stolen base record of 104. Brock stole his 893rd base in 1977, breaking Ty Cobb's career record. When Lou turned in a .221 campaign in 1978, at age 39, he refused to retire on a down note. He returned for a final season in '79, batted .304 at age 40, earned his 3,000th hit, and stole 21 bases in 123 games. He ended his career with 938 stolen bases, and was present when Rickey Henderson broke both records. Brock earned eight stolen base titles, scored over 90 runs 10 times, batted .300 in eight seasons, and had over 200 base hits four times. Lou was inducted into the Hall of Fame in 1985.

DAN BROUTHERS

★

By any standard, Dan Brouthers was the greatest hitter in the game's first period, from 1871 (the founding of the National Association) to 1893, when the pitcher's mound was established at its present 60'6" distance from home plate. Brouthers captured five hitting titles and was at one time or another a league leader in every major batting department.

Dennis Joseph Brouthers (1858-1932) was initially a pitcher. He reached the National League in 1879 with the Troy Trojans. After three undistinguished twirling efforts, he was converted to a full-time first baseman.

Unlike most great hitters, Brouthers struggled at the plate in the majors at the outset, returning to semipro ball in 1880 for further seasoning. Back in the NL the following year with Buffalo, Big Dan teamed with Deacon White, Hardy Richardson, and Jack Rowe to give the Bisons an attack so devastating that the quartet came to be labeled "The Big Four." Brouthers soon emerged as the acknowl-

Opposite page: Lou Brock. *Above:* Brock breaks Maury Wills's single-season stolen base record by swiping No. 105 in 1974 against the Phillies as Larry Bowa awaits the throw from the catcher.

edged club leader and one of the game's first great stars by topping the circuit in batting in 1882 and 1883.

When Buffalo encountered severe financial problems in 1885, the entire Big Four was sold to Detroit in mid-September for $7,500. National League president Nick Young attempted to void the deal, believing it would swing the pennant unfairly to Detroit. When the quartet refused to return to Buffalo, however, Young allowed them to remain in Detroit provided they not play in any games against pennant contenders. So, the Big Four had to sit out the last three weeks of the season as all Detroit's remaining games were with teams in the race for the flag.

Allowed to play for Detroit in 1886, Brouthers led the league in homers. The following season, he sparked the Wolverines to their only pennant. Poor attendance forced Detroit to fold after a fifth-place finish in 1888. The Big Four broke up as a result, with Brouthers being awarded to the Boston Beaneaters. In his first year in the Hub, Big Dan promptly won his third batting title. In 1890 Brouthers won a flag with the Boston Reds in

the Players' League, and the following season he was on the pennant-winning Boston Reds in the American Association. He played on one last pennant winner in 1894 with the fabled Baltimore Orioles. Brouthers had a career .342 batting average, and he knocked in 1,057 runs and scored 1,523 runs in 1,673 games. He was elected to the Hall of Fame in 1945.

Dan Brouthers, the top hitter of his time, notched not only the best pre-1893 batting average, at .342, but also the highest slugging average at .519.

MORDECAI BROWN

★

Three Finger Brown was one of a kind. He became a great pitcher because of, rather than in spite of, a crippling injury.

At the age of seven, while visiting his uncle's farm in Indiana, Mordecai Peter Centennial Brown (1876-1948) accidentally stuck his right hand under a corn chopper. Before he could retrieve the hand, half of his index finger was torn off and the thumb and middle finger were permanently impaired.

The damaged hand hampered Brown whenever he tried to play his preferred position of third base but strangely seemed to work to his advantage when he turned to pitching in his early 20s. Brown found that the unnatural grip he had to employ on the ball caused many of his straight pitches to behave like knuckleballs and imparted an extra dip to his curves. The irony is that Brown lacked a major-league fastball and might never have risen above semipro competition were it not for his uncle's corn chopper.

Brown joined the Cardinals in 1903. Thinking that his

crippled hand would handicap him in the long term, the Cardinals dealt him to the Cubs before the 1904 season. With Chicago, Brown achieved almost instant stardom and became the linchpin of the mound staff.

On June 13, 1905, Brown and Christy Mathewson of the Giants hooked up in one of the greatest pitching duels ever. Brown surrendered just one hit but came out a loser, 1-0, when Mathewson held the Cubs hitless. To Mathewson's dismay, it turned out to be the last time he bested Brown until the 1909 season. In between, Brown topped the great Matty on nine consecutive occasions.

With Brown's right arm leading the way, the Cubs won four pennants between 1906 and 1910 and two World Series. The second and last championship came in 1908 against Detroit and saw Brown win two games and post a perfect 0.00 ERA. Two years earlier Brown came through the regular season with a 1.04 ERA to set a 20th-century National League record.

Used not only as a starting pitcher but also as the Cubs' stopper, Brown topped the NL in 1911 with 53 appearances while compiling a 21-11 record. It was the last of his six consecutive 20-win seasons. Brown returned to the Cubs in 1916 after two years in the Federal League. Fittingly, his final big-league appearance came on Labor Day that season against Mathewson, who was also making his final bow. Matty, for once, took Brown's measure, winning 10-8. Brown had a career 2.08 ERA to go with his 239-129 record.

Mordecai Brown was a good hitter for a pitcher, compiling 235 career hits and a .206 batting average. As with other fine-hitting pitchers of his era, Brown sometimes batted ahead of his catcher.

ROY CAMPANELLA

★

Roy Campanella—along with Jackie Robinson and Don Newcombe—was a pioneering black ballplayer who boosted a Dodger organization that to this day is acknowledged as one of the finest teams in baseball history.

Born in Philadelphia, as a youngster Roy Campanella (1921-1993) decided to become a catcher because no one else had signed up for that position in school. He played well enough that in 1937 the 15-year-old backstop was catching on the weekends for the semi-pro Bacharach Giants. He moved to the Baltimore Elite Giants, with whom he played most of his career in the Negro Leagues. By the mid-1940s, Campy challenged Josh Gibson as the best catcher in the Negro Leagues.

Campanella was approached about signing with the Brooklyn organization late in 1945 but was unwilling because he thought that he would be playing with the Brooklyn Brown Dodgers Negro League team. Eventually, Campanella was convinced to sign and played the 1946 season with Class-B Nashua, where he was the Eastern League MVP. In 1947, he was the International League MVP while with Montreal.

Campy was a success from the day he arrived in Brooklyn in mid-1948. The stocky catcher had a rocket for an arm, a powerful bat, and handled a legendary pitching staff to five pennants in 10 years. Campanella was a prime reason the 1950s Dodgers were the exceptional team in the National League. In 1951, Campanella won the first of three Most Valuable Player awards, a feat accomplished by only a tiny group of stars. He batted .325 with 33 homers and 108 RBI. His 1953 MVP season was among the best ever recorded by a catcher, as he led the league with 142 RBI, clubbed 41 homers, scored 103 runs, and batted .312.

Campy chipped a bone in his left hand in spring training in 1954, and he hit only .207 in 111 games that year. He rebounded in 1955 to win his third MVP by batting .318, with 32 homers and 107 RBI. Starting in 1956, his hand injury dating back to 1954 had caused nerve damage, and his hitting suffered further decline in 1957. He hoped for a return

Big Roy Campanella barrels into the commissioner's box while chasing a foul pop-up at the 1955 World Series, while commissioner Ford Frick (first row) looks somewhat disquieted.

to form in 1958, but it never happened. Campanella was paralyzed in a car crash during the winter between the 1957 and 1958 seasons and never played again. Confined to a wheelchair, he eventually went to work for the Los Angeles Dodgers. Inducted in 1969, Campy summed up his love for the game by saying, "You got to be a man to play baseball for a living, but you got to have a lot of little boy in you, too."

ROD CAREW

★

In 1977, Rod Carew made a valiant run at the .400 mark last topped by Ted Williams in 1941, though Rod fell just short at .388. He topped the .300 plateau 15 times and the .330 mark 10 times, winning seven batting titles along the way. Carew was a master of the base hit, as he posted 200-plus hits in four seasons.

Born in the Panama Canal Zone in 1945, Rodney Scott Carew moved to New York when he was 17. After high school he joined the Twins' organization in 1964. Promoted to Minnesota in 1967, Carew won the Rookie of the Year Award when he hit .292. He established his bat wizardry early, winning a batting title in 1969. Minnesota won the AL West in 1969 and '70; Carew and Co. ran into the Baltimore buzz saw both years.

Carew won four straight AL batting titles from 1972 to 1975. As a second baseman, he was weak on the double play and had a below average arm but compensated with good range. Unfortunately, the slightly built Carew took a pounding

Campy never played any other position but catcher in the majors, and in seven of his 10 seasons he caught more than 120 games. He pinch batted only 45 times in his career and had 15 pinch hits.

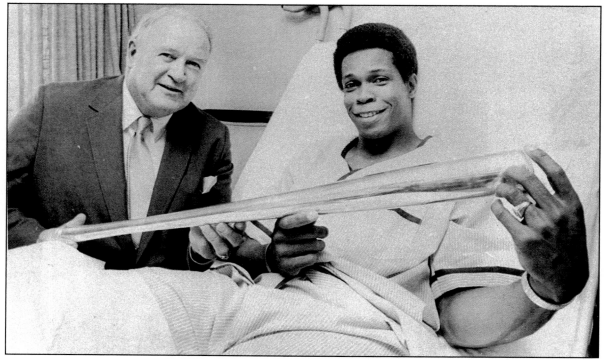

Above: Rod Carew (right), while convalescing in 1970, received a silver bat from AL president Joe Cronin for winning the 1969 bat crown. *Opposite page:* Carew hit over .300 in 15 different seasons and over .350 in five.

at second. Twins manager Gene Mauch moved Rod to first base to extend his career. In 1977, he responded with a serious run at a .400 season, hitting .388 and a league-leading 16 triples, 239 hits, and 128 runs. It was his sixth batting title, and the next closest hitter to Carew's .388 mark was NL batting champ Dave Parker at .338, making it the largest margin in baseball history. Carew was a runaway choice for the league's Most Valuable Player.

Rod was a master bunter—when he won the title in 1972

he had 15 bunt-hits, but not a single home run—and would astonish teammates by putting a handkerchief at various spots up and down the foul lines and dropping bunts onto it. In 1969, he stole home seven times, tying Pete Reiser's record. Carew had seasons of 35 swipes in 44 attempts and 27 in 35, and stole at least 23 in six out of seven seasons. He won his final batting title with a .333 mark in 1978.

After that season, Carew forced his own trade and ended up with the California Angels,

where owner Gene Autry was trying to build a winner with veterans. The 1979 Angels went to the ALCS, and though Rod hit .412, they lost to the Orioles in four games. He failed to hit .300 during the 1984 season for the first time in 15 years. He returned in 1985 and hit .285, and became only the 16th man to collect 3,000 hits. He retired after the 1985 season with 3,053 hits. In 1991, Carew became the 22nd player to be elected to Cooperstown in his first year of eligibility.

STEVE CARLTON

★

*T*im McCarver, Steve Carlton's catcher, once said that Carlton "does not pitch to the hitter, he pitches through him. The batter hardly exists for Steve. He's playing an elevated form of catch."

In 1967, his first full season, Stephen Norman Carlton (born in 1944) was 14-9 for the Cardinals, with 168 strikeouts in 193 innings. He gave the world-champion Redbirds a powerful one-two punch, along with team ace Bob Gibson. Carlton started the fifth game of the 1967 World Series against Boston, where he yielded just three hits in six innings but was tagged for a loss.

Carlton won 13 games in 1968 as the Cardinals defended their National League crown. In 1969, the 6'4" flame-thrower notched a 17-11 record with a 2.17 ERA (second best in the league). A slump dropped Carlton to 10-19 in 1970. After he bounced back to a 20-9 record in 1971, he wanted a fitting pay raise, but the Cards balked. Because of the contract dispute, Carlton was traded to Philadelphia for Rick Wise.

Steve Carlton compiled seasonal earned run averages under 3.00 with at least 190 innings pitched in eight different seasons, and he had more than 200 strikeouts in eight years, with 190-plus in three others.

Carlton's 27-10 record and 15-game winning streak for the last-place Phillies immediately soothed critics of the trade, who prized Wise, a fan favorite. Dubbed "The Franchise," Carlton accounted for an incredible 45.8 percent of Philadelphia's 59 victories, setting a modern record. He was the NL leader in wins, ERA (1.97), starts (41), complete games (30), innings pitched (346), and strikeouts (310). Only Sandy Koufax had broken the 300-strikeout barrier in the NL before Carlton, and only five other pitchers had ever won 20 or more for a last-place club. Carlton won his first Cy Young and was rewarded with a $150,000-a-year contract.

In 1976, Philadelphia won the NL East, with Carlton going 20-7. He won his second Cy Young Award in 1977, with a 23-10 record, as the Phils won their second straight division title.

It took a league-leading performance of 24 wins from Carlton in 1980 to send the Phillies to their first World Series in 30 years. He won his third Cy Young, striking out a league-best 286 batters.

In 1982 the Phillies faltered despite Carlton's achievements.

Steve Carlton receives his first Cy Young Award for his work in the 1973 season. He was to receive a record four Cy Youngs altogether.

He won an unprecedented fourth Cy Young Award, going 23-11 with league highs in strikeouts (286) and innings pitched (295). Carlton slipped to 15-16 in 1983, but he sent the Phillies to another World Series with two playoff victories. Carlton's last winning season came in 1984. He won 13 games, but the sore-shouldered hurler had to cope without his once-wicked slider, the pitch that made him famous. He retired in 1988.

During his career, Carlton accumulated six 20-win seasons and earned seven All-Star Game selections. He led the NL in strikeouts five times and wins four times. He was inducted into the Hall of Fame

GARY CARTER

★

Gary Carter, one of the best backstops of the 1980s, was a savior for the Mets in the mid-1980s. While they seemed ready to challenge for a NL title, they needed one more good hitter and a capable catcher to guide a talented but inexperienced pitching staff. Before the 1985 season, New York shipped four players to Montreal for Carter. That year, he topped the Mets in homers (32) and RBI (100), hitting an impressive .281 and leading league backstops in putouts and chances per game.

Another superb season by Carter in 1986 helped the Mets win their first divisional crown since 1973. The Mets finished with a stunning 108-54 record, while Carter posted 24 homers and 105 RBI. Carter hit two homers in the fourth game of the World Series and led the New Yorkers to a world championship with nine RBI.

A third-round draft pick by the Montreal Expos in 1972, Gary Edmund Carter (born in 1954) played catcher, first base, third base, and outfield in three minor-league seasons before making the big leagues. Carter began his major-league career as an outfielder. In his rookie year of 1975, he played 92 of his 144 games in the Montreal outfield. At bat, he hit .270 with 17 homers and 68 RBI.

Six weeks on the disabled list blighted Carter's sophomore season, but in 1977 his play was so inspired that the Expos traded starting catcher Barry Foote in June and gave the job to Carter.

The new responsibilities brought out the best in Carter, and he hit .284 with 31 homers and 84 RBI. Carter proved that he could handle the defensive expectations of a full-time major-league catcher. He paced league catchers in assists, putouts, and double plays. In 1978, he had 20 homers and 72 RBI. In 1979 he batted .283 with 22 homers and 75 RBI, and again he led league catchers in assists, putouts, and double plays.

In 1980, the Expos finished second in the East with a 90-72 record (only one game behind the division-winning Phillies). Carter sparked Montreal that year with 29 homers and 101 RBI. Defensively, he led NL catchers in putouts, assists, and fielding percentage

(.993). In 1981 Carter had an off year, but the the Expos came within inches of the World Series. In a special divisional playoff, the Expos nipped the Phillies in five games, before losing the NLCS to the Dodgers.

Carter hit 29 homers and 97 RBI in 1982. Although he hit just 17 homers in 1983, Carter had a league-best .995 fielding average. In his last year in Montreal, 1984, he hit .294 with 27 homers and a league-leading 106 RBI.

Gary Carter never batted .300 but was dangerous with a bat in his hands nevertheless. He slugged at least 20 home runs in nine different seasons, had at least 100 RBI in four different seasons, notched more than 80 RBI in seven seasons, and scored at least 75 runs six times.

OSCAR CHARLESTON

★

Oscar Charleston put punch in the lineups of no less than a dozen teams in his 35-year career. He was a barrel-chested man of great strength, a long-hitter who could hit for average and run like the wind. Only Josh Gibson, who's memory is fresher, challenges Oscar's reputation as a slugger, and only Cool Papa Bell is mentioned with him when the best center fielders of the Negro Leagues are named.

Born in Indianapolis, Oscar McKinley Charleston (1896-1954) began his career in organized baseball in 1912 at age 15 in the Philippines as a member of the Army. Two years later, he was the only African American in the Manila League. Discharged in 1915, Charleston signed on with the Indianapolis ABCs.

John B. Holway wrote, "There were three things Oscar Charleston excelled at on the field: hitting, fielding, and fighting. He loved all three, and it's a toss-up which he was best at." Each of the three is documented. Charleston's lifetime average is .357. Newt Allen said, "He hit so hard, he'd knock gloves off you." Charleston's 11 homers against major-league pitchers in exhibition games ties for the highest total recorded, and he hit them for distance, too. In the field, Oscar was just as impressive, with an arm more accurate than strong, and the speed to run down drives in any part of the park easily. Right fielder Dave Malarcher, who played alongside Charleston, said: "He could play all the outfield. I just caught foul balls. I stayed on the lines." Charleston's spectacular catches are legendary.

Infielders got out of Oscar's way as he sped around the bases. They knew he would use all his considerable strength and speed against them and that he had a mean streak. Off the field he was just as formidable. Cool Papa Bell said that Charleston ripped the hood off a "mouthy" Klansman in Florida in 1935; the Klansman elected to drop the matter. Charleston is also remembered as a genial, good-natured fellow who was attracted to the good life.

Charleston stayed on into the 1940s as a player-manager, mainly with the great Pittsburgh Crawfords and the Homestead Grays. Charleston was elected to the Hall of Fame in 1976.

Like other great players such as Ernie Banks and Stan Musial, Oscar Charleston switched to first base at the end of his career.

ROGER CLEMENS

★

*R*oger Clemens was the top pitcher in the American League in the late 1980s and early 1990s. His fastball was one of the best in the league. With a curveball, a forkball, and a change-of-pace, "The Rocket" was a complete hurler.

William Roger Clemens (born in 1962) in the 1981 draft was a 12th-round choice by the Mets out of San Jacinto Junior College, but instead he went to the University of Texas and helped the Longhorns in 1983 win the NCAA championship by beating Alabama in the finals. That year, he was the 19th player selected, by the Boston Red Sox.

The Red Sox rushed Clemens through their minor-league system, and he was in Boston by 1984. His rookie season was beset by a forearm muscle pull during September. Nevertheless, he went 9-4 with five complete games and 126 strikeouts in 133⅓ innings. In 1985 Clemens was hampered by a bad shoulder and needed surgery at season's end. He had an unspectacular 7-5 record with a 3.29 ERA.

From 1986 to 1992, Roger Clemens notched at least 200 strikeouts a year. His streak of seven consecutive seasons with 200 Ks tied an AL record held by Rube Waddell and Walter Johnson. Clemens also tied a mark held by Grover Alexander by leading his league in shutouts and ERA three consecutive seasons.

Clemens returned healthy and revitalized for the 1986 season and helped Boston coast to its first World Series in a decade. He had a 24-4 record (a league-leading .857 winning percentage) with 10 complete games, 238 strikeouts, and a league-best 2.48 ERA. He also set a major-league record by striking out 20 Mariners on April 29, 1986. Boston went from 81 wins in 1985 to 95 in '86, and Clemens was named the Cy Young winner and the MVP. He threw seven shutout innings against the Angels in the decisive seventh game of the American League Champi-onship Series to send the Red Sox to the World Series. He struck out 17 Angels during three starts and established an AL record by pitching 22⅔ ALCS innings. He was winless in two World Series starts against the world-champion Mets.

In 1987 Clemens became the first Red Sox pitcher to have back-to-back 20-win seasons since Luis Tiant in 1973 and '74. Besides his league lead in victories, Clemens's 20-9 record gave him a league-best .690 winning percentage. His 18 complete games and seven shutouts were also AL highs.

Again, he was the Cy Young winner.

A late-season slump stopped Clemens from earning his third straight 20-win season in 1988. However, he finally led the league in strikeouts with 291. He won 17 games in 1989.

In 1990, Clemens led the BoSox to the ALCS again with a 21-6 record and a 1.93 ERA, but Bob Welch won the Cy Young Award. The next season, Clemens was for him an unre-markable 18-10 with a 2.62 ERA, but his performance was still the best in the loop that year, and he received his third Cy Young trophy.

Roger Clemens signs autographs before a game.

ROBERTO CLEMENTE

★

*R*oberto Clemente took being a role model seriously, sending out 20,000 autographed pictures a year to kids. He had one of the strongest outfield arms in history, won four batting titles, and notched 3,000 base hits. On Dec. 31, 1972, he was on a cargo plane from Puerto Rico airlifting emergency relief supplies, bound for earthquake-torn Nicaragua. The plane crashed a mile off of the Puerto Rico coast and there were no survivors. Clemente left behind his wife, three young sons, and millions of fans. He was elected to the Hall of Fame in a special election held just 11 weeks after his death; he was named on 93 percent of the ballots.

Roberto Clemente y Walker (1934-1973) grew up near San Juan, Puerto Rico. He developed his strength as a youngster by unloading grocery trucks and by squeezing a rubber ball. He started playing for a pennant-winning Santurce team in 1952, and when he was 19 years old, his outfield mate was Willie Mays. In 1954, Clemente signed with the Dodgers, who attempted to hide him by assigning him to their top minor-league club in Montreal and playing him sparingly. The Pirates unearthed him and drafted him in 1955.

Clemente joined the Pirates that year, and he was a good player for several years. By 1960, he began to emerge as a star, achieving personal bests in runs, home runs, RBI, and batting average. He hit .310 as the Pirates beat the Yankees in the World Series. He raised his game another notch in 1961, hitting .351, the first of five

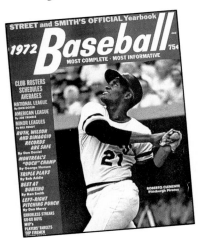

Above: Roberto Clemente was featured on the cover of *Street and Smith's* 1972 yearbook after his astounding performance in the 1971 World Series, in which he hit .414 and was chosen Series MVP. *Opposite page:* An outstanding hitter, Clemente batted over .300 in 13 consecutive seasons, won four batting titles, and was chosen to the All-Star team 12 times.

times he was to hit above .340.

No one who saw Clemente throw the ball could forget the power and accuracy of those throws. His arm was a deadly weapon that he could unleash from impossible angles and distances. He won Gold Gloves every year from 1961 through 1972.

Roberto won four batting titles, hit 240 homers, and was the National League Most Valuable Player in 1966. He has perhaps the greatest defensive reputation of any right fielder in history, playing more games in right field than any player in National League history.

Although Clemente was troubled by a bad back, bone chips, and shoulder troubles throughout his career, he posted the highest batting average for the decade of the 1960s with a .328 mark. Clemente hit .312 in 1972, at age 38, and rapped his 3,000th hit on Sept. 30, becoming just the 11th man to reach that level. Clemente felt a duty to his fans, particularly his compatriots. He once said, "A country without idols is nothing." Clemente was and still is an idol for many people in many countries.

TY COBB

★

When the first Hall of Fame vote was taken in 1936, Ty Cobb was named on 222 of the 226 ballots cast, to lead all candidates for enshrinement. The shock was not that "The Georgia Peach" outpolled every other player in major-league history to that time, including Babe Ruth and Honus Wagner, but that four voters could ignore Cobb's towering credentials.

This slight is understandable only when it is taken into consideration that many consider him to be the greatest player ever and all know that he is also the most despised.

Tyrus Raymond Cobb (1886-1961) contended that he was far from being a great athlete. What made him such a superb player was his unparalleled desire to achieve, to excel, and, above all, to win. No story better illustrates this than the one told about a 1905 fracas between Cobb and Nap Ruck-

er, his roommate while both were playing in the minors for Augusta. Rucker returned to their hotel room ahead of Cobb after a game and drew a bath for himself. When Cobb found Rucker in the tub and began upbraiding him, Rucker only looked bewildered. "Don't you understand yet?" Cobb roared. "I've got to be first all the time—in everything."

About any other player but Cobb such a tale might seem apocryphal. But as a result of his unquenchable thirst to win

Teammates Ty Cobb, left, and Harry Heilmann, right, sandwich Shano Collins, Ike Boone, and Joe Harris of Boston, about 1924. Heilmann was extensively tutored in hitting by Cobb and became one of Cobb's few friends in baseball.

and his reckless slides with spikes high whenever he tried to take a base, he was shunned by other players. Some—such as Sam Crawford, who played beside Cobb in the Detroit outfield—went years without speaking to Cobb. Yet, if wanting to be first was what ignited Cobb, no one can deny that he got his wish. When he retired in 1928 after 24 seasons in the majors, he held almost every major career and single-season batting and baserunning record. Most have since been broken, owing largely to the longer schedule now played, but one that almost certainly never will be is his mark for the highest career batting average. Precious few players in the past half century have managed to hit .366 for one season, let alone a 24-year period.

Cobb's deepest regret was that he never played on a World Series winner. The closest he came to it was in 1909, when the Tigers took the Pirates to seven games before succumbing. Only age 22 at the time and playing on his third consecutive American League champion, Cobb seemed destined to play in many more World Series before he was done. Sadly, the 1909 classic

Notorious for sharpening his spikes and then sliding with them high, Ty Cobb was a truly great baserunner. He was not only the single-season and career stolen base leader when he retired, he also swiped home 35 times and stole second base, third base, and home in the same inning three times.

proved to be his last taste of postseason competition.

Whether playing for an also-ran or a contender, though, Cobb gave the same relentless effort. It was thus difficult to credit a story that surfaced after he was fired as the Tigers player-manager following the 1926 season. Reportedly both he and Tris Speaker had helped rig a 1919 game between Detroit and Cleveland. The only part of the story that was consistent with the Cobb everyone knew was that it had been fore-

ordained that Detroit would win the contest. Cobb, not even for all the money in the world, would ever have agreed to finish less than first in something.

Despite the 1926 scandal, Cobb was allowed to sign with the Philadelphia Athletics. He retired after two seasons in Philadelphia, never again to have a full-time job in baseball. For the next 33 years he continued to live on the terms under which he had played, comfortably fixed but essentially alone.

MICKEY COCHRANE

★

*M*ickey Cochrane laid claim throughout his career to being the best-hitting catcher in baseball.

In the spring of 1923, Gordon Stanley Cochrane (1903-1962) signed his first professional contract in the Eastern Shore League under the name Frank King. Mickey used an alias not to protect his college eligibility—he had already graduated from Boston U., where he had been a five-sport star—but to guard his ego.

However, Cochrane did well at Dover, although it took him several weeks to learn his true position was behind the plate. Once he became a catcher, he caught the eye of Connie Mack. So certain was Mack of Cochrane's future greatness that he took over Portland in the Pacific Coast League in order to give Mickey a place where he could hone his skills without danger of the Athletics losing him.

Joining the Mackmen in 1925, Cochrane caught a rookie-record 134 games, while hitting .331. Mickey was the first major leaguer to play a full season on a pennant-winning team managed by Connie Mack and then later to manage a pennant-winner himself. Cochrane was still a long way from being a polished maskman, however. Some felt that he never did fully master his trade. When Pepper Martin ran wild for the Cardinals against the A's in the 1931 World Series, Philadelphia pitcher George Earnshaw publicly blamed Cochrane for the embarrassment; others felt that the responsibility belonged to the A's hurlers.

Mickey might have been the best-hitting catcher of all time. His .320 batting average and .419 on-base percentage are career records for a catcher, and his .478 slugging average is an AL record. Cochrane also had an exceptional batting eye—he walked four times as often as he struck out.

Cochrane played on five pennant winners, three in Philadelphia and two more after he was traded to Detroit following the 1933 season. He had early success as a pilot—Cochrane won flags in 1934 and '35, his first two seasons at the Detroit helm. On May 25, 1937, Mickey was beaned by Bump Hadley of the Yankees and hovered near death for more than a week before recovering. Cochrane was eager to get back into action, but Detroit owner Walter Briggs would not permit it, especially since doctors had warned that a second beaning could prove fatal. Cochrane was named to the Hall of Fame in 1947.

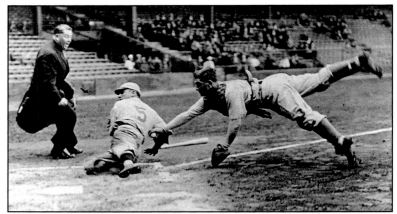

Early in his career, Mickey Cochrane was not a very good defensive catcher, but he worked hard at the craft and became accomplished at many aspects of the position. He was one of the best at tormenting batters. He also led league catchers six times in putouts and twice in double plays and assists.

EDDIE COLLINS

★

*J*ohn McGraw once said that Eddie Collins was the best ballplayer he'd ever seen. Connie Mack (who managed both Collins and Nap Lajoie) called Collins the best second baseman he ever saw. Those are strong endorsements coming from two men who saw a lot of baseball. Collins played in 25 seasons, and is arguably the greatest second baseman in history.

Edward Trowbridge Collins Sr. (1887-1951) was a college star for Columbia, but evidence that he appeared as a professional under an assumed name in six games in 1906 ended his amateur status. He joined Connie Mack's Philadelphia Athletics after graduation. Eddie teamed with Jack Barry at shortstop, Stuffy McInnis at first, and Frank Baker at third to form the famous "$100,000 Infield." In Collins's first World Series, in 1910, he hit .429 and set four hitting records, after a regular season that included a then-record 81 stolen bases. In all, he won three championships with the A's.

When the Athletics were broken up and sold off after the devastating salary raids of the upstart Federal League, Collins fetched the highest price paid for a player until Babe Ruth went to the Yankees. The White Sox gave $50,000 for "Cocky" after his MVP 1914 season. He led the Sox to a World Series triumph in 1917. One of the clean players on the 1919 Black Sox, Eddie never forgave the eight players who sold out. The 1919 World Series was Eddie's last, but he left behind a stack of World Series records.

Collins hit for average and not power but played in an era when power was not as much a part of the game as now. He

Eddie Collins finished in the top six of MVP voting seven times. There was no voting before 1911 and between 1915 to 1921.

A great fielder, Eddie Collins led AL second baseman in one or another fielding category every year from 1909 to 1922 save for one.

finished with a .333 lifetime batting average and a .406 career on-base average. He hit over .340 10 times, and he almost never struck out. Collins owns many fielding records for second basemen, including most putouts, assists, and total chances.

Collins was named player-manager of the White Sox in 1924 and remained two years at the helm. He returned to Philadelphia in 1927 but played less and less until he retired from playing in 1930. After retiring, Collins persuaded long-time friend Tom Yawkey to buy the Boston Red Sox. As the Red Sox general manager, Collins signed Ted Williams and Bobby Doerr. Eddie was enshrined in Cooperstown in 1939.

SAM CRAWFORD

★

*I*n Sam Crawford's time the mark of a great slugger was still not how many home runs he hit but how many triples. By that standard Crawford was the dead-ball era's most prolific long-ball hitter. He left the majors in 1917 with 312 triples. Crawford also was the first player in this century to lead both major leagues in home runs.

Born in Wahoo, Nebraska, Samuel Earl Crawford (1880-1968) was tagged "Wahoo Sam" early in his professional career and grew so fond of the nickname that he asked that it be inscribed on his Hall of Fame plaque. Crawford first played pro baseball in 1899 and did so well that Cincinnati purchased him near the end of the season. Still just 19 years old when he made his debut with the Reds on Sept. 10, 1899, Crawford hit .307 in the 31 games that remained and collected eight triples in just 127 at bats.

After the 1902 season, Crawford seized what might be his last chance to escape the lowly Reds, a cellar finisher in 1901 despite his loop-leading

16 homers. He jumped to Detroit in the American League. Wahoo Sam promptly hit .335 in his first year with the Bengals and cracked 25 triples, an AL record that stood until 1913 when Joe Jackson notched 26 three-baggers, a total that Crawford himself matched a year later. Even, with Crawford's slugging, Detroit remained a second-division team until it added Ty Cobb to its cast in 1905. While not the hitter for average that Cobb was, Crawford was his superior as an extra-base-hit producer. Playing side by side in the same outfield, the pair spearheaded the 1907 to '09 Tigers, the first team in American League history to garner three consecutive pennants.

Sam Crawford led his league in triples in six different seasons, starting in 1902 with the Cincinnati Reds and ending in 1915 with the Detroit Tigers.

Crawford fashioned a .309 career batting average in 2,517 games and logged at least 10 triples in every full season he played. He was a loop leader in three-baggers six times and also topped the AL on three occasions in RBI.

During his long tour of duty with Detroit, Crawford became very popular with Motor City fans, to the envy of Cobb. The relationship be-tween the two grew so strained that purportedly the only time they spoke to each other was when a ball was hit between them. Their animosity lasted even after both retired, but ironically it was Cobb who campaigned the hardest for Crawford when Sam continued to be passed over for selection to the Hall of Fame. In 1957, Crawford received the long-overdue honor.

Sam Crawford never led his league in slugging percentage, but he finished in the loop's top five in 11 different seasons.

JOE CRONIN

★

At age 20, in 1926, Joe Cronin sat on the bench in Pittsburgh, was farmed out, and then sold. In 1959, he became president of the American League. Between, he turned in a Hall of Fame career as one of the best hitting shortstops in history.

Joseph Edward Cronin (1906-1984) was born in San Francisco a few months after the great earthquake. Coming from a low-income back-ground, Joe grew up an all-around athlete. He won a city-wide tennis championship as a youngster, and in high school he played soccer and basketball, along with baseball. He played semipro baseball after gradua-tion. A Pittsburgh Pirates scout signed Joe in 1925, and he played one good season for Johnstown, Pennsylvania, in the Mid-Atlantic League. Pro-moted to the Pirates the next year, he sat behind Glenn Wright in Pittsburgh for two seasons.

After his trials in the Na-tional League, Cronin finally landed in Washington in the American League in 1928. As the regular shortstop in 1929,

While it took Joe Cronin (throwing) several years to find his place as a starting player in the big leagues, once he located a spot he batted over .300 in eight straight seasons.

he had a decent season, and followed it up with a year that was to earn him *The Sporting News* Most Valuable Player Award in 1930, when he hit .346 with 127 runs and 126 RBI. Joe reached the 100-RBI mark in eight seasons, remarkable for a shortstop with his fielding ability. Cronin compiled a lifetime .301 batting average by hitting over .300 in 11 seasons, and was a spectacular doubles hitter. He socked 51 in 1938 and hit 515 in his career. He was a fine defensive player and was named the outstanding major-

league shortstop by *The Sporting News* seven times.

Cronin was active in an era when player-managers were common, and he served a long term in that role, as skipper of the Washington club in 1933 and 1934, and bossing the Red Sox for 13 years after his sale to the Boston club in 1934. His maiden voyage as a manager produced a pennant in 1933, and Cronin hit .318 as Washington lost to the Giants in the World Series. Ted Williams said after Cronin had quit playing he was "the great-

est manager I ever played for." Cronin also had many doubts about his double duty and tried to resign after his first season. He didn't finish first again until 1946, the year he stepped down as a player, when he brought Boston its first pennant since 1918. A broken leg finally took him out of the lineup for good.

In 1959, Joe was elected president of the American League, the first former player to be so honored. He was inducted into the Hall of Fame in 1956.

DIZZY DEAN

★

One of the most entertaining players in the history of baseball, and a member of the Gashouse Gang of the old St. Louis Cardinals, Dizzy Dean blazed across the baseball sky for five seasons. He was the last pitcher to win 30 games in a season before Denny McLain in 1968. Diz was the league's Most Valuable Player in 1934 and finished second in the voting in 1935 and 1936.

Jay Hanna Dean (1911-1974) was born in Arkansas to an itinerant farm worker, and the Dean family traveled the Southwest. Diz and his brothers (his kid brother Paul was also a pitcher) went to work in the fields at early ages. Jay picked up his nickname (given for obvious reasons) and his knowledge of pitching while in the army. After serving, he moved to Texas and pitched for a company team. A Cardinals sleuth spotted him and signed him to a St. Louis organization contract for the 1930 season. He had a combined 25-10 record that year in the minor leagues before pitching a three-hit shutout for the Cardinals on the final day of the season. After winning 26 games in 1931 at Triple-A Houston, he was called up to stay for the 1932 campaign. Dizzy won 18 games and led the NL in shutouts, innings pitched, and strikeouts, the first of four con-

Dizzy (left) and his brother Paul "Daffy" Dean were a great one-two starting combo for the 1934 Cardinals. Dizzy won 30 and Daffy had 19.

secutive strikeout titles he would earn.

Dizzy was not dumb and was a shrewd negotiator. Once, he staged a holdout during the 1934 championship season for his brother Paul, also a Cardinal, whom Diz felt was underpaid. Despite missing some starts during the holdout, the elder Dean went 30-7, and rookie Paul was 19-11.

The Dean brothers won four World Series games as the Cards beat the Tigers. While pinch-running in game four, Dizzy was beaned in the forehead while breaking up a double play. It was feared that he would miss the remainder of the Series until the headlines

the next day ran "X-Ray of Dean's Head Reveals Nothing." Dizzy ended up pitching a shutout and scoring the only run he would need in the seventh game.

During the 1937 All-Star game, a line drive off the bat of Earl Averill broke Dizzy's toe. He tried to come back too soon, which altered his motion and, as a result, injured his right arm. He never fully recovered and never again won more than eight games in a season. He retired in 1941 at age 30.

Dizzy became a popular broadcaster in St. Louis with a gift for memorable malapropisms. He was elected to the Hall of Fame in 1953.

Dizzy Dean in 1933 struck out 17 Cubs, setting a major-league record for most strikeouts in a game; it has since been broken.

BILL DICKEY

★

Until Yogi Berra came along, Bill Dickey was not only known as the greatest Yankee catcher but one of the greatest catchers of all time.

Born in Bastrop, Louisiana, William Malcolm Dickey (1907-1993) grew up in Arkansas. After playing the infield in high school, he attended Little Rock College in 1925, where he was a pitcher and catcher. Lena Blackburne, manager for Little Rock in the Southern Association, spotted Dickey and signed him that year. For several seasons thereafter, Bill played with both Little Rock and their associate teams in the lower minors. Since Little Rock was an unofficial tributary team for the White Sox, most major-league teams took little notice of him. Of course the Yankees scouted him, and when their investigation proved worthwhile, purchased him in 1928. He caught in 10 games at the end of that season, joining one of the greatest teams of all time.

Dickey's first full season, in 1929, he batted .324 and completed the outstanding lineup. He was Lou Gehrig's roommate, and they were a matched set—quiet and consistent. Dickey was a steady .300 hitter, 10 times topping the .300 mark. His mark of .362 in 1936 was a record for backstoppers. Over the four-year period from 1936 to 1939, the left-handed Dickey took advantage of the short right field porch in Yankee Stadium to pop 20-plus homers a year and drive in 100-plus runs.

A hard worker and a fierce competitor, Dickey handled Yankee pitching staffs on eight World Series teams, winning seven championships. His 17-year career spanned the era from Ruth to DiMaggio. Bill caught 100 or more games for 13 consecutive seasons, a record that would stand until Johnny Bench appeared. At the time of Dickey's retirement, he held the records for putouts and fielding average.

A quiet leader and generally calm on the field, Bill lost his cool one day in 1932 and received a one-month suspension and a fine after he broke baserunner Carl Reynolds's jaw with one punch after a collision at home plate. After catching only 71 games during the 1943 season, Dickey hit a two-run homer in the fifth and final game of the Series that fall against the Cardinals to propel the Yanks to the title.

Bill enlisted in the Navy at age 36, missing the 1944 and 1945 seasons. He returned but played in only 54 more games to finish his career in 1946. When the Bombers were working with a young kid named Berra, Bill was called in to show the youngster the way to do it. Dickey was named to the Hall of Fame in 1954.

Bill Dickey has the reputation as one of the finest handlers of pitchers in baseball history. He was also a great fielder, leading the AL three times in fielding average and assists, and five times in putouts.

Bill Dickey hit more than 20 home runs in four different seasons, compiling at least 100 RBI in each of those years. He batted at least .300 in 11 seasons, he batted at least .325 in five seasons, and he had only 289 strikeouts in 6,300 at bats.

MARTIN DIHIGO

★

Since the Negro League teams obtained such slender profit margins, often teams carried only 14 to 18 players. The most valuable player to a team was usually the one who could play several positions adequately. Martin Dihigo could pitch and play all the infield and the outfield positions at an All-Star quality level.

Born in Matanzas, Cuba, Martin Dihigo (1905-1971) began his pro career in 1923 in the Cuban Winter League as a strong-armed but weak-hitting outfielder. There is a legend that he won a distance-throwing contest against a jai alai player who was allowed to use his wicker-basket cesta. He is compared very favorably to Roberto Clemente by those who saw both players throw from the outfield. Like the American-born Negro League players, Martin crossed and re-crossed the 90 miles of water between the two countries to ply his trade; he also played in Puerto Rico, Mexico, and Venezuela. From the time he came to America in 1923 through 1936, he made only

Martin Dihigo was one of the most versatile players in history, ranking with Babe Ruth. In 1935-36 in the Cuban League, Dihigo performed a rare double feat, leading the circuit with a .358 batting average and with 11 pitching wins.

occasional forays to the pitching mound, having some success with his good fastball and control.

Dihigo pitched more often when he was in the Latin American countries. His pitching stats include an 18-2 record and an 0.90 ERA in 1938, and a 22-7 record and a 2.53 ERA in 1942. He twirled the first no-hitter in Mexican League history. According to the albeit unsubstantiated records found by historians thus far, he prob-

ably won 256 games while dropping only 136.

From his early troubles at the plate, Martin developed into a great hitter by age 20. He made his lasting impression with his bat in the United States. He was a fine hitter—he hit over .400 three times and led two different leagues in batting average—and he hit a 500-foot round-tripper in Pittsburgh in 1936. Dihigo grew to over 210 pounds and led his league in homers at least twice, in 1926 and in 1935. He tossed runners out at home plate with frightening regularity.

He posted a .316 career batting average in the Negro Leagues. He often left the outfield to pitch relief, especially when he was managing. Dihigo was a manager for the New York Cubans, in Mexico, and in Cuba until 1950. He also played all nine positions in one game on several occasions.

After his retirement, Dihigo became a broadcaster and the Minister of Sport in Cuba. One of Latin America's most admired players, he died in 1971. Martin is the only player to be in the Cuban, Mexican, and American Baseball Halls of Fame.

JOE DiMAGGIO

★

*I*f Joe DiMaggio wasn't the greatest all-around player in baseball history, he almost certainly was the most majestic.

Joseph Paul DiMaggio (born in 1914) was a native of San Francisco, where he and his brothers, Vince and Dom, played baseball on the sandlots hour after hour. Joe left high school early to work in a cannery and to play semipro baseball. At age 17, he signed with the San Francisco Seals (for whom brother Vince played) at the end of the 1932 season. Joe played in three games and batted .222. The next season, he had a .340 batting average, 28 homers, and 169 RBI in 187 games. Joe was a local hero.

DiMaggio batted .341 in 1934, but he suffered a knee injury that scared some big-league clubs away from him, especially at the price that the Seals were demanding. The Yankees had no such qualms; with their superior financial position, the Bombers were able to risk the $25,000 and five minor-league players for Joe. The Yankees assigned him back to San Francisco for the 1935

season, and he had a .398 average, 34 homers, and 154 RBI—raising the hopes of Bronx fans.

DiMaggio lived up to even tough New York standards in his 1936 rookie season, joining Lou Gehrig to power the Yankees to the first of four consecutive world championships. Although he was severely ham-

pered by Yankee Stadium's cavernous left field, The Yankee Clipper twice led the team in home runs and in slugging. He hit only 148 of his 361 lifetime home runs at home.

DiMaggio was an outstanding and beautiful defensive outfielder. He played center field with grace and threw the ball with terrific power. He led

Above: Joe DiMaggio led the American League in scoring only once, in 1937 with 151 runs scored. He scored more than 100 runs in eight seasons, however. *Opposite page:* DiMaggio was in the top five of American League slugging percentage leaders in 11 seasons, and he notched a career .579 slugging percentage.

the league in assists with 22 his rookie year, and had 21 and then 20 before the league apparently got wise and stopped running on him.

Joltin' Joe won his first Most Valuable Player Award in 1939, when he had his career-best .381 batting average. When he won his second MVP in 1941 he had 76 walks and only 13 strikeouts. He also hit in a record 56 consecutive games, a feat considered the greatest by some observers. No other hitter has ever hit in more than 44. He almost never struck out—his high was 39, his rookie year—and actually came close to having more lifetime homers than Ks, with 369 strikeouts to his 361 round-trippers.

If Yankee Stadium depressed his career totals, World War II was even more of a factor as Joe lost three seasons. He won his third MVP and the Yankees won another championship in 1947 (it was Joe that hit the drive that made Al Gionfriddo famous), but a heel injury slowed Joe in 1948, and he couldn't return to the lineup until June of 1949. His return was memorable, as he was 5-for-11 with four homers and nine RBI in a double-header. Another world championship

Joe DiMaggio, left, confers with Yankee shortstop and future fellow Hall of Famer Phil Rizzuto. DiMaggio was highly respected by teammates and foes alike, because although he was profusely talented, he worked hard to enhance his proficiency. Was DiMaggio consulting with Rizzuto about hitting? In 1950 and 1951, Phil actually had a higher batting average than did Joe.

BUCK EWING

⭐

At a glance, Buck Ewing's career seems noteworthy but in no way extraordinary. He led the National League in home runs in 1883 and in triples in 1884, but his accomplishments otherwise appear modest. In Ewing's case, however, statistics are deceiving. In 1919, Francis Richter, one of the top sportswriters of his day, deemed Ewing, Ty Cobb, and Honus Wagner the three greatest players in baseball to that time. Richter went on to say that Ewing might have been the best of them all according to "supreme excellence in all departments—batting, catching, fielding, baserunning, throwing, and baseball brains—a player without a weakness of any kind, physical, mental, or temperamental."

William Ewing (1859-1906) was one of the first players from the Cincinnati area to become a major-league star. A weak hitter early in his career, Ewing batted only .178 in a brief trial with Troy in 1880 and finished at an even .250 the following year in his first full big-league season. Any hitting

Joe DiMaggio's and Marilyn Monroe's wedding in 1954 drew much publicity to the normally reticent Joe after he retired from baseball. While their marriage lasted but nine months, DiMaggio was always there for Monroe when she needed support.

followed, the first of five straight for the Yanks, but DiMaggio would only stick around for three of them. Injuries and the grind of the road drove Joe into retirement after the 1951 season. He was succeeded in center by Mickey Mantle.

With the passing of time, Joe's legend continued to grow to an enormous magnitude.

Ernest Hemingway used Joe as a symbol in *The Old Man and the Sea*. Musicians from Les Brown to Paul Simon wrote about DiMaggio in songs. Marilyn Monroe married Joe. He became a promoter for a national product, Mr. Coffee, that became part of the American vocabulary. DiMaggio was inducted into the Hall of Fame in 1955.

Bill James, in his *Historical Baseball Abstract*, describes Buck Ewing, here on an Old Judge card, as one of the top players of his time when taking into account the opinion of Ewing's contemporaries. Francis Richter and John Foster, two guide editors, each stated that Ewing was baseball's greatest player.

EWING, C., New Yorks
Copyright by Goodwin & Co., 1888.
OLD JUDGE
CIGARETTE FACTORY.
GOODWIN & CO., New York.

BOB FELLER

★

ob Feller was probably harmed more than any other great player by World War II. While serving in the Navy he lost nearly four full seasons just as he was entering his prime. Had Feller's career been allowed to proceed without interruption, he might now be considered the greatest pitcher in history.

Born in 1918 at Van Meter, Iowa, Robert William Andrew Feller was signed by Cleveland while still a 16-year-old high school student, in 1935. The signing was illegal according to the rules of the time and would have cost the Indians the rights to Feller had commissioner Kenesaw Mountain Landis not feared a gargantuan bidding war among the other teams if Feller was made a free agent. For even as a teenager, he was renown for the blazing fastball that would soon gain him the nickname "Rapid Robert."

No one could have taught Feller what he possessed when he debuted with Cleveland in a July 1936 exhibition game against the Cardinals. Though only 17, Feller was already so swift that he fanned eight Red-

Buck did was a bonus, however. From the very outset of his career, he was viewed as an outstanding defensive catcher, the most demanding position on the diamond.

Ewing was one of the first catchers to catalogue each opposing batter's weakness and then share the knowledge in pregame clubhouse meetings. John Foster wrote that "as a thrower to bases, Ewing never had a superior. Ewing was the man of whom it was said, 'he handed the ball to the second baseman from the batter's box.'"

Great as Ewing was behind the plate, he could not play there every day. The position was so physically taxing that catchers in the last century seldom worked more than half

their team's games. While most backstops simply took that day off, Ewing customarily played another position. So versatile was Buck that he could fill in anywhere on the diamond. In 1889, with the Giants in a drive for the pennant, Ewing even pitched and won two complete games. He jumped to the Players' League the following year and was named manager of the New York Giants. The 1890 season was Ewing's last as a regular catcher.

Ewing finished his playing career in Cincy in 1897. A player-manager at the time, he remained with the Reds for two more years as a manager. In 1936, he tied for first place in the initial vote of the old-timers for the Hall of Fame. Buck was inducted in 1939.

Although the Indians signed Bob Feller as a high school student, which was against the rules of the time, commissioner Kenesaw Mountain Landis acquiesced to letting Feller become an Indian not only because Landis feared a bidding war but because Feller himself wanted to stay with the Tribe.

he topped the major leagues with 240 strikeouts and also set a modern single-game record when he fanned 18 Tigers in his last start of the season. Despite his remarkable feat, Feller lost the contest, due in part to walks. Along with his record-shattering strikeout performance, Rapid Robert also set a new modern mark for bases on balls in 1938 when he gave up 208 walks.

His control slowly improving, Feller paced the American League in wins during each of the next three seasons and then went into the Navy. His pre-war high and low points both came in 1940. That year Feller tossed the first Opening Day no-hitter in AL history but then ended the season with a 1-0 loss to Detroit that killed Cleveland's hope for its first pennant since 1920.

Returning from the war, Feller had his finest season in 1946 when he won 26 games and logged 348 strikeouts. An arm injury in 1947 curtailed Bob's fastball thereafter, but he continued to be one of the game's top hurlers until 1955. He was the author of three career no-hitters and 12 one-hit games. Feller was selected to the Hall of Fame in 1962.

birds in the three innings he hurled, causing home plate umpire Bob Ormsby to label him the fastest pitcher Ormsby had ever seen, Walter Johnson included.

All did not come easy, though, for Bob. Batters quickly learned that while he was virtually unhittable, they could nevertheless reach base simply by waiting for walks. In 1938,

ROLLIE FINGERS

★

After bringing Rollie Fingers up from the minors in 1969, the Oakland A's were uncertain what to do with him. For three seasons the A's shuttled him between the bullpen and periodic starting roles. Finally in 1971, after he was able to finish only four of his 35 career starts to date, Oakland manager Dick Williams decided Fingers was best suited for relief work. Rollie responded with a team-leading 17 saves that year and 21 saves in 1972. In 1973, Williams again briefly tried Fingers as a starter before recognizing once and for all that Rollie's proper job was as a fireman. In the 11 remaining years of his career, Rollie Fingers never made another starting appearance.

Clean shaven when he first appeared on the major-league scene, Roland Glen Fingers (born in 1946) soon became known for having the longest mustache from tip to tip in major-league history. His career high-point came in the 1974 World Series for the A's against the Dodgers. With the Athletics shooting for their

Rollie Fingers was one of the first relievers to demand that his work per game be limited so that he may be stronger for more games. In that way, Fingers himself helped create the modern relief specialist.

third successive world championship, Fingers won the first game of the Series with a four and one-third inning relief stint and then came through with two saves in the final two games. For his efforts, Fingers earned the Series Most Valuable Player trophy.

After two more seasons with the A's, Rollie became a free agent at the end of the 1976 campaign. He signed a five-year pact at an estimated $1.5 million with the Padres. In each of his first two seasons in San Diego, he topped the senior loop in saves. His personal high of 37 saves came in 1978. In 1980, Fingers was swapped to the St. Louis Cardinals and then immediately shipped to the Milwaukee Brewers.

Fingers had his finest season in the strike-abbreviated 1981 campaign. In 47 appearances, he collected a major-league-leading 28 saves and etched a 1.04 ERA. His banner year garnered him both the MVP and the Cy Young Awards but narrowly missed bringing Milwaukee a division crown. When the Brewers broke through the next year to win their first pennant, an ailing elbow forced Fingers to watch their World Series loss to the Cardinals from the sidelines.

Elbow problems shelved Fingers for all of the 1983 season, but he rebounded strongly in 1984 to post 23 saves and a 1.96 ERA. The 1985 campaign proved to be his last, however, when he sagged to a career-worst 1-6 record and 5.04 ERA, with 17 saves. At the time of his retirement, he had a major-league record 341 saves. Fingers was voted to the Hall of Fame in 1992.

CARLTON FISK

★

*C*arlton Fisk retired as the all-time leader in games caught and home runs by a catcher, but he will best be remembered for his game-winning home run in game six of the '75 World Series.

In that game, the Reds and the Red Sox were tied 6-6 in the bottom of the 12th inning, when Fisk stepped to the plate against Reds pitcher Pat Darcy.

While Carlton Fisk is best remembered with a bat in his hands, some of his best moments came as a catcher. His fielding was big-league caliber almost from day one.

The image of Fisk swinging, watching the ball sail, and waving his arms to encourage it to stay in fair territory is truly memorable.

After spending a little time at the University of New Hampshire on a basketball scholarship, native New Englander Carlton Ernest Fisk (born in 1947) was drafted by the Boston Red Sox in 1967, spent 10 months in the military, and began his pro baseball career at age 20 in 1968.

After four years on the farms, Fisk immediately distinguished himself as a big-league rookie in 1972, leading the circuit with nine triples—the only offensive category in which he would ever lead a league in his 24-year career. He was also tops among league catchers with 72 assists and 846 putouts—and 15 errors. This wasn't a big enough obstacle to keep him from snaring American League Rookie of the Year accolades.

In 1973 Carlton slammed 26 homers, but he missed nearly the entire 1974 season and quite a bit of the 1975 regular season with injury. Following a subpar 1976 season (a .255 average, 17 homers, and 58 RBI), Fisk rebounded in

Carlton Fisk displayed the ability to hit homers as a White Sox. In 1985 he had 37 homers in 543 at bats. In 1988, despite missing 70 games with a broken hand, Carlton had 19 home runs in 253 at bats for a 7.5 home run percentage. In 1990 and 1991 he had 18 homers each year in 452 and 460 at bats, respectively.

1977, hitting .315 with 26 homers and 103 RBI.

After the 1980 season, Fisk became a free agent when the Red Sox failed to offer him a new contract before the December signing deadline. The Chicago White Sox secured Fisk's services with a five-year, $2.9 million deal. The White Sox were desperate not only for offense but for an on-field general with some major-league experience and natural leadership. Fisk was just what they were looking for.

He helped the Sox to a 1983 division title by hitting .289 with 26 homers and 86 RBI. His finest season in Chicago came in 1985. He was plagued by injuries in 1984, during which he had 21 homers but only 43 RBI, breaking a record for the fewest RBI by someone with 20 or more home runs. In '85, though, he came back with career highs in homers (37) and RBI (107). He credited his comeback to his extensive training program, pumping iron through the winter.

In 1990 Fisk broke Johnny Bench's record of most homers by a catcher; in 1993 Carlton broke Bob Boone's record of most games caught.

WHITEY FORD

★

The "Chairman of the Board," Whitey Ford was the ace pitcher for the 1950s Yankees. His .690 winning percentage is the best of any modern 200-game winner, as his teams won 11 pennants and seven World Series. Ford captured 15 Series records, including a streak of 33 scoreless innings.

Edward Charles Ford (born in 1926) grew up in New York City. He started pitching only as a senior in high school. The Yankees discovered him in 1946 playing in the sandlot Queens-Nassau League after school, but they had to out-bid the Red Sox and the Dodgers to the tune of $7,000 for Ford's services. He started his pro career in 1947 by notching a 13-4 record; he was 16-8 in 1948, and he led the Eastern League with a 1.61 ERA while going 16-5 in '49.

Ford was summoned to New York in mid-1950 after a 6-3 record. He teased New York fans with a brilliant 9-1 record in 12 starts, and he notched a shutout in the World Series. He then served two years in the military, leaving be-hind the greatest of expectations. When he returned in 1953 he more than measured up, going 18-6 as the Yankees won an unprecedented fifth straight world championship.

Whitey didn't just win, he won spectacularly. During his first 14 seasons, only twice did he post a record that was as low as three games over .500, and in 12 seasons he was at least six games over .500. He led the AL with 18 wins and 18 complete games in 1955. In 1956, he had the league's best ERA

Whitey Ford was not an overpowering pitcher; he was 5'10" and 180 pounds. His stock-in-trade was keeping opposing batters off base. Opponents had on-base percentages under .300 in eight seasons in which Ford hurled at least 190 innings. He had an assortment of changeups to go with his average fastball.

at 2.47. Manager Casey Stengel didn't let Ford pitch more than 250 innings a season, usually starting him against first-division teams.

When Ralph Houk took the Yankees reigns in 1961, he unleashed Whitey. Ford went an AL-top 25-4 with a league-high 39 starts and 283 innings pitched, winning the Cy Young Award. He had a 24-7 record in 1963, again leading the AL with 37 starts and 269 ⅓ innings pitched.

Ford was a superb craftsman with excellent control. He used several pitches, and although some weren't legal, the threat that he fixed some balls kept hitters guessing, helping him more than actually throwing doctored balls.

Whitey, his best buddy Mickey Mantle, Billy Martin, and other Yankees were well known about town. "When Whitey pitched he always felt like unwinding that night after the ballgame," Mickey Mantle said. He added that he was ready to celebrate if Whitey won the game. "Lucky for both of us, he won 236 games when he was pitching for the Yankees." Ford was inducted into the Hall of Fame in 1974, the same year as the Mick.

Known throughout his career as a big-game pitcher, Whitey Ford was 10-8 in 22 World Series starts, with a 2.71 ERA, three shutouts, seven complete games, 146 innings pitched, 94 strikeouts, and 34 bases on balls.

JIMMIE FOXX

★

*I*n an era of big hitters, Jimmie Foxx won four home run titles and two batting titles. He was the first American Leaguer to win consecutive MVP Awards and the first man to win the Award three times.

James Emory Foxx (1907-1967) grew up on a farm in rural Maryland. He enjoyed both high school track and baseball, and through his athletic ability and immense home runs he became celebrated. Frank "Home Run" Baker—the former Athletics and Yankees third baseman who was the manager for Easton, Maryland, of the Eastern Shore League—scouted Foxx pitching in both high school and semipro games. In 1924, Baker sent Jimmie a penny postcard reading, "Would you be interested in becoming a professional ballplayer? If you are, contact me." Jimmie signed a contract at age 16, and Baker, short of catchers, put Foxx behind the plate. He caught 76 games, batting .296 with 10 homers.

Both the Yankees and Athletics were interested in Foxx,

Jimmie Foxx won three batting and on-base titles and was in the top five in the AL in batting average six times and on-base average 10 times.

but Baker steered Jimmie to the A's as a favor to Connie Mack. Foxx joined Philadelphia in 1924, sitting on the bench next to Mack to learn the American League. Jimmie began the 1925 season in Philadelphia but was soon optioned to Providence of the International League. He hit .327 there, though curiously he had only one home run in 101 at bats. He was back in Philadelphia in

1926, and from '26 to 1928 he was a utility player, backing up Mickey Cochrane at catcher and playing first and third.

By the time Foxx became the regular first baseman in 1929, the A's were a powerhouse. "Double X," Al Simmons, and Lefty Grove formed the heart of Mack's last great team, and appeared in three consecutive World Series from 1929 to 1931. Foxx and Simmons combined for 192 home runs, and Grove was 79-15 in those three years. Jimmie won consecutive MVPs in 1932 and '33. He had 169 RBI and 58 homers in 1932, and he earned the Triple Crown in 1933 with 48 homers, 163 RBI, and a .356 average. The A's won two championships before bowing to St. Louis in seven games in 1931. That was to be Foxx's postseason swan song—he hit .344 and slugged .609 in 18 World Series games.

Because Connie Mack suffered economically during the Depression, he sold Foxx to Boston in 1936. Jimmie hailed his arrival by hitting 41 homers and 143 RBI that year.

Foxx had enough left for a final burst. After "slumping" to 36 homers, 127 RBI, and a career-low .285 average in 1937, he bounced back in 1938. Foxx hit 50 homers and led the league in RBI and average, winning his third MVP Award. Appendicitis shortened his terrific 1939 season, and 1940 was his last decent year. By 1945, his eyes had been failing him. When he retired he had 534 homers and 1,921 RBI, and only Ruth had more home runs. Foxx was inducted into the Hall of Fame in 1951.

FRANKIE FRISCH

★

rankie Frisch was a football and baseball star at Fordham University, with a degree in chemistry and a competitive drive that made him a natural leader on the field. There could be only one leader on a team managed by John McGraw, but McGraw realized that the talents of "The Fordham Flash" could help the New York Giants. In 1919 Frisch joined the club, and by

Pepper Martin (left) and Frank Frisch have a slight disagreement with an umpire. As a Giant, Frisch and manager John McGraw were close. When the two had a falling out, in 1926, Frisch was dealt to the Cards. As a manager, Frisch was similar to McGraw, especially in that both loved to badger umpires.

1921 the Giants won the first of four straight pennants.

Frank Francis Frisch (1898-1973) was born in the Bronx and attended Fordham Prep before going to the university. He briefly left college during World War I to join the Student Army Training Corps. Back at school, Frankie learned how to play baseball under former New York Giant third baseman Art Devlin, Fordham's baseball coach. Devlin tipped McGraw to Frankie, and when all reports were positive, Frisch was signed to a professional contract.

McGraw's Giants won the World Series in 1921 and 1922, with Frisch hitting .300 and .471 in the two tournaments. Frisch captured the imagination of baseball fans with his slick fielding (he played third in 1921 and second in 1922) and his timely hitting. In 1923 he led the league with 223 hits, establishing himself as one of the great stars of the day.

The lively ball era began to produce terrific power numbers, but Frisch was not a slugger. He never hit more than a dozen home runs in a season, but hit over .300 13 times, including 11 in a row, from 1921 to 1931.

Frank Frisch was equal to Rogers Hornsby at bat, whom he was traded for, but Frisch, no slouch, lasted longer. He was a starter for the Cards for the next nine years, while Hornsby was a regular for only three years.

Frisch was an exceptional fielder. *The New York Times* called him "possibly the flashiest second baseman of any day" after one of the most talked-about trades of the time. Frank had a serious clash with McGraw and walked off the club in 1926. After suspending Frisch, McGraw traded him in 1927 to St. Louis for Rogers Hornsby, equally at odds with the St. Louis club. The fiery Frisch had finally worn out his welcome with McGraw, though the Flash later said, "I could have flopped as a ballplayer under any other teacher."

Frisch had learned to win, and as the second baseman for the famous "Gashouse Gang," he appeared in four World Series, winning one in 1931, and leading the team to another in 1934, a year after becoming player-manager. Well-respected by his contemporaries, Frisch in 1931 won the first MVP Award in the American League, after a year that was not his best (a .311 average, 96 runs, 82 RBI, and 28 steals). Frankie's playing career lasted through the 1937 season, but he managed for 16 years, winning 1,137 games.

LOU GEHRIG

★

On June 2, 1925, when New York Yankees backup first sacker Fred Merkle, who was giving the club's long-time regular Wally Pipp a day off, seemed about to collapse from the heat, manager Miller Huggins called on rookie first baseman Lou Gehrig as a late-inning replacement. Merkle never started another game in the majors and Pipp never got his job back. Gehrig played a record 2,130 consecutive games for the Yankees. He did not always play all nine innings and he was not always stationed at first base, but one way or another his name always appeared on the lineup card before the game was over. Only very rarely did he play for the sole reason of extending his monumental streak. He played because he was the best all-around first baseman in baseball history.

Born in Manhattan, Henry Louis Gehrig (1903-1941) starred in all sports at the High School of Commerce. Upon graduation, he signed a professional baseball contract with Hartford of the Eastern League under the name of Lewis. Re-

Above: This trophy was presented to Lou Gehrig by his teammates on Lou Gehrig Day. *Opposite page:* Gehrig was an amazing run producer, helped in part because he always seemed to have teammates on base. He is No. 2 all time in RBI per game, at .922, opposed to Sam Thompson's .923 RBI per game.

gardless of the disguise he chose, he could not hide his prodigious talent, and the ruse was soon discovered. As a consequence, he was declared ineligible for sports at Columbia University, where he had been counted on to play both football and baseball.

Gehrig accepted a bonus of $1,500 from the Yankees against his father's wishes and began playing with Hartford under his own name. A two-year stint in the minors was all he needed before he was ready to take his place among the game's greats. In his first full season, Gehrig hit .295, scored 73 runs, and knocked home 68 teammates. He would never again tally under 100 runs or collect less than 100 RBI in a full season. He averaged the highest number of runs and RBI per game of any 20th-century player.

In 1931, Gehrig established an AL record when he netted 184 RBI, breaking his own old mark of 175 set in 1927. The following year he became the first player in the 20th century to clout four home runs in a game. He also once had three triples in a game that was rained out in the fourth inning before it became an official contest. When Lou left baseball he had 493 home runs, second at the time only to Babe Ruth.

Gehrig's slugging exploits were only part of the story. He was also both an excellent baserunner and a solid first baseman. When he was se-

lected the AL's Most Valuable Player, as he was twice, it was for his overall performance.

In 1934, Gehrig won the Triple Crown while copping his only batting title with a .363 mark. Two years later he garnered his final home run crown with 49 four-baggers, tying his own personal high. When Gehrig's batting average slipped to .295 in 1938 and his RBI and homer totals also dipped, it seemed just an off year at first. The strange slump persisted into the next season, restricting him to a meager four singles in his first eight games. When teammates began congratulating him for making routine plays, Lou knew the time had come to step down. On May 2, 1939, he took himself out of the lineup for the first time in nearly 14 years. A few weeks later he entered the Mayo Clinic for tests, which revealed that he had amyotrophic lateral sclerosis— a hardening of the spinal cord. The rare disease has no known cure and is terminal. Knowing he would soon die, Gehrig retired formally on July 4, 1939, in a special ceremony at Yankee Stadium. Tearfully, he told the packed house, "Today, I consider myself the luckiest man on the face of the earth."

Following the 1939 season, Gehrig took a job with the New York City Parole Commission. He continued to work with youth groups and to play bridge with his wife, Eleanor, and close friends until just a few weeks before his death on June 2, 1941. That same year he was inducted into the Hall of Fame.

Lou Gehrig notched at least 200 base hits in a season eight times, at least 40 homers in five years, and more than 100 walks 11 times.

CHARLIE GEHRINGER

★

Never flamboyant and the possessor of an almost Sphinx-like demeanor, Charlie Gehringer might have gone virtually unnoticed on the baseball diamond but for one remarkable quality. He gave the same quietly outstanding performance day in and day out. Gehringer's unceasing excellence led to his being nicknamed "The Mechanical Man." Mickey Cochrane, after managing Charlie for two years in Detroit, said of him, "He says hello on Opening Day and goodbye on closing day, and in between he hits .350."

Charles Leonard Gehringer (1903-1993) was raised about 60 miles north of Detroit. After starring in high school, he played both football and baseball for one year at Michigan University and then decided his future lay in professional baseball. On the recommendation of former Tiger Bobby Veach, Gehringer was given a tryout by none other than the great Ty Cobb, then the Detroit player-manager. Signed by the Tigers in 1924 as a third baseman,

Charlie Gehringer notched 100 RBI in seven seasons, had a .400 on-base average in nine seasons, and scored 100 runs in 12 seasons. He also led AL second basemen in fielding average seven times.

Gehringer was soon moved to second base and became the club's regular there in 1926. For the next 16 years Charlie broke the hearts of all the other keystone aspirants in the Detroit organization. After hitting .277 as a rookie, he batted over .300 every other season but one until he began to fade in 1941.

Gehringer's high-water mark came in 1937 when he rapped .371 to win the American League batting crown. At age 34, he was the oldest first-time winner of a hitting title in history. Before 1937, Gehringer had also paced the junior loop on several occasions in runs, hits, doubles, triples, and stolen bases. His play in all departments was of such high caliber that he was voted the AL second baseman for the first All-Star game in 1933. Gehringer played in six All-Star games altogether and had 10 hits in 20 at bats. He displayed the same steady brilliance in his three World Series appearances with the Tigers. In 81 at bats, Charlie hit .321, one point higher than his overall career batting average of .320.

Reduced to a utility role by 1942, Gehringer retired at the end of the season, even though he still had enough of his old batting skill left to lead the AL in pinch hits. Following three years in the Navy during World War II, Gehringer went to work for an auto dealer in Detroit. Two years after he was elected to the Hall of Fame in 1949, Charlie returned to the Tigers as the team's general manager. Gehringer subsequently served as a Tigers vice president until 1959.

BOB GIBSON

★

*I*n the 1960s, when power pitchers ruled the game, there were few as dominant as Bob Gibson. He was among the most exciting and successful of World Series performers, setting records and winning championships for the St. Louis Cardinals.

Robert Gibson (born in 1935) grew up in the slums of Omaha, Nebraska, and overcame a heart murmur and asthma as a child to become an outstanding athlete in both baseball and basketball. The Kansas City Monarchs offered him a contract after his high school graduation, but he turned it down to play both sports at Creighton University. The Cardinals signed him to a contract in 1957, and he played an unimpressive season in their farm system. After the season, he played basketball with the Harlem Globetrotters, which he did for only one year. From 1957 to 1960, he was generally unimpressive on the mound, and he didn't receive many starts. In 1961, Johnny Keane became the Cardinals manager, and he put Gibson in the starting rotation to stay.

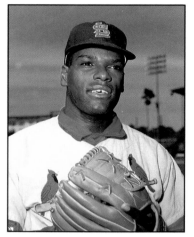

Above: Bob Gibson had extreme self-confidence. Tim McCarver said, "I remember one time going out to the mound to talk with Bob Gibson. He told me to get back behind the batter, that the only thing I knew about pitching was that it was hard to hit." *Opposite page:* Gibson had more than 200 strikeouts and fewer than 100 walks in eight seasons.

Though Bob led the league in walks that year, he won 13 games. The following season he struck out 208 hitters, the first of nine seasons of 200-plus Ks, on his way to the record for strikeouts during the decade. In 1963, he went 18-9. In 1964, he was 19-12 and led the Cardinals to a World Series.

Gibson was intimidating in World Series play, winning a National League record seven games and losing only two as the Cards won two world championships, in 1964 and 1967, and lost one in 1968.

He won two games in the 1964 fall classic, and notched an ERA of 1.00 while winning three games in 1967.

In 1968, Gibson won both the MVP and Cy Young Awards (as did Denny McLain in the AL), helping to prompt a lowering of the mound and a reduced strike zone. His record was 22-9, with a NL-record 1.12 ERA, and a league-best 268 strikeouts. He pitched 13 shutouts, and one-fifth of all his decisions were shutouts. In the World Series that year, he had a single-game record 17 strikeouts.

Pride played a role in Gibson's character and his success. He had to stay in a private home during his first major-league spring training in 1958, and the struggle to overcome racial barriers stayed with him. He helped force the Cardinals' Florida hotels to accept black players in the early 1960s.

Gibson won another Cy Young in 1970 for his 23-7 showing. He had over 20 wins in five seasons and had double figures in 14 consecutive years. He was a tremendous athlete, with 24 lifetime home runs and nine consecutive Gold Gloves. Gibson was inducted into the Hall of Fame in 1981.

TREASURY OF BASEBALL

JOSH GIBSON

★

Possibly the best known of the Negro League sluggers, Josh Gibson's tape measure home runs rattled off the seats at a rate that could not be ignored.

Joshua Gibson (1911-1946) was born in Buena Vista, Georgia. Josh's father, wishing to give his children a better chance in life, moved the family to Pittsburgh, where Josh grew up. Gibson maintained that the greatest gift his father gave to him was to let him grow up in Pittsburgh. An outstanding athlete, he won medals as a swimmer before turning full attention to baseball. Working at an air-brake factory at age 16, he was a star for an all-black amateur team.

Josh was playing semipro ball by 1929. He was watching a Homestead Grays game when their catcher split a finger. They pulled Gibson, who had already acquired some small fame for his long hits, out of the stands and put a Grays uniform on him. Within two years he was one of the team's biggest stars. Though he was barely in his 20s, Gibson was hitting around 70 home runs a year. He was

lured to the Pittsburgh Crawfords in 1932, where he caught for Satchel Paige for five years.

Gibson was a catcher from the beginning, but he was not polished from the start. Since

he played more than 200 games a year, with summer in the States and winter in either Mexico or the Dominican Republic, Josh became a veteran backstop in little time. Walter

By all accounts, Josh Gibson had one of the best throwing arms of all catchers of his era. While he had some problems with pop-ups behind the plate, his 800-plus home runs made those problems easier to tolerate.

Johnson said Gibson was a better receiver than Bill Dickey. "[Gibson] catches so easy he might as well be in a rocking chair," said the Big Train. Roy Campanella called Gibson "not only the greatest catcher but the greatest ballplayer I ever saw."

Gibson reached distances in major-league parks undreamed of by other top sluggers of his day. He is credited with hitting a ball out of Yankee Stadium, and his longest hits are variously estimated between 575 and 700 feet. His career total is uncertain, but even the lowest estimates put him ahead of Hank Aaron, with 800 to 950 career homers. Gibson's lifetime average is one of the highest in the Negro Leagues, at .354, .379, or .440 depending on the source. Against major-league pitching in 16 exhibition games, he hit .424 with five homers.

Gibson went back to the Grays in 1936, but began to suffer from headaches. He drank more than was his habit, partly in a search for relief from what was finally diagnosed a brain tumor. He died at age 36 in 1947, one day after Jackie Robinson played his first game for Montreal in the Dodger farm system.

GOOSE GOSLIN

★

Goose Goslin was the only American Leaguer between 1921 and 1939 who was on five pennant-winning teams despite never playing for the Yankees or under Connie Mack.

Nicknamed Goose both because of his last name and because of his large nose, Leon Allen Goslin (1900-1971) grew up on a small farm in Salem, New Jersey. Originally a pitcher, he was converted to the outfield when his first professional manager thought that Goose's bat had more promise than his arm.

While in the midst of leading the Sally League in hitting during his second season in the loop, Goslin was bought by Washington for $6,000. A successful trial at the end of the 1921 campaign gave Goose hope of winning a big-league job in 1922. He injured his arm while heaving a shotput during spring training of 1922, however, and was never again able to throw with his old ability. Goslin, however, became a competent outfielder.

Goose quickly emerged, though, as a standout slugger. In 1923 he led the American League in triples. A year later he was the loop's RBI king, his 129 ribbies topping even Babe

Goose Goslin was in the top five in slugging percentage in the AL for five straight seasons while he was playing in Washington.

Ruth and preventing the Babe from winning a Triple Crown. Playing in Washington, Goslin had no hope of ever winning a Triple Crown himself. The outfield fences in his home park—Griffith Stadium—were so distant that no Washington player won an AL home run crown until the 1950s when changes were made in the park's contours. Indeed, Goslin hit 17 homers in 1926 on the road and none on his home soil.

The Senators in those years were good enough to win without the long-ball, however, taking back-to-back pennants in 1924 and 1925. When a drought followed, Goslin was dealt to the Browns early in the 1930 season, only a year and one-half after he won the AL batting title.

Reobtained on Dec. 14, 1932, Goslin helped the Senators to win their third and last pennant the following summer.

Swapped to Detroit in 1934, Goslin played on flag winners in each of his first two seasons in the Motor City and produced the hit in the 1935 World Series that brought the Tigers their first world championship. Goose was selected to the Hall of Fame in 1968.

HANK GREENBERG

★

Of the many players who lost playing time and had their career totals diminished by World War II, Hank Greenberg may have lost the most. He was active for nine and one-half seasons, serving in the Army for four and one-half years, but was able to produce Hall of Fame numbers.

Henry Benjamin Greenberg (1911-1986) was raised in the Bronx, and the Yankees offered the 18-year-old a contract in 1929. With Lou Gehrig at first base for the Yanks, Greenberg chose to sign with the Tigers.

In his first two farm seasons, he was a .300 hitter with average power. In the Texas League in 1932, though, he hit 39 homers with 139 RBI. He was the Tiger first baseman in 1933.

In 1934, Greenberg led the league with 63 doubles and drove in 131 runs. In 1935, the Tigers won a world championship, as Hank won his first MVP Award, leading the league with 36 homers and 170 RBI. For the next four years the Tigers vainly chased the Yankees before sinking to the second division. High RBI totals became Greenberg's special gift. His 183 in 1937 is the third highest total in his-

A rabbi counseled Hank Greenberg that he could play on Rosh Hashanah, which he did, but not on Yom Kippur, which he did not.

Hank Greenberg drove in 183 runs in 154 games in 1937, which was the third-highest percentage of RBI per game in the 20th century, at 1.19.

tory, and his career rate of .92 RBI per game is matched only by Gehrig in this century. Greenberg challenged Babe Ruth's single-season home run record by clubbing 58 in 1938.

In 1940, Hammerin' Hank led the Tigers to a pennant as he grabbed his second MVP Award, leading the league in doubles, homers, and, of course, RBI. He also made the shift from first base to left field in order to accommodate Rudy York, and the originally apprehensive Greenberg found the outfield to his taste. Though Hank hit .357 in the World Series, the Tigers bowed to Cincinnati in seven games. He played in only 19 games in 1941 before going to war.

He returned to lead the Tigers to the world championship in 1945, cracking a grand-slam homer on Sept. 30 to clinch the pennant. He hit .304 in the Series as Detroit felled the Cubs. In 1946, he led the league in home runs and RBI, but it was to be his last good season.

A salary dispute sent Greenberg to Pittsburgh in 1947. He promptly retired, but Pittsburgh officials were desperate for his drawing power (the club had just been sold). The Pirates met Greenberg's every demand, and Hank played one more year before retiring. While with the Pirates he worked extensively with Ralph Kiner. Hank also encouraged Jackie Robinson; Greenberg withstood his share of prejudice, being the greatest Jewish star of his day.

LEFTY GROVE

★

Generally acknowledged to be the greatest left-handed pitcher ever, Lefty Grove is considered by many authorities to be the greatest pitcher, period. The holder of the highest career winning percentage among pitchers who posted 300 or more career victories, Grove in addition compiled a 112-39 record in the minors to give him a combined winning percentage of .696, which is far and away the highest of any pitcher in organized baseball history.

Born in Lonaconing, Maryland, Robert Moses Grove (1900-1975) quit school in the eighth grade to work in a coal mine. Later an apprentice glass blower and railroad worker, Lefty was age 20 before he decided that baseball might offer a brighter future. After six games with Martinsburg in the Blue Ridge League, he was purchased by Jack Dunn, owner of the Baltimore Orioles in the International League.

For the next four and one-half years, Grove was trapped in Baltimore, unable to move up to the majors because International League teams at that time were exempt from the draft system and allowed to retain their stars for as long as they wished. Although Grove was paid better by Dunn than he would have been by several major-league owners, he was nevertheless impatient to leave Baltimore. Finally, after the 1924 season, Connie Mack of the Philadelphia A's agreed to pay Dunn $100,000 for Grove's contract, plus an extra $600 to make the purchase higher than the amount the Yankees paid the Red Sox for Babe Ruth.

For all his minor-league training, Grove was still not quite ready to become a major-league star. The control problems that had beset him in Baltimore persisted during his first two seasons with the A's. But in 1927, Grove for the first time in his career gave up less than three walks per game. Not coincidentally, he also won 20 games for the first time in the majors that season.

The following year, Lefty topped the American League in wins for the first of four occasions. In 1929, he paced the AL in winning percentage for the first time, a feat he was to repeat on five occasions. That year Grove also led the loop in strikeouts for the fifth of what would soon be seven straight seasons. It was his stinginess with runs that was Grove's greatest forte, however. On nine separate occasions he topped the American League in earned run average.

Grove had his finest season to date in 1930 when he won 28 of 33 decisions and led the AL in winning percentage, ERA, and strikeouts. It seemed that he had surely reached his pinnacle, but incredibly his 1931 season was better. That year, Lefty had a 31-4 mark and an .886 winning percentage, the highest in history by a 30-game winner. The real topper, though, was his 2.06 ERA that was 2.32 runs per game below the league average of 4.38. As a consequence of his extraordinary performance, Grove received the first MVP Award given to an AL player by the Baseball Writers Association of America.

Traded to the Red Sox by the A's after the 1933 season

Opposite page: Lefty Grove led the AL four times in allowing the lowest on-base average, finishing in the top five nine times in that category.

Chicago Tribune writer Westbrook Pegler said that Lefty Grove "could throw a lamb chop past a wolf."

GABBY HARTNETT

★

Until Johnny Bench came along, Gabby Hartnett was considered the greatest catcher in the history of the National League. He couldn't run, would talk your ear off—they didn't call him Gabby for nothing—and lasted for years on a lot of bat and a lot more savvy. Burleigh Grimes said Gabby "had as good an arm as ever hung on a man."

Born in Woodsocket, Rhode Island, Charles Leo Hartnett (1900-1972) grew up in Massachusetts the oldest of 14 children. Gabby's father, Fred, was a semipro catcher, and he taught seven of his children how to catch well enough to play organized ball (four boys and three girls). Gabby's first pro assignment was with Worcester of the Eastern League, where he caught 100 games and batted .264 in 1921. The Giants rejected the backstop because of his small

when Connie Mack wanted to unload his high salary, Grove was never again the game's dominant hurler, although he collected four ERA crowns and one winning percentage crown with Boston. In his later years, Lefty developed a great curveball when arm trouble reduced his fastball's blazing speed. After winning his 300th game in 1941, he officially retired that fall on the day that Pearl Harbor was attacked. Although his retirement announcement was overshadowed as a result, little else he did during his career escaped notice. Elected to the Hall of Fame in 1947, Lefty devoted himself for years to working with young players and financially supporting youth baseball leagues.

Gabby Hartnett had a career .297 batting average, a .370 on-base average, a .489 slugging average, 236 homers, and 1,179 RBI.

hands, so the Cubs bought his contract in 1922. Gabby needed a few years to develop his batting, but Bob O'Farrell was able to hold the spot, having his best two years at the plate in 1922 and '23. When Hartnett took over in 1924, he held the position until the late 1930s, save for an injury-plagued 1929.

Gabby became a reliable stickman for several years after taking the position. He batted in the .275 range with some power. After getting an arm injury in 1929, he exploded in 1930, hitting .339 with 37 homers and 122 RBI.

In 1935, Hartnett was the National League MVP, though his power stats would not stand with those of the heavy hitters of his day. His .344 average was third in the league, and he led league receivers in assists, double plays, and fielding average as he guided Cub pitchers to 100 wins and a pennant. His last three years with the Cubs were as player-manager.

Hartnett left a host of career fielding records, but is best known for the "Homer in the Gloamin'" in 1938. As player-manager of the Cubs he led his team from nine games out in August to wrest the pennant

Gabby Hartnett led NL catchers in fielding average six times, and he was widely regarded to have the NL's best arm before Roy Campanella.

away from the Pirates. As *The New York Times* reported it: "In the thickening gloom, with the score tied and two out in the ninth inning today, red-faced Gabby Hartnett blasted a home run before 34,465 cheering fans to give his Cubs a dramatic 6-5 victory over the Pirates." The Cubs won four pennants during Gabby's time with them: in 1929, 1932, '35, and '38.

Red Smith wrote, "[Hartnett] was so good that he lasted 20 years in spite of the fact that he couldn't run. All other skills were refined in him."

RICKEY HENDERSON

★

*R*ickey Henderson swiped Lou Brock's single-season and all-time stolen base titles, and in the process became acknowledged as the consummate leadoff hitter.

As a high school senior in 1976, Rickey Henley Henderson (born on Christmas Day 1957) received two-dozen scholarship offers to play college football. Instead, he signed with hometown Oakland that year, after being drafted in the fourth round. In the minors he became the fourth player in professional baseball history to steal seven bases in a single game. He won a starting spot in Oakland by June 1979, stealing 33 bases in 89 games while hitting .274.

In 1980, Henderson became the third major leaguer ever to steal 100 bases in a season, a target he'd later surpass not once, but twice. The next year brought Henderson's first Gold Glove, and league bests in hits (135), runs (89), and stolen bases (56). His steals more than doubled in 1982, when Brock's record of 118 pilfers in a single season was shattered by

Rickey Henderson in 1984 stole 108 bases and was caught only 19 times; in 1988 he stole 93 bases and was caught just 13 times.

telligent baserunner, he stayed above the 80 percent mark in successful steals throughout his career.

In December 1984, the Yankees gave up five players (including Jose Rijo) to get Henderson from Oakland. Oakland was unable to sign Rickey to a long-term contract, so the team traded him before losing him to free agency. Despite a month's worth of injuries in early 1985, Henderson finished his first Yankee season with personal highs in homers and RBI (24 and 72), which he would surpass the following year with 28 dingers and 74 RBI. It was after these two years—when he scored 146 and 130 runs—that talk of Henderson being the best leadoff man of all time was taken seriously. Early in his career, he was considered one of the finest fielders in the AL, using his speed to turn hits into outs. Henderson never had a great arm, but he was always more than competent with the glove.

The A's reacquired him in mid-1989 as they were making their pennant run. In 1993, he moved to Toronto for the Jays' World Series bid, then moved back to Oakland in 1994.

Henderson's 130. Rickey also led the AL in walks that year (116). He snatched 108 bases in 1983.

Henderson topped the league in stolen bases every season from 1980 to 1991, save for 1987, when he spent two months on the disabled list. These season totals range from 56 steals in 1981 to a record-breaking 130 in 1982. An in-

ROGERS HORNSBY

★

*W*ith the lone exception of Ty Cobb, no superstar was more disliked than Rogers Hornsby. Hornsby was aloof, independent, and brutally honest. As a consequence, he was probably the least understood great player. Modern authorities cite his defensive lapses as a drawback, but Hornsby was the greatest right-handed hitter in history.

Rogers Hornsby (1896-1963) was given his unusual first name by his mother, whose maiden name was Rogers. He began as a shortstop in the Texas-Oklahoma League in 1914. Weighing 140 pounds at age 18, he hit .232. In 1915, Rogers was still a light-hitting shortstop, but the Cardinals saw enough to pay $500 for his contract.

After putting on weight in the off-season, Hornsby hit .313 for St. Louis as a rookie and played a surprisingly adequate shortstop. In 1917, his second full season, he topped the National League in slugging and was second in batting. Moreover, he led all league shortstops in double plays.

Hornsby slipped below the .300 mark for the only time in his major-league career in 1918, but continued to rank high in all slugging departments. Moved to third base in 1919, "The Rajah" again finished second in the NL batting race. The following spring, Hornsby earned the batting and RBI crowns in his first season as a second baseman. His .370 average was the highest in the 20th century by an NL second baseman.

No one expected Rogers to duplicate that figure in 1921, and he did not. Instead he hit .397 and then followed up by hitting .401 in 1922, .384 in 1923, .424 in 1924, and .403 in 1925 to make him the only player in history to average over .400 for a five-year span. During the 1920s, Hornsby hit below .361 on just one occasion. That came in 1926 after he was made player-manager of the Cardinals. The dual responsibility held Rogers to a .317 mark, but the Cardinals nevertheless brought the first pennant in National League history to St. Louis under his leadership.

A fierce dispute with St. Louis owner Sam Breadon resulted in Hornsby being traded to the Giants before the 1927 season. In his lone season in New York, Hornsby set a new Giants season batting average record. Hornsby quit as a full-time player after the 1931 season with a .358 career batting average, 301 homers, and 1,584 RBI. Rogers was elected to the Hall of Fame in 1942.

Rogers Hornsby was an above-average fielder and a great hitter.

CARL HUBBELL

★

Carl Hubbell was a winner. He had to be to earn a nickname like "The Meal Ticket." In his 16 years with John McGraw's Giants, Hubbell won 253 games and lost 154, while posting a remarkable 2.97 earned run average.

Carl Owen Hubbell (1903-1988) grew up on a pecan farm in Oklahoma. He started pitching for an oil company team after high school before getting a chance in the Oklahoma State League in 1923. He made it to Oklahoma City of the Western League by 1925, going 17-13. Hubbell threw a screwball, breaking toward lefty batters, unlike a curve, which breaks away from lefty batters. Carl was sold to the Tigers in 1925, who did not permit him to use his screwball, fearing it would ruin his arm. His performance was inferior, he was optioned to the minors, and his confidence collapsed shortly thereafter.

After two years of mediocre pitching in minor-league ball, Hubbell received his outright release from Detroit in 1928 and began pitching in the Texas

Above: Carl Hubbell led the NL in lowest on-base percentage allowed for seven seasons. *Opposite page:* In nine seasons Hubbell was in the top five in the league in allowing the fewest walks per game.

League. Giants scout Dick Kinsella was a delegate to the Democratic National Convention in Houston that year and took in a Texas League game. He discovered Hubbell, and Giants skipper John McGraw paid $30,000 for the hurler, a record for that loop.

Hubbell put the league on alert, tossing the league's only no-hitter in 1929, but his big years didn't begin until 1933. He registered five straight 20-plus victory seasons starting in 1933. That season, King Carl pitched a record 18-inning shutout against the Cardinals, won two games in the World

Series, pitched 20 Series innings without allowing an earned run (he tossed a Series-record 11-inning shutout), and was chosen the league's Most Valuable Player.

The following season he had his most famous moment. In the second All-Star Game, in 1934, Hubbell fanned Babe Ruth, Lou Gehrig, Jimmie Foxx, Al Simmons, and Joe Cronin in succession, electrifying the fans and prompting fellow NL All-Star Gabby Hartnett to call down to the AL dugout, "We gotta look at that all season."

Hubbell won the MVP again in 1936 when he turned in one of the best pitching records in history at 26-6. The Giants returned to the World Series that year and in 1937, losing to the Yankees both times. Hubbell had finished 1936 with 16 straight wins and won his first eight in 1937, for a 24-game winning streak. Throwing his screwball for so many years had turned his left arm around, and he underwent elbow surgery after the 1938 season. He never was the same, although he won 11 games each year from 1939 to 1942. Carl was inducted into the Hall of Fame in 1947.

SHOELESS JOE JACKSON

★

The debate still rages over how Shoeless Joe Jackson should be remembered. Some fans prefer to remember him as a sweet-swinging hitter who was one of the greatest outfielders of all time. Others simply recall that he was one of eight men accused of throwing the 1919 World Series.

Joseph Jefferson Jackson (1889-1951) started working at a cotton mill as a child. The Philadelphia Athletics discovered him playing on the mill's baseball team. He agreed to play in Philadelphia, but the largely uneducated Jackson was uncomfortable with the fast pace of big-city life. After just 10 games in two years, the A's released the unhappy slugger. He fared better in Cleveland, where he stayed until early 1915, when the financially strapped team had to sell off players to raise funds.

Throughout his 13 seasons in the majors, played mostly with the Indians and the White Sox, Jackson was consistently among the league's top hitters. For a four-year stretch in his prime, he averaged better than

Joe Jackson had one of his best batting seasons at age 31 in 1920, when he hit .382 with 12 homers, a loop-best 20 triples, 42 doubles, a .444 on-base average, a .589 slugging average, 105 runs, 121 RBI, and only 14 strikeouts.

.390. In 1911 he batted .408, only to lose the batting title to Cobb, who hit .420. The following year Jackson came back with a .395 average, but once again Cobb topped the .400 mark. Just 31 years old when he was banned, Jackson batted .382 in 1920, his final season, compiling a .356 lifetime average. Only Ty Cobb and Rogers Hornsby earned higher lifetime batting averages.

After the White Sox won the 1919 AL pennant, they were a heavy favorite to beat the Reds in the World Series. Instead, the White Sox lost five games to three. Immediately, accusations flourished about noticeably uninspired performances of several White Sox players. Over the course of the 1920 season, it was charged that eight members of the White Sox, including Jackson, had accepted bribes to throw the Series. Alledgedly, Jackson had accepted $5,000 from the mobsters but never got the $20,000 he was promised.

The eight members of the White Sox were accused of participating in the fix and were banned from baseball for life. Even though a grand jury acquitted the eight (with signed confessions of Jackson and others mysteriously missing), commissioner Kenesaw Mountain Landis still refused to reinstate the eight "Black Sox."

Jackson maintained his innocence until his death, and he had many supporters. The top batter in the Series, he had 12 hits in 32 at bats, a .375 average. But skeptics pointed out the two costly errors Jackson made in the field.

After being banned, Jackson returned home to South Carolina. He played baseball for semipro teams under assumed names and then lived comfortably. His supporters have made continuous but unsuccessful attempts to convince the baseball establishment that Jackson belongs in the Hall of Fame.

REGGIE JACKSON

★

When Reggie Jackson was a kid, his father sent him to an ice cream stand for a vanilla, strawberry, and chocolate cone. Not finding all three flavors, Reggie traveled to several stores for separate quantities of each flavor, so as to avoid having to go home empty-handed. Failure was not an option in the Jackson household; it was understood that the job would get done.

It was from that environment that Jackson grew into a player who viewed himself as a horse who could carry the load. Reginald Martinez Jackson was born in 1946 in Wyncote, Pennsylvania. His father, Martinez, was a ballplayer in the Negro Leagues, no doubt passing on to his son ample athletic talent as well as the sturdy upbringing. Jackson would need all of those attributes in the employ of Charles Finley and George Steinbrenner.

Jackson was an outstanding high school football player, receiving 51 scholarship offers. He went to Arizona State as a football defensive back and a baseball player, starred for a couple of years, and was the second player picked in the 1966 draft, by Kansas City. He made his debut in 1967 as a member of the A's. He blossomed as the franchise moved to Oakland in 1968, hitting 29 homers with 74 RBI. With the nucleus of Oakland's dynasty forming, including Catfish Hunter, Reggie became a superstar in 1969, leading the league with 123 runs and a

Reggie Jackson in 1969 slugged 47 homers and notched a .608 slugging percentage, which was 19 points higher than No. 2 Rico Petrocelli.

Reggie Jackson retired as the all-time career leader in strikeouts, with 2,597. Nevertheless, he knocked in more than 100 runs in six seasons, had more than 30 homers in seven seasons, and had over 20 homers in 16 seasons. He had 563 career homers, 1,702 RBI, and a career .490 slugging percentage.

.608 slugging percentage. In 1971, Oakland won the first of five straight West Division titles. Jackson hit 32 homers, not including the shot off the light tower in the All-Star Game. He matched his 32-homer output in 1973, when he won the AL MVP. The years from 1972 to 1974 brought three straight world championships as the A's, united in a dislike for owner Finley, brawled their way to a dynasty.

Free agency broke up the A's, and Jackson was traded to Baltimore for the 1976 season. After playing out his option, he joined the Yankees, where he clashed with manager Billy Martin and Steinbrenner. Jackson called himself "The Straw that Stirs the Drink," alienating himself from his teammates. But in game six of the 1977 World Series, Jackson hit three homers on three swings to deliver the title to the Yanks; that feat assured him of his "Mr. October" designation.

After five years in New York, Jackson moved to the California Angels, helping them to a first-place finish in 1982 and 1986. The spotlight again found Jackson in 1993 as he was the only player inducted into the Hall of Fame that year.

FERGUSON JENKINS

★

$\mathcal{A}$ master of control, Ferguson Jenkins never walked more than 83 hitters in a season. He won 20 games a season from 1968 to 1972, on his way to 284 career wins, and he is the only pitcher in baseball history to fan more than 3,000 batters while walking fewer than 1,000.

A 6'5" right-hander out of Chatham, Ontario, Canada, Ferguson Arthur Jenkins (born in 1943) was discovered by the Phillies in 1962. He labored in the Philadelphia minor-league organization for three and one-half years before being promoted in 1965. The Phillies used Fergie as a reliever, and after the Chicago Cubs obtained him from Philadelphia during the 1966 season, they put him in the bullpen. Cubs manager Leo Durocher decided to move Jenkins into the starting rotation at the end of the season, and he responded with two complete games. In 1967, he was 20-13 with a 2.80 ERA for the Cubs, the first of six consecutive 20-win seasons. He led the NL with 40 starts in 1968, and he went 20-15.

Fergie Jenkins finished what he started. He led his league in complete games four times, had 30 completions in 1971, and had 20 complete games or more in eight seasons. In 1968 he lost a record five games by 1-0 scores.

Jenkins's best season with the Cubs was 1971, when he led the league with 325 innings pitched and 24 wins, and posted a 2.77 ERA to earn the Cy Young Award. He was 20-12 in '72, but slipped to 14-16 in 1973. The Cubs, deciding that they needed a replacement for third baseman Ron Santo, sent Jenkins to Texas for Bill Madlock.

Fergie had one more outstanding season left in his arm. In 1974, he led the American League with a career-high 25 wins, lost 12, and fanned 225. Though he never won 20 games again, he continued to pitch effectively. In '75, he was 17-18 with a 3.93 ERA. Boston traded three players for him that winter, and, although Jenkins hurt his foot, he was 12-11 with a 3.27 ERA. He had a run-in with Red Sox manager Don Zimmer in 1977, and Fergie was shipped back to Texas. He went 18-8 in 1978, won 16 and 12 games the next two years, and was back with the Cubs in 1982.

Jenkins led the league in strikeouts in 1969 and fanned more than 200 six times. Like other control pitchers, he gave up many homers; his 484 home runs allowed are the second most in history. Curiously, his highest total allowed in a season, 40, occurred in 1979 when he was with Texas. His career made him a fine Hall of Fame candidate, but an arrest for drug possession in Toronto in 1980 made his election problematic. In 1991, Jenkins was elected to the Hall of Fame by one of the closest margins in Cooperstown history.

JUDY JOHNSON

★

Judy Johnson has perhaps the weakest batting stats of the Negro League players recognized by the Hall of Fame. His fielding at third base is usually described as steady or intelligent rather than spectacular. Yet everyone who played with him or saw him play agreed that he was a great ballplayer.

William Julius Johnson was born Oct. 20, 1900, in Snow Hill, Maryland. He started his career in 1918 as a semipro, getting his break when World War I called many black players away from baseball. He was a worthy fill-in during the war, but he still needed seasoning, and by 1918 was playing for the Madison Stars, a farm team.

He returned to one of the powerhouse teams in the East, the Philadelphia Hilldales, in 1921. He started as a shortstop, but his range was limited for that position. He was moved around the infield, eventually taking over the third base job. He was a line-drive hitter who drove in a high number of runs, despite not hitting a great amount of homers.

Known as steady rather than spectacular, Judy Johnson was considered the top third baseman in the 1920s and '30s. After retiring he went on to be a scout for the Philadelphia Athletics.

Johnson played for Philadelphia 11 years (from 1921 to '29 and 1931 and 1932) and played winter ball in Cuba. He hit a career-high .406 in 1929, a year in black baseball that matched white baseball in 1930 for unprecedented offensive totals. He was chosen MVP by sportswriter Rollo Wilson for the season. Judy moved to the Homestead Grays as a player-manager for the 1930 season. His best move as a skipper was to insert young Josh Gibson into the catcher's job.

Johnson was a member of

perhaps the best Negro League team in history when he joined Gus Greenlee's Pittsburgh Crawfords in 1932. Greenlee built the first stadium completely owned by an African American. To fill his new ballpark, Greenlee was determined to have the best talent that he could find, raiding the Pittsburgh-based Homestead Grays and other teams for the best black players money could buy. The Crawfords were managed by Oscar Charleston and included Josh Gibson, Satchel Paige, and Cool Papa Bell. Johnson finished his playing career with the Crawfords in 1938.

Later, Johnson became one of the most astute scouts for the majors, when white baseball began to accept black players. "I could have gotten Hank Aaron [for the Athletics] for $3,500," said Judy. "I got my boss out of bed and told him I had a good prospect and he wouldn't cost too much, and he cussed me out for waking him up at one o' clock in the morning." He later landed Dick Allen for the Phillies, and Johnson went to spring training with the Phils until he retired in 1974. There he passed on his knowledge to many players.

WALTER JOHNSON

*W*hen Walter Johnson joined the Washington Senators in August 1907, they were the worst team in the American League. Then in their seventh year of existence, the Senators had yet to finish higher than sixth place or have a pitcher who won 20 games in a season.

Walter Perry Johnson (1887-1946) soon remedied the latter shortcoming, but not even his mammoth talents could immediately lift the team.

The Senators finished last or next to last in each of Walter's first five seasons with them, even though he twice won 25 games. Then in 1912, Washington vaulted all the way to second place as Johnson seemingly had a career season with 32 wins, 303 strikeouts, and a 1.39 ERA. When Walter surpassed belief the following year, winning 36 games and posting a 1.09 ERA, the lowest in American League history by a pitcher with more than 300 innings, the Senators repeated their second-place finish. Eleven years would pass, however, before Washington again returned

Walter Johnson's accomplishments were all the more admirable when you consider that he never deliberately threw at a batter, and he refused to argue with an umpire.

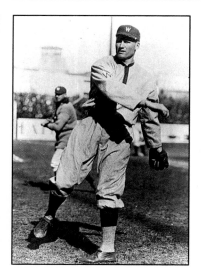

Johnson, one of the fastest hurlers in the game, once said, "You can't hit what you can't see."

to contention, and by then Johnson seemed nearly done. He was age 36 and had not won more than 17 games in a season for four years.

Those who had written Walter off, though, were in for a surprise. In 1924, with Washington locked in a season-long battle with the Yankees for the pennant, Johnson paced the junior loop in winning percentage, strikeouts, and ERA. More important, his league-leading 23 wins played an essential role in bringing the Senators their first flag. In the World Series that fall, Johnson was beaten twice by the New York Giants but recovered to win the deciding seventh game in relief. The following season he spurred

Washington to a second consecutive pennant when he again was a 20-game winner. He also batted .433 that year with 20 RBI in 36 games. The Pirates, however, proved him mortal in the World Series, topping him in the seventh game after he had twice bested them in earlier rounds.

Nicknamed "The Big Train" by Grantland Rice, Johnson was also called "Barney" by intimates. Although race-car driver Barney Oldfield was the source for the name, it was not inspired by Johnson's fastball but rather by the manner in which he drove.

In his 21 years with the Senators, Johnson won 416 games. No other pitcher in this century has won so many. More to the point, no other pitcher could have won nearly as many games with the teams for which Johnson played. Except for 1926, Johnson's winning percentage exceeded his team's winning percentage in every season that he worked 200 or more innings. Most of the time the difference was well over 100 points. Johnson was elected to the Hall of Fame in 1936 along with Ty Cobb, Babe Ruth, Honus Wagner, and Christy Mathewson.

AL KALINE

★

There is a storybook quality to the career of Al Kaline, who joined the Detroit Tigers as an 18-year-old boy and retired a 40-year-old legend. He hit for average, hit for power, and was a near-perfect defensive player with an arm like a rocket launcher. He is among the brightest—and best loved—in a galaxy of Detroit stars.

Albert William Kaline (born in 1934) was raised to be a baseball player; his grandfather, father, and uncles had all been semipro players. Al played on so many extracurricular teams that he would play three or four games on any given Sunday, changing uniforms in the car. All of that extra work paid off, though, because he hit .488 in his senior year in high school. Every team was interested in obtaining him, but he chose to sign with the Detroit Tigers, for $30,000.

Al never played an inning of minor-league ball, since the bonus rule required that he stay on the big-league roster for at least two years. He was tossed into his first big-league game as a pinch-hitter the day he

In Kaline's second full season, 1955, he proved he was also a major-league hitter. He won the batting title that season, hitting .340 with a league-high 200 hits and 27 home runs. He established himself as a premier player, and finished a close second in the MVP vote. Al batted .314 in 1956, with 194 base hits, 27 homers, and a career-high 128 RBI.

As good as Kaline was—and he had some good teammates, too, like Norm Cash, Jim Bunning, and Rocky Colavito—the Tigers were only a mediocre team. In-season management changes were a regular occurrence. From 1957 to 1967, Kaline batted from .280 to .300, with 18 to 25 homers and 70 to 100 RBI.

The Tigers jelled in 1968, winning the pennant, but Kaline broke his leg and played in only 102 games. In the World Series, Tiger manager Mayo Smith gambled that outfielder Mickey Stanley could handle shortstop so Al could play right field. The gamble paid when Kaline batted .379, slugged .655, and drove in eight runs as the Tigers won their first world championship since 1945. Kaline was inducted into the Hall of Fame in 1980.

When the Tigers offered Al Kaline their first $100,000 contract in 1971, he responded, "I don't deserve such a salary. I didn't have a good enough season last year. . . . I'd prefer you give it to me when I deserve it."

signed, right out of high school. He was a big-league defender from day one, and he knew it: "The first time I went out to play with the outfielders, I said, 'Hey, I'm as good as any of these guys. I can throw better than anybody here, and I can go get the ball with any of them.' "

TIM KEEFE

★

As virtually all the 19th century's 300-game winners, Tim Keefe had the luxury of playing for good teams for the better part of his career. In an era when most quality pitchers started upward of 50 games a season, winning 30 games with a contender was a routine matter, provided a hurler was durable, and Keefe was certainly that. In his first nine full seasons in the major leagues, he labored 4,103 innings and racked up 285 victories. Although he posted only a 57-51 record for the remaining five seasons of his 14-year career, he totaled 342 wins, the eighth most in history.

Born in Cambridge, Massachusetts, Timothy John Keefe (1857-1933) played for local amateur teams until he was 22 years old. He joined the Utica team of the National Association in 1879. By the middle of the following season, he was in the majors with the Troy Trojans of the National League. In 1880, Troy already had an outstanding rookie pitcher in Mickey Welch, and Keefe seemed destined to become no more than the club's second-

Iron-arm wonder Tim Keefe. In 1883, he pitched 68 complete games in 68 starts. On July 4 that year, he threw a one-hitter in the morning and a two-hitter in the afternoon.

line hurler. Early in the 1881 season, however, Keefe slowly but steadily began to prove himself the more tireless worker.

When the Troy franchise moved to New York in 1883, the pitching duo of Keefe and Welch was split up, with Keefe going to the Metropolitans, the New York representative in the rival American Association. After the Metropolitans won the Association pennant in 1884, Keefe and several other of the team's stars were quickly transferred to the National League entry in New York,

soon to be renamed the Giants. What made the shift an easy matter, albeit somewhat unethical, was that both Gotham clubs were under the same ownership.

Reunited in 1885, Keefe and Mickey Welch helped carry the Giants to National League pennants in 1888 and 1889. On both occasions, New York beat the American Association champion in the World Series with comparative ease, giving Gotham fans cause to believe a dynasty was in the making. After the 1889 season, though, the Brotherhood revolted and formed the Players' League. Along with most of the other Giants stars, Keefe jumped to the New York franchise in the Brotherhood circuit, which was managed by Buck Ewing, his former catcher on the Giants.

Although the best team on paper, Ewing's club could finish no better than third when Keefe was held to 17 victories by arm trouble. Returning to the National League after the Players' League failed, he pitched three more seasons without much distinction, then became an umpire. Keefe was named to the Hall of Fame in 1964.

HARMON KILLEBREW

★

*T*he top right-handed home run hitter in AL history with 573 round-trippers, Harmon Killebrew had over 40 home runs in eight seasons and over 100 RBI in 10 seasons.

Born in 1936, Harmon Clayton Killebrew was an All-State quarterback in Idaho and semipro baseball star. When he was age 17, he was recommended to Clark Griffith of the Senators by Idaho Senator Herman Walker, who wanted to see his young constituent in the majors. Killebrew blasted a 435-foot homer for scout Ossie Bluege, who found out that Harmon was batting .847 with half of the hits being home runs. Bluege signed "Killer" immediately.

Killebrew was a bonus baby and didn't get a chance to play full-time until 1959. Under the rules of the time, the Senators had to keep him in the bigs for two years, and he sat on the bench in 1954 and 1955, getting in only 47 games, and then spent most of the next three seasons in the minors. He was a third baseman when he came

Harmon Killebrew changed defensive positions often. It didn't seem to affect his hitting, however, as he led the league in homers for six seasons and RBI for three. The 1969 MVP was an All-Star 11 times.

Greatness abounds. From left, Harmon Killebrew, Mickey Mantle, Jim Lemon, and Roger Maris pose for a photograph. This awesome collection of power hit a total of 1,548 home runs and 4,473 RBI during their careers.

back up, and though he eventually played more games at first base than third, he had significant playing time at the hot corner until 1971. He eventually earned outstanding AL left fielder, third baseman, and first baseman honors from *The Sporting News.*

"Killer" was ready when he played as a regular in 1959, leading the league with 42 home runs during his first full season and hitting 31 the next year, after which the Senators became the Minnesota Twins. A dead pull hitter, he hit 46 for

his new fans in 1961, but that year Roger Maris went on his spree. Killebrew led the league in 1962, 1963, and '64, hitting 142 in the three seasons and driving in 333 runs. The Twins rocketed to first place in 1965 with 102 wins, though Killer had one of his poorest years due to an elbow injury, and the Twins lost the World Series.

Killebrew had established himself as a major star with his consistent slugging, and won the AL MVP Award in 1969 when he hit 49 homers, drove in 140 runs, and drew 145

walks, leading the league with a .430 on-base average. His walk totals were impressive, and though he drew criticism for his less-than-impressive batting averages, his on-base averages were usually among the best in the league.

The Twins won the AL West division its first two years of existence, but failed to return to the World Series. Knee problems began to slow Harmon, and after a final year with Kansas City as a designated hitter, he retired after the 1975 season.

RALPH KINER

★

*T*he greatest slugger in those years immediately after World War II, Ralph Kiner had a National League record seven straight home run titles. Only Babe Ruth has a career home run ratio that is better than Kiner's.

Ralph McPherran Kiner (born in 1922) was a renown semipro baseball player in Alhambra, California, as both a pitcher and a hitter. After he graduated from high school in 1940, he was approached by several ballclubs, who all wanted him to sign with a Class-D affiliate. Instead, Ralph signed with the Pirates, who offered to start him in Class-A. He played in the minors for two and one-half seasons, making it to the Triple-A International League before joining the Navy in mid-1943.

After his release in December 1945, Ralph said, "I began preparing for spring training, and I got myself into just sensational shape. Sure enough, I had a spring training like no one's ever had." In 1946, Kiner became the Pirate's left fielder, and he hit 23 home runs to lead the league.

Ralph Kiner gave his all to the game. Even with a losing club, he was largely responsible for bringing over 5 million fans.

In 1947, Pittsburgh acquired Hank Greenberg, and the Pirates moved the left field fence in from 365 feet to 335 feet (an area known as "Greenberg's Garden"). Kiner's 23 homers began to look like small potatoes. Ralph hit 51 homers in 1947, while he found a mentor in Greenberg. Hank retired after the '47 season, and left field became known as "Kiner's Korner." Ralph slugged 40 homers in 1948, and 54 in 1949. Though his slugging was aided by Forbes Field, he twice set road home run records. He walked 100 times or more in six straight seasons to post an excellent lifetime on-base percentage of .397, which in turn helped him to six seasons of at least 100 runs scored. The Pirates were usually in the second division during Kiner's tenure, but he was recognized as one of the game's greatest stars.

Kiner was a hard and inno-

SANDY KOUFAX

★

Sportswriter Arthur Daly once likened Kiner to "Huckleberry Finn in a baseball uniform."

vative worker. "I remember back in 1941 or 1942, I obtained a filmstrip of Babe Ruth's swing, broken down frame by frame, which I copied carefully and practiced whenever I got the chance," he said. Kiner later had films taken of his own swing in order to spot flaws and took hours of extra batting practice. Though he had an unimpressive throwing arm, he was a four-time *Sporting News* All-Star. He was also a mover in the players' movement, which led to the pension plan and the financial bonanza of modern players. Later, Ralph would become a broadcaster for the Mets. He was inducted into the Hall of Fame in 1975.

Sandy Koufax put together one of the most dominating stretches of pitching in baseball history. Over a five-year span, he led the NL in ERA five times and compiled a 111-34 record, before arthritis forced him to retire at age 30.

Sanford Koufax was born in Brooklyn in 1935, and while he liked baseball, he was very interested in basketball. In 1953, he went to the University of Cincinnati on a basketball scholarship. He also pitched for the baseball team, and he had tryouts with several clubs interested in a lefty with such a great fastball. Late in 1954, he signed with his hometown Dodgers for $25,000, even though the Braves offered more. He knew that as a bonus baby he would have to serve his apprenticeship in the majors, and he thought he would more easily adjust at home.

Koufax started only five games in 1955, showing bursts of brilliance surrounded by intervals of wildness. His schooling continued for the next two seasons, when he got 10 and 13 starts and received much of

his work out of the bullpen. The Dodgers moved to Los Angeles before the 1958 season, and Koufax posted an 11-11 mark with a 4.40 ERA in 26 starts. He had 23 starts, an 8-6 mark, and a 4.05 ERA in 1959. He was 8-13 with a 3.91 ERA in 1960.

In spring training of 1961, catcher Norm Sherry advised Koufax to slow his delivery, to throw changeups and curveballs, and to relax. Following that advice, Sandy recorded his first record over .500, going 18-

Above: Joy abounds for Sandy as he wins his fourth career no-hitter. The lefty hurler threw one each season from 1962 to '65. *Opposite page:* Despite the advancement of arthritis, Sandy Koufax won two of his three Cy Young Awards in 1965 and '66.

TREASURY OF BASEBALL

13 and leading the league in Ks with the eye-popping total of 269. In 1962, the Dodgers moved to Dodger Stadium. Sandy developed a frightening numbness in his left index finger, due to a circulatory ailment. He could make just 26 starts; had he gone on he very well could have lost the finger. He was 14-7 with a league-leading 2.54 ERA that year and pitched a no-hitter.

The 1963 season was his triumph. Sandy went 25-5, leading the NL with 25 wins, a 1.88 ERA, 11 shutouts, and 306 strikeouts. He won both the MVP and Cy Young Awards. He tossed his second no-hitter and won two games in the Dodgers' World Series victory. In 1964, he was 19-5 with a league-best 1.74 ERA. That year, a deteriorating arthritic condition in his left arm first became conspicuous. He continued to pitch, with the help of cortisone shots and ice, for two more seasons, winning Cy Young Awards in 1965 and '66. He had league-best ERAs of 2.04 and 1.73, and he won 26 and 27 games. He also tossed two more no-hitters, including a perfect game. He was inducted into the Hall of Fame in 1972.

NAP LAJOIE

★

*I*n 1896, Napolean Lajoie (1874-1959) was purchased by the Phillies from Fall River of the New England League. By Nap's fifth year with the Phillies, the club seemed ready to mount a serious pennant bid. A salary hassle with Phillies owner Colonel Rogers, however, induced Lajoie to jump to the Philadelphia Athletics of the fledgling American League when A's

As a testimony to his brilliant career, Nap Lajoie was the sixth player elected to the Hall of Fame in 1937. He hit .339 lifetime.

manager Connie Mack offered him a four-year, $6,000-per-season pact. It seemed as if this was sufficient enticement for Lajoie, who went on to set a 20th-century record by batting .422 and winning the Triple Crown in 1901, the AL's first campaign as a major league.

The Phillies, however, were not about to surrender their great second sacker. After considerable litigation, a state court injunction prohibited Lajoie and another former Phillies star, Elmer Flick, from playing with any other team in Philadelphia. Since the injunction applied only in the state of Pennsylvania, Mack sent Lajoie and Flick to Cleveland, for which they could play in every other AL city but Philadelphia. Owing to all the legal wrangling, Lajoie got into only 87 games in 1902. Nap swiftly made up for the setback by winning the hitting titles in 1903 and 1904.

In all, Lajoie won three American League bat crowns, with one, in 1910, that is still in dispute. That year, Nap edged Ty Cobb by a single point after making eight hits in a season-ending doubleheader, six of them bunts that Lajoie was able to beat out because St.

Louis Browns third baseman Red Corriden was playing deep on orders from his manager Jack O'Connor to deny the hated Cobb the hit title.

None of Lajoie's many other accomplishments is tainted or diminished, however. For the first 13 years of the 20th century, he was the American League's equivalent of Honus Wagner—the greatest fielder of his time at his position who was also one of the game's greatest hitters.

Unlike Wagner, who played on four pennant winners in Pittsburgh, Lajoie was never on a championship team. The closest he came was in 1908, when Cleveland lost the pennant to Detroit by a half-game. Lajoie was then in his fourth season as Cleveland's player-manager. He was so popular in the Forest City that the team was renamed the "Naps" in his honor.

Although Lajoie stepped down as manager following the 1909 season, he remained with Cleveland for five more seasons as a second baseman. He concluded his major-league career with a two-year stint with the A's. Lajoie had a career .338 batting average and was elected to the Hall of Fame in 1936.

BUCK LEONARD

★

*B*uck Leonard was a left-handed power-hitting first baseman in the Negro Leagues who often drew comparisons to Lou Gehrig. Buck was a key ingredient to the domination by the Homestead Grays in the 1930s.

Walter Fenner Leonard (born in 1907) was born to a railroad fireman in Rocky Mount, North Carolina. Buck also worked on the railroad until the Depression forced him out of a job. He played semi-

Buck Leonard (above) teamed with Josh Gibson on the Homestead Grays to form the Thunder Twins. Buck's lefty power at the plate is legendary.

pro baseball with clubs in North Carolina and Virginia until 1933, when the Baltimore Stars signed him. He traveled with the team until it ran out of money in New York and disbanded. Stuck in New York, he was lucky to find a position with the Brooklyn Royal Giants for the rest of the season. Leonard stopped in a New York tavern owned by Joe Williams, a retired player who had starred on Cum Posey's Homestead Grays. Williams now had his eye open for talent, because the Grays had been all but wiped out by player raids and retirement.

Leonard had a tryout, and he signed to play first base for the Grays. The team began to regain respectability, and when Josh Gibson came aboard in 1937, the Grays caught fire, winning nine consecutive flags. And when Gibson jumped ship to play in Mexico in 1940, Leonard carried the club, hitting .392 in 1941 to lead the Negro National League. He led the Grays to back-to-back World Series wins in 1943 and 1944 over the Birmingham Black Barons. He won another batting title, in 1948, when he was 40 years old, at .395, and a pair of home run titles in his long career. The Grays won their final World Series in 1948.

Buck was fairly well paid for his services. The Homestead Grays were based both in Pittsburgh and Washington, playing games in Forbes Field when the Pirates were out of town and in Griffith Stadium when the Senators were on the road. Since the Grays were able to fill both stadiums, they were able to pay their stars more than other Negro League teams. The lure of Mexican baseball was also a boon to Leonard. The Grays were forced to match the salary that he was being offered to play south of the border, and he was able to command over $1,000 per month in 1942, and even more later, good amounts for the Negro Leagues. He stayed with the Homestead Grays for his entire career, instead of jumping to other teams as other Negro League stars had done.

Buck played in Mexico, Cuba, Puerto Rico, and Venezuela in the winter, and he also barnstormed with Satchel Paige's all-stars. Leonard played in Mexico in the early 1950s after he retired from the Grays. In 1972, Leonard was selected for the Hall of Fame.

POP LLOYD

★

Pop Lloyd jumped from semipro baseball to the black professional leagues in 1905 at age 21, and was a good enough player to play semipro until he was age 58. He was a fine defensive shortstop for most of the early days in his career, and he showcased a line-drive stroke that drove his average to dizzying heights.

Born in northeast Florida, John Henry Lloyd (1884-1964) started playing semipro ball in his midteens. Moving to the Cuban X-Giants in 1905, Pop, like other gifted players of his generation, began his career as a catcher. By 1907, he was a shortstop and a cleanup hitter. Lloyd played for whatever team could pay him. He spent time on various Philadelphia teams, New York teams, and with the Chicago American Giants, among others. As a star player, Lloyd was in demand for All-Star games and tours to Cuba and the West Coast, but the financial situation of the black leagues forced him to miss spring training at times in order to work a regular job.

In a 1910 12-game exhibition series in Cuba against the

Pop Lloyd was a force to be dealt with offensively and defensively. When asked to pick the premier player of all time, Babe Ruth said, "I'd pick John Henry Lloyd."

Detroit Tigers, Lloyd went 11-for-22. While the Bengals won seven games, Ty Cobb (who batted .370) was sufficiently embarrassed to vow never to play against blacks again. In 1914, Rube Foster enticed Pop to play for the Chicago American Giants. In the Windy City he teamed with "Home Run"

Johnson in a legendary double-play combination. Lloyd helped lead the American Giants to championships in 1914 and 1917.

Lloyd was often likened to Honus Wagner, a comparison Wagner was proud to acknowledge. It was an apt analogy, because, like Honus, Lloyd was highly regarded, was a terrific hitter, and was known to scoop up dirt and pebbles along with ground balls. From his playing days in Cuba, Pop's other nickname was *El Cuchara,* Spanish for "The Shovel."

At age 44 in 1928, still in the pros, Pop hit .564 in 37 games, with 11 homers and 10 steals. The next year, he hit .388. Pitcher Sam Streeter said "Everything he hit was just like you were hanging out clothes on a line." Not only was Pop a great hitter, but he had an intimate knowledge of the game. In 1915, Lloyd had the first of many stints as a player-manager, and in 1921 he took charge of the short-lived Columbus, Ohio, franchise in Rube Foster's new Black National League. It was there that he finally acquired his nickname, and he was mentor to a new generation. He was named to the Hall of Fame in 1977.

CONNIE MACK

★

*C*onnie Mack had the longest career on a baseball field that any man has ever had—66 years as a player and manager, starting in the 19th century and lasting through the first half of the 20th.

Like many managers, Cornelius Alexander Mack (born McGillicuddy, 1862-1956) was a catcher in his playing days, a soft hitter who lasted 11 years starting in 1886. Mack became player-manager in 1894 with the Pittsburgh Pirates, taking over a talented but disappointing team. The club

remained in relatively the same position the next two years that he was the manager, and he was fired after the 1896 season.

At that point one of Mack's friends, Western League commissioner Ban Johnson, invited Connie to pilot the Milwaukee franchise, which he did for four years. In 1901, when Johnson elevated the status of the minor circuit to the major American League, he gave the Philadelphia franchise to Connie. Mack remained the A's manager through the 1950 season.

Mack first gained attention for his "White Elephants" in 1901 by buying star Napoleon Lajoie away from the crosstown NL Phillies. Lajoie was gone

Connie Mack, pictured here between Mickey Cochrane, left, and Lefty Grove, saw baseball as a business. This did not mean that he didn't like to win. His efforts helped put together teams that won five World Series.

in 1902, but Mack built a championship club around pitchers Eddie Plank, Rube Waddell, and Chief Bender to win pennants in 1902 and 1905. Behind hurlers Bender and Jack Coombs, and the "$100,000" infield (featuring second baseman Eddie Collins), the A's won three world championships in 1910, 1911, and '13.

When the upstart Federal League had begun to raid the two established leagues, Mack could see his team unraveling as Boston swept them in the 1914 Series. "If the players were going to cash in and leave me to hold the bag, there was nothing for me to do but to cash in too," Mack said. Selling off his best players, he doomed the club to a record seven straight last-place finishes.

Mack's method was to buy hot prospects from the flourishing minor-league teams of the times, trusting his ability to discover stars. In the mid-1920s, Mack's charges were usually in pennant races. By 1929, the A's exploded. Young stars such as Al Simmons, Jimmie Foxx, Mickey Cochrane, and Lefty Grove won three straight pennants and the World Series in 1929 and 1930.

Unfortunately for Mack, the Depression forced him to sell many of his best players to better-heeled teams. He wallowed in the second division for the rest of his career. "The Tall Tactician," who dressed in his severe dark suits, was age 87 when he managed his last team. He compiled a career 3,731-3,948 record as a manager. Always the gentleman, Mack was beloved by his players and was among the first people inducted into the Hall of Fame, in 1937.

Connie Mack spent an amazing 66 years in baseball. Mr. Mack, with Ira Thomas at right, was sometimes called the 10th man due to his expertise in moving players around in the field. His personal experience helped, too, as he played every position except pitcher and third base.

MICKEY MANTLE

★

Mickey Mantle was the most feared hitter on the most successful team in history, and overcame great pain in his quest to satisfy his fans, his father, and himself.

Mickey Charles Mantle was born in 1931 in Spavinaw, Oklahoma, the son of Mutt Mantle, a lead miner who had dreams of a good life for his youngster. Mickey (named after Mickey Cochrane) was a standout schoolboy player, but a football injury nearly derailed his career—and his life. He suffered from osteomyelitis, a condition that weakened his left leg; he may have lost the leg if his mother had not procured a then-new treatment with a revolutionary drug, penicillin.

The Yankees signed Mickey to a contract in 1949, and the shortstop hit .313 that year, and committed 47 errors. The next year with Joplin, he led the Western Association with a .383 batting average, 141 runs scored, 199 base hits, and 55 errors at shortstop in 137 games. His 26 homers and 136 RBI led Casey Stengel to pro-

The Commerce Comet—the finest switch-hitter in baseball and the consummate all-around player. Mickey Mantle led the league four times in home runs, was a member of 16 All-Star teams, participated in 12 World Series, and posted lifetime marks of 1,509 RBI, 536 homers, and a .298 batting average.

claim Mickey the top prospect in baseball.

Mantle opened the 1951 season in right field (after extensive defensive tutoring by former Yankee outfielder Tommy Henrich). Mickey did not live up to his advance billing and was sent to the American Association in midseason. Discouraged, he wanted to quit,

but it was Mutt that goaded Mickey's pride and put him back on the path to stardom.

Mantle had enormous forearms and blazing speed, and he became a superb center fielder, taking over for Joe DiMaggio in 1952. Mantle was possibly the fastest man in the game during his early years. In his best seasons, and there were

Mickey Mantle, Casey Stengel, Yogi Berra, and Hank Bauer of the Yankees. Stengel had this to say of the young Mick: "They're been a lot of fast men but none as big and strong as Mantle."

Mantle's high school leg injury, torn knee cartilage in 1951, and many other injuries he suffered after that, shortened his career and were a constant source of pain. After two painful seasons in 1967 and 1968, The Mick retired, with a .298 average, 536 homers, and 1,509 RBI. Mantle was inducted into the Hall of Fame in 1974.

many, Mantle was simply a devastating player. He could run like the wind and hit tape measure homers, like his famous 565-footer in Washington in 1953. He led the Yanks to 12 fall classics in 14 years, and seven world championships. He still owns records for most homers, RBI, runs, walks, and strikeouts in World Series play. He led the AL with 129 runs in 1954 and got his first homer title in 1955 with 37. He was a free-swinger who struck out often, but could also take a walk, drawing 100 10 times.

In 1956, Mantle had one of the greatest seasons ever at bat. He hit 52 homers with 130 RBI and a .353 average to win the Triple Crown. He also led the league with 132 runs and a .705 slugging percentage. He had 112 walks and won the first of three Most Valuable Player Awards. He won the MVP in 1957, hitting .365 with 34 homers, 94 RBI, 121 runs scored, and 146 walks.

Mantle notched homer crowns in 1958 and 1960, then raced Roger Maris in 1961 to break Babe Ruth's single-season home run mark. While Maris's 61 was the winner, Mick led the league with a .687 slugging percentage and 132 runs scored. Mick won an MVP Award in 1962 with a .321 average and 20 homers.

Above: Who else could have replaced Joe DiMaggio but another legend in the making. *Opposite page:* After he retired, Mantle had a recurring dream of being locked out of the ballpark with no way in. He'd wake up in a sweat after hearing, "At bat, No. seven, Mickey Mantle."

TREASURY OF BASEBALL

JUAN MARICHAL

★

Juan Marichal won more games than any pitcher during the 1960s, with 191. He was the greatest control pitcher of his time—he walked just 709 men in over 3,500 innings—with a delivery that defied logic. The timing oddities and whirl of motion that resulted from his high-kick windup baffled hitters for 16 seasons, leading to a 243-142 career record with a 2.89 ERA.

Juan Antonio Marichal y Sanchez (born in Laguna Verge, Dominican Republic, in 1937) as a youngster learned to pitch using a homemade baseball. Signed by the Giants' organization in 1958, he led the Midwest League that year with 21 wins and a 1.87 ERA, and he led the Eastern League in '59 with 18 wins and a 2.39 ERA. In half a season at Tacoma of the Pacific Coast League, he was 11-5.

Called up to San Francisco in 1960, Marichal was immediately an effective pitcher. He was 6-2 with a 2.66 ERA that year, and had his worst ERA of the decade in 1961 when he was 13-10 with a 3.89 ERA.

Above: Juan Marichal and his famous high leg kick. *Opposite page:* Although Marichal was tough on the Dodgers, he actually spent his last season, 1975, in Los Angeles.

In 1963, Marichal led the league in wins, going 25-8. That year he lost to a Sandy Koufax no-hitter, but Marichal won his next start by no-hitting Houston. He also encountered Warren Spahn, with each going all the way in a 16-inning Giants win. It was the first of six 20-win seasons in seven years for "Manito," each season posting ERAs under 3.00.

On Aug. 22, 1965, with the Dodgers and the Giants in a tight pennant race, Marichal was pitching against Koufax. That historic feud erupted in a brawl two days earlier. Juan had thrown a couple of purpose pitches, and when Dodger catcher John Roseboro asked Koufax to dust Marichal, Sandy refused. Marichal, apparently convinced that Roseboro's return throw to Koufax came too close to hitting him in the ear, took the bat and cracked the Dodger receiver in the head a couple of times. The benches emptied, erupting into one of the most vicious brawls in baseball history. Willie Mays played peacemaker, leading Roseboro from the fray, May's uniform stained with Roseboro's blood. Marichal was suspended and fined, and since the Giants finished just two games back, his absence was costly.

The incident may have prevented Marichal from doing better in awards voting ("The Dominican Dandy" never won a Cy Young Award), as well as in his Hall of Fame induction, for which Roseboro campaigned. Juan was inducted in 1983. He was one of the best right-handers of the 1960s, finishing in the top three in wins five times and ERA three times. He was particularly tough on the Dodgers, beating them in 37 of 55 lifetime decisions.

TREASURY OF BASEBALL

EDDIE MATHEWS

★

Eddie Mathews is best remembered as teaming with Hank Aaron to form the Braves' one-two punch that dominated the NL in the 1950s and early 1960s. Mathews was the best-hitting third baseman before Mike Schmidt.

Edwin Lee Mathews (born in 1931) was a muscular high school baseball and football star in 1949 in Santa Barbara, California. He was pursued by the Brooklyn Dodgers, who offered a $10,000 contract, although signing a free agent for more than $6,000 meant that he had to stay on the major-league roster for two seasons. He was also courted by the Boston Braves, who offered $6,000. Eddie researched the rosters and decided that the Braves would give him the best opportunity to start quickly; he didn't want to sit on a major-league bench for two years. Mathews batted .363 with 17 homers in 1949, in his first season in pro baseball, and he had 32 homers and 106 RBI for Atlanta of the Southern League in 1950.

Mathews was promoted to Boston in 1952, and though

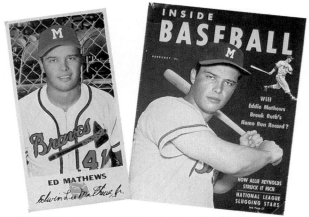

Above left: Eddie Mathews on a 1954 Johnson's Cookie Card. *Above right:* A cover of *Inside Baseball* featuring Mathews. *Opposite page:* On his induction into Cooperstown, he said, "My mother used to pitch to me and my father would shag balls. If I hit one up the middle, close to my mother, I'd have some extra chores to do. My mother was instrumental in making me a pull hitter."

he fanned a league-high 115 times his rookie season, he also cracked 25 homers. The next season, the franchise's first in Milwaukee, he won his first homer title, hitting 47. He provided power the next three seasons, getting 37 or more homers and 95 or more RBI from 1954 to '56. In 1957, he batted .292 with 32 homers and 94 RBI, as the Braves won the world championship. He hit .251 with 31 homers as the Braves won the pennant in 1958. Eddie won the homer crown in 1959 with 46.

Mathews hit at least 30 homers in nine seasons, four times hitting over 40. He led the league in walks four times, had 90 or more bases on balls nine times, and scored at least 95 runs in 10 straight seasons. One reason he was scored so much was that he batted ahead of Aaron. Playing with Henry may have obscured Mathews's performance, but while together, they hit 863 home runs, more than Babe Ruth and Lou Gehrig. Mathews was Aaron's manager in 1974, the year Hank broke Ruth's career home run record. Mathews had 512 homers and 1,453 RBI in his career.

When Mathews joined the Boston Braves in 1952, he played the hot corner poorly, but he matured into a capable third baseman. He led the NL in putouts twice, assists three times, and fielding average once. Eddie was inducted into the Hall of Fame in 1978.

TREASURY OF BASEBALL

CHRISTY MATHEWSON

★

Christy Mathewson left Bucknell University in 1899 to sign his first baseball contract. Seventeen years later he retired with 373 wins and an almost universal recognition as the greatest pitcher in National League history to that time.

Christopher Mathewson (1880-1925) probably did more than any other performer of his day to enhance the image of a professional baseball player. Educated, intelligent, and a real gentleman, he seemed almost too good to be true.

Mathewson was originally the property of the New York Giants but was drafted by Cincinnati for $100 when he won 20 games for Norfolk of the Virginia League in 1900, after doing poorly in an early-season trial with the New York club. John Brush, who owned a piece of the Reds and knew he would soon be serving the Giants in a similar capacity, clandestinely arranged to return Matty to New York for a badly worn Amos Rusie.

After winning 20 games for the Giants in 1901, Matty

Mathewson walked only 1.6 batters per nine innings.

tumbled to just 14 victories the next year. After that, however, he reeled off 12 straight seasons in which he won 20 or more games. "Big Six" won over 30 games on four occasions, with a high of 37 in 1908. The net result of his epic run of success was that he had 300 career victories by the time he was 32 years old.

Sometimes, though, Mathewson seemed to have trouble winning the big games. In his last three World Series appearances—1911, '12, and '13—Matty won just two games while losing five. In his defense,

the Giants consistently displayed defensive lapses at crucial moments when he was on the mound and scored only seven runs in the last 39 innings he hurled in Series play.

However, Mathewson's work in championship contests did not always end in disappointment. In 1905, his first World Series appearance, he twirled a record three complete-game shutouts and 27 scoreless innings against the Athletics to lead the Giants to victory in their first 20th-century post-season affair. Matty's feat is considered by some to be the most outstanding performance in World Series history.

In 1916, with his famed screwball, or "fadeaway," no longer effective, Mathewson was traded to Cincinnati so that he could become the Reds player-manager. After only one mound appearance in the Queen City, he became a bench pilot only. Matty entered the Army in August of 1918. While serving overseas in World War I, he accidentally inhaled poison gas, permanently damaging his lungs. He died on Oct. 7, 1925. In 1936, Christy was among the first group of five players elected to the Hall of Fame.

WILLIE MAYS

★

few players have combined grace, popularity, and accomplishment like Willie Mays. He was a beautiful fielder, a tremendous power hitter, an outstanding outfield thrower, a canny baserunner, a huge drawing card, and a durable champion.

Born in 1931 in Westfield, Alabama, Willie Howard Mays was so advanced that when he was 14 years old he competed with the men on his father's steel mill team. He played semipro ball at age 16, and was on the Birmingham Black Barons by 1947. He was one of the last players, and likely the best, to come from the Negro Leagues to the big leagues. In 1950, the Giants signed him and sent him to the Inter-State League, where he batted .353. In 1951, he was batting .477 at Minneapolis of the American Association when the Giants promoted him. The New York front office published an apology in the Minneapolis paper, understanding the impression Willie had made on Millers fans.

Leo Durocher demanded that Mays be promoted after

"Don't get me wrong," Mays once said, "I like to hit. But there's nothing like getting out there in the outfield, running after a ball, and throwing somebody out trying to take that extra base. That's real fun."

the Giants started at 6-20. Although Willie started out 0-for-12, he had a galvanizing effect on the Giants. They came from 13½ games back to force a playoff with the front-running Dodgers, beating them on Bobby Thomson's home run (Willie was on deck) in the culmination of "The Miracle on Coogan's Bluff." Mays hit 20 homers, perfected center-field play, and won the Rookie of the Year Award. He also won the hearts of teammates and fans alike for his enthusiasm, good humor, squeaky voice, and incredible play.

Mays was in the Army for most of 1952 and all of 1953.

Above: Willie Mays fearlessly slides into home. *Above right:* The Say Hey Kid was one of the dominant sluggers of the 1950s and '60s. *Opposite page:* A happy, high-spirited person, Mays was beloved by many.

With those years, Willie is almost certain to have broken Babe Ruth's lifetime home run record. In 1954 Willie returned to win the MVP Award, leading the league with a .345 average and a .667 slugging percentage and hitting 41 homers. His catch of a Vic Wertz drive in the Giants' World Series victory has become one of baseball's most admired moments.

Willie led the NL in homers with 51 in 1955. He hit over 35 homers in 11 seasons, 40 homers six times, and won five slugging crowns. In addition to everything else, add speed; he won four stolen-base and three triples titles. His biggest victory came over the skeptical San Francisco fans. When the Giants moved out to the West Coast in 1958, Bay Area fans remembered Joe DiMaggio. Willie melted all resistance by his play.

In 1962, Mays and the Giants again found themselves in a tie with the talented Dodgers. Willie led a powerhouse team to another playoff victory, scoring four runs in the ninth to earn the right to face the Yankees in the World Series. It was one of Willie's best seasons, as he hit 49 homers and drove in 141 runs. In 1964, he won his second MVP by batting .303 with 35 homers and 111 RBI. Mays finished among the top six in MVP voting 12 times.

Mays won a dozen Gold Gloves in a row for his outfield play, from 1957 to 1968. Mickey Mantle, the man Mays would be compared to most often, said, "you have to work hard to be able to make things look as easy as Willie makes them look." Mays retired with records for games, putouts, and chances for center fielders.

The "Say Hey Kid," Mays led the league in walks, hit 18 homers, and was 23 for 26 as a basestealer—at age 40. He spent his final two seasons in New York with the Mets, and he appeared in one final World Series. He was a near-unanimous selection to the Hall of Fame in 1979.

BILL MAZEROSKI

★

The 1960 World Series between the Yankees and the Pirates was one of the most unusual fall classics ever. The Bronx Bombers exploded for 91 hits and 55 runs in the seven-game Series; won three games by scores of 16-3, 10-0, and 12-0; and outscored the Pirates 55-27. But the Bucs won the tourney when, in the bottom of the ninth inning of a tied game seven, Bill Mazeroski hit a Ralph Terry offering over the left field wall for a home run, giving the Pirates a dramatic 10-9 triumph. While Maz's most important moment came with his bat, he was the top-fielding second sacker of his time, and maybe of all time.

William Stanley Mazeroski (born in 1936) played for 17 seasons in the big leagues, all of them with the Pirates, beginning in midseason in 1956. In his 81-game debut with the Pirates, he hit .243, replacing Johnny O'Brien at second base. During his first full season, in 1957, Maz played in 148 games, hitting .283 with eight homers and 54 RBI. He received his first All-Star invitation in 1958, hitting .275 with

Bill Mazeroski, eight-time Gold Glove winner, retired with several records for second sackers, including most double plays in a single season and most career double plays. In 1987 the Bucs retired his No. 9.

19 homers and 68 RBI, and leading NL second sackers in assists and chances.

Mazeroski in 1960 led the league in five defensive categories, including a sterling .989 fielding percentage. Offensively, he batted .273 with 11 homers and 64 RBI. In the World Series Mazeroski batted .320 with eight hits and a team-leading five RBI while fielding flawlessly. His two-run homer in the fourth inning provided the Bucs with a 6-4 victory in the Series opener.

From 1961 to 1968 his average danced between .251 and .271. He hit 10 or more homers in six campaigns

(1958, 1960, 1961, 1962, 1964, and 1966). In 1966, he had 16 and a career-best 82 runs batted in.

Mazeroski was an eight-time Gold Glove winner. He retired after the 1972 season with several major-league records for second sackers, including most double plays in a single season (161 in 1966), most career double plays (1,706), most seasons with the league lead in assists (nine), and most seasons leading the league in double plays (eight). As a hitter, Mazeroski ended his career with 2,016 hits, 138 homers, and 853 RBI. In 1987 the Pirates retired his No. 9.

JOE MCCARTHY

★

Joe McCarthy's .615 managerial career winning percentage and his .698 World Series winning percentage are both the best of all time.

Joseph Vincent McCarthy (1887-1978) attended Niagara University for two years. He left in 1907 after signing with Wilmington of the Tri-State League. He showed enough talent to move up to the high minor leagues for four years as a utility infielder. In 1913, Wilkes-Barre of the New York State League made Joe a player-manager. He guided them into second place while hitting .325. He then returned to the high minors for five seasons—as a player only.

In 1919, Joe was with Louisville of the American Association, when in midseason they made him player-manager. He guided the team into third place, and he stayed with Louisville for six more seasons, winning two pennants. Louisville won 102 games in 1925, while the Cubs won 68, and Chicago signed McCarthy.

McCarthy's first action with the Cubs was cutting Grover Alexander, establishing a repu-

Joe DiMaggio said, "Never a day went by when you didn't learn something from McCarthy."

tation as a disciplinarian. But "Marse Joe" was very much a man behind the scenes, which was partly responsible for his low profile, despite the great success of his teams. Joe improved the Cubs each year, and the acquisition of Rogers Hornsby in 1929 gave Chicago the final ingredient to win the pennant. The Cubs were destined for second the next year, but McCarthy left the club with four games to play, and Hornsby took over. McCarthy assumed control of the Yankees, skipperless after the death of Miller Huggins.

Babe Ruth wanted the Yankee manager job very badly, and

it is a tribute to McCarthy's ability that he was able to deflect the Babe's resentment and make the team his own. The Yankees finished second in 1931, but in 1932 the Yanks beat McCarthy's old Chicago team in the World Series. Three second-place finishes followed, then in 1936 Joe DiMaggio joined the team, and the Yankees won four straight Series, winning 16 games while losing just three. In 1941, they won it all again.

McCarthy was one of the first to get significant pitching help from his bullpen, and the 1941 team had no 20-game winner. He brought them to the Series again in 1942 and 1943, winning his final championship in 1943. While the Yankees were talented, Joe increased their achievements by making them disciplined and prepared.

McCarthy left the Yankees in 1946 for health reasons, and in 1948 went to Boston. Ted Williams felt that the two frustrating second-place finishes in 1948 and '49 took the heart out of Joe. "He finally quit during the '50 season, I think out of his own extreme disappointment," Williams said. McCarthy had a 2,125-1,333 record and was inducted into the Hall of Fame in 1957.

WILLIE McCOVEY

★

The "other" Willie on the 1960s San Francisco Giants, Willie McCovey was one of the great sluggers of the decade, averaging 30 homers each year and leading the league in round-trippers three times and in home run percentage four times.

Willie Lee McCovey (born in 1938) was such an outstanding baseball player that as a youngster he played on men's teams in his Mobile, Alabama, hometown. He was signed by the Giants in 1955, and led the Georgia State League with 113 RBI, in 113 games. He made it to the Pacific Coast League by 1958, where the first baseman hit .319 with 89 RBI that year. While that performance should have earned him a spot in San Francisco in 1959, he was assigned to the PCL again; the Giants had '58 NL Rookie of the Year Orlando Cepeda playing first base. After McCovey batted .372 with a league-best 29 homers and 92 RBI in 95 PCL games in 1959, he was called up by San Francisco. In the last 52 games of the 1959 season, "Stretch"

Above: More soft-spoken than some of his teammates, Willie McCovey preferred to let his bat do the talking. He was well-respected for his dead-pull hitting and ability to send one out of the park almost at will. *Opposite page:* Big Mac won the 1969 MVP Award and led the NL with a 9.2 home run percentage, one of the highest ever.

belted 13 homers with a .354 average and was voted the NL Rookie of the Year.

In 1960, though, McCovey's performance took such a dive he was returned to the minors. In 1961 and '62 he hit pretty well, socking a combined 38 home runs in about a season's worth of at bats. But in the same two years, Cepeda hit 81 homers with 256 RBI. They were both first basemen—and unsatisfactory outfielders—but they took their turns at first and in the outfield

until Cepeda's knee injury in 1966 prompted his trade to St. Louis.

The Giants won the pennant in 1962. In the ninth inning of the seventh game, McCovey was at bat with the winning run on second. He hit a line drive—"the hardest ball I ever hit," he said—directly at Yankee second baseman Bobby Richardson. A hit to either side would have given the Giants a championship, and Stretch would have been the hero. Unfortunately, a World Series victory never came. In 1971, the Giants lost to the Pirates in the NLCS, though Willie hit .429 with two homers. McCovey won the National League MVP Award in 1969, during a span of outstanding production. He led the circuit in slugging percentage three years, from 1967 to '69.

Stretch, as popular as he was, was traded to the Padres in 1974, where he spent most of three seasons. In 1977, he returned to the Giants and had one more good season, batting .280 with 28 homers and winning NL Comeback Player of the Year. He tied Ted Williams on the all-time home run list with 521. Willie was elected to the Hall of Fame in 1986.

TREASURY OF BASEBALL

JOHN MCGRAW

★

John McGraw was the most controversial, notorious, hateful, inspiring manager in baseball history, and he is the winningest manager in National League history.

John Joseph McGraw (1873-1934) played in an era when "rowdyism" was rampant, and he was among the worst offenders as he battled with opponents, umpires, and fans for any edge he could grasp. He played mostly third base from 1891 to 1906; a spike wound cut short his playing career. His infamous Baltimore Oriole club twice won the Temple Cup. He had his first taste of managing in 1899, when he steered the club along with teammate Wilbert Robinson.

McGraw and Robinson were sold to St. Louis in 1900, but elected to leave in 1901 to join the nascent American League, taking over the new Orioles. McGraw did not get along with AL founder Ban Johnson and began to listen to the siren song of the firmly established National League. He persuaded John Brush to buy an interest in the Orioles and

In John McGraw's 29 full seasons as the skipper of the New York Giants, the New Yorkers finished first in 10 seasons, and they placed second in 11 other campaigns. McGraw's Giants won at least 90 games in 14 of his 29 full seasons and finished within 10 games of the pennant winners in nine of the 19 seasons that they did not win the flag.

then release McGraw and some of the team's bright young stars. They went to New York, and Brush sold his Cincinnati club and bought the restocked Giants. McGraw was then age 29, and he managed the team for the next 30 years.

Fans anticipated fireworks when McGraw and young, gentlemanly pitching sensation Christy Mathewson met, but the two became fast friends. The Giants won pennants in 1904 and 1905. There was no World Series in 1904, as owner Brush scoffed at the AL. In 1905, the Giants beat Philadelphia for the first of three world championships for the

McGraw-led Giants, though McGraw was doomed to lose six World Series in his career.

In 1908, "Merkle's Boner" cost the Giants a pennant, though many historians think that the accountability lay with McGraw. "Little Napoleon" put together three pennants from 1911 to '13, and another in 1917. McGraw was a fine field general who knew all the tricks for manufacturing runs in that low-scoring era. He was the "absolute czar" of the team, relying on discipline and fear. John once said, "nine mediocre players pulling together under one competent head will do better work than nine individuals of greater ability without unified control." His record is dotted with problems with umpires, and his violent nature often got him into trouble off the field and on.

McGraw built a powerhouse in the early 1920s, winning a record four straight pennants from 1921 to '24, with World Series victories in 1921 and 1922. With the advent of lively ball strategies, baseball changed, and the '24 pennant was to be his last. He retired in 1932 with a 2,784-1,959 record. McGraw was elected to the Hall of Fame in 1937.

JOHNNY MIZE

★

Hard-hitting first baseman Johnny Mize was a link from the great 1930s Cardinals teams to the great Yankees dynasty of the 1950s.

John Robert Mize was born in 1913 in Demorest, Georgia. He played a good deal of basketball as a youngster, because his hometown was small enough to make gathering enough players for baseball difficult. He played baseball well enough while in high school to sign with Greensboro of the Piedmont League in 1930. In 1933, while at Rochester of the International League, he suffered painful leg cramps that would haunt him for the next several years. In 1935, he underwent surgery to remove a growth on his pelvis. Thus cured, he moved up to the St. Louis Cardinals.

Mize joined the Cards in 1936, batted .329, had 93 RBI, and clubbed 19 home runs, a total he was to increase each year for the next four. He surpassed the .300 mark for the next eight years, peaking at .364 in 1937. In 1939, Johnny led the league in homers (28)

Johnny Mize struck out only 524 times in his career in the majors. He hit three home runs in a game six times, becoming the only man to do so. He homered in all 15 parks in use at the time.

and batting average (.349). In 1940, "The Big Cat" walloped 43 dingers to top the senior circuit and drove home 137 runs, also the league lead. He finished second in the MVP voting to Frank McCormick. Mize led the NL with three consecutive seasons of .600-plus slugging percentages— 1938 to 1940. With the Cards, from 1936 to 1941, Mize had 100 or more RBI every year but one, his 1936 rookie year.

Traded to the New York Giants before the 1942 season for three major leaguers and $50,000, Mize led the NL that season with a .521 slugging percentage and 110 RBI. He served three years in the Navy during World War II. He returned from the service to top the NL twice in home runs, including 51 round-trippers in 1947, tying Ralph Kiner for the league's top spot. Mize, however, still paced the loop in RBI (138) and runs scored (137).

Toward the end of the '49 season, the Yankees acquired Mize for $40,000. He went 2-for-2 in the 1949 World Series with two RBI. The Yanks looked like geniuses. Mize was even a bigger hero in the 1952 Series. In a wild battle with the Dodgers, he hit .400 with six RBI and three homers in 15 at bats, grabbing the Series MVP honor. A part-time first sacker and pinch-hitter, Johnny led the AL in pinch hits from 1951 to 1953.

In all, "The Big Cat" won five World Series rings with the Yanks. He retired after the 1953 season, at age 40. The only slugger in history to hit three home runs in a game six times, Mize was named to the Hall of Fame in 1981.

JOE MORGAN

★

Little Joe made the Big Red Machine go. Joe Morgan is best remembered for being a catalyst for the world champion Reds in 1975 and 1976. He also is second to Eddie Collins for most games at second base.

Joe Leonard Morgan was born in 1943 in Bonham, Texas, but his family moved to Oakland, California, when Joe was very young. His first hero was Jackie Robinson, but later Morgan emulated the play and the determination of Nellie Fox. After attending the same high school that produced Frank Robinson, Morgan signed with the Astros in 1963. In 1964, he was the Texas League MVP, batting .319 with 42 doubles, 12 homers, and 90 RBI.

In 1965, Morgan was the Houston second baseman. Houston coach Fox taught Joe a "chicken flap" of his left elbow while taking his batting stance, to remind him to keep his elbow high. Morgan hit .271 that year, with 14 home runs, 100 runs scored, and an NL-leading 97 bases on balls, and he finished second in

Above: Little Joe's diminutive size (5'7" and 150 pounds) did not diminish his ability at the plate. *Opposite page:* Speedy Joe Morgan understood the importance of posing a threat on the basepaths. "A good basestealer," he once said, "should make the whole infield jumpy."

Rookie of the Year voting to Los Angeles second baseman Jim Lefebvre. Joe notched 89 walks in 1966 despite missing time with a fractured knee cap. In 1968, he lost almost the whole season when he tore ligaments in his knee. He returned in 1969 to get 94 runs

that year, 102 runs in 1970, and 87 runs in 1971. The Astros and the Reds tied for fourth place in 1971, and each team was looking for a change. In one of the blockbuster trades of the decade, the Reds sent second sacker Tommy Helms and first baseman Lee May to

TREASURY OF BASEBALL

Houston for outfielder Cesar Geronimo, pitcher Jack Billingham, and Morgan.

When Joe got out of the Astrodome, his stats were enhanced. The 5'7" second baseman hit 16 homers in 1972, 26 in '73, and 22 in 1974. His walk totals those years were 115, 111, and 120, and he scored 122, 116, and 107 runs.

Morgan was the only second sacker in baseball history to win back-to-back MVP Awards, in 1975 and '76. In 1975, he batted .327 with 17 homers, 107 runs scored, 94 RBI, 67 stolen bases, and a league-best 132 walks as the Reds won 108 games. Morgan batted .320 with 27 homers, 113 runs scored, 111 RBI, 60 swipes, and 114 walks in 1976.

Joe was a steady fielder and won five straight Gold Gloves from 1973 to '77. He led the Reds to another playoff berth in 1979. He then moved back to Houston in 1980, again appearing in the NLCS. In 1983, he joined the Phillies and appeared in his last World Series. Joe led the NL in walks four times and runs once. He never led the circuit in stolen bases, but he finished in the top three eight times. Joe was elected to the Hall of Fame in 1990.

DALE MURPHY

★

*D*ale Murphy was one of the National League's most gifted outfielders of the 1980s, as well as one of baseball's finest ambassadors.

Selected by the Braves in the first round of the June 1974 draft, Dale Bryan Murphy (born in 1956) spent more than three years in the Braves' farm system trying to become a catcher. While he had the physical ability to be a catcher, he wasn't able to overcome some

In 1983, Dale Murphy captured his second consecutive MVP Award. At the time he received the honors, he was only 27 years old, making him the youngest player to take the Award in back-to-back seasons.

mental roadblocks. He was switched to first base, and during his first full season in Atlanta, in 1978, he had 23 homers and 79 RBI. The following year, Murphy led the league with 20 errors but had 21 round-trippers.

Murphy in 1980 earned All-Star honors in his first season as a center fielder. He finished third in the homer battle with 33. In 1981, Murphy tied the major-league record for most double plays by an outfielder (four), a feat he would repeat in 1985.

Named the NL MVP in 1982, he led the league in RBI with 109, while notching a .281 batting average, 36 homers, and 113 runs scored. He won a Gold Glove that year, his first of five in a row. In 1983, he captured his second consecutive MVP Award, at age 27 the youngest player to take the Award back-to-back. He led the league in slugging percentage (.540), RBI (121), and (for the second straight year) games played (162). He also matched his 1982 effort of 36 homers.

Murphy's lineup of charitable endorsements and contributions was as lengthy as his major-league stats. In 1985 he earned the Lou Gehrig Memo-

Dale Murphy was the personification of a complete player. He created one of baseball's longest consecutive playing streaks when he played in 740 consecutive games (Sept. 27, 1981 through July 9, 1986).

rial Award as the player who best exemplified the spirit and character of Gehrig.

Murphy led the league in home runs for the first time in 1984, with 36. In '85 he led the loop with 37 dingers, 118 runs scored, and 90 bases on balls. He also had 185 hits, a 15-game hitting streak, and a healthy .300 average that year. In 1987 he had a personal best of 44 homers. Starting in 1988, his career started a downward decline, though he was able to drive in at least 77 runs a season from '88 to 1991. He retired during the 1993 season, with 398 homers and 1,266 RBI.

EDDIE MURRAY

★

Eddie Murray averaged 28 homers a year in his 12 seasons as a Baltimore Oriole, from 1977 to 1988, and he could be counted on to drive in at least 78 runs every year.

Standards of excellence were set early for Eddie Clarence Murray (born in 1956), who played baseball at Locke High School in Los Angeles with future major-leaguers Ozzie Smith, Darrell Jackson, Gary Alexander, and younger brother Rich Murray. Brothers Eddie and Rich followed three older brothers—Charles, Venice, and Leon—into the higher echelons of organized ball, and both surpassed their elders by making it to the majors. Eddie won seven games pitching as a senior, and he was also a center on his school basketball team.

A third-round pick by the Orioles in 1973, Murray earned minor-league All-Star honors on three occasions. A natural right-handed batter, he taught himself to switch-hit to become more effective at the plate. In 1977, at age 21, when he broke into the bigs, he did it with style, becoming the

When Eddie Murray broke into the bigs, he did it with style, becoming the fourth Oriole to capture American League Rookie of the Year honors. He was also the first player to snare that trophy while appearing mostly as a designated hitter.

a dazzling fielder. He won three straight Gold Gloves, from 1982 to '84. He was among the best at fielding bunts and gaining force-outs at second base. Murray appeared in his first World Series in 1979, reaching base seven of his first eight at bats against the Pirates, but then he went hitless for the remainder of the Series.

From 1980 to '83 Murray seemed to get hotter as the seasons progressed. He ended this run with career highs in home runs, runs, and walks. The Orioles, also powered by shortsop Cal Ripken, beat the Phillies in the 1983 World Series.

Except for the 1981 strike year, when Murray led the AL with 78 RBI, he had at least 84 RBI every year for the 12 years he was an Oriole, five times surpassing the 100 ribbie mark. He continued that consistent production after his days in Baltimore.

Murray didn't have good relations with the press for years, but he was involved in community work during his various stops in the majors. He was nominated for the Roberto Clemente Humanitarian Award in 1984 and '85 for sponsoring medical, educational, and religious foundations.

fourth Oriole to capture American League Rookie of the Year honors. He was also the first player to snare that trophy while appearing mostly as a designated hitter.

Placed at first base in 1978, Murray continued his excellent production at bat while thriving in the field. During his years as a first sacker with the O's, he gained a reputation as

STAN MUSIAL

★

Stan "The Man" Musial starred for the St. Louis Cardinals for 22 seasons and was the first National League player to win three Most Valuable Player Awards.

Stanley Frank Musial was born in 1920 in Donora, western Pennsylvania, an area which produced many great athletes. When Musial was a youngster he was the batboy for a local team, until they gave him the opportunity to pitch, and he rang up 13 Ks in six innings. When he was just 18 years old, in 1938, he went to see the Pirates play the Giants, and he turned to his friend and said that he thought that he could hit big-league pitching. That year, Musial joined the Cardinals' organization as a pitcher.

Assigned to Daytona Beach in the Florida State League in 1940, Stan was pitching very well and hitting over .300. He played in the outfield on the days that he didn't pitch. During the season, he attempted a diving catch and injured his left (pitching) shoulder so badly that his career on the mound was over. The Cards, aware of his great athletic talent, moved

him to the outfield full time, and he performed so well that he was in the majors by the end of 1941.

In 1942, the emerging Cardinal powerhouse won the first

After Musial got hit 3,000, he said, "I never realized hitting a little ball around could cause so much commotion. I now know how Lindbergh must have felt when he returned to St. Louis."

of three straight pennants and the World Series as the rookie Musial hit .315. In 1943, he won his first MVP Award, leading the league with a .357 batting average, 220 base hits, 48 doubles, and 20 triples. He again led the NL in hits and doubles in 1944.

Musial had good home run power, terrific doubles power, and for his time, was a spectacular triples hitter. He was terrifically fast—one of his nicknames was "The Donora Greyhound"—and was a fine fielder, in left and later as a first baseman. Though he never led the league in homers, he won six slugging titles and in 1954 hit five round-trippers in a double-header. His unique batting corkscrew stance, described by Ted Lyons as "like a kid peeking around the corner to see if the cops are coming," resulted in seven batting crowns. Musial posted a lifetime .416 on-base average, scoring at least 105 runs in 11 straight seasons.

In the Navy in 1945, Stan the Man came back to win his second MVP in 1946 as the Cards won another world championship. He led the league with a .365 batting average, 50 doubles, 20 triples, and 124 runs scored. He won

Stan the Man batted over .300 for 16 seasons in a row. Then, just before turning 42, he tossed in a .330 effort for good measure.

his third Most Valuable Player trophy in 1948. He missed the Triple Crown by a single home run, hitting a career-high 39 to Johnny Mize's and Ralph Kiner's 40. Musial had a .376 average (the NL's highest since Bill Terry hit .401 in 1930), 230 hits, 46 doubles, 18 triples, 131 RBI, and 135 runs, all of which led the NL. Besides winning three MVPs, Musial finished second four times.

Several of the other NL organizations gained ground on St. Louis and its farm system by the early 1950s. Stan won batting crowns from 1950 to 1952 (with averages of .346, .355, and .336), but the Cardinals could finish no better than third. Stan won his final batting title in 1957 when he was age 37, and the Redbirds finished second. But while Stan maintained his excellence, St. Louis from 1953 to '59 would get no closer than fourth place. Musial hit .330 in 1962, when he was 42 years old. In his final season, 1963, he hit a home run in his first at bat after becoming a grandfather. Musial was voted the Player of the Decade in 1956 for the period from 1946 to 1955. Stan the Man was elected to the Hall of Fame in 1969.

KID NICHOLS

★

When he first joined the Boston Beaneaters in 1890, Charlie Nichols looked so youthful and so physically unprepossessing that he was called "Kid." The nickname stuck with him for the remainder of his life. Nichols is the only 300-game winner in major-league history who got by with just one pitch, his fastball (later in his career, Nichols developed a changeup but rarely used it). And at that, it was by no means an overpowering fastball. What Nichols did possess in spades, however, was control. When he walked a batter, it was usually only because he was afraid to let him hit.

Charles Augustus Nichols (1869-1953) began his career in 1887 with his hometown Kansas City club in the Western League. After two years, Nichols landed with Omaha in the Western Association, managed by 29-year-old Frank Selee (already a keen judge of talent). Selee was hired as the Beaneaters' manager the following year and proceeded to sign Nichols.

Nichols topped the 25-win mark in each of his first nine seasons.

Nichols won 27 games as a rookie in 1890 and 273 games in his first 10 seasons, more than any other pitcher during the decade of the 1890s. On eight occasions he collected 30 or more victories, reaching a high of 35 in 1892. Never a strikeout or an ERA leader, Kid nevertheless topped the National League three times in shutouts and always ranked among the leaders in both complete games and saves (staff leaders were also often used as stoppers then).

The Boston Beaneaters were the most formidable team in the game in the 1890s, and no one had more to do with Boston's success than Nichols, who had 10 straight winning seasons. In 1898, Ted Lewis, Vic Willis, and Nichols teamed up to win 82 games, bringing the Beaneaters their fifth flag in the decade. The club began to falter after that, however. When team owner Arthur Soden lost several stars to the AL by refusing to match the offers made them by junior-loop clubs, Nichols quit the Beaneaters and bought a part interest in the Kansas City team in the Western League.

After two years as a player-manager with Kansas City, Kid was lured back to the majors by the Cardinals, who offered him the same dual role, and he won 21 games in 1904. Despite winning 361 games, Nichols was not named to the Hall of Fame until 1949.

Using basically one pitch, the Kid used control to become the youngest pitcher in the history of the game to win 300 major league contests.

MEL OTT

⭐

Mel Ott stood out even in an era of great sluggers, for his youth, his stance, and his consistent performance over nearly two decades.

Melvin Thomas Ott (1909-1958) was born in Gretna, Louisiana, and was a three-sport star at Gretna High. At age 16, Mel tried out for New Orleans in the Southern Association but was rejected as too small. He played semipro ball that summer for a team owned by Harry Williams, who was another participant in John McGraw's vast scouting network.

Williams tipped McGraw, who gave Ott a tryout. Even though Mel had an odd batting technique, McGraw was impressed with Ott's hitting ability and signed him. McGraw refused to send Ott down to the minors to develop, because McGraw was afraid that a farm skipper would alter Ott's stance, thereby "ruining" him. Under the wing of McGraw, who knew how to groom players, Ott became a star.

Ott's stance was one of the most unique in baseball. He

Mel Ott's stance was one of the most unique. Until his record was surpassed by Willie Mays in 1967, Master Melvin was the all-time NL home run leader.

lifted his front foot before swinging, his hands held low, almost below his belt. The result was a level swing with terrific power, amply announced in his first season as a regular, in 1929, when he hit 42 home runs with 152 RBI. He also led the league with 113 walks, a sign of the discipline that would lead to a lifetime on-base average of .410. He was only

20 years old, and his youthful appearance and size (he was a compact 5'7", 160 pounds) reinforced the impression of youth that was to stay with him throughout his career.

Ott was a fine outfielder with perhaps the best arm of his day. Though he was not slow he had a way of running on his heels that caused him some leg problems, but he managed to circle the bases 1,859 times, one of history's highest totals. Ott also totaled 1,860 RBI. He did benefit greatly from his home park, hitting "only" 187 road homers to 324 round-trippers at home. Though he missed out on McGraw's pennant-winning teams, Mel was a World Series hero when Bill Terry managed the club in 1933, hitting .389 with two homers, one winning the final game in the 10th inning. He returned to the Series twice more, coming up empty against the Yankees both times.

Mel became player-manager of the Giants in 1942 but failed to win a pennant. For a man known for his sweet disposition, he was a hard taskmaster as a manager. Ott was inducted into the Hall of Fame in 1951.

SATCHEL PAIGE

★

Sometimes it seems that Satchel Paige was more a mythological being than a flesh-and-blood man. He was the most popular baseball player in the Negro Leagues. After Jackie Robinson and Larry Doby integrated the majors, Paige was still baseball's biggest draw. He was ageless, could do anything with a baseball, and all who faced him acknowledged his greatness.

Leroy Robert Paige (1906-1982) was born in Mobile, Alabama, one of 11 children. His birthday is recorded as July 7, 1906, but even that is shrouded in the mists of legend. Negro League star Ted "Double-Duty" Radcliffe, who was born in Mobile in 1902, said that he was younger than Paige. Satchel got his nickname because he worked as a porter at the train station when he was a boy. In 1918, at age 12, he was sent to a state reform school, where he learned to pitch.

Released from the reform school in 1923, Paige was signed by the semipro Mobile Tigers in 1924. His reputation

In four decades of play, Satchel saw many changes. Reflecting on some of them, he said, "I never threw an illegal pitch. The trouble is, once in a while I toss one that ain't never been seen by this generation."

spread, and by 1926 he was hurling for the Chattanooga Black Lookouts. He jumped to the Birmingham Black Barons in 1927, all the while pitching exhibition games and in the Caribbean and Mexico in the winter. He stayed with Birmingham until 1930.

Paige had two fastballs that were overpowering: "Long Tommy," which was supersonic, and "Little Tommy," which was merely unhittable. He also threw his "bee ball," named be-

cause it would "be where I want it to be."

Paige gained fame when he joined the Pittsburgh Crawfords in the early 1930s, with battery mate Josh Gibson and a host of other stars. Crawfords owner Gus Greenlee would hire Paige out to semipro clubs that needed an attendance boost for a day. When Paige barnstormed around the country or pitched in the Dominican Republic, he was so popular that fans would not come to see his

Page is often quoted as saying, "Age is a question of mind over matter. If you don't mind, it don't matter."

teams unless he pitched, so he would pitch every day. He would promise to fan the first nine men he faced, and often delivered. He also regularly got the best of the likes of Dizzy Dean and Bob Feller, proving that he could pitch against the best in the major leagues. Paige would walk hitters to get to Joe DiMaggio. DiMaggio said Satchel "was the best I ever faced." Paige was fantastically well paid for the times, earning close to $50,000 a year.

All those innings in all those games gave Satchel a sore arm, and by 1939 the fastballer looked to be through as a dominant hurler. J.L. Wilkinson, the owner of the Kansas City Monarchs, signed Paige primarily as a gate attraction to pitch for the Monarchs' traveling "B" team. During that year, Satchel developed several off-

speed pitches. He also used several hesitation deliveries that were so convincing that hitters were helpless. When his arm recovered the next season, he was a better pitcher than he had been in the 1930s. Satchel pitched for the Monarchs in the 1940s, but he was more an independent operator than a team member.

Finally, in 1948, Bill Veeck, who had long coveted Negro League players, signed Paige to a contract. He asked Browns manager Lou Boudreau to take some swings against Paige, and when Boudreau failed to get good wood on the ball, he became enthusiastic. Paige was pitching before packed houses, as the Browns won the pennant. Satch was disappointed that he didn't get a start in the World Series, which the Browns won, though he did pitch two score-less innings. Many who had cried that Veeck was pulling a publicity stunt were forced to eat their words.

Paige was a colorful speaker and original thinker; his six rules for "How to Stay Young" became famous, the sixth being: "Don't look back. Something might be gaining on you." Paige was inducted into the Hall of Fame in 1971.

JIM PALMER

★

The image of Jim Palmer as a sex symbol, cultivated in his famous briefs advertisements, tends to diminish the ability the Baltimore right-hander held as one of the game's top hurlers. Palmer won 20 games in eight seasons, won 15 games a dozen times, and gave up less than three earned runs a game in 10 seasons.

James Alvin Palmer (born in 1945) received only one year of minor-league seasoning before the Orioles promoted him in 1965. He was stationed in the bullpen most of that year. In 1966, he was inserted into the starting rotation (replacing Milt Pappas) and responded with a 15-10 record for the pennant-winning Birds. Jim gained his first bit of fame at age 20 by shutting out the Los Angeles Dodgers in game two of the World Series. The losing pitcher of that contest was Sandy Koufax, pitching in the final game of his career.

Palmer missed most of the 1967 and '68 seasons with an arm injury. After surgery corrected the problem, he came back in 1969 to win 16 games

Jim Palmer won three Cy Young Awards and four Gold Gloves.

and lose only four, leading the AL with an .800 winning percentage. In 1970, he began a streak of four consecutive 20-win seasons. He led the league with a 2.40 ERA, going 22-9 for the 1973 Orioles to win his first Cy Young Award. Palmer had elbow problems in 1974, and went 7-12 with a 3.27 ERA. In 1975, for the second time in his career, he rebounded to become one of the top hurlers in baseball. He led the

AL with a 2.09 ERA and 23 victories to win his second Cy Young. He led the league in victories in 1976 (earning another Cy Young) and 1977, and he had 20 wins in 1978.

Jim subscribed to the theory that most batters couldn't handle his high, tight fastballs, and he was right. He allowed his share of home runs, but in 3,984 innings he never gave up a grand slam. Despite his various injuries, he led the league in innings pitched in four seasons. He started eight games over six World Series in his career. With Palmer on the staff, the Orioles won the AL West from 1969 to 1971, 1973, '74, and 1979. Palmer had a 268-152 record with a 2.86 ERA.

Jim and the Oriole manager for those AL West crowns, Earl Weaver, were both highly competitive and self-confident men. The two, thus, had many run-ins. Their relationship was not as rocky as believed by the fans of the day; the fact that Weaver and Palmer were quotable and were on the same team for 14 years added weight to that perception. Palmer retired in 1984, and he was named to the Hall of Fame in 1990. In spring training of 1991, he staged an ill-advised comeback attempt.

GAYLORD PERRY

★

Gaylord Perry—the only pitcher in history to have won the Cy Young Award in both leagues—fooled hitters and umpires for 22 years. He was an admitted proponent of the spitball and entitled his autobiography *The Spitter and Me.* He contended that he rarely threw it, however, maintaining the idea that he might use a spitball was enough to put the hitter at a disadvantage. He heightened suspicion by his odd, herky-jerky delivery.

Gaylord Jackson Perry was born in 1938 in Williamston, North Carolina, the younger brother of Jim Perry by two years. Gaylord spent four years in the Giants' farm system, and he was first called to San Francisco in 1962 as a part-time starter. He was age 25 in 1964 when he became a regular starter, and he responded well, with a 2.75 ERA for the 1964 Giants. The next year his ERA ballooned to 4.19, but he rebounded with a 21-8 mark and a 2.99 ERA in 1966. He kept his ERA under 3.00 for four straight years, and he tossed a

The only Cy Young Award winner in both leagues, Gaylord Perry is infamous for the use of a spitball. When he retired from the game, he shared this thought, "The league will be a little drier now, folks."

no-hitter in 1968 and led the league with 23 wins in 1970.

The Giants traded Perry to the Indians before the 1972 season (for Sam McDowell, on the way out by then). Perry responded by winning the Cy Young Award, at 24-16 with a 1.92 ERA. He was 19-19 in 1973, and in 1974 he was joined by his brother, Jim, on the Cleveland staff. Jim had pitched for the Tribe from 1959 to 1963, and in '74 he turned in a 17-12 record with a 2.96 ERA. Gaylord went 21-13 that year, and their 38 victories represented half of Cleveland's win total that year.

Although Gaylord won 70 games for Cleveland in just over three years, he was then traded to Texas. Three years later, he was traded back to the National League, and in 1978 he won the NL Cy Young Award with a 21-6 season for the Padres. Perry finally drew a suspension in 1979 for his foul play, then went calmly back to work. He kept moving, landing in Seattle in 1982, where he won his 300th game. He won his final four games for Kansas City in 1983 using a "puff ball" that had so much rosin on it that it billowed on its way to the plate.

Perry won 314 games with a remarkable 3.11 ERA, while playing on only one pennant-winning club. Jim had 215 career wins, and the brothers' 529 total was the highest until the Niekro brothers surpassed it in 1987. Gaylord's 3,534 strikeouts and his 5,351 innings pitched ranked him in history's top 10 when he retired. Perry retired after the 1983 season and was elected to the Hall of Fame in 1991.

EDDIE PLANK

★

Before enrolling at Gettysburg College, Eddie Plank had no organized baseball experience. Moreover, he was age 21 at the time and had spent his entire life on a farm in Gettysburg. However, the Gettysburg coach was Frank Foreman, a former major-league pitcher whose roots in the game reached back to the old Union Association in 1884. Foreman cajoled Plank into trying out for the team and soon realized that he had a prize pitcher.

Although nearly age 26 when he graduated from Gettysburg in 1901, Edward Stewart Plank (1875-1926) was signed by Connie Mack of the Philadelphia A's, who were about to embark on their first season in the fledgling American League. Proceeding straight to the A's without a day in the minors, Plank won 17 games as a rookie and quickly became a bane not only of enemy hitters but also of American League umpires. Although his pitches were quite straightforward—he had only

Having never spent a single day in the minor leagues, Gettysburg Eddie proceeded directly to the Philadelphia A's. He won 17 games as a rookie. He theorized that a deliberate delivery would rattle the batters, thus giving him the upper hand.

a fastball and a curve—he worked so deliberately that he seemed to take forever between deliveries. Plank claimed that he slowed the pace of the game to rattle hitters. Additionally, he kept them off balance by talking to himself on the mound. Sportswriters found him poor copy; he was so colorless he was almost dull.

Plank's feats, though, were anything but lackluster. He won 20 or more games in a season seven times for the A's, a club record that he shares with Lefty Grove. Plank nevertheless failed to lead the AL in wins, ERA, or strikeouts.

After slipping to 15 wins in 1914 and losing the second game of the World Series that fall, a heart-breaking 1-0 verdict to Bill James of the Miracle Braves, Plank deserted the A's that winter to play in the renegade Federal League. Thus it was that his 300th win came in the uniform of the 1915 St. Louis Terriers.

The following year, the St. Louis Browns signed Plank, and he finished out his career with them in 1917, the first southpaw in major-league history to win 300 games.

Eddie was elected to the Hall of Fame in 1946.

PEE WEE REESE

★

Pee Wee Reese was the leader of the 1940s and '50s Brooklyn Dodgers. He was a great shortstop who stood so tall among his teammates that he was able to silence a team revolt against Jackie Robinson in 1947.

Harold Henry Reese was born in Louisville in 1918. He was a city marbles champion at the age of 12, was tagged with the Pee Wee nickname, and it

stuck with him the rest of his life. He was a very good player on the same church-league team that sent Billy Herman to professional ball. Pee Wee was signed by the Louisville club of the American Association in 1938 and spent two solid seasons there. The Red Sox owned the rights to Reese, and when they were not ready to purchase him, Branch Rickey of the Dodgers spent $75,000 to obtain him.

While Reese wasn't a great player immediately, he became

On his birthday in 1955, the 35,000 fans wished Pee Wee a happy birthday with song and lit candles in a darkened Ebbets Field.

important to the Dodgers, as a hitter, a fielder, and a leader. In 1941, Pee Wee took the first misstep in the legendary Dodger-Yankee rivalry, when he was caught stealing in the World Series, killing a Dodger rally. It was the first of five Series losses to the hated Yanks.

Reese spent three years in the Navy during World War II, but returned to the Dodgers to become the old man of the Boys of Summer, the "Little Colonel" of the team that won six pennants in Reese's 12 postwar seasons. Though his batting stats don't indicate a big hitter, he was a three-time league leader, once in runs, once in walks, and once in stolen bases. He was a complete player who helped make the offense go and was an anchor on defense. His play won him top 10 mention in MVP voting eight times.

Reese's teammates were lavish in their praise. Though at first he was among the many to request a trade upon the signing of Jackie Robinson, Reese quickly changed his mind. When the rebellion continued, Pee Wee befriended Jackie, and the other Dodger players fell in line. Reese was inducted into the Hall of Fame in 1984.

CAL RIPKEN

★

Cal Ripken felt he had a job to do, and that he should go to the ballpark every day and do it. With his consecutive-game streak, he is the only player that has come close to Lou Gehrig in terms of persistence.

While many ballplayers of his time were derided for not putting enough effort into their jobs, Ripken's insistence on doing his job every day incredibly was looked upon by some as somewhat selfish, something that is not team oriented. His consecutive-game streak and consecutive-innings streak began on May 30, 1982. He had played 8,243 frames before sitting out the last two innings of a Sept. 14, 1987, blowout against the Blue Jays. The O's were leading 18-3 and didn't need to risk Ripken.

Picked by the Orioles in the second round of the June 1978 draft, Calvin Edwin Ripken Jr. (born in 1960) made his debut at Bluefield in the Class-A Appalachian League, batting .264 with zero homers in 63 games. He found his power stroke by 1980 and was an Oriole by the end of the 1981 season.

Above: In 1991, Ripken earned his second MVP Award. *Following page:* Cal's consecutive-game streak began on May 30, 1982.

In 1982, his first full season as a big leaguer, he notched 29 home runs and 93 RBI, an accomplishment that helped him secure the AL Rookie of the Year Award. He started the year as the club's top third baseman, playing that position for 72 games, before moving to shortstop. At 6'4" he was the tallest full-time shortstop in major-league history.

In 1983, as a shortstop, Ripken was selected as the

American League Most Valuable Player, and he led Baltimore to the 1983 World Series. He led the loop with 211 hits and 47 doubles, and had a .318 batting average, 27 homers, and 102 RBI.

Ripken had his second straight .300-plus season in 1984. His .304 mark was accented by 195 hits, 103 runs scored, 27 homers, and 86 RBI. And he set a new mark for American League shortstop assists with 583. Ripken had led the league in assists, putouts, double plays, fielding percentage, and chances per game at various points in his career. He also won a few Gold Gloves.

For more than five years, his brother, Billy, was the Oriole second baseman. Only four brother combinations in history have been keystone combinations for one team. Their father, Cal Sr., was the Baltimore third-base coach and, for a short while, manager.

After a few mediocre years, Ripken in 1991 hit .323 with 34 homers and 114 RBI to win his second MVP Award. Ripken in 1993 surpassed Ernie Banks as the player with the most career homers as a shortstop.

ROBIN ROBERTS

★

Robin Roberts won 20 or more games each season from 1950 to 1955. He pitched in the majors for 19 years and never failed to win at least 10 games in any of the 17 seasons in which he had at least 30 starts.

Robin Evan Roberts (born in 1926) was raised in Springfield, Illinois, and was a good high school basketball player. He attended Michigan State University on a basketball scholarship in 1945 after his discharge from the Air Force. He found his way to the diamond and eventually dominated. He threw two no-hitters at MSU and by 1948 was the subject of a bidding contest. The Phillies offered him a $25,000 bonus, and Robin signed.

Roberts spent just part of the 1948 season in the Inter-State League, giving up 82 hits plus walks in 96 innings, and fanning 121 for a 9-1 record. Late that season, he joined a Phillies team that was on the rise. Philadelphia finished sixth in '48, finished third in '49, and in 1950 finished first.

In 1950, Roberts was 20-11 and was among the league leaders in nearly every significant category. His 20-win season that year was the first of six consecutive 20-plus win seasons as the "Whiz Kids"—so known because of youthful stars Roberts, Curt Simmons, and Richie Ashburn—bowed to the Yankees in the World Series. Roberts gave up just one run in the first nine innings of his sole start, losing to a Joe DiMaggio homer in the 10th. It was to be Robin's only shot at a title, as his teams only twice finished as high as third during the rest of his career.

In 1952, Roberts was 28-7, leading the league by 10 wins. From 1953 to 1955, he led the NL with 23 wins a year. He led the league in games started from '50 to '55, and complete games from 1952 to '56. He also led the NL with 198 strikeouts in 1953 and 185 Ks in 1954. He had outstanding control and extraordinary durability, leading the league in innings in four straight seasons. After a few down years, he again was a top pitcher from 1958 to 1965, save for 1961. He had a 286-245 record with a 3.41 ERA. Roberts was inducted into the Hall of Fame in 1976.

Robin Roberts won 20 games for six years in a row.

BROOKS ROBINSON

★

Brooks Robinson revolutionized the third base position. He was a soft-handed, accurate-armed man who did with reflexes and intelligence what can't be accomplished with just a strong arm. He won the Gold Glove 16 times and earned 15 straight All-Star Game starts. Upon his retirement, Robinson held most fielding records for third basemen: most games (2,870), highest fielding average (.971), most putouts (2,697), most assists (6,205), and most double plays (618).

Born in Little Rock, Arkansas, in 1937, Brooks Calbert Robinson was discovered while playing second base in a church league. The Orioles signed him in 1955 and brought him up after he hit .331 in the Piedmont League. He hit .091 with Baltimore that year. He split several more seasons between Baltimore and the minors, and by 1960 was the regular Oriole third baseman. For the next four years, he was not a stellar offensive performer but a very respectable one, hit-

Above: Mr. Impossible was one exciting player to watch play the game. *Opposite page:* While Brooks could hit well enough (.267 lifetime), it was his fielding that gained him distinction. He won Gold Gloves from 1960 to '75 and was an All-Star selection each of those years, as well.

ting for decent average and some power. He had a .303 batting average and 23 home runs in 1962.

In 1964, Robinson batted .317 with a career-high 28 homers and a league-leading 118 RBI. His offensive production, as well as his sterling glove work that year, earned him AL MVP honors, though the Orioles finished third. Frank Robinson joined the Orioles in 1966, and Baltimore went to its first World Series. Brooks hit .269 with 23 homers and 100 RBI that year. In 1968, Earl Weaver became the Baltimore manager, and Brooks had the chance to star

for a team that would finish first or second in eight of the next nine years.

Robinson's work in the 1970 World Series earned him MVP honors; he hit .583 in the ALCS, and .429 in the fall classic with two homers and a highlight reel full of defensive gems. The vanquished Reds nicknamed him "Hoover" after the affair, expounding on his tag of the "human vacuum cleaner."

Robinson was the Orioles regular third baseman for 19 years. In 23 big-league seasons, he had over 20 homers six times and had over 80 RBI eight times. He collected 2,848 hits, 268 home runs, and 1,357 RBI. He topped the .300 mark only twice, finishing his career at .267. He led American League third basemen in fielding average in 11 seasons, including five years and then four years consecutively. He also led circuit hot corner men in assists eight times, putouts and double plays three times, and total chances per game twice. After retiring in 1977, he became a baseball broadcaster in Baltimore. Robinson's induction into the Hall of Fame in 1983 drew one of the largest crowds ever.

TREASURY OF BASEBALL

FRANK ROBINSON

★

Frank Robinson holds two distinctions; he was the first to win Most Valuable Player Awards in both leagues and was the first African-American manager in major-league baseball.

Born in 1935, Frank Robinson signed with the Cincinnati Reds in 1953, after a career as a three-sport star at Oakland's McClymonds High School, where he played with Curt Flood and Vada Pinson (both signed by the Reds). That year with Ogden of the Pioneer League, Frank batted .348 with 17 homers and 83 RBI in 72 games. He led the '54 Sally League with 112 runs scored.

By 1956, Robinson was with Cincinnati and won the Rookie of the Year Award by leading the league with 122 runs and hitting .290 with an NL-rookie-record-tying 38 homers. He was a fine defensive outfielder (winning a Gold Glove in 1958) and was very quick on the bases. He produced similar offensive stats from 1957 to 1960, solidifying his position as one of the top outfielders in the NL.

Frank led the Reds to a pennant in 1961, leading the league with a .611 slugging percentage. He also batted .323 with 37 homers, 117 runs scored, 124 RBI, and 22 stolen bases. He was named National League MVP. He led the NL with a .624 slugging percentage in 1962, the third consecutive season he led the circuit in that category. He also led the league with 51 doubles, a .424 on-base average, and 134 runs scored. He had his worst season statistically as a Red in 1963, when he hit .259 with 21 homers and 91 RBI in 140 games.

In 1966, when Robinson was 30, the Reds traded him to the Orioles. Reds general manager Bill DeWitt said, "Robinson is not a young 30 years of age." All Frank did that year was win the Triple Crown, become the only man to win MVP Awards in both leagues, and hit .286 with two homers as the O's beat the Dodgers in the 1966 World Series. In 1968, Earl Weaver took the helm in Baltimore, and they won three straight pennants

Above: In 1966, Frank Robinson was the first Triple Crown winner since Mickey Mantle in '56. *Opposite page:* Robinson often challenged pitchers by crowding the plate. He usually won such contests of will.

TREASURY OF BASEBALL

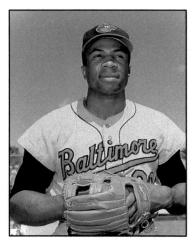

Despite recurring arm problems, Frank Robinson won a Gold Glove in 1958. The 11-time All-Star continued to contribute to the game as a manager for the Indians, Giants, and Orioles.

and another championship in 1970. Robinson not only played fine baseball but displayed outstanding skills as a team leader. By 1973, he had moved to the Angels, and that year he smacked 30 homers and drove in 97 runs.

In 1974, Robinson went to the Cleveland Indians on waivers, and in '75 became the first African-American manager in baseball as player-manager of the Indians. He batted over .300 nine times, had over 30 homers 11 times, and had over 100 RBI in six seasons. Only Babe Ruth, Willie Mays, and Hank Aaron socked more homers. Robinson earned the respect of everyone in baseball.

JACKIE ROBINSON

★

During the first half of this century a color line excluding African Americans extended to nearly every significant field of endeavor. There was a great inertia that needed to be overcome in order to create the integrated society promised in the Constitution. That first high-profile integration came on a diamond, and the first black man to cross the white lines was Jackie Robinson.

Jack Roosevelt Robinson (1919-1972) grew up in Pasadena, California, in a poor neighborhood. His brother, Mack, participated in the 1936 Summer Olympics in Berlin. Jackie, too, was an outstanding athlete; he went to UCLA and starred in four sports. He broke the Pacific Coast Conference record in the broad jump and twice was the PCC's leading scorer in basketball. He led the nation in yards per carry in football and was a baseball star. In 1941, he played pro football. After Pearl Harbor, Jackie attended Officer Candidate School in Kansas, making it to second lieutenant. In 1944, he

was threatened with a court martial, because he refused to sit in the back of an army bus; he instead received an honorable discharge.

Robinson joined the Kansas City Monarchs of the Negro Leagues after his discharge. At $100 per week, it was the best-paying job he could get. When he was approached by Dodgers

Above: Jackie Robinson, Rookie of the Year in 1947 and MVP in 1949. *Opposite page:* "Above all else," Jackie said, "I hate to lose." His courage and strength changed the game—and the country—forever.

general manager Branch Rick-ey's representative, Clyde Suke-forth, Jackie was initially dis-believing and disinterested. "Suddenly I became disgusted with myself," Robinson said. "Why the reluctance? Why the hesitancy? After all, it was a gamble; you don't get anyplace in life if you don't take a risk once in a while." Rickey chose Robinson to be the first African American in the major leagues for many reasons, but aside from being an outstand-ing athlete and baseball player, he had many character strengths. Rickey impressed upon Jackie the need to turn the other cheek. From the be-ginning, Jackie was everything Rickey wanted.

Robinson first broke the color line with Montreal of the International League in 1946, and led the league with a .349 batting average and 113 runs scored as his team won the lit-tle World Series.

With the Dodgers in 1947, Robinson was Rookie of the Year. He said his lowest day that year was his first visit to Philadelphia. He could "scarcely believe my ears. Almost as if it had been synchronized by some master conductor, hate poured forth from the Phillies' dug-

Jackie Robinson endured much in being the first player to break the color barrier. He once said, "I'm not concerned with your liking or disliking me. . . . All I ask is that you respect me as a human being." Jackie let his talent speak for itself and became the best second baseman in history.

out." He said he was never closer to quitting. "How could I have thought that barriers would fall, that my talent could triumph over bigotry?"

Jackie was also combative after the most overt racism had faded. He refused to be someone he was not, refused to conform to an image of a man who "knew his place." It is important to his memory that he not only took the first step to integrate the majors, but he took the next step, too. He was not afraid to let his talent speak for itself, and to be himself.

Jackie won a batting title in 1949 at .342 on the way to being named the league's Most Valuable Player. Though he played just 10 seasons, he helped the Dodgers to six World Series, winning one. Robinson was the most devastating baserunner of his day and a fine basestealer. He had dangerous home run power and was exceptionally difficult to strike out. He played his first season for the Dodgers at first base, an unfamiliar position, and set a rookie record for double plays. Later he became one of the very best second basemen in history. Robinson retired in 1957 and was inducted into the Hall of Fame in 1962.

PETE ROSE

★

*P*ete Rose is the all-time leader in career hits, in 1985 passing Ty Cobb's 4,192 and ending with 4,256.

Rose, like Cobb, squeezed every inch of production from his talent then squeezed some more. Rose, like Cobb, seemed out of place anywhere but on a diamond. And Rose, like Cobb, had adversity at the end of his career with gambling. Commissioner Kenesaw Mountain Landis exonerated Cobb. Commissioner Bart Giamatti, in August 1989, banned Rose from the game for life. Evidence suggested that Rose had bet on baseball games while a manager, but nothing was ever proven in court (though Rose went to jail for five months for tax evasion).

The Reds signed 140-pound Cincinnatian Peter Edward Rose (born in 1941) in 1960; he did little in his first pro year, hitting .277 and leading his league with 36 errors at second base. He spent the offseason pumping iron, and his next two years in the minors were highlighted by a .330 batting average, improved fielding,

and circuit leads in runs, hits, and triples (a career high of 30 in 1961).

Rose started the 1963 season as the Reds second sacker. His enthusiasm immediately endeared him to the hometown fans. Taking a walk, he would dash to first because he saw Enos Slaughter run to first; when Whitey Ford saw Rose

Above: Pete Rose acknowledges the hometown Cincinnati crowd after breaking Ty Cobb's career base hit record.

TREASURY OF BASEBALL

Above: A pack of power. From left, Tony Perez, Johnny Bench, Joe Morgan, and Rose. On his love of the game, Pete said, "I'd walk through hell in a gasoline suit to keep playing baseball." *Opposite page:* Pete provided the spark that drove the Big Red Machine as a player and as a manager.

do this in a spring training game Ford dubbed Rose "Charley Hustle." Rose copped a .273 batting average with 101 runs and a Rookie of the Year Award in '63.

A sophomore slump hit Rose in 1964; his batting average was .269, his fielding average was .979, and he struggled to turn the double play. He spent that winter playing Venezuelan ball, and in 1965 he was back with the Reds, leading the league in hits (209)

and putouts (382). He was named to his first of 17 All-Star teams, appearing in a consecutive 10 from 1973 to 1982. He was an All-Star at a record five different positions (second, third, first, left, and right). In 1967 the Reds moved Rose to the outfield, and in 1968 and '69 he posted batting titles.

Rose led the "Big Red Machine" to four World Series over seven years beginning in 1970. In 1973, he collected

230 hits, and the NL MVP. In 1975 Rose moved to third base so George Foster and Ken Griffey could play, and the Reds won the world championship, with Rose named the Series MVP for batting .370. He also led the Reds to a championship in 1976. He amassed a 44-game hitting streak in 1977. A free agent after the 1978 season, Rose signed with the Phillies; he led them to a championship in 1980 and an NL title in 1983.

BABE RUTH

★

In 1917, when Babe Ruth was age 22, he was 6'2" and a slim 180 pounds of muscle, and a superb left-handed pitcher who had a lifetime record of 94-46. His prowess with the bat, however, prompted his manager to cut in half the number of starts of this young ace in 1918, and give him 317 at bats playing as a regular outfielder. He went 13-7 pitching and led the league with 11 home runs. The kid became the talk of both leagues. The finest player in the history of the game was just beginning to flex his muscles, but everyone already knew about Ruth.

In 1919, George Herman Ruth (1895-1948) set a single-season record with 29 home runs and led the league in RBI and runs for the Boston Red Sox. Red Sox owner Harry Frazee's financial needs prompted Ruth's sale to the New York Yankees. "The Sultan of Swat" brought $125,000, more than twice the price of any previous player, and a $300,000 loan. The Red Sox, winners of the 1916 and 1918 World Series (Ruth was 3-0 as a pitcher in the fall classic), have not won a World Series since, but the New York Yankees went on to become the most successful franchise in history.

In 1920 Ruth took New York, baseball, and America by storm. His 54 home runs were more than any other American League team total. His .847 slugging average still stands as the single-season record, and he hit .322 with a league-leading 158 runs and 137 RBI. He dominated the AL almost up to his 1935 retirement. He had a batting title in 1924, 12 home run titles, eight times

When asked if he believed in any superstitions, Babe said, "Just one. When I hit a home run, I make sure I touch all four bases."

leading the league in runs, six in RBI, and 13 times in slugging. He had a career .342 batting average, with 506 doubles, 714 homers, and 2,211 RBI.

He might have won more honors, but in 1922 he was suspended by the commissioner for barnstorming, and he played in only 110 games. He was limited to only 98 games in 1925, when he was sidelined with an intestinal abscess; "Babe's Bellyache" was front page news across the country. Despite his big swing, the Bambino never struck out 100 times in a season, and he led the league in walks 11 times, including a record 170 in 1923. He still holds lifetime marks in walks and slugging. He led the way for a new, high-powered-offense baseball that packed in fans in record numbers, and helped heal the wounds left by the 1919 Black Sox scandal.

The Babe led the Yankees to seven World Series appearances and four championships. He teamed with Lou Gehrig to form the most feared one-two punch in baseball history, and in 1927 the fabled "Murderers Row" of the Yankees won 110 games and lost just 44. Ruth set a record that year

It has been said that it was more exciting to see Babe Ruth strike out than to see someone else hit a home run. Here, a youthful Ruth at the plate. He once said, "What I am, what I have, what I am going to leave behind me—all this I owe to the game of baseball, without which I would have come out of St. Mary's Industrial School in Baltimore a tailor, and a pretty bad one, at that."

that was to capture the imagination like no other, hitting 60 home runs in a single season. He further added to baseball lore in the 1932 World Series, when, as legend has it, he made his famous "Called Shot." He reportedly pointed to the center-field bleachers before slam-ming a two-strike home run into center against the Cubs.

Beyond his on-field heroics, Ruth—one of the first five players inducted into the Hall of Fame in 1936—was a legend for his off-the-field adventures as well. He was genial and absent-minded, with an ap-petite for life that led him to every excess. He made friends everywhere—while he ate everything, drank everything, tried everything. He was the best and the most beloved player ever to play the game. The Hall of Fame was created for players like Babe Ruth.

"A man who has put away his baseball togs after an eventful life in the game," Babe said, "must live on his memories, some good, some bad." He gave more than his share of memories to the fans as well. The Bambino lives on through history as one of the greatest to ever play the game.

NOLAN RYAN

★

The single-season (383 in 1973) and all-time (5,714) strikeout leader, Nolan Ryan was one of the hardest throwers in baseball history, and he used that fastball to garner seven no-hitters and 324 career wins over his 27-year career.

The Mets drafted Lynn Nolan Ryan (born in 1947) in 1965 in the fifth round. He first appeared in the major leagues for a three-game stint in 1966, and he returned to the majors permanently in 1968. The following year he was a key member of the "Miracle Mets" of 1969, setting an NLCS record for most strikeouts by a reliever by fanning seven Braves. He concluded his sophomore season with a world-championship ring.

Ryan was traded to the Angels in 1971 for Jim Fregosi; Nolan did not experience his first winning season for California until 1972, when he was 19-16 with a league-leading 329 Ks. In 1973 he set a record for most strikeouts by a pitcher in a single season with 383 and collected his first 20-win season. It was during this

Baseball's all-time strikeout king, Nolan Ryan. Despite a persistent blister problem and a month on the DL, he threw out 133 batters in 134 innings in 1968 for the Mets.

time that his heater picked up the "Ryan's Express" appellation, referring to the movie *Von Ryan's Express*. In 1977 Ryan was the AL Pitcher of the Year, going 19-16 with a 2.77 ERA.

During his eight seasons with the Halos, he led the loop in strikeouts seven times (and in walks on six occasions).

Ryan in 1980 signed a free-agent deal with the Astros to be close to his home in Alvin, Texas. He grew up there and raised his own family there. Ryan thrived at the Astrodome, leading the NL with a 1.69 ERA in 1981. He also led the loop in ERA in 1987 with a 2.76 mark; unfortunately, he also had an 8-16 record that year, despite leading the league with 270 strikeouts (and allowing only 87 walks). It was in his years at the Astrodome that he was able to cut his walks allowed from the league-leading totals (as high as 204) that he suffered in California down to levels under 100. He signed as a free agent with Texas in 1989 and pitched for the Rangers for the final five years of his career.

Ryan was the first pitcher to have three straight seasons with 300 or more strikeouts (from 1972 to 1974), and he is the only hurler to have more than four no-hitters. His fifth no-hitter, bettering Sandy Koufax's four, came on Sept. 26, 1981; it was special to Ryan. "The fact that this one came in a pennant race, on national TV, and in front of my mom makes it that much more significant," he said. His seventh no-no came in 1991 against the Blue Jays, when Ryan was 44.

The Express became the first million-dollar-per-year player when he signed with the Houston Astros in 1980. He thrived at the Astrodome, leading the National League with a 1.69 ERA in 1981.

RYNE SANDBERG

★

*I*n one of baseball's great ironies, Bill Giles, president of the Phillies, was so eager to trade Larry Bowa to the Cubs after the 1981 season for the less-than-immortal Ivan DeJesus that he threw in Ryne Sandberg, who went on to become the best second baseman in baseball for most of the 1980s and the early '90s.

Ryne Dee Sandberg was born in 1959 in Spokane, Washington, and he starred in three sports in high school (in 1978 he was a *Parade Magazine* High School All-American in football). A 20th-round choice by the Phillies in that year's draft, he signed his first pro contract only four days after agreeing to attend Washington State on a football scholarship.

In his 1982 debut with the Cubs, Sandberg played 140 games at third base. He batted .271 and scored 103 runs—a record for Cub rookies. Moved to second base in the last month of the season, he quickly adapted to his new position. In 1983, Sandberg became the first player in National League history to win a Gold Glove

In 1989, smooth fielder Ryne Sandberg broke Manny Trillo's record of 89 consecutive games of errorless play at second base.

after his first season at a new position.

In the 1984 season, Sandberg led Chicago into the NLCS for the first time by clubbing 19 home runs, batting .314, winning another Gold Glove, scoring a league-leading 114 runs, and smacking a league-high 19 triples. He was named NL MVP.

In 1985 Sandberg became the third player in major-league history to total 25 or more home runs and to steal 50 or more bases in a single season.

Opposite page: In 1990, Ryne Sandberg powered a loop-best 40 homers to become the first second baseman with 40 since Davey Johnson tagged 40 home runs in 1973. Ryno was the first second sacker since Rogers Hornsby in 1925 to lead the league in homers, and Sandberg was the first ever to have consecutive 30-homer seasons.

Sandberg's 54 stolen bases were the most by a Cub since Frank Chance stole 57 in 1906.

In 1986 Sandberg broke an NL record by making just five errors all season, for a .9938 fielding percentage. In 1989 he led the Cubs with 30 homers on their way to an NL East title. In 1990 Sandberg powered a loop-best 40 homers to become the first second baseman since Davey Johnson of Atlanta in 1973 to hit 40 homers. Ryne was the first second sacker since Rogers Hornsby in 1925 to lead the league in homers, and Sandberg was the first ever to have consecutive 30-homer seasons.

Sandberg in 1991 won his ninth consecutive Gold Glove. His ability at bat alone propelled him to the top of the list of the second basemen of his era; Ryne was also at or near the top defensively every year, and he is greatly respected by teammates and foes alike.

RON SANTO

★

Ron Santo will best be remembered by Cubs fans as the leader of the '69 squad who would click his heels after a Chicago victory. From 1960 to 1973 he stalked the left side of Wrigley Field's infield.

The Cubs gave Ronald Edward Santo (born in 1940) his first chance in the mid-1960s after less than two full seasons of minor-league ball. Santo batted .327 with 11 homers and 87 RBI at San Antonio in 1959. He was called up from Houston in 1960 after just 71 games, and he batted .251. In his first full season, in 1961, Santo batted .284 with 23 homers and 83 RBI.

The seven-time All-Star came into his own as a hitter in 1963. In 162 games Santo batted .297 with 25 homers and 99 RBI. In 1964 he hit 30 dingers with 96 RBI while batting a personal best of .313. He reeled off four straight seasons of 30 or more homers through 1967. Meanwhile, his RBI totals didn't drop below 90 until 1971. Santo drove in more than 100 runs four times—his high mark was 123 in 1969. He never led in any major hitting departments (aside from his loop-best 13 triples in 1964). However, he always

Due to the "Santo Clause," Ron was not traded from the Cubs to the Angels, but rather to the crosstown rivals, the White Sox.

ranked in the top five of several categories each year.

Santo was a victim of the Cubs youth movement following the 1973 season, even though he had a respectable season—with 20 home runs, 77 RBI, and a .267 average in 149 games. The Cubs tried to trade him to the Angels, but he became the first player to invoke the five-and-10 clause in the standard contract that allowed players with 10 years experience and five on the same club the right of approval for trades (and it was dubbed the "Santo Clause"). He wanted to stay in Chicago, so the Cubs traded him to the crosstown White Sox. He ended his career there after just one season. The Sox futilely tried to make Santo into a second baseman and then a utility infielder. That role hindered Santo's hitting; he batted just .221 before retiring. In his career, Santo had 2,254 hits, a .277 batting average, 1,108 walks, 365 doubles, 342 homers, 1,138 runs, and 1,331 RBI.

Santo was the best defensive third baseman in the National League during the 1960s, and he ranked with such players as Brooks Robinson and Clete Boyer during an outstanding decade of top glovemen at the hot corner. Santo won five straight Gold Gloves from 1964 to 1968.

During his time in baseball, though he never said much about his physical well-being, Santo battled with diabetes. His quiet courage in the face of the affliction was an inspiration. Following his retirement Santo became an oil company executive and an announcer for his beloved Cubs.

As a Cub infielder, Ron Santo said, "Funny, but there is less pressure being three or four games behind in a pennant race than three or four ahead. Last year, we kept looking over our shoulder."

MIKE SCHMIDT

★

*I*n 1973 Mike Schmidt was Philadelphia's starting third baseman. He hit 18 homers but batted a paltry .196 and fanned 136 times in only 367 at bats. From that wretched beginning, Schmidt went on to become the best third baseman in baseball.

Michael Jack Schmidt (born in 1949) was a college All-American at Ohio University, where he earned a bachelor's degree in business. The Phillies drafted him in the second round in June 1971. He had little success in a half-season with Reading in 1971, hitting just .211, but he prospered in Eugene in 1972, posting a .291 average with 26 home runs and 91 RBI. When he appeared in 13 games for Philadelphia near the end of the season, he batted just .206.

After his dismal 1973 season, Schmidt could have easily lost his job and his future in Philadelphia. But in 1974, the faith the Phillies had invested in Schmidt paid off. He won his first National League home run crown with 36 blasts. He drove in 116 runs and pumped his average up to a healthy .282.

After a rough start, Mike Schmidt went on to be a three time MVP, a 12-time All-Star selection, and winner of 10 Gold Gloves.

TREASURY OF BASEBALL

He won homer crowns in 1975 and '76 with 38 dingers each year, and he took a walks title with 120 in 1979. Mike always took his share of bases on balls, and he posted fine on-base averages throughout his career. Before 1988 he never fell below 21 homers or 78 RBI in one season (both totals coming in a subpar 1978).

Schmidt's best season came in 1980, when he posted a league-leading 48 dingers and 121 RBI. He also led the Phillies franchise to its first world championship after 97 years of existence. In the World Series he batted .381 with three homers and seven RBI. He was named the NL Most Valuable Player and the World Series MVP that year.

Only Hank Aaron and Willie Mays hit more National League round-trippers than Schmidt, who had 542. He topped 30 homers on 13 occasions—the same number of seasons that Babe Ruth had turned the trick. Schmidt surpassed the 35-homer barrier 11 times—as many times as Aaron had (Ruth managed to do it a record 12 times). Only Ruth won more league home run titles than Schmidt. Ruth led the American League nine times, while Schmidt paced the National League eight times. Schmidt holds the record for most career home runs by a third baseman.

Schmidt was not a one-dimensional star all those years. He was the best-fielding third baseman in the league many of the seasons that he played, winning 10 Gold Gloves; he also broke NL records for career double plays, assists, and total chances at third base.

Above and opposite: About the fans in Phillie, Mike said, "They read their sports pages, know their statistics, and either root like hell or boo our butts off. I love it. Give me vocal fans—pro or con—over those tourist-types who show up in Houston or Montreal and just sit there."

TOM SEAVER

★

When Tom Seaver won 25 games to spirit the New York Mets to a stunning pennant in 1969 (earning the nickname "Tom Terrific"), he set a Mets record. The previous mark had been 16, established by Seaver in his 1966 rookie season. Over the ensuing 17 seasons, Seaver would set a multitude of team and National League pitching records.

Unlike most pitching greats, George Thomas Seaver (born in 1944) was a virtual nonentity in high school. Not until he had served a Marine hitch and enrolled at the University of Southern California did he first begin to attract the notice of major-league scouts. The Braves thought so highly of his collegiate mound work that they offered him a $40,000 bonus in 1966 to sign. His contract with the Braves was voided, however, by commissioner William Eckert, who ruled that the rights to Seaver would go in a specially arranged lottery to any team that agreed to match or top the Braves' bonus offer. By the luck of the draw, the Mets won the privi-

Terrific Tom! He struck out 200 or more batters in 10 seasons (nine in a row from 1969 to 1976) and was the 17th 300 game winner in history.

lege of signing Seaver for a $50,000 bonus.

Seaver was the Mets' staff ace for 10 seasons. On three occasions (1969, 1973, and 1975) he won the Cy Young Award, and he twice hurled the Mets to a pennant. The team's second flag came in 1973 when Seaver earned his second Cy Young honor despite winning just 19 games, five fewer than Giants ace Ron Bryant. Seaver's stats in 1973 were bolstered, however, by both the

Above and opposite: In addition to his career with the Mets, Seaver also pitched for the Reds, White Sox, and Red Sox. The 11-time All-Star finished with a 311-205 record overall.

Like many of the best players, Tom took the game seriously. Of wasted talent, he said, "If you don't think baseball is a big deal, don't do it. But if you do, do it right." Obviously, he thought it was a big deal.

NL ERA and strikeout crowns. In all, Seaver paced the senior circuit five times in whiffs. The last occasion, in 1976, marked the ninth consecutive season in which Tom had fanned at least 200 hitters to set a major-league record.

During the 1977 season, Seaver was traded to Cincinnati to the shock of Mets fans. Although he twice led the NL in winning percentage, Seaver failed to bring the Reds a pennant. After six years in Cincy, he was reacquired by the Mets before the '83 season. At age 39, Tom seemed destined to finish his career as a Met. Instead, after one season in New York, he was drafted by the White Sox when the Mets, thinking him too old to be at risk, did not put his name on their list of protected players.

Seaver won 31 games in his first two seasons in the AL. When he started poorly in 1986, he was dealt to Boston. He retired with a 311-205 record, a 2.86 ERA, and a .603 career winning percentage, the highest of any 300-game winner in the past half century. In 1992 he was named on 98.8 percent of the ballots for enshrinement into the Hall of Fame.

AL SIMMONS

★

*A*l Simmons's career .334 batting average made mincemeat of critics who believed that he would never be able to hit good pitching with his peculiar penchant for striding toward third base when he swung rather than toward the mound. The unorthodox batting style caused him to be tagged "Bucketfoot Al."

Born Aloys Szymanski (1902-1956) in a Polish section of Milwaukee, Wisconsin, Simmons never wanted to be anything but a baseball player. In 1922, he signed his first professional contract with the Milwaukee Brewers of the American Association. When Al hit .398 for Milwaukee in a 24-game trial at the end of the 1923 campaign, the Brewers found themselves with hot property on their hands and were able to sell him to the Philadelphia Athletics for around $50,000.

In 1924, his rookie year with the A's, Simmons batted .308 and knocked home 102 runs. The following year, he collected a league-leading 253 hits and hiked his average to

Simmons realized the importance of determination. Regretting times he had not given 100 percent, he imparted these words of wisdom to a young Stan Musial, "Never relax on any time at bat; never miss a game you can play."

.387. Moreover, he became the first player in AL history to drive in 100 or more runs in each of his first two seasons.

Not only an outstanding hitter, he was also an able outfielder with a strong throwing arm. When Ty Cobb joined the A's in 1927, he helped Al to develop even further as a hitter. Like Harry Heilmann, another great right-handed hitter during the 1920s, Simmons found it remarkably easy to befriend the much-shunned Cobb. In his single-minded dedication to becoming the best player he possibly could be, Simmons himself acquired the reputation for not being overly personable.

When the A's copped their first of three consecutive pennants in 1929, Al enjoyed the first of five straight seasons in which he made 200 or more hits, at the time an American League record. The following year he won his first of two consecutive batting crowns and was generally regarded as the American League's most valuable player.

Simmons was traded to the Chicago White Sox in 1933 when A's manager Connie Mack began to break up his dynasty for economic reasons. Later in his career Al played for Detroit, Washington, and Boston before spending one season in the National League. He returned to the A's in 1944, then retired with a .334 lifetime batting average, 307 homers, and 1,827 RBI.

A coach for the A's during the late 1940s, Simmons also acted as the club's unofficial manager when Connie Mack wasn't necessarily on top of his game. In 1953 Al was elected to the Hall of Fame.

GEORGE SISLER

★

George Sisler was one of the best first baseman who ever played the game, despite performing at peak capacity for only about half of his career. He had amply demonstrated, though, that he might well have been the greatest hitter of them all.

George Harold Sisler (1893-1973) grew up in Akron, Ohio, and signed a contract with the Akron entry in the Ohio-Penn League while still in high school, though he received no money. He later enrolled at Michigan to play under Branch Rickey, and soon Sisler was considered one of the best college players. His Akron

contract became the property of the Pittsburgh Pirates, but after college George signed with the St. Louis Browns, now managed by Rickey. After much controversy, the National Commission ruled in favor of the Browns, because George was a minor when he signed the Akron contract.

Like Babe Ruth, George began his career as a pitcher. Shortly after joining St. Louis, Sisler beat Walter Johnson in a classic pitchers' duel. Stationed at first base in 1916, Sisler hit .305 in his first full season. After three successive seasons in which he batted around .350, George went wild in 1920. Not only did he top the American League with a .407 average, but he collected an all-time record 257 hits and set a

In addition to possessing a wicked bat, Gorgeous George fielded with seemingly effortless grace. He topped the AL in assists seven times. No stranger to the double play, he topped the league three times.

George Sisler in his 15-year career notched a .340 batting average, a .379 on-base average, and a .468 slugging percentage.

age and averaged 240 hits over the three years. With all Sisler's heroics, the Browns still could not land their first pennant, losing to the Yankees by a single-game margin. Sisler finished his career without ever appearing in a World Series.

After the 1922 season, George began to develop double vision, stemming from his infected sinuses. An operation only partially remedied the problem. When Sisler returned to the Browns in 1924 as a player-manager, he slumped to .305. He rebounded somewhat in 1925 when he batted .345 and knocked home 105 runs. He quickly regressed, falling to .290 in 1927, his lowest average ever for a full season's work.

Sold to Washington in 1928, Sisler played just 20 games for the Senators before finishing his career with the Boston Braves. He had a lifetime .340 batting average with 425 doubles, 100 homers, and 1,175 RBI. His son Dick hit a dramatic three-run homer on the final day of the 1950 season to give the Phillies the NL pennant. Sisler's other two sons, David and George Jr., also became professional players. Dad George was elected to the Hall of Fame in 1939.

new 20th-century mark for first basemen with 19 home runs.

In 1921 Sisler batted .371 and led the junior loop with 18 triples. The next season he again cracked the .400 barrier when he soared to .420. Since he also paced the AL in runs, hits, and triples, he became the natural choice for the league's MVP Award. He compiled an astounding .389 batting aver-

OZZIE SMith

★

The Wizard of Oz made everything look easy, just like the Wiz in St. Louis, Ozzie Smith. Throughout his career he fielded almost flawlessly at shortstop, switch-hit with ability, and stole bases with ease. The exuberance he brought to the game was worth its weight in Gold Gloves.

Osborne Earl Smith (born in 1954) did not sign a pro contract until age 22 because he wanted to finish college at Cal State Poly first. The Padres picked him in the fourth round of the June 1977 draft.

After just one-half year in the minors, Smith started 1978 as San Diego's regular shortstop. He notched 40 stolen bases, a league-leading 28 sacrifice hits, and a second-place finish in Rookie of the Year balloting. He also registered 548 assists—the first of a record eight seasons he'd tally 500 or more assists. One of the greatest plays of Smith's career came against Atlanta in April of that year. When Jeff Burroughs scorched a grounder up the middle, Smith dived to his left. As the ball bounced up, he

Above: When the Wizard of Ah's is on the case, he'll get the job done. *Opposite page:* In addition to contributing a near-perfect glove, Smith, owner of a keen batting eye, is an ever-present threat at the plate.

grabbed it bare-handed and threw Burroughs out at first.

In 1979 Smith led the NL shortstops with 555 assists. He batted only .230 in 1980 but won his first Gold Glove. Smith also stole 57 bases, making him and Padres Gene

Richards and Jerry Mumphrey the first trio of teammates in NL history to have 50 steals apiece in a season. In 1981 Smith led the league in at bats and three defensive categories.

On Feb. 11, 1982, Smith was traded to the Cardinals for shortstop Garry Templeton, a player who was younger than Ozzie, was seemingly more talented at the plate (he led the NL in hits in 1979), and was pretty good but more erratic with a glove. While some thought that San Diego got the better of the trade, the Cards were very happy. Smith in Busch Stadium became probably a more valuable defensive asset than he had been in San Diego, and he became more productive at bat, leading the Cards to a world championship that year.

Ozzie continued to improve at the plate every year. In 1985 he hit .276 with six homers. His home run in game five of the NLCS that year was his first in more than 3,000 lefty at bats. Smith's best season came in 1987, with a .303 average, 104 runs scored, and 75 RBI; he was second in the league's MVP balloting. Smith won 13 Gold Gloves in a row, from 1980 to 1992.

DUKE SNIDER

★

There was an unprecedented concentration of talent playing center field in New York in the 1950s. The Yankees had Mickey Mantle, the Giants had Willie Mays, and in Brooklyn, Duke Snider was king. In the four years the three played in the same city together, Duke took a back seat to no one. From 1954 to 1957, Snider had the most homers and RBI of the three, and he totaled more home runs and had more RBI than any player in the 1950s. He also was an excellent center fielder with an amazingly powerful arm.

An outstanding athlete as a youth in Compton, California, Edwin Donald Snider (born in 1926) signed with the Dodgers in 1944 after high school, and he led the Piedmont League in homers. He was in the Navy in 1945 and part of 1946, returning to the Texas League for part of the year.

The Duke played his first game for the Dodgers on the same day in 1947 that Jackie Robinson did. Snider, though a good minor-league hitter, was batting only .241 with 24

Above: The Earl of Flatbush. Snider joined Babe Ruth and Ralph Kiner as the only men to ever hit at least 40 homers in five straight seasons (from 1953 to 1957). *Opposite page:* The Dodgers retired the Duke's uniform number after his playing days came to an end.

strikeouts in 83 at bats at Brooklyn before he was sent down to St. Paul. In 1948, Snider spent most of the season in Montreal. Branch Rickey put Snider through a strict regime, having Duke stand and watch pitch after pitch go by without swinging to learn the strike zone.

When he mastered the strike zone, Snider became the left-handed power for the Boys of Summer. He hit .292 with

23 homers in 1949, and he led the NL with 199 base hits while getting 31 homers in 1950. He led the league in runs scored in 1953, '54, and '55. He joined Babe Ruth and Ralph Kiner as the only men with at least 40 homers in five straight seasons (from 1953 to 1957). His streak ended when in 1958 the Dodgers moved to the L.A. Coliseum with its vast right field—440 feet to right-center.

The Duke was a regular on six Dodger pennant winners, turning in awesome World Series performances. He hit four homers twice in World Series competition, once in the Dodgers' first world championship when they beat the hated Yankees in 1955. He ranks fourth on the all-time World Series home run list with 11.

Duke played in the 1959 World Series, but he injured his knee and was reduced to part-time play in 1960. In 1961, he broke his elbow, and he was never again a dominant player. He spent a year with the Mets in 1963, and retired after a year with the Giants in 1964, with 407 career homers and 1,333 RBI. He was inducted into the Hall of Fame in 1980.

TREASURY OF BASEBALL

WARREN SPAHN

★

Warren Spahn won more than 20 games in 13 of the 19 years in which he had at least 30 starts, on his way to winning more games than any lefty in history (363). He was the best hurler, and often the only good pitcher, on two decades of Braves teams, from Boston to Milwaukee, as he led the league in wins a record eight times and complete games a record nine times.

Warren Edward Spahn was born in Buffalo in 1921 to a father who was an avid amateur baseball player. Warren grew up as a first baseman, but he was unable to win the first base job in high school, so he switched to pitching. Signed by the Braves in 1940, he struck out 62 Class-D batters in 66 innings. In 1941, he moved up to Evansville and led the Three-I League with 19 wins and a 1.83 ERA.

Spahn was called up to Boston in 1942 and did not win in four appearances that year. When he failed to knock down Pee Wee Reese in a game, Braves manager Casey Stengel said, "Young man,

Above and opposite: Warren Spahn's outstanding efforts were evidenced with the numerous times he led the league in wins, ERA, and strikeouts. Returning after WW II, he said, "I felt like, wow, what a great way to make a living. If I goof up, there's going to be a relief pitcher come in there. Nobody's going to shoot me."

you've got no guts." Stengel later said it was his worst miscalculation. Spahn was off to war for the next three years, where he earned a Bronze Star and a Purple Heart.

Warren returned in 1946 and went 8-5 with a 2.94 ERA. He bloomed in 1947, winning 21 and leading the NL with a 2.33 ERA. In 1948, he teamed with Johnny Sain in the famous "Spahn and Sain and pray for rain" rotation. Sain won 24 games to lead the league, Warren went 15-12, and the Braves won the pennant, losing to Cleveland in the Series.

In 1949, Spahn led the NL with 21 wins, 25 complete games, 302 ⅓ innings, and 151 strikeouts. He led the NL with 21 wins and 191 Ks in 1950. He won 22 games in 1951, a league-leading 23 in 1953, 21 in 1954, and 20 in 1956. He began to lose some velocity on his fastball in the early 1950s, but he compensated by developing new pitches and researching the league's batters.

The Braves—with Eddie Mathews, Lew Burdette, and Hank Aaron—were a pennant-caliber team in the late 1950s. Spahn went 21-11 in 1957 and the Braves won the World

TREASURY OF BASEBALL

"Spahn and Sain and pray for rain" was the rallying cry of the Boston Braves in the late '40s. These two hurlers, who sometimes threw on two days' rest due to lack of pitching depth, were the driving force of the team.

TRIS SPEAKER

★

Whether Tristram E Speaker was the greatest fielding center fielder of all time is an argument that can never finally be settled. All the statistical evidence shows that he was the best outfielder of his era, if not ever, and there is no dispute that he revolutionized outfield play more than any other performer in history. His achievements as a defensive player, however, are so prodigious that they can mask the fact that he was also an outstanding hitter.

Born in Hubbard, Texas, Speaker (1888-1958) broke his right arm so badly as a child that he had to relearn how to bat and throw left-handed. Originally a pitcher, Speaker was moved to the outfield and played such a shallow center field that he was in effect a fifth infielder at times. In the deadball era, when long drives were rare, other outfielders copied Speaker in order to cut down on bloop hits. With the coming of the lively ball era in the early 1920s, however, many observers believed that Speaker's style of play would be rendered outdated. In a sense, they were

Series. They returned to the fall classic in 1958 (with Spahn going 22-11), and he pitched beautifully (a 2-1 record with a 2.20 ERA); 1957 would be Warren's only World Series win, and '58 his last appearance. He won more than 20 games, though, in 1959, 1960, '61, and '63. "You don't make concessions," Spahn once said. "If you concede one little thing, pretty soon you find yourself conceding another, then another." He was elected to the Hall of Fame in 1973.

After a salary dispute that questioned his ability to bat, Tris Speaker left the Red Sox and signed with Cleveland. He averaged .354 over the next 11 years. In 1920, Speaker batted .388 as he led the Indians to their first World Series.

home runs, and on-base percentage. During his career, "The Grey Eagle" topped the junior circuit in two-base hits a record eight times, amassing 792 doubles, more than any other player in history.

A salary dispute resulted in his being traded to Cleveland after the 1915 season. In his first year with the Indians, he wrested the batting crown from Ty Cobb. In July 1919, the Indians named Speaker player-manager. Under his guidance Cleveland shot up to second place. In 1920, Cleveland gained its first pennant with Tris batting .388.

In December 1926, he suddenly quit the Indians without explanation. A few weeks later it emerged that he feared being implicated in an alleged plot with Ty Cobb to fix a game in 1919 between Detroit and Cleveland. The two were exonerated, though, when Dutch Leonard, a former pitcher who bore a grudge against both Cobb and Speaker, refused to confront the pair in person with his accusation. Tris retired as a player in 1928 with 3,515 career hits, a .344 batting average, 1,881 runs scored, and 1,559 RBI. In 1937, he was named to the Hall of Fame.

right. The sudden explosion of long hits made playing shallow impossible—for virtually every outfielder but Speaker.

Tris joined the Boston Red Sox near the end of the 1908 season. A lackluster team at the time, Boston quickly vaulted back into contention because of Speaker's presence. In 1912, he played on his first of two world championship teams in the Hub while pacing the American League in doubles,

WILLIE STARGELL

*W*illie Stargell was one of the most potent power hitters of his time, performing as a mainstay of the Pirates for 21 years, and retiring among the all-time leaders in home runs, slugging, and RBI.

Wilver Dornel Stargell (born in 1940) grew up in Alameda, California, and was a middle linebacker for his school's football team, until he broke his pelvis in 1958. He signed with the Pirates in 1959, and he gradually increased his power through four stops in the minor-league chain. He hit .276 with 27 home runs and 82 RBI in 1962 with Columbus of the International League, and he was called up to Pittsburgh for good that year.

Stargell took over left field for the Bucs in '63 and had 11 homers and 47 RBI that year. Playing half his games in Forbes Field curbed his power stats, but he still started a string of 13 straight 20-homer seasons in 1964, even though he played in only 117 games.

It was after the Pirates moved to Three Rivers Sta-

dium in 1970 that the country took notice of Willie. After a good season in 1970—and a division title for the Pirates—Stargell exploded in 1971. The Pirates won the pennant, and Willie led the league with 48 homers and had 125 RBI, though he managed just a .208 average in the Series. The Pirates went back to the playoffs in 1972, 1974, and 1975. In 1973, he led the league with a .646 slugging percentage, 43 doubles, 44 homers, and 119 RBI. He is the only man to hit two balls out of Dodger Stadium, and his 269 homers were to be the most in the 1970s. But as his age started to catch up with him, his power began to wane. From 1974 through 1977, his home run totals fell steadily. In 1978, the 38-year-old "Pops" reached back, slugging .567 in 122 games with 28 homers and 97 RBI.

Left: One of Willie Stargell's lesser-known records. *Opposite page:* Willie was a powerhouse from his earliest days. He sent the ball so far that they called his long-distance shots "collect calls." When in Detroit for an All-Star game in 1971, Sparky Anderson said of him, "He's such a big, strong guy, he should love that porch. He's got power enough to hit home runs in any park, including Yellowstone."

In 1979, Stargell led the Bucs to the world championship. Though he played in just 126 games, he hit 32 homers and .281, and then hit over .400 in the playoffs and Series with five homers. He was tied with St. Louis first baseman Keith Hernandez in the voting for the NL MVP Award, and won both the NLCS and World Series MVPs. Willie was honored as much for his leadership as for his production. He was the leader of a team that was a family, as he encouraged the Pirates by example, drive, and handing out "Stargell Stars" to stick on their caps when they contributed to a victory. He suffered from a deteriorating arthritic condition and retired after the 1982 season, gathering 475 homers and 1,540 RBI. Willie was inducted into the Hall of Fame in 1988.

TREASURY OF BASEBALL

CASEY STENGEL

★

Renowned for his unique misuse of the English language, Casey Stengel was as smart a field general and judge of talent as baseball ever produced.

Born in Kansas City, the source of his nickname, Charles Dillon Stengel (1890-1975) played his way to Brooklyn by 1912, and he was a part-time outfielder for 14 years. He launched two game-winning homers for John McGraw's Giants in the 1923 World Series, after which McGraw promptly sold him to the Braves. Casey said, "if I'd hit three homers McGraw might've sent me clear out of the country."

In 1925 Stengel was hired as president, manager, and out-fielder for Worcester of the Eastern League. After the season, Stengel the president released Stengel the outfielder and fired Stengel the manager, and then resigned. He moved to Toledo of the American Association in 1926, staying for six years. He coached in Brooklyn for two seasons, and got his first major-league managing stint in 1934 with the Dodgers. Casey managed

Casey Stengel, best known for managing the Yankees, was first a player. In fact, he launched two game-winning homers for John McGraw's New York Giants in 1923. His playing days were over two years later.

Brooklyn from '34 to 1936, finishing in second division each year. In 1938, the Boston Braves hired him, and again he had no first-division finishes from 1938 to 1943. By 1944, Stengel was managing back in Triple-A, where he stayed for five years.

In 1949, Yankees general manager George Weiss sur-prisingly hired Casey to run a

Yankee team with Yogi Berra and Joe DiMaggio, and with Mickey Mantle and Whitey Ford waiting in the wings. Even that collection of talent could not account for the Yankee stretch of five straight World Series wins. Stengel was largely responsible for the revival of platooning, out of favor for almost two decades. He always wanted to get big years out of as many players as possible. In his 12 years with the Bombers they won 10 pennants and seven World Series, success unmatched in professional ball. The Yankees job came to an end when they lost the World Series in 1960. "I commenced winning pennants when I came here, but I didn't commence getting any younger," said "The Old Perfesser," age 70.

George Weiss in 1962 hired Casey to run the Mets. The 1962 Mets lost 120 games, but Stengel took it with a smile. Stengel had a way with words that can't be imitated, dubbed "Stengelese" by the press. He saw the bottom and the top, and as he said himself: "There comes a time in every man's life and I've had plenty of them." He compiled a 1,905-1,842 record and was inducted into the Hall of Fame in 1966.

Casey Stengel, pictured here pondering life during the Yankees World Series against the Pirates in 1960, once said, "The secret of managing is to keep the guys who hate you away from the guys who are undecided."

SAM THOMPSON

★

Samuel Luther Thompson (1860-1922) was already 24 years old and seemingly destined to spend his life as a carpenter in his hometown of Danville, Indiana, when a scout for the Evansville club in the Northwest League bade him to give professional baseball a try. The scout was more interested in Thompson's older brother Cy, then demurred when he discovered that Cy was past age 26.

After playing only five games with Evansville, Sam ended up out of a job when the club folded. Thompson signed with Indianapolis of the Western League in 1885. When Thompson got off to a fast start in 1885, manager Hustling Dan O'Leary, an off-season resident of Detroit, convinced Detroit owner Fred Stearns to purchase Big Sam.

Joining the Wolverines in early July, Thompson tallied 11 hits in his first 26 at bats and claimed the club's right field job. He led Detroit in batting in 1886, his first full campaign in the majors. In 1887, he paced the entire National League as he hit .372 and

Sam Thompson was one of the best rightfielders of his time.

bagged a 19th-century record 166 RBI. Still, Thompson's talents as a hitter went largely unrecognized in his time (RBI totals were kept on an informal basis). As a result, it was not until long after Thompson retired that historians revealed him to be the most prolific of any player ever at driving in runs—.921 per game. The

home run, another Thompson specialty, was regarded as a minor feat by many of the game's authorities in the late 1800s.

Thompson, however, was not merely a slugger. He also led the National League on three occasions in hits, twice in doubles, and once in triples. A good outfielder, he had one of the strongest arms in the game. The Detroit franchise collapsed after the 1888 season, and Sam was sold to the Phillies.

In the early 1890s, Big Sam was joined by Ed Delahanty and Billy Hamilton, giving Philadelphia a trio of future Hall of Fame outfielders. While Hamilton batted .399, the other two topped the .400 mark in 1894. The following year, Thompson hit .392 and led the National League with 18 homers and 165 RBI, coming within one marker of tying his own 19th-century record. A bad back shelved him early in the 1897 season. He made several unsuccessful comeback attempts, the final one with Detroit in 1906. Then 46 years old, Thompson found himself playing beside 19-year-old Ty Cobb for a few days. Thompson was named to the Hall of Fame in 1974.

ARKY VAUGHAN

★

A nine-time All-Star, Arky Vaughan was one of the greatest offensive shortstops in baseball history. He led the NL three times in walks, triples, runs, and on-base percentage. He also led the loop in putouts and assists thrice, proving that he was no slouch with the glove.

Born in Clifton, Arkansas, where he received his nickname, Joseph Floyd Vaughan (1912-1952) was raised in Fullerton, California. After he played a few years in semipro ball, he was signed in 1931 by Wichita of the Western Association, where he hit .338 with 21 homers and 145 runs scored. The Pirates made Arky their starting shortstop in 1932.

Vaughan retired with a .318 career batting average, the second highest in history by a shortstop. It is also the second highest by a shortstop on the team for which he played most of his career. Because he broke in with Pittsburgh, Arky invited immediate comparison to Honus Wagner, a comparison that he and every other shortstop could not but suffer for the

In 1935, Arky Vaughan batted .385 with 19 homers, 99 RBI, and 108 runs.
In 499 at bats that season, he struckout only 18 times.

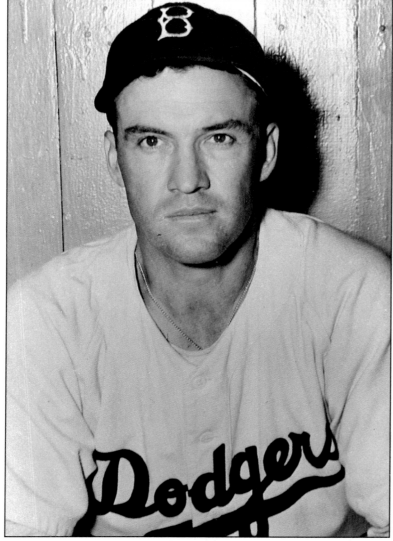

Nicknamed after his home state of Arkansas, Vaughan was a quiet, well-controlled player. He did, however, have a falling out with manager Leo Durocher. That dispute led to his retirement from the game.

the National League with 122 runs scored in 1936.

In the 1941 All-Star game at Briggs Stadium in Detroit, Vaughan became the first player to hit two home runs in a mid-summer classic when he rapped a two-run clout in the seventh inning and then repeated his feat in the eighth.

In 1943, Vaughan paced his loop in stolen bases. After being traded to the Dodgers the previous year, Vaughan was just age 31 and still at his peak. He could not abide having to play for Brooklyn manager Leo Durocher, nonetheless. Unable to get Brooklyn to trade him, the mild-mannered Vaughan opted to retire quietly. He sat out all of the next three seasons, returning only in 1947 when Durocher was suspended for the year. After slumping to .244 in 1948, he retired again, this time for good.

Vaughan scored more than 100 runs in five seasons, batted .300 or better in 12 seasons, and had a .370 on-base percentage or better in 11 seasons. He notched a career .406 on-base average.

In 1952, Vaughan drowned in a fishing mishap. He was selected in 1985 to the Hall of Fame.

making. Although never Honus's equal in the field, Arky gave Wagner a close run offensively. Vaughan's incredible .385 season in 1935 not only achieved the National League batting crown but set a 20th-century loop record for the highest average by a shortstop. He also led the league with a .491 on-base percentage, a .607 slugging average, and 97 walks in '35. A year later, he garnered 118 bases on balls to carve out another National League record for shortstops. He led

HONUS WAGNER

★

Growing up in a small Pennsylvania German community, John Peter Wagner (1874-1955) was commonly known as Johannes or Hans. Once he became a pro baseball player, Hans gave way to Honus.

Wagner was a rarity, the son of an immigrant father who thought baseball was an acceptable profession. One reason the elder Wagner held such a sanguine opinion was that Honus's older brother Albert had previously tried his hand at the game with fair success. But Albert, nicknamed Butts, was nearly age 29 before he reached the major leagues and then only for one season, in 1898. By that time Honus was already an established star with the Louisville Colonels of the National League. Good as he was as a hitter, though, Honus had something of a problem: He could not find a regular position. The Colonels used him at first base, second base, third base, and the outfield during his three seasons with them.

WAGNER, PITTSBURG

Honus Wagner never wanted his picture on this tobacco card.

When the franchise folded after the 1899 season, owner Barney Dreyfuss, who also owned the Pittsburgh Pirates, was permitted to take his best players to the Steel City with him. Dreyfuss naturally retained Wagner, a .336 hitter in 1899.

Player-manager Fred Clarke used Wagner mainly in the outfield in 1900 and was rewarded when Honus won the first of his record eight National League batting titles and also led the loop in doubles, triples, and slugging average. When Bones Ely slumped to .208 in 1901, Wagner spelled him for nearly half the season at shortstop. It was the first time Honus had played the position

In 1909, this trio (from left, Honus Wagner, Tommy Leach, and Fred Clarke) teamed to lead Pittsburgh to a World Series win. Honus batted .333 and stole six bases (even home) to beat Ty Cobb and the Tigers.

in the majors. In 1902, he was returned to the outfield as Wid Conroy handled the shortstop post for most of a season that saw the Pirates win the pennant by a record 27 ½ games. The team was so strong that it could survive several defections to the American League and still triumph for a third successive season in 1903. When Conroy was one of the players to jump ship, Clarke had a hole again at shortstop. Remembering that Wagner had filled the gap reasonably well two years earlier, Clarke decided to give Honus the job on a permanent basis. Finally, for the first time in his career, Wagner had a position he could call his own, and the rest is history.

Since Wagner's retirement as a player in 1917, his name has appeared in the shortstop slot on almost everyone's all-time All-Star team. Some go even further and rate him the greatest player ever.

Even in his time Wagner was regarded as a folk hero. A model of clean living, he once had a baseball card of him removed from circulation because it was distributed in cigarette packs. The few copies of the card that survive are now each worth more than the total

Above left and right: The Flying Dutchman was actively involved in baseball in Pittsburgh for 56 years. He was a player for 17 years, a manager for an additional 39. He loved to play baseball and dominated his league. He never argued with the officials. Once he said, "In all my years of play, I never saw an ump make an unfair decision. They really called them as they saw 'em." *Opposite page:* Wagner said: "There ain't much to being a ballplayer, if you're a ballplayer."

amount of salary Wagner made during his career.

Wagner was so great a shortstop that contemporary players must have considered it a cruel act of providence that he was also blessed with such incredible talent as a hitter. During his 21-year career Wagner was a league-leader at least twice in every major offensive department except home runs and walks. When he retired he had compiled more hits, runs, total bases, RBI, and stolen bases than any player in history to that point. All these career records have since been broken, but no other shortstop in the game's long history has even approached Wagner's overall achievements.

Honus was among the elite group of five players named to the Hall of Fame in 1936 when the first vote for enshrinement was conducted. For some 15 years afterward he continued to serve as a Pirates coach, a job he had first begun on a regular basis in 1933. Wagner died on Dec. 6, 1955, in Carnegie, Pennsylvania, the town where he was born.

ED WALSH

★

Originally, Edward Augustine Walsh (1881-1959) had an overpowering fastball and little else. In 1904, however, while in spring training with the Chicago White Sox, he learned how to throw a spitball from teammate Elmer Stricklett, reputedly the first hurler to master the pitch. Walsh's spitter became so effective that Sam Crawford once said of it, "I think the ball disintegrated on the way to the plate, and the catcher put it back together again."

Besides acquiring the best spitter in the game, Walsh also worked overtime to improve his fielding. A liability to himself early in his career, Walsh by 1907 had become his own biggest asset. That year he collected 227 assists, an all-time record for pitchers. Walsh also won 24 games in 1907 and worked 422 innings, but both figures were dwarfed by what he did the following year.

In 1908, Walsh labored an American League record 464 innings, hurled 42 complete games, and became the last pitcher in major-league history

Ed Walsh was a true workhorse. In 1907, he went 24-18 and led the league with a 1.07 ERA. But it was 1908 that would prove to be his busiest year. No AL hurler has worked more innings than he did in that season. A master of the spitball, Big Ed threw 464 innings and won 40 games that year. He accomplished this by working almost every other day, pitching in a total of 66 games.

to notch 40 victories in a season. Notwithstanding his superhuman achievement, the White Sox finished third. The team's problem, a weak attack, was most glaringly in evidence on Oct. 2 when Walsh ceded Cleveland just one run and fanned 15 batters but lost 1-0 because his mates were unable to get a single man on base against Addie Joss.

The Joss perfect-game defeat was typical of Walsh's fate all during his career with the White Sox. Two years later,

Three of the most feared righthanded pitchers of their time—Ed Walsh sandwiched between Jim Scott (left) and Ed Cicotte. Walsh was 2-0 for World Series play with a 1.80 ERA. His propensity for overwork led to an early retirement.

when he led the American League with a magnificent 1.26 earned run average, he nonetheless had a losing record (18-20) as the Sox hit just .211 and scored a meager 457 runs in 156 games.

Despite a woeful dearth of offensive support, Walsh never lacked for confidence in his own ability. Charles Dryden called him the only man who "could strut while standing still." Another Chicago writer, Ring Lardner, made Big Ed his model for Jack Keefe, the cocky bumpkin hero of *You Know Me Al*, the classic baseball novel of the dead-ball era.

Playing for the notoriously penurious Charlie Comiskey, Walsh never earned more than $7,000 in a season and usually had to pitch well over 400 innings just to avoid having his salary cut. By 1913, overwork had taken its toll, and he was never again a front-line hurler. Although Ed hung on until 1917, he won only 13 games in his last five seasons and thus ended his career five short of 200 victories. What he lacked in wins, however, he more than compensated for in other departments. His 1.82 career ERA is the lowest of all-time. Walsh was elected to the Hall of Fame in 1946.

PAUL WANER

★

Because Paul Waner, at 5'9", 150 pounds, was bulkier than his brother Lloyd, he was called "Big Poison" and Lloyd "Little Poison." The nicknames supposedly were Brooklynese for the word "person" and stemmed from a moment early in their careers when a Dodgers fan, bemoaning the pastings the Waners gave Brooklyn pitchers, said something like: "There goes that big and little poison again."

The elder brother, Paul Glee Waner (1903-1965), left East Central Teachers College in Oklahoma against his father's advice to pursue a professional baseball career in 1923. Originally a pitcher, he switched to the outfield when he hurt his arm while training that spring with the San Francisco Seals of the Pacific Coast League. In his third year with the Seals, Waner paced the PCL with a .401 batting average and 75 doubles.

Sold to Pittsburgh along with infielder Hal Rhyne for $100,000 and three players, Paul began immediately to demonstrate that he was cheap even at that enormous price,

Big Poison. Paul Waner had speed, a strong arm, and hit .333 lifetime.

one of the largest ever paid for a minor leaguer to that time. In 1926, his rookie season, he hit .336, higher than any other National League regular that year, but missed the batting crown when it was awarded to Cincinnati Catcher Bubbles Hargrave, who had only 326 at bats. Waner's performance spurred the Pirates to buy his younger brother Lloyd. The

two combined to amass a sibling record 460 hits in 1927, but more important, their offensive production helped bring Pittsburgh the National League pennant. That year, Paul led the NL with a .380 average, 237 hits, 17 triples, and 131 RBI, winning the MVP Award.

Paul developed into one of the finest hitters in National League history. He not only won three hitting titles but led the NL at one time or another in every major batting department except home runs and walks. En route to accumulating 3,152 career hits, he set an NL record by tabulating 200 or more hits in a season on eight separate occasions. He was an outstanding flycatcher, combining a center fielder's speed with one of the strongest arms in the league.

An imbiber, Waner one year foreswore liquor. When his average hovered at .250, his manager brought Paul to the nearest tavern and bought him a drink. He had 3,152 hits in his career, with a .333 batting average, 603 doubles, 1,626 runs scored, and 1,309 RBI. Named to the Hall of Fame in 1952, Waner wrote a book on hitting in the early 1960s that was well received.

HOYT WILHELM

★

Hoyt Wilhelm blazed the way for the modern relief specialist and was the first career reliever to enter the Hall of Fame. He got into more games than any pitcher in history and retired with more relief wins than any other major leaguer.

James Hoyt Wilhelm (born in 1923) was a native of Huntersville, North Carolina. He grew up listening to radio broadcasts of the Senators, and he became a fan of Washington pitcher Dutch Leonard, who was one of the first pitchers to rely almost exclusively on the knuckleball. Wilhelm studied a 1939 newspaper article that described the mechanics of throwing the pitch and eventually became a master. He was successful in his first pro season with Mooresville in the North Carolina League in 1942, but World War II intervened. Wilhelm served three years and saw action in the Battle of the Bulge.

A winner of the Purple Heart, Wilhelm returned to Mooresville in 1946, had two good seasons, and moved to the Sally League in 1948. He was bombed but returned the next season and flourished. He moved up to Minneapolis of the American Association in 1950. He stayed for two seasons, had a .500 record, and allowed four and one-half runs a game.

In 1952, Hoyt made the Giants as a reliever. He burst out of nowhere to lead the National League with 71 games pitched, 15 relief wins, a 2.43 ERA, and an .833 winning percentage. He had 11 saves that season. On April 23, during the first at bat in his career, he smashed a home run. In his second at bat, he smacked a triple. When he retired 21 seasons later, he had totaled one career home run and one career triple. He led the league in appearances in 1953, and he notched 15 saves. In 1954, he had a 2.10 ERA and a league-

Knuckleballer Wilhelm claimed his piece of history by being one of the best relievers of all time. He posted a 2.52 lifetime ERA.

best 12 relief wins as the Giants won the World Series. Wilhelm recorded a save in the Series, the only postseason appearance in his career.

Wilhelm lasted until he was age 49. From 1962 to 1968, he posted ERAs below 2.00 in six of the seven years. In his long career he had just 52 starts, most of which came with Baltimore in 1959 and 1960. He had a no-hitter in 1958 and led the AL with a 2.19 earned run average as a starter in 1959. He had a career-high 27 saves for the 1964 Chicago White Sox.

Like many pioneers, Wilhelm's career records will be eclipsed. But he opened the door for relievers who will follow him into the Hall of Fame. He was inducted in 1985.

Despite a 21-year career, Hoyt hit his only big league home run in his first major league at bat on April 23, 1952.

TED WILLIAMS

★

Ted Williams once said that he had a dream of walking down the street and having people point to him and say, "There goes Ted Williams, the greatest hitter who ever lived." Some baseball historians make that claim, with his competition being Babe Ruth. Williams holds the distinction of working harder at hitting than anyone.

Born in 1918 in San Diego, Theodore Samuel Williams spent most of his solitary, difficult childhood playing baseball on the sandlots. His renown in that city swelled to the point that, in 1936 at age 17, Williams signed with his hometown San Diego Padres of the Pacific Coast League and hit .271. In 1937, he batted .291 with 23 homers. Signed by the Red Sox, the brash, young Williams in 1938 spring training alienated some veteran BoSox. When Ted was sent down to Minneapolis, he said, "Tell them I'm going to make more money in this game than all three of them put together." He then won the American Association Triple Crown with a .366 average, 43 homers, and 142 RBI.

Williams made an immediate impact in Boston. He fin-ished his rookie 1939 season with a .327 average, 31 homers, and a league-leading 145 RBI. He led the AL with 134 runs scored while batting .344 in 1940. In 1941 he hit .406, the last man to hit over .400. Going into the last day of the year, he was at .39955. Manager Joe Cronin gave Ted the opportunity to sit out the double-header to save his average, which would have rounded up to .400, but Williams played both games and went 6-for-8 to raise his mark to .406. In 1942, Williams got his first major-league Triple Crown, with a .356 average, 36 home runs, and 137 RBI. Ted, however, finished second in MVP

Ted Williams was the finest slugger in the game for two decades. In 1941, his single best season and perhaps the best ever, he hit .406.

TREASURY OF BASEBALL

voting to Yankees second baseman Joe Gordon.

Early in his career Williams became disenchanted with the Boston press and fans. Disenchantment turned to antagonism when, in 1942, he was labeled a slacker for filing for military deferment because he was the sole supporter of his mother. He often went public with his anger at times, spitting and making obscene gestures.

Williams spent three years as a pilot in World War II, returning in 1946 to lead Boston to his only pennant, winning his first MVP Award. That year he first encountered "The Williams Shift," a defensive scheme invented by Indian manager Lou Boudreau that loaded the defense against Williams pulling the ball, forcing him to hit the other way. Teddy Ballgame captured his second Triple Crown in 1947 (with a .343 batting average, 32 home runs, and 114 RBI) but was denied the MVP, losing to Joe DiMaggio. Ted won the batting crown in 1948 (.369 average), and another MVP in 1949, hitting .343 with a league-leading 43 homers, 159 RBI, 150 runs, and 162 walks. In 1950, he fractured his elbow and played only

Opposite page and above: "Baseball," said The Splendid Splinter, "is the only field of endeavor where a man can suceed three times out of 10 and be considered a good performer."

half a year, totaling just 28 homers and 97 RBI.

In 1952, when Ted was 34 years old, he was recalled for the Korean War, where he flew 39 missions, missing most of two more seasons. Back from Korea, he missed out on two more batting titles in 1954 and 1955 because requirements for the league crown counted at

bats and not plate appearances. He got two more batting crowns when he hit .388 (with 38 homers) in 1957 when he was 39 years old, and .328 in '58 at age 40. At age 41, he hit a career-low .254 and was urged to retire by almost everyone, even owner Tom Yawkey. Williams was too proud to retire with such a bad final season, and returned in 1960, hitting .316 with 29 home runs, including one in his last at bat.

Despite missing five years to military duty, his career numbers are astounding: the highest on-base average in history at .483, with five seasons when he got on base over half the time (his high was .551 in 1941); the second-highest slugging average at .634; the second-highest number of walks at 2,019; and he hit 521 home runs. Hitting was a science to Williams, who wrote a highly regarded book on the subject. The Thumper was elected to the Hall of Fame in 1966. He managed the Washington Senators from 1969 to 1974.

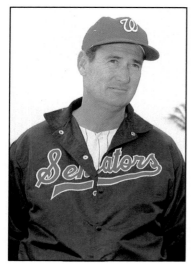

Right before becoming the Senators manager, Ted said, "All managers are losers; they are the most expendable pieces of furniture on earth."

DAVE WINFIELD

★

Dave Winfield was an amazing athlete, and he added determination to his ability to become one of the finest outfielders of his generation.

Born in St. Paul, Minnesota, in 1951, David Mark Winfield was drafted by the Orioles in 1969 out of high school. Instead of signing, the 6′6″, 210-pound gifted athlete spent four years at the University of Minnesota playing baseball—he was better known as a pitcher than an outfielder—and basketball. More contenders for his services emerged in 1973 (especially after he became an All-American in baseball). Winfield was a first-round pick of the Padres. Football's Minnesota Vikings made him a 17th-round choice. The Atlanta Hawks chose him in the 50th round of the NBA draft, and the Utah Jazz in the sixth round of the ABA's draft.

Winfield signed with the Padres, gaining an automatic berth in the Padres' lineup. His rookie batting average was .277, with three homers and 12 RBI in 56 games. Full-time outfield work followed in 1974, and he

Above: Dave Winfield experienced fantastic individual success in the 1980s. His bat was on fire and he won seven Gold Gloves. He drove in over 100 runs each year from 1982 through '86. *Opposite page:* Winny was an All-Star selection from 1977 through 1988.

led the league with 12 errors; his redemption came by way of 20 homers and 75 RBI. In 1975 he hit .267 with 15 homers and 76 RBI; in 1976 he hit .283 with 13 homers and 69 RBI.

Winfield broke loose with 25 homers and 92 RBI in 1977. His sixth and seventh seasons of 1978 and 1979 fea-

Multitalented Dave Winfield. After his senior year of college, he was drafted by four teams in three different sports.

tured identical .308 averages. He tallied respective totals of 24 and 34 homers. His RBI totals zoomed from 97 to a league-leading figure of 118. His fielding kept improving, and he earned a Gold Glove in 1979, his first of seven. Winfield concluded his stint with the Padres in 1980. His final season in San Diego consisted of 20 homers and 87 RBI.

A free agent, Winfield was the chief topic of hot-stove dis-

cussions following the season. The Yankees finally snared him with a 10-year contract for $13 million, making him baseball's highest-paid player at that time. In New York, he was successful on the field and controversial out of uniform. Winfield wrote a biography in 1988 that offered frank insights about teammates and unbridled criticism for team owner George Steinbrenner. Lawsuits and countersuits flew when Winfield accused Steinbrenner of reneging on an agreement to donate to Winfield's charitable foundation. Steinbrenner countersued, alleging that charitable funds may have been misspent.

Winfield hit 37 dingers in 1982 and 32 in 1983; from 1982 to '89, his low for RBI was 97. He had to sit out all of the 1989 season because of a herniated disk. In 1990, at age 38, he came back and batted .267 with 21 homers and 78 RBI, winning the Comeback Player of the Year Award for California. In 1992, he was the first 40-year-old to collect 100 RBI in a season, as he led the Blue Jays to the world championship. In the game six finale of the World Series, Winfield drove in the game-winning RBI.

EARLY WYNN

★

It took Early Wynn eight tries to win his 300th game. The Chicago White Sox released him after the 1962 season, when he had 299 career wins. He was not picked up in 1963 until June, when his former club, the Indians, contacted him. He started five games for the Indians, winning his 300th game on July 13. He retired after that season.

Early Wynn was born in Hartford, Alabama, in 1920. His father was an area semipro ballplayer. As a youngster, Early lifted 500 pound bales of cotton after school for a dime an hour. At age 17, he signed a pro contract with the Senators after attending a tryout camp. He worked often in the minor leagues, though he wasn't overly impressive. Although he pitched three games for the Senators in 1939, he didn't stay in the bigs until 1941. He produced one good year with Washington, 1943, when he went 18-12 with a 2.91 ERA.

After nine frustrating years in Washington, compiling a 72-87 record, Wynn joined the Cleveland Indians in 1949, and

"That space between the white lines," said 300-game winner Early Wynn, "that's my office. That's where I conduct business."

changed the course of his career. In 1951, he won 20 games for the first time. He then won 23 in 1952, a league-leading 23 in 1954, and 20 in 1956. With the 1954 Indians he was to become a member of a legendary pitching staff, as he joined with Bob Lemon, Mike Garcia, Art Houtteman, and

Bob Feller. Wynn won Cleveland's record 111th game, carrying a no-hitter into the ninth, and led the league with 23 wins, his third 20-win season in four years. The frustrated Senators pitcher had become a star. Wynn had nine winning records in the 10 years he pitched in Cleveland.

Wynn was among the meanest headhunters in the game; calling home plate his office, he would not hesitate to move batters off the plate. "Gus" would also throw at a man on first base if he felt the need, disguising the beanball as a pick-off throw. He once said he would knock down his own grandmother if she dug in against him. In Cleveland he learned control, pitching patterns, and the curveball from Mel Harder. Wynn's strikeout totals rocketed, and his 1,544 were the most Ks in the 1950s. He was wild as well, and may have been a bigger winner if he hadn't retired with a then-record for most career walks.

Wynn went to the White Sox in 1958 and was 1-1 for them in the 1959 World Series. He helped them get there with his last fine season, going 22-10. Wynn was elected to the Hall of Fame in 1972.

CARL YASTRZEMSKI

★

A great hitter for several seasons and a very good hitter for many years, Carl Yastrzemski performed the impossible: replacing Ted Williams.

Carl Michael Yastrzemski (born in 1939) grew up in Southampton, New York, the son of an amateur baseball player. Carl played shortstop beside his third baseman father on the local team, and when Carl was age 18, he was pursued by several pro teams. He spurned them to attend Notre Dame in 1958, but after one year he decided that he wanted to turn professional. He visited a Yankee tryout camp and felt that he wasn't treated well, so he signed with the Red Sox. In 1959, he led the Carolina League with a .377 batting average, and in 1960 led the American Association with 193 base hits.

Williams retired after the 1960 season, and "Yaz" was moved into his left field spot. Carl batted .266 in his first season, in '61, and improved to a

Carl Yastrzemski was a brilliant player. Although he garnered many honors throughout his career, he is perhaps best remembered for his 1967 efforts. That year he led the league in batting average, home runs, and RBI; was an All Star; won the Gold Glove Award; and was the league's MVP.

.296 batting average and 94 RBI in his sophomore year. He won his first batting title in 1963 with a .321 average, and showed good power and a good eye. In 1965, he led the AL with a .536 slugging percentage and 45 doubles, and in '66 led the circuit with 39 doubles.

The Red Sox, a ninth-place team in 1966, won the pennant on the last day of the 1967 season, in the tightest race in American League history. Yaz won the Triple Crown that year, hitting .326 with a career-best 44 homers and 121 RBI, the last man to win a Triple Crown. He hit .522 with five home runs and 22 RBI in the final two weeks of the season. He was devastating in the final series against the Twins, going 7-for-8 and playing stellar defense. He was named the AL MVP. In the World Series, he hit .400 with three homers, but the Sox lost in seven games.

In 1968, Carl won the batting title with the lowest average ever, at .301. In 1969 and 1970 he hit 40 homers. Aside from his Triple Crown season, he only hit as many as 28 one other time. He had an upright, distinctive stance, his bat almost straight up-and-down. Ted Williams said that Yaz "re-

Yastrzemski once told umpire Ed Runge, "Ed, you're the second best umpire in the league. The other 23 are tied for first."

minded me of myself at that age—I mean he positively quivered waiting for that next pitch." Yaz swung a potent bat for 23 seasons, patrolling left field expertly for the Red Sox as the master of the Green Monster. Yastrzemski was the first AL player to total more than 3,000 hits and 400 home runs. He was inducted into the Hall of Fame in 1989.

CY YOUNG

★

Shortly after being signed by Canton of the Tri-State League in 1890, the 23-year-old Cy Young was spotted warming up against a wooden fence on a farm near Gilmore, Ohio. The ensuing damage to the barrier, as legend has it, was likened to that of a cyclone hitting a wall. A sportswriter shortened "cyclone" to "Cy," and Young would never again be known by any other name.

Denton True Young (1867-1955) made his big-league debut with the Cleveland Spiders on Aug. 6, 1890. Most of the game's stars were playing in the Players' League that season; one of those who were not was Cap Anson, player-manager of the Chicago White Stockings, Young's foes in his inaugural outing. Anson had scouted Young while he was at Canton and rejected him as being "just another big farmer." When Cy beat the White Stockings 8-1 and allowed only three hits, Anson strove to purchase him from Cleveland.

Throughout the 1890s, Young, Kid Nichols, and Amos Rusie vied for recognition as

Denton True Young's career spanned 22 years. He claimed farm chores in the off season helped him stay fit. Perhaps that was the secret to his incredible success.

the top pitcher in the game. Although Nichols pitched for the best team and collected the most wins, and Rusie regularly logged the most strikeouts and lowest ERAs, it was Young who reached the top of the league in all three departments. He blended stamina, guile, and control in almost equal measures to make him a pitcher who rarely had a bad game. A pennant for the Spiders never materialized, however, and when attendance sagged in Cleveland, Young and most of the team's other stars were shipped to St. Louis in 1899.

Turning 33 years old in 1900, Young slipped to just 19 wins, his lowest output since his rookie season. Speculation that he was nearly through gave St. Louis some consolation when Young deserted the club to sign with Boston in the newly reorganized American League. The rumors of Young's imminent departure from the game soon were dispelled after he led the yearling major league in wins in 1901, then repeated his feat the next two years.

Cy went on to win 20 or more games six times for the Boston Americans, pitch on two pennant winners, and participate in the first modern

World Series in 1903. Perhaps the finest effort of his career came on May 5, 1904, when he pitched a perfect game to beat Rube Waddell of the Athletics 3-0.

Sold to Cleveland at age 42 in 1909, Young again defied time by leading the Naps mound staff with 19 wins. It was his last good season. Two years later, after winning seven games in a campaign split between Cleveland and the Boston Braves, Young retired with 511 career victories. To the day he last took off his uniform, he boasted that he had never had a sore arm or spent a single minute on the trainer's table. He was inducted into the Hall of Fame in 1937.

Cy Young was a blend of stamina, guile, and excellent control. This made him a pitcher who rarely had a bad game. He won 511 games in his career, three of which were no-hitters. He once said, "A pitcher's got to be good and he's got to be lucky to get a no-hit game."

ROBIN YOUNT

★

Robin Yount mastered two defensively challenging positions—shortstop and center field—well enough to be named the AL's Most Valuable Player while playing each of those spots. He was the third player—after Hank Greenberg and Stan Musial—to win MVP Awards at two positions.

In 1982 Yount escorted the Brewers to their first AL pennant, batting .331 with 29 home runs and 114 RBI. He led the league in slugging percentage (.578), total bases (367), hits (210), and doubles (46), and was among the leaders in virtually every offensive category. It was also his first Gold Glove-winning year, as he led loop shortstops with 489 assists. He was the runaway choice for the American League's MVP Award. Yount that year became the first player in World Series history to have two four-hit games.

Because of a chronic shoulder injury, Yount in 1985 needed to switch to a position that would put less stress on his body. The Brewers decided to put Robin in center field full-

Above and opposite: Yount was only 18 when he won Rookie honors in 1974. When he concluded his 20th season in 1993, he was the only player to have 200 hits against every team he played against.

time, and by 1989 he won his second MVP. He batted .318 with 21 homers, 101 runs scored, and 103 RBI.

Robin R. Yount was born in Danville, Illinois, in 1955. The Woodland Hills, California, High School Player of the Year in 1973, he was the third player selected in the June 1973 free-agent draft—behind David Clyde and John Stearns, and just ahead of Dave Winfield. Yount spent the rest of the 1973 season in the minors, and at 18 years old Robin became

the Brewer starting shortstop in 1974.

That year, "Robin the Boy Wonder" hit .250 with three homers and 26 RBI in 107 games, and his fielding average was .962. He led the AL in 1975 with 44 errors, but he hit .267 with eight home runs and 52 RBI. It was about this time that he started to pump iron, and the increased strength helped him to increase his productivity in 1977, batting .288 with 66 runs scored.

Yount held out for a better contract in 1978, threatening to quit baseball and play professional golf instead. The Brewers relented, and he won his first postseason All-Star honors for a .293 batting average, nine homers, and 71 RBI. In 1980 he led the AL with 49 doubles, and he had 23 homers, 121 runs scored, 87 RBI, and a .293 average.

Robin got his 3,000th base hit on Sept. 9, 1992. After a lackluster 1993 season, he decided to hang up his spikes rather than be mediocre. He had a .285 batting average, 1,632 runs scored, 251 homers, and 1,406 RBI in his career. His brother, Larry, had a one-game career as a pitcher with the 1971 Astros.

TREASURY OF BASEBALL

Leaders of Baseball

THOSE WHO MADE A DIFFERENCE

While fans focus on the players' struggles, important persons have clashed in the back rooms. Albert Goodwill Spalding, a leader in the sports world, faced the paramount labor challenge led by John Montgomery Ward of the Players' League. Ban Johnson was the only man to challenge the NL and win. Yet he had to encounter Kenesaw Mountain Landis, who became commissioner in 1920. Landis's foe over myriad matters was "The Mahatma"—Branch Rickey. In 1969, Bowie Kuhn became commissioner, leading to rewards and reversals. Kuhn's adversary was Marvin Miller, a labor leader like Ward. These figures changed the way America views baseball.

Baseball has had many thrilling confrontations off the field that matched the intensity of the greatest 3-2 ninth-inning strikeout of the slugger by the hard-throwing relief pitcher. In comparison, the off-the-field battles lacked some of the immediate drama and were seldom face-to-face, but these scraps between heavyweight superstars changed the game forever.

One of the first, and most significant in the history of the game, was the conflict between Albert Goodwill Spalding, probably the country's most important figure in 19th-century sports, and John Montgomery Ward, founder of the Brotherhood, the first union movement in baseball. The issue was Ward's Players' League of 1890, the challenge to the way baseball paid and treated its players.

Both men had been highly successful players. Spalding was one of the game's first great pitchers, and led his Boston team to four of the five championships in the National Association, the first organized baseball league. Ward was a superb pitcher in his own right; he threw only the second perfect game in major-league history. His lifetime 2.10 ERA is fourth best of all time. When Ward's arm went bad, he became one of the game's premier shortstops. And both men had outside interests: Ward was a lawyer; Spalding owned the world's largest sporting goods company, in addition to running the National League the way John D. Rockefeller ran Standard Oil.

Al Spalding in the 1880s believed he *was* baseball, and few could claim otherwise. He was the most powerful man in the game. As president of the Chicago team from 1882 through 1891, he had successfully led the move to clean up the game, reducing the longstanding practice of gambling in the stands. He hired private

Monte Ward studied at Columbia University in his off-seasons, and in 1887 he earned both a bachelor's degree in political science and a law degree. He served as a manager, a team business manager, and a team president, and came within a single vote of being named NL president.

Left: Monte Ward (far left) pitched the second perfect game in NL history, in 1880. After winning 164 games as a pitcher, he was versatile enough to become a starting shortstop and second baseman for 11 years, leading his league in fielding once and stolen bases twice.

detectives to check up on players he felt were consorting with the wrong types. And even though he himself had jumped a contract to join the National League when it began in 1876, no one was clearer on the absolute necessity of the owners controlling the players. In 1881, he stated, "Professional baseball is on the wane. Salaries must come down or the interest of the public must be increased in some way. If one or the other does not happen, bankruptcy stares every team in the face." Spalding was a giant of his time. He often spoke in epigrams: "Baseball [is] the exponent of American Courage, Combativeness, Confidence; American Dash, Discipline, Determination; American Energy, Eagerness, Enthusiasm; American Pluck, Persistency, Performance; American Spirit, Sagacity, Success; American Vim, Vigor, Vitality."

Trying to cross Albert Spalding was asking for big trouble. He had the absolute self-confidence that only the successful self-made man can possess. His motto, hung on the wall of his office, stated it clearly: "Everything is possible to him who dares."

John "Monte" Ward came from a different background. Ward was highly educated. Through off-season study he earned degrees in political science and law from Columbia University by the time

Al Spalding was convinced that baseball was going to be a worldwide sensation, so he financed tours of teams stocked with all stars to England, Ireland, Australia, Egypt, and elsewhere.

he was 27. He spoke five languages. Early in his career he had been notorious for hotheaded behavior, but as he matured, that personal passion transmuted into a special kind of charisma. One writer said, "He exuded honesty and purity in every gesture." At the age of 25, Ward and Ned Hanlon helped organize some of the players into a rudimentary labor organization, the Brotherhood of Base Ball Players, which originally began its existance as a benevolance organization. Two years later he tried unsuccessfully to get his team to sign black pitcher George Stovey.

In 1887 Ward was asked by a magazine to write an article answering the question, "Is the Ball Player a Chattel?" In it he attacked the concept of the reserve clause and the blacklist, which prevented any team from signing a player who turned down his original team's contract offer. "For the mere refusal to sign upon the terms offered by the club, the player was to be debarred entirely, and his name placed among those disqualified because of dissipation and dishonesty! Has any body of sane men ever before publicly committed itself to so outrageous a proposition?" In this and other articles Ward let the baseball establishment know the players would not sit still for this kind of treatment.

Albert Spalding parlayed his big name (he was a star pitcher in the 1870s) and close ties to the National League to create a virtual sporting goods monopoly. He was president of the Chicago franchise in the NL from 1882 to 1891.

Spalding, ever in love with the glory of the game, sent two teams of all-stars to travel the world in the 1888-89 off-season, spreading the baseball sacrament to the heathens. Ward was captain of one of the teams. The excursion was far from a success, critically or financially. Worse yet, while many of the game's stars were overseas, they received word of "The Brush Plan," a salary structure devised to cut costs.

In the plan, every player would be graded from "A" to "E." The "A" players could make the top salary of $2,500. No one could make more. Ward himself had made $4,000 the year before, as had other stars. The "E" players would make $500, and would be expected to help with other duties, such as collecting tickets before the game or sweeping up afterwards. Not surprisingly, the players were outraged. The Brotherhood wanted to strike.

Returning from the junket, the shrewd Ward recommended otherwise. He realized a strike could only elicit a few concessions. He told the players not to sign new contracts, essentially "playing out their option." And he began to organize financiers to back a new league in which the players would share the costs and the wealth—The Players' League.

When the owners realized that the players were serious about forming a new league, they dropped the Brush rules like a hot grounder. But it was too late. An eight-team league was formed, and more than 100 of the best players joined Ward in the new venture. The National League and American Association bribed two dozen or so to come back.

In true imperious leader style, Spalding refused to believe the players were serious, and threatened lifetime banishment for any who joined them. Every legal challenge the establishment could throw at the new league was batted down by the courts, however.

Spalding started taking the situation more seriously. He announced, "I am for a war without quarter. I want to fight until one of us drops dead." And he fought with all the power he had. He purchased *The New York Sporting News* and installed virulently

John T. Brush was a bitter foe of the American League. Owner of the New York Giants, he resisted reconciling with the AL, and he opposed the AL's shift of the Baltimore franchise to New York. He showed his displeasure by refusing to play in the 1904 postseason.

anti-Players' League writer O.P. Caylor as its editor. Spalding also had Francis Richter, editor of the influential *Sporting Life*, in his hip pocket. Longtime Spalding pal Henry Chadwick railed against the radicals in print. And even though the upstart *The Sporting News* of St. Louis was pro-Brotherhood, it wasn't enough. The Players' League announced their schedule first; Spalding rewrote the NL schedule to create as many direct conflicts as he could. Spalding threatened newspaper owners around the country that he would withdraw all of his sporting goods company's advertising from their papers if they printed boxscores from the "terrorist" league.

Amazingly, the Players' League outdrew the National, but the competition was expensive for both sides. Spalding had to personally contribute money to keep the New York Giants afloat, and he had the other owners kick in to help Boston and Pittsburgh.

Ban Johnson, right, attempted but failed to become a lawyer, so he instead became a sports editor for a newspaper in Cincinnati before becoming a league commissioner.

Late in the season Spalding called for a meeting with several of the most powerful Players' League owners. John Ward wanted to meet with Spalding, too, but he was rebuffed. "It is time for the moneyed men to sit down with the moneyed men," Spalding said. Spalding never admitted that his league had lost money. By offering under-the-table deals to PL owners, though, he successfully shut the new league's doors forever. And while he was at it, he saw the chance to get rid of the American Association, too, which had been a bothersome "equal" for 10 years. The way he structured the return of players from Ward's league effectively wiped out the Association.

In his book *The Answer Is Baseball*, Luke Salisbury asks the question, "Was Ward's experiment hamstrung by his character?" The answer, obviously, is yes. Ward, obsessed with propriety and respectability, could not stoop to the level of the ruthless Spalding. Al Spalding's baseball playing career ended before John Ward's began. So they never faced each other as pitcher and batter or rival moundsmen. When Spalding and Ward faced off over the Players' League, however, Spalding was the clear winner. Players did not again offer a serious labor challenge until the 1960s.

After Spalding squashed the Players' League and wiped out the American Association by appropriating its four best teams, the 12-team National League ruled supreme for almost 10 years. The "moneyed men" counted their money, but baseball foundered. Good pennant races were rare. Second-division teams often were out of the race by July Fourth, and attendance suffered as a result. Baseball's next great leader arose: Byron Bancroft "Ban" Johnson.

Like Spalding, Johnson was tough, ruthless, and uncompromising. Originally a sports editor for a newspaper, Johnson was hired

Above: John McGraw was a very good player, usually one of the best third basemen in the 12-team National League in the 1890s. Not naturally gifted, he used every edge he could to gain an advantage, including tripping baserunners and baiting opposing pitchers.

Left: From left: Wee Willie Keeler, Hughie Jennings, Joe Kelley, and John McGraw—with an unidentified suit in the middle—were the leaders of Ned Hanlon's famous 1890s Baltimore Orioles, whose "inside" brand of winning baseball dominated three decades of strategy.

Cy Young had won 286 games in 11 years and was 34 years old before he jumped to the American League in its inaugural season, in 1901. He was not close to being finished, however, and his star power for 11 more seasons and 225 more wins helped confirm the AL's credibility.

by the Western League, a high minor league, in 1894 to help smooth out problems for one year. He stayed. Johnson saw that the future of baseball was as a family game, so he did everything in his power to keep his league clean. He instituted tougher rules for umpire behavior and stood firmly behind his arbiters in any disputes, to reduce rowdy behavior and counter the ever-present danger of gambling. When the National League decided to lop off four teams before the 1900 season, Johnson saw his chance to go for the big time. He put franchises in Baltimore, Washington, and Cleveland, which the NL had abandoned, signed players left adrift by the realignment, and called his group the American League.

Nearly 90 players—enticed by salaries above the NL maximum of $2,400—jumped to Johnson's league, including stars such as Nap Lajoie, Cy Young, John McGraw, Ed Delahanty, and Willie Keeler. Two years of all-out war ensued. When the NL owners petitioned for peace late in 1902, Johnson strutted in holding all the cards. His league had outdrawn the older group in every city in which it competed head-to-head. His league was cleaner, thanks to his diligence, and he knew the NL bosses wanted that.

The NL owners offered a merger, but Johnson held firm. His only concession was an agreement not to open a team in Pittsburgh; and he moved the Baltimore team to New York, where they later became the greatest team and greatest drawing card in the sport's history. To administer the agreement, a three-man commission was instituted. Two members were Johnson and the NL president. The third was Garry Herrmann, owner of the NL Cincinnati team but a longtime pal of Johnson's. It was pretty clear to most people that Johnson was baseball's true czar.

He and Herrmann ruled the game for nearly 20 years. Johnson's haughtiness was the perfect counterpart for Herrmann's beer-loving sociability. When Johnson ruffled feathers with his fist-slamming and hot temper, Herrmann smoothed them with savvy political wisdom and another round.

Late in the decade of the 1910s, both Johnson and Herrmann were challenged by owners irate over their decisions. Johnson tried to halt the trade of surly Carl Mays (later to become famous for throwing the pitch that killed Ray Chapman); a group of owners effectively overruled him. And when the Black Sox scandal broke in 1920, baseball went outside its ranks to find a man who would clean up the game with no questions asked.

That man was Federal Judge Kenesaw Mountain Landis, the man with the craggy visage and stern demeanor, who would rule the game with an iron hand for the next 25 years. Landis, named after a Civil War battle, was not highly educated. His first law degree came from the Y.M.C.A. law school in Cincinnati. As a lawyer he rapidly earned a reputation for fearlessness. He would

Judge Kenesaw Mountain Landis loved the pageantry surrounding the game. Not highly regarded as an adjudicator, pageantry helped earn Landis a federal judgeship. It was about Landis that Heywood Broun said, "His career typifies the heights to which dramatic talent may carry a man in America if only he has the foresight not to go on the stage."

take on anybody, and his bombast enlivened many an Illinois courtroom. He used his caustic wit to poke holes in his opponents' cases. His tactics did not sit well with many judges; several times he was nearly ruled in contempt of court.

He became a judge because of his political connections, and he wasn't especially good at it. He was known for being tough, and his looks certainly underscored that sentiment. But his most famous case, in which he handed down a $29,240,000 fine to Standard Oil for illegal rebate practices—the largest fine of its kind ever—was quickly overturned by a superior court.

Landis had caught baseball's eye in 1915. When the Federal League filed an antitrust suit against the National and American Leagues, major-league baseball's moguls were worried they would lose antitrust status (as they still are today). The Feds picked Landis's courtroom because of the Standard Oil case; it gave him the reputation of a "trust buster." Landis solved baseball's problem, however. He sat on the issue, making no ruling, and thereby giving the leagues time to work out a negotiated settlement. Baseball's unique status was preserved.

It didn't hurt that he was also known as a tremendous baseball fan. As a lawyer, he once said to opposing counsel, "Can't we get this postponed till tomorrow? Brownie [Mordecai Brown] is pitching against Matty [Christy Mathewson] today, and I don't want to miss that."

Dead-ball-era star pitchers Smokey Joe Wood (left) and Christy Mathewson clashed in the 1912 fall classic, with Wood going 3-1, including a win over Matty in the deciding game-eight that featured the "$30,000 Muff" by Fred Snodgrass.

Landis accepted the new job as commissioner of baseball on one condition: that he have absolute final say in any matters regarding the best interests of the game. The owners, delighted to be rid of Johnson's fire and Herrmann's smoke, and fearful of public outcry over the scandals, had no choice but to agree.

In Landis's first year he banished 15 players for life, including the eight "Black Sox." Yet despite his imposing presence and grim looks, he was actually a big fan of players, and usually gave them all the help he could to get them off the hook in case of disputes. The story goes that he missed the beginning of the garbage incident in the 1934 World Series because he had just learned to spit chewing tobacco by closely studying a player do it. With owners he was much different. Opposed to the idea of farm systems, he did everything he could to prevent them, freeing more than 200 players from contracts he felt were unfair, and fining the owners who had signed them.

Leo Durocher (left) and Branch Rickey worked together for the Dodgers during the 1940s despite having little in common. What each man possessed in spades, however, was an unquenchable desire to win.

Naturally the white-maned commissioner and the feisty Ban Johnson would not see eye to eye. Landis helped AL owners reduce Johnson's power. When Johnson brought to Landis's attention the claim by Dutch Leonard that he, Ty Cobb, Tris Speaker, and Smokey Joe Wood had fixed a game or two in 1919, the Judge ruled the evidence was insufficient to penalize some of the game's greatest stars. It was all Johnson could stand. He retired shortly thereafter.

Landis's opposition to farm systems caused major battles with another strong figure in the game's history—Branch Rickey. Rickey was the Cardinal farm director in 1938 when Landis set 91 St. Louis farmhands free, among them Pete Reiser, in what has become known as the "Cedar Rapids" decision.

While Spalding, Ward, Johnson, and Landis were men who seemed above nicknames, Rickey received one that perfectly summed up his style: "The Mahatma." Rickey was smart, and had a superb ability to recognize baseball talent when he saw it. His style was something else altogether. He pontificated in long windy sentences that baffled sportswriters and stupefied players. He could squeeze a dollar very tight, and "persuade" players to settle for less pay than they deserved. Historian A.D. Suehsdorf said that Rickey had "the air of a con man playing a parson. [But] essentially he was that traditional American type, the sharp trader."

His given first name was "Wesley," after John Wesley, founder of the Methodist Church. Rickey was a deeply moralistic and religious man. He had vowed to his mother he would never play in a game or attend one on Sunday, and he never did, although he always made sure he knew what the Sabbath's gate receipts were. As a professional catcher he was miserable; in one game in 1907 the opposition stole 13 bases against him, still a record. As a scout, coach, and manager, however, he was in a class by himself. He worked his way through college as a scout and coach. With the Cards, by 1940 he had built the largest farm organization ever—33 teams. Of course Branch was playing things to his advantage: When he sold a player to another team he got to pocket part of the purchase price. This arrangement led to Card owner Sam Breadon firing Rickey, and Branch's move to the Dodgers. Under Rickey's eye for talent and control of the purse strings, the Cardinals had won six flags and been world champs four times.

As president and general manager of Brooklyn, Rickey took the same approach. He signed a lot of people and built up a sensational farm system. Rickey realized what a lot of people seemed to miss during World War II: that someday the war would be over and baseball would need players. So he signed hundreds of young men before they went overseas. Landis felt that farms could block

Sam Breaden was part of an ownership group that bought St. Louis Cardinals in 1916, and was majority owner and president from 1920 to 1947. An activist owner, he made 14 managerial changes in his 27 years, despite winning nine pennants.

a player's natural progression. Rickey was also an innovator in equipment and training techniques.

His greatest "innovation" was the return of blacks to baseball, when he signed Jackie Robinson and made him a Dodger in 1947. Baseball had closed its doors to blacks in the 1890s. Given Rickey's unique personality blend of preacher and horse trader, it is difficult to determine if he was motivated by a higher sense of justice or a bigger bottom line. His plan to reintegrate the game could not have seen fruition without the help of an unlikely ally—baseball's second commissioner, Albert "Happy" Chandler.

Chandler was no Landis, nor did the owners want him to be. He was a glad-handing politician of the "good old boy" Southern school. No one ever sported a more appropriate nickname than "Happy." He served as Kentucky's governor and its Senator. While he was in the Senate, he was a frequent visitor to Griffith Stadium. He was firm in his belief that baseball should continue during World War II, even if it had to play with 4-Fs.

Chandler's style immediately generated awkwardness with the millionaires who owned the game. As Lee Lowenfish and Tony Lupien put it, "A commissioner willing to sing 'My Old Kentucky Home' at a moment's notice embarrassed the urbanites. . . . In commissioner Chandler [the owners] had a leader of no great force or distinction, which suited them perfectly."

The owners voted solidly against Rickey's plan to bring Robinson to the majors, but Chandler overruled them, in a slightly remarkable display of moral courage for a man born and raised in the grand tradition of Southern gentry, a man to whom principles were often something else to negotiate. Chandler thought of all the African Americans who had fought bravely to preserve American freedom during the war.

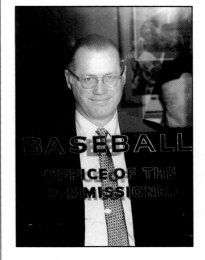

A descendant of the old West figure Jim Bowie, Bowie Kent Kuhn worked the scoreboard at Griffith Stadium as a youngster and as a lawyer had the National League as a client for his New York law firm for almost 20 years before he was appointed in 1969 the commissioner of baseball.

The next great leader of baseball came along in 1969. Bowie Kuhn was a commissioner in the Landis sense. Kuhn believed in making decisions that he felt were best for baseball, and he didn't seem to worry whom he offended. He made many owners angry with some of his calls, when he restructured trades to make them fairer. He made everyone upset when he banned legends Willie Mays and Mickey Mantle from baseball employment because they were working as "greeters" at casinos.

During Kuhn's tenure baseball reaped its richest rewards and suffered through its most trying turmoils. And baseball had never had a bigger fan in the commissioner's chair than Bowie Kuhn. His first job had been as a scoreboard operator in Griffith Stadium. He later said it was the best job he had ever had. He made his love of the game part of his career. Within months of receiving his first job as a lawyer, he asked to work on the major-league baseball account. He spent 19 years there helping baseball fight off the persistent antitrust charges filed against it. Hired as a temporary commissioner just to restructure the way baseball did its business, he stayed 15 years.

Kuhn's greatest problem was public relations. He acted like a professional lawyer (something sportswriters had no idea how to deal with), and he looked like a shill for the owners, with his 6'5" bearing and slightly pompous style. When he ordered that all World Series games begin at night, the TV cameras loved showing him sitting in his box, wearing no top coat on chilly October evenings, looking ridiculous. Many fans today probably think of Kuhn as an idiot, although nothing could be further from the truth.

Kuhn, though, ran into two other people who led him into stinging battles to determine the nature of the game. He was the victor in the contests against the first, but he (and some would say baseball) was the bitter loser in confrontations with the latter.

Bowie Kuhn was not at ease in front of the media. He was awkward and stilted. Yet there are several authorities who think that Kuhn turned out to be the most proficient commissioner in baseball history.

Top left: Charles Finley, with his mule Charley O, made his fortune selling life insurance.

Charley Finley was a baseball fan who made several million dollars in one day in a brilliant insurance deal. Although the owners kept voting him down when he tried to buy a team, he finally won out when Arnold Johnson died within months of obtaining the Kansas City Athletics and Finley snapped up 52 percent of the team. Finley was a hustler—street-smart and tough. He was also forward-looking. He once said, "The day Custer lost at the Little Big Horn, the Chicago White Sox beat the Cincinnati Red Legs 3-2. Both teams wore knickers. And they're still wearing them today." He looked for innovations. Some, like orange baseballs for night games, an electronic umpire, and a mechanized rabbit to deliver fresh balls to the home plate ump, seem as foolish today as they did then. He also pushed for the designated hitter and for World Series night games, equally radical ideas for their time.

However, his style was pushy and boorish: He berated his players in public. He hired a mule as team mascot and instructed

Vida Blue was sold by Finley to the Yankees and then the Reds in 1976, and Bowie Kuhn voided both sales.

broadcaster Harry Caray to drop his signature "Holy Cow!" in favor of "Holy Mule!" Finley gave Catfish Hunter his nickname and then asked Vida Blue to change his first name to "True."

The flamboyant Finley could not believe that anyone could tell him what to do with his players. Kuhn did, however, over and over. Reggie Jackson, Blue, Mike Andrews, Jackson and Blue again, Joe Rudi, and Rollie Fingers: All were treated in such a way by Finley that Kuhn felt he had to step in and make things right. Kuhn admitted later that helping get Charley Finley out of baseball was the act as commissioner that he was most proud of.

Marvin Miller, right, in the 1940s served on the War Labor Board and in the federal conciliation service, and as an authority on pensions working for a steelworkers union he was suited to the players' union leader job that he took in 1966.

Marvin Miller was a different story. Miller was a brilliant student who graduated from high school when he was just 15. Trained in the law, he took a job with the United Steel Workers Union and soon became a top aide to USWA presidents David McDonald and I.W. Abel. Miller learned the tough ways of dealing with management in negotiations. He was even hired by the U.S. government to train labor negotiators. In 1966 the Major League Players Association hired him as its director. According to one analyst, "Miller may have had more influence on the game than anyone in this half century." Miller took a nearly invisible organization of athletes and made it successful.

The MLPA had been founded in 1953, the fifth attempt for major leaguers to organize. Until Miller, however, the union had all the power of a wet noodle. Concerns such as the length of spring-training road trips and the location of water fountains in bullpens were the stuff of its "negotiations" with the owners.

Miller changed all that. Baseball management had always feared a union. Miller gave them real reason to worry.

Miller was the owners' worst nightmare. He admitted he was no baseball fan, but what did that matter. He railed against the owners' outright ownership of players. "Unlike most antitrust agreements," he said, referring to the terms of the standard baseball contract, "this one is written down on paper, and even printed." Even more importantly, Miller was able to unite the players. A baseball player builds his career on his individual skills; close attachments to others are usually bad business.

The owners steadfastly refused to believe Miller could bend the group of players to his will and keep them there. It cost them in a big way. When the players actually went on strike in 1972, the owners were dumbfounded. Instead of viewing Miller as a serious adversary, they reacted like a town bully who had been upended by a skinny newcomer: They vowed vengeance. Miller's great skill at riling the owners' feathers kept them always on the defensive. In addition, Miller was a master of dealing with the press to manipulate public sentiment in favor of the players. He would call the owners stupid, greedy, un-American, or all three. The stuffy Kuhn was made to look ridiculous. The press loved painting Kuhn as a buffoon. Red Smith sharpened his wit with such lines as, "An empty car pulled up and Bowie Kuhn got out."

In his 16 years as director of the MLPA, Miller changed the game forever. The players were no longer "chattel" of management, as Monte Ward had argued in 1887. They were in some ways more powerful than the men who owned their contracts.

Ray Grebey, chief management negotiator, holds up a newspaper signaling the end to the 1981 strike. Grebey was hired in 1978 to provide the owners with a headstrong advocate that would provide a counterbalance to Marvin Miller.

Baseball Highlights

THE BEST
BETWEEN THE LINES

The cycle of baseball's significant moments endures. Cookie Lavagetto became a hero for breaking up a no-hitter and winning game four of the 1947 World Series. Bill Bevens, who lost the game, is not remembered in the same way as Don Larsen—revered for tossing a perfect game in the 1956 fall classic. Kirk Gibson's homer to win the first game of the 1988 World Series echoed not only Lavagetto's hit but also Bobby Thomson's "Shot Heard 'Round the World," while Joe Carter's homer to deliver the 1993 World Series paralleled 1960 as Bill Mazeroski delivered the championship to Pittsburgh. Events such as these reveal the magic of the game.

NAP LAJOIE TAKES AL TRIPLE CROWN

◆

The American League opened for business as a second major league in 1901 and raided National League rosters for established "name" players. It was a young star, however, that did the most to validate the credibility of the new league.

Napoleon "Nap" Lajoie was a slick-fielding, 26-year-old second baseman who had batted .326, .361, .324, .378, and .337 in his first five seasons for the Philadelphia Phillies (very good, but not unthinkable batting averages for the high-scoring late 1890s). His career, however, had given little hint of what was to come. Playing for the Athletics in 1901, the Phillies' crosstown American League competitors, Lajoie put on a one-man slugging exhibition and won the century's first Triple Crown. He led the AL in hitting at .426, in home runs with 14, and in RBI with 125.

This Triple Crown is retrospective, since the concept did not exist in 1901; triples, not home runs, were the power stat of the day, and the RBI did not become official until 1920. But in 1901 there was no shortage of important offensive categories dominated by Lajoie. He led the new league in runs with 145, hits with 232, doubles with 48, on-base average at .463, and slugging percentage at .643. His .426 batting average is the highest mark of this century. Besides Lajoie,

Nap Lajoie was a top player in the NL when he jumped to the nascent American League in 1901. He had led the NL in slugging in 1897 and RBI in 1898. He jumped from the NL Philadelphia Phillies, where he was making $2,400 (the NL's maximum), to the Philadelphia Athletics, where he was offered $6,000.

only Rogers Hornsby in the 20th century has won the Triple Crown with a batting average over .400. While some say that Lajoie's 1901 numbers were inflated because American League competition was still a cut below National League standards and because foul balls were not counted as strikes in 1901, it must be remembered that this was no less true for Lajoie than for all of the men he outhit, including Mike Donlin, Jimmy Collins, and Socks Seybold.

Lajoie could not single-handedly win the pennant; the A's pitching let them down, and they finished fourth. But Phillies' fans followed him to the new league in droves. He helped plant a secure AL foothold in one of the three key markets (the others were Chicago and Boston) in which the AL had chosen to take on National League teams on their own turf. Lajoie's contract status then became the main battleground in the war between the leagues when the Phillies sued to get him back and obtained an injunction from the state courts that forbade Lajoie from playing for any team but the Phillies in 1902. A's manager Connie Mack, knowing how important Lajoie's drawing power was to the AL's survival, hit upon the ingenious dodge of sending Lajoie to play for AL Cleveland, where he would be outside the Pennsylvania court's jurisdiction. There, with the exception of away games in Philadelphia, he played out the 1902 season, batting .378. After the two leagues made peace in 1903, Lajoie remained with Cleveland for 12 years and won three more batting titles.

Nap Lajoie

AL SOCKS SENIORS IN INITIAL WORLD SERIES

◆

The 1903 season began on a note of good will, with the NL and the AL agreeing to coexist. During the season two of the more sporting owners, Barney Dreyfus of Pittsburgh and Henry Killilea of Boston—whose teams were running away with their leagues' pennants—agreed to play a best five-of-nine postseason series. This competition was fierce, unlike the meaningless Temple Cup series of the 1890s.

The AL's Boston Pilgrims seemed to be overmatched against one of the greatest dynasties in NL history. Pittsburgh won its third straight pennant in 1903, with player-manager Fred Clarke; hitting stars Honus Wagner, Ginger Beaumont, and Tommy Leach; and a brilliant pitching staff of Deacon Phillippe, Sam Leever, and Ed Doheny. In 1902 Clarke's wrecking crew had taken the flag by 27½ games in a 142-game schedule. Pittsburgh was 91-49 in 1903, winning the loop by six and one-half games.

The 16,242 Pilgrim fans who filled Boston's Huntington Avenue Grounds for game one hung their hopes on a number of late-season injuries to key Pirates: Leever had hurt his shoulder, Doheny had suffered a mental breakdown and was hospitalized, and the great Wagner had a bad leg. Nevertheless, the visitors beat Cy Young 7-3, as Leach's two triples and Jimmy

Fred Clarke

Sebring's home run picked up the slack, and Phillippe struck out 10 and walked none on a six-hitter. After Boston evened matters behind Big Bill Dinneen in game two, Phillippe returned on a day's rest to win again in game three 4-2. Incredibly, Clarke started Phillippe again in game four, played in Pittsburgh only three days later on Oct. 6. Though his arm was showing signs of strain (he struck out only one in nine innings), he won again, beating Dinneen 5-4. The Series now stood at Boston one game, Phillippe three.

The tide turned in games five and six, when Young shut down the Pirates 11-2 and Dinneen won 6-3. The two Boston pitchers then took complete control of the rest of the Series as their team won four straight to become world champions, five games to three. Young and Dinneen allowed the opposition a total of five earned runs in the final four contests and twice defeated an exhausted Phillippe, who received little support from his teammates either in the field or at bat.

Phillippe started five of the eight World Series games, winning three and completing all five. He pitched 44 innings over 13 days, and he gave up only three walks and had 22 strikeouts, allowing 14 earned runs for a 2.86 ERA.

The 1903 edition of the Pirates was one of the best of the early 1900s Pittsburgh dynasty, which was started in 1900 with the transfer of such players as Honus Wagner, Fred Clarke, and Deacon Phillippe from the Louisville franchise.

HAPPY JACK FAILS TO COLLECT 42nd WIN

◆

Pitcher Jack Chesbro is remembered today for setting the modern record for wins in a season, with 41. In his own time, however, Chesbro was famous for a very different exploit—a wild pitch that lost an AL pennant for the New York Highlanders. Strangely enough, he performed both of these feats in the same year, 1904.

Boston and New York took turns in first place down the stretch of the 1904 pennant race. The two clubs had little else in common. Under Hall-of-Famer Jimmy Collins, Boston fielded the same star-filled lineup that had won the 1903 flag by 14½ games. Clark Griffith's Highlanders finished dead last in Baltimore in 1902 before moving to New York in 1903. With a patchwork of no-name rookies and such older players as Wee Willie Keeler and Griffith himself, New York's 1904 squad resembled an expansion team more than a dynasty.

The greatest difference between the teams was pitching. Boston had a solid four-man rotation. The thin Highlander staff became a two-man show of Chesbro and Jack Powell, who started 96 games between them and completed 86. Chesbro led the AL in innings with 455, games with 55, and complete games with 48. On that final day against Boston, Griffith gave Chesbro the ball one more time.

Boston brought a slim game and one-half lead into New York for two final games on Monday, Oct. 10. With no tie possible, it was doubleheader sweep or nothing for the Highlanders; the 15,000-seat Hilltop Park was filled beyond capacity.

Chesbro dueled Boston pitcher Bill Dinneen until the fifth inning, when New York scored twice; two innings later, Boston tied it up when second baseman Jimmy Williams threw away Dinneen's easy grounder with runners on second and third.

It was still 2-2 in the Boston ninth when a single, a sacrifice, and an infield out moved a man to third with shortstop Freddy Parent at bat. With the count at 1-2, Chesbro let fly with his out-pitch, a hard-sinking spitball. But the pitch eluded the catcher, young Red Kleinow, and Boston won the game 3-2 and the pennant.

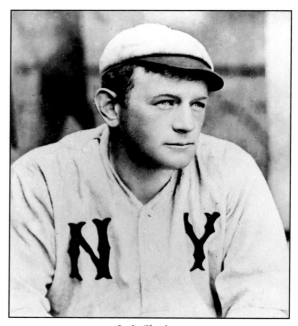

Jack Chesbro

MATHEWSON HURLS THREE WORLD SERIES SHUTOUTS IN 1905

◆

Red Kleinow

New York won what must have been a very dreary second game 1-0 in 10 innings.

Many contemporary authorities contend that Kleinow should have handled the pitch and that Chesbro's selection as the goat was unfair. Even after Chesbro's death, in 1931, Chesbro's wife and others campaigned to have the scorer's decision changed from wild pitch to passed ball. Regardless, there are other points in Chesbro's defense: The Highlanders still had the bottom of the ninth to come back, there was Williams's key error, and New York still had to win the second game.

Chesbro's good name seems to have been restored simply because his 41-12 season is still in the record books.

It was a pitchers' year in the American League in 1905. That year hitters batted a combined .241, and the pennant-winning Athletics led the league with a .255 batting average and only 623 runs scored. After a tough pennant race in which Philadelphia barely survived a late surge by Chicago—which compiled a 1.99 team ERA—Connie Mack's A's were looking forward to facing the New York Giants pitching in the World Series.

The pre-Series wisdom rated the New York pitching staff, with Christy Mathewson (31-8, 1.27 ERA) and Joe McGinnity (21-15, 2.87 ERA), about even with the Philly rotation—including Rube Waddell (27-10, 1.48 ERA), Eddie Plank (24-12, 2.26 ERA), and Chief Bender (18-11, 2.83 ERA). But that was before the eccentric Waddell hurt his shoulder while playfully wrestling with a teammate and put himself out of action. As it turned out, John McGraw and his Giants embarrassed Philadelphia four games to one. The New York pitchers so dominated the Series that the only difference a healthy Waddell would have made was if he notched a few hits.

Mathewson, a 26-year-old righty with a mystifying screwball, was in top form in game one and beat Plank 3-0, allowing four hits and no walks in nine innings. He also stopped the most direct scoring threat he faced in the Series by fielding a bunt and throwing out a baserunner at home. Bender evened the Series with a shutout of his own, winning 3-0 over McGinnity. The roof then fell in on the A's. Matty threw another four-hitter to win game three 9-0. He walked one batter, but no Athletic got past first base. McGinnity won game four 1-0 on third baseman Lave Cross's error in the fourth inning. Mathewson clinched the Series by scattering six hits and defeating Bender 2-0. Matty retired the last 10 batters that he faced in the Series.

Besides setting a still-unchallenged record by pitching three shutouts in a single Series, Mathewson allowed 14 hits and just one walk in 27 innings; he struck out 18. While he was on the mound, not a single Athletics runner reached third. And Mathewson did this all in six days.

John McGraw skippered the 1905 Giants to 105 wins and 48 losses. The Giants had the No. 2 ERA in the loop that year, but they were No. 1 in runs scored.

Christy Mathewson

The Series composite score, 15-3, which could be mistaken for the score of one game, underlines the irony that 1905 was one of the best-pitched World Series of all time—and yet it was one of the most lopsided. The A's hit no triples and no home runs; they had 23 more strikeouts than RBI. Six Philadelphia regulars batted under .200. Adding in McGinnity's 17 innings of work and Ames's one, the New York pitchers allowed the A's a grand total of 25 hits and five walks in 45 innings.

Years later, McGraw would say that of all his great teams, this team came nearest to perfection. Certainly none improved on the 1905 Giants' Series ERA—0.00.

MERKLE MAKES MISERABLE MISTAKE

◆

Fans in 1908 saw two of the most exciting pennant races ever. Three NL teams finished within one game of first; Detroit won a four-team AL race by .004, the smallest margin of victory in history. Both feats were overshadowed, however, by the "Merkle Blunder."

Fred Merkle was a competent first baseman who hit .273 over a 16-year career. But Giants fans never stopped calling him "Bonehead" and saying "So long, Fred. Don't forget to touch second." Merkle took the heckling so hard that later he admitted it was tough to play.

On Sept. 23, 1908, Merkle was a substitute in a game against the Cubs, who trailed New York in the standings by .006. With two out in the bottom of the ninth inning in a 1-1 game, Merkle singled Moose McCormick over to third. Al Bridwell then singled to center, McCormick scored the winning run, and Merkle made for the Giants' clubhouse to avoid the crowd, which was spilling onto the infield. He didn't bother to touch second. Today, thanks to Merkle, every player makes sure to touch second under these circumstances; otherwise the defense can tag the base for the force-out and nullify the run.

According to the Cubs, this is just what happened. Second baseman Johnny Evers somehow, in the midst of the postgame confusion, retrieved the ball and tagged second in view of plate umpire Hank O'Day, who told base umpire Robert Emslie to call the absent Merkle out. With resumption impossible, O'Day ruled the game a tie and ignited a firestorm of protests and counterprotests. There were some witnesses who said they saw Merkle touch the base. Others claimed that the ball Evers retrieved came from the Cub dugout.

Significantly, Evers had had a run-in with O'Day in an identical situation in a game against Pittsburgh two weeks earlier. There O'Day had declared that the run counted, but he felt personally stung when Chicago protested officially to league President Harry Pulliam. Though O'Day's call in Pittsburgh was upheld, it is doubtless that the protest intimidated O'Day. One thing is sure—Merkle's play was a blunder only in retrospect. Merkle could never have sus-

Fred Merkle

Star second sacker Johnny Evers was a fanatical rules reader. It was said that Evers went to bed at night with a copy of the baseball rules book.

SNODGRASS'S MUFF JINXES THE GIANTS

◆

The National League was under a postseason jinx throughout the 1910s, losing eight out of 10 World Series. This was never more apparent than in the exciting, strange, and—for seven games and nine innings—well-played 1912 edition. John McGraw's New York Giants won 103 games, leading the NL in runs scored and ERA. In the World Series, the Giants outhit the Boston Red Sox .270 to .220 and allowed a full earned run less per game. Yet somehow they managed to lose four games to three.

In game one McGraw sacrificed rookie spitballer Jeff Tesreau to Smokey Joe Wood—who was coming off an overpowering 34-5 season—with the Giants losing 6-4. The tactic misfired when Christy Mathewson was wasted in a second-game 6-6 tie that was halted by darkness. Giants pitcher Rube Marquard won game three 2-1, and Wood beat Tesreau again. Young Hugh Bedient won over Matty in another 2-1 game, and Marquard won his second game 5-2 in game six. Wood pitched against Tesreau in game seven but was unexpectedly shelled by the Giants, who won 11-4 to force an eighth-game showdown between Mathewson and Bedient.

Opposite page: Fred Snodgrass was blamed for losing the 1912 World Series, though other Giants could have worn goat horns.

pected that O'Day would call him out on a never-before-enforced technicality, that his team would finish tied with Chicago, that there would be a postseason replay, or that the Giants would lose that game and the pennant.

The Merkle affair was painful all around. O'Day was reviled by colleague Bill Klem, who called it "the worst call in the history of baseball." Fans and the press debated the matter all winter. Many thought Giants manager John McGraw should have known about the Pittsburgh incident and cautioned his players. Eventually, however, baseball seems to have agreed to scapegoat Merkle and leave it at that.

For nine innings both teams threatened in nearly every turn at bat, banging out a combined total of 14 hits, but could only push across two runs. In the fifth, Boston's Harry Hooper made a game-saving play when he leapt into the stands and brought back a Larry Doyle home run—*bare-handed.* Mathewson and Wood, who came in after the seventh, walked a 1-1 tightrope into extra innings. Then in the Giants half of the 10th, slugging outfielder Red Murray doubled and Fred Merkle singled him home. Now it was New York's turn to feel confident, with the great Mathewson needing to go just one more inning to clinch the Series.

In that inning, though, normally steady Giants center fielder Fred Snodgrass dropped an easy fly ball to put leadoff batter Clyde Engel on second. Hooper later said that mistake "could have happened to anybody" but has been immortalized as the "$30,000 Muff" (after the Series winners' share). Snodgrass made a great catch on the next batter that erased an extra-base hit, but when the time came to choose a goat for the Giants' 3-2 defeat, this play was forgotten and Snodgrass was the unanimous choice.

There were other villians. Mathewson got Tris Speaker to pop up in foul territory near first base, but Matty confused first baseman Merkle and catcher Chief Meyers by calling for Meyers—who was farther from the play—to take it. Neither made the catch. Speaker then singled the tying run home and the go-ahead run to third; Larry Gardner won the Series with a sac fly that should have been the third out.

WALTER JOHNSON DRUBS THE 1913 AL

Walter Johnson threw his sidearm fastball for two decades. He won 417 games—110 by shutouts—while losing only 279. Yet Johnson's team, the Washington Senators, was a second-division team for most of his career. Washington finished seventh or eighth five times in five years between 1907 and 1911. Peak performances by "The Big Train" during the early 1910s propelled the Senators no higher in the standings than second.

Walter Johnson won 36 in 1913.

Senators hurler Walter Johnson's amazing 1913 season featured league-leading performances in six categories. However, he couldn't carry the load by himself, and the Senators finished second to Connie Mack's Philadelphia Athletics in the race for the AL flag.

The Big Train arrived in the big leagues in 1907 as green as could be. After conquering early wildness, (he threw 21 wild pitches in 1910), he hit his stride in 1912, going 33-12 and striking out 303 to help Washington move up five places in the standings to second.

The following year, Johnson topped his fine 1912 season with the best performance of his career and one of the greatest pitching seasons in history. He went 36-7 and led the 1913 AL in wins, ERA (1.14), and strikeouts (243) to become one of only six American League pitch-

ers ever to win the "pitching triple crown." His 1.14 ERA, the fourth-lowest of all time, combined with his league-best 11 shutouts and 55 ⅔ consecutive scoreless innings (a record that stood until 1968) demonstrates Johnson's utter dominance of AL hitters.

After the blazing fastball, The Big Train's biggest weapon was control. Though his strikeout total dropped by 60 from the previous year, he cut his walks in half to 38 and wild pitches down to three. His opponents batted only .187 against him and had an on-base percentage of .217; the league batting average was .256 and on-base percentage was .325. Still, even with their No. 1 pitcher 29 games over .500, the Senators won only 90 games and finished six and one-half games behind Philadelphia. The drop-off in talent from Johnson to the rest of the 1913 Senators is shown by the shocking differential in their winning percentages; Johnson's stood at .837 and the rest of the team 351 points lower at .486.

In 1913 Johnson also led the league in complete games with 29, innings with 346, fewest hits allowed per nine innings with 6.03, and fewest bases on balls allowed per nine innings with 0.99. His ratio of baserunners per nine innings was 7.26, the best in the 20th century.

His greatest season more or less told the story of the rest of Johnson's career. Though he won 20 or more games for the next six years, Washington settled back into the second division. It wasn't until 1924 that the Senators won the world championship.

BOSTON BRAVES EARN 1914 MIRACLE

According to the sports pages and fan conversations, to win a pennant you need only hustle, clutch hitting, and defense. The 1914 "Miracle Braves" came from last place to prove that point.

The story of the underdog Boston Braves' journey from last place in July to the pennant begins and ends the same way: with a fit of pique. Disappointed in his team's third-place finish in 1913, Cubs owner Charles Murphy traded star second baseman Johnny Evers to the Braves. Evers became, along with hard-fighting shortstop Rabbit Maranville, the heart of the Boston club. Evers was voted the NL's MVP for 1914, beating out his double-play partner by six votes. Evers led the team with 81 runs and a .390 on-base average. He led the league second basemen in fielding, and he and Maranville led in double plays. Boston had a scrappy offense, one of the best defensive teams ever, and an innovative manager in George Stallings.

Stallings was a great motivator and an early practitioner of platooning. Boston had very good pitching, led by Bill James and Dick Rudolph, but no sluggers to speak of. Maranville set an NL record for putouts and the major-league record for total chances at shortstop, and he had a team-high 78 RBI with a .246 average and only 33 extra-base hits.

Despite a popgun offense and a thin mound staff, the 1914 "Miracle" Braves rose up
from fifth place in 1913 to win the NL pennant by 10½ games.

Boston Braves manager George Stallings is flanked by his two top pitchers, Bill James and Dick Rudolph. The two hurlers combined for 53 of Boston's 94 wins in 1914 and won two more each in the dramatic World Series sweep of Philadelphia.

With Maranville out sick, the 1914 Braves won only four of their first 22. By mid-June they were still in last place, but the front-running New York Giants had been unable to move away from the pack. The Braves then began a dizzying 34-10 pennant drive with eight straight wins. On July 21 the Braves moved into fourth. Another winning streak, this time nine games, brought them within six and one-half games of the Giants. On Aug. 10 Boston passed Chicago and St. Louis to capture second place. A sweep of the Giants, climaxed by an extra-inning 1-0 defeat of Christy Mathewson, lopped another three games off the Braves' deficit. Finally, Boston moved past New York into first place for good on Sept. 8. Stallings drove his team to 94 wins and a 10½-game lead over the Giants.

The 1914 Braves had one more dramatic upset in them. Behind the pitching of James, Rudolph, and Lefty Tyler (who combined for a 1.15 ERA) and the hitting of Evers, Maranville, and catcher Hank Gowdy, Boston demolished the mighty A's in four games. A's owner Connie Mack angrily sold off most of his stars and condemning his team to seven straight last-place finishes.

TWO HURLERS VIE IN 26-INNING TIE

◆

According to most baseball historians, by 1920 the pitching-dominated dead-ball days were over. But someone must have forgotten to tell the Boston Braves or the Brooklyn Robins. On May 1 of that year, they played the deadest game in dead-ball history, a 26-inning 1-1 tie.

"From 3 o'clock until near 7 in the evening," led the *Boston Post* the next day, and proceeded to give its readers the shocking news that the game had taken three hours and 50 minutes to play 26 innings. Today, nine innings can

Brooklyn's Leon Cadore

take that long. The game's low walk and strikeout totals (nine and 14, respectively) show that the pitchers, in true dead-ball fashion, were throwing strikes. That only two runs were scored on 25 hits shows why; with an extremely high proportion of all hits being singles, dead-ball era pitchers were free to put the ball in play without risking a game-breaking home run. This obviously speeds up play, allowing an average of less than nine minutes per inning.

Most amazing, though, is the fact that both teams' starting pitchers, Leon Cadore for the Robins and Joe Oeschger for the Braves, pitched all 26 innings. This was unusual, even for those days of iron-man heroics; neither starting catcher went the distance. Strangely enough, Oeschger

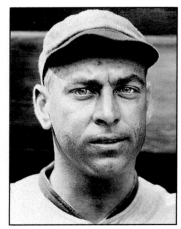

Boston's Joe Oeschger

had survived a 20-inning game the year before, and perhaps the experience helped; the veteran right-hander allowed a mere nine hits, and in only one inning, the 17th, did Brooklyn put two hits together. Cadore lived a little more dangerously, allowing 15 hits and relying on his superb defense to bail him out of trouble. With one out in the ninth and the bases loaded, second baseman Ivy Olson killed a Boston rally by fielding a grounder, tagging the runner going by, and then getting the force at first. In the sixth, Boston had tied up the score and was threatening to take the lead, but third baseman Tony Boeckel was cut down at the plate by a brilliant relay from the outfield.

So it went until umpire William McCormick declared a tie on account of darkness, setting the record for the most innings in a single game. How long could Cadore and Oeschger have gone on? Neither allowed a run over the final 20 innings or even a hit over the final six. Later, Oeschger said that he felt tired after the 18th, but his teammates kept telling him, "Just one more inning, Joe, and we'll get a run." Cadore claimed that his arm could have gone a few more innings, but admitted he was "growing sleepy."

WAMBY PERFORMS TRIPLE PLAY IN 1920 WORLD SERIES

◆

Cleveland won its first pennant in 1920. Led by player-manager Tris Speaker (who hit .388 with 50 doubles), Elmer Smith, and Larry Gardner, the Indians had the AL's top offense with 857 runs. Their pitching staff featured the 31-game winner Jim Bagby and Stan Coveleski, as well as Ray Caldwell (20-10) and "Duster" Mails.

But the Indians' success was overshadowed by the Black Sox scandal and the death of Cleveland shortstop Ray Chapman, killed by a pitch from Yankee Carl Mays.

Wilbert Robinson's Brooklyn Robins won the NL pennant behind spitballer Burleigh Grimes and hosted Cleveland in game one of the best five-of-nine Series on Oct. 5. Coveleski defeated former Giant ace Rube Marquard 3-1. After Grimes and Sherry Smith beat Bagby and Caldwell in games two and three, Coveleski won his second of three victories to even things.

The Indians extended their theme of famous firsts in game five, the turning point of the Series.

Bill Wambsganss had a long career but is known today for one spectacular play.

Elmer Smith took Grimes deep with the bases loaded in the opening inning for the first grand slam in World Series history. The score remained 4-0 until Indians starter Bagby added a three-run shot in the fourth, the first World Series home run by a pitcher. Brooklyn rallied in the fifth after lead-off hitter Pete Kilduff reached base on a hit and catcher Otto Miller singled him to second with none out. The stage was now set for Cleveland's greatest first of all.

With left-handed relief pitcher Clarence Mitchell up next, Robinson decided against a pinch hitter; Mitchell could hit, going six for 18 that season as a pinch hitter himself. Expecting that Mitchell would be able to pull the ball off of the righty Bagby, second baseman Bill Wambsganss moved back onto the outfield grass and toward first. Mitchell, however, lined a shot up the middle to his backhand side and both runners took off. Wambsganss lunged and made the catch on a fly to retire Mitchell. Wamby then let his momentum carry him to second base before Kilduff could return to the base for the easy second out. Then Wamby turned, saw a stunned Miller standing a few feet away, and applied the tag for the third out. It took the Cleveland crowd a few seconds to grasp that they had just seen the first unassisted World Series triple play.

Brooklyn's luck didn't change in the rest of the Series—they were shut out in games six and seven. Neither did Mitchell's. His next time up, he grounded into a double play, to account for 19 percent of his team's outs in only two at bats.

OLD PETE ERASES LAZZERI, YANKEES

◆

Over his 20-year career, Grover Cleveland "Pete" Alexander won 373 games, including eight 20-win seasons and three 30-victory campaigns. But despite all those wins, the greatest moment of his Hall of Fame pitcher's career came when he saved a game as a relief pitcher during the 1926 World Series between the St. Louis Cardinals and the New York Yankees.

At the beginning of the '26 season, the man who in his prime had been called "Alex the Great" was now "Old Pete." He had spent time that winter in a sanitorium due to epilepsy and

Hall-of-Famer Grover Alexander

alcohol abuse. He was age 39 when he reported to spring training with the Cubs. But Alexander broke his ankle during camp, argued with manager Joe McCarthy once the season started, and was released by June.

When it appeared his career was over, Cardinals player-manager Rogers Hornsby plucked Alexander from the scrap heap and put him into the Cards rotation. Alex gave to "The Rajah" everything that he had left in his aging right arm, producing nine victories and helping the Redbirds to their first pennant and a World Series meeting with the Yankees.

After the Cardinals lost game one of the Series, Alexander brought his team back with a 6-2 win, retiring the last 21 Yankees in order. When the Bronx Bombers won two of the next three games, it was up to Alexander to keep his team in the Series. He came through with a 10-2 victory and, legend has it, did a hefty amount of drinking that night, confident his work for the Series was over.

In the deciding seventh game, Jesse Haines pitched the Cardinals to a 3-2 lead after six innings. But with two out in the seventh frame, Haines suddenly walked the bases loaded. Up next for the Yanks was the year's outstanding rookie, Tony Lazzeri, who during the regular season was second on the team to Babe Ruth in RBI with 114.

Hornsby remembered that Alexander had struck out Lazzeri four times the day before and, to the amazement of 38,093 fans in Yankee Stadium, called Alex in from the bullpen to

Star Yankee infielder Tony Lazzeri

stop the Yankee threat. After ball one, Lazzeri swung and missed at a curve. The next pitch was a fastball and Lazzeri hit a line drive that was almost a homer but veered just a few feet foul. On the next delivery, Alex went back to his curve ball and Lazzeri went down on strikes—again.

The Yankees would not threaten to score again. Alexander kept the Yankees off the bases until two out in the ninth, when he walked Babe Ruth. Ruth uncharacteristically tried to steal second and was thrown out. Alexander saved the game and the Cardinals won the Series.

BABE BLASTS 60 FOR '27 YANKEES

◆

Not counting his short but impressive early stint as a pitcher with the Boston Red Sox, Babe Ruth's career reached not one, but two peaks. After setting new home run records with 11 in 1918, 29 in 1919, 54 as a Yankee in 1920, and, finally, 59 in 1921, Ruth had revolutionized baseball and set a standard no succeeding slugger has been able to match. The legendary "Bambino" made home run hitting one of those rare arts—like epic poetry and tragedy—whose earliest practitioners are ranked by posterity as the greatest.

Ruth faded a bit in his late 20s, perhaps worn down by drinking, partying, and general excess as well as his frequent squabbles with Yankee management and the commissioner. The Babe's home run totals dropped into the 40s in 1923, '24, and '26, and below that in 1922 when he was suspended for illegal barnstorming, and in 1925, when stomach surgery and another suspension limited him to 98 games.

However, those who thought that he might be through were mistaken. In 1927, at the age of 32, Ruth hit his 60th home run of the sea-

Above: Babe Ruth pitches for Boston.
Opposite page: Ruth's famous swing produced 60 homers in 1927.

son off pitcher Tom Zachary (who had also given up No. 22 and No. 36) to reach his greatest home run total ever. His major-league record stood for 32 years, until Roger Maris hit 61 homers in 1961. Ruth also batted .356 with 138 walks, 158 runs scored, and 164 RBI.

Ruth may well have been spurred on by the competition of budding Yankee power-hitter Lou Gehrig, then in his third full season and batting behind Ruth in the clean-up slot. In 1927, the 24-year-old first baseman—who had never hit more than 20 home runs or batted over .313—hit .373, drove in a league-high 175 runs, and nearly kept pace with Ruth in home runs until September, when Ruth put on a unique long-ball stretch drive by swatting 17 (including three on Sept. 6 and two each on Sept. 7, 13, and 29). In a historical sense, however, Ruth's competition was never with anyone but himself. And if even he could not duplicate his 1920 and 1921 seasons—the only years in history in which he or anyone else has slugged over .800—the Babe of 1927 came close, with a .772 mark. In 1961, Roger Maris slugged only .620. Ruth's 60 homers in 1927 represented 38 percent of the Yankees' AL-leading total and 14 percent of the league's total—*more than any other single team.* After Gehrig's 47 home runs, third place went to Lazzeri with 18.

TREASURY OF BASEBALL

WILSON ERUPTS FOR 190 RUNS BATTED IN

◆

Although the home-run era may have begun in 1920, its effects continued throughout the Roaring Twenties, as the number of runs scored shot up year after year until 1930. The baseball was deadened the next season, ensuring that 1930 would go down in history as the absolute peak of the major-league batting outburst.

It was fun while it lasted. The American League batted .288; the National, .303; AL pitchers compiled an ERA of 4.65; the NL hurlers, an ugly 4.97. The St. Louis Cardinals finished first with an ERA of 4.40 and 1,004 runs scored. Incredibly, last-place Philadelphia outhit them .315 to .314. A short list of individual single-season hitting records set in 1930 comprises six of the all-time top-30 seasons in RBI, six of the top 30 in total bases, four of the top 20 in slugging average, and two of the top 20 in home runs.

If Ty Cobb was the symbol of the dead-ball era and Babe Ruth the hero of 1920, the personification of the combustible 1930 season was Lewis "Hack" Wilson. The free-swinging, home-run-bashing, and utterly eccentric Chicago Cubs center fielder put together one of the few National League seasons that can be compared with the best of Ruth and Lou Gehrig. Wilson was a legendary carouser who was once

reprimanded by commissioner Kenesaw Mountain Landis for reputedly socializing with Al Capone. After failing to impress the Giants, Hack came to Chicago in 1926. There the 5'6", 220-pound barrel-chested and spindly legged outfielder blossomed, batting over .300 and upping his home run totals each year until 1930.

Wilson had an overwhelming year in 1930. He drove in a major-league-record *190* RBI, clobbered a National League-record 56 home runs, drew 105 walks, and scored 146 runs. He batted .356 and slugged .723. If not the National League's best hitter that year—an argument could be made for Chuck Klein—Wilson was the most flamboyant. Chicago fans reveled in the sight of the comically stubby Wilson wildly flailing at the ball with his favored 40-ounce tree trunk of a bat. In the spirit of the times in which he lived, Hack swung away with abandon.

Hack beat the previous NL record for RBI, set by Sam Thompson with 166 in 1887, by 24 ribbies. Wilson broke the major-league record held by Lou Gehrig, who set it in 1927 with 175. Wilson drove in 1.23 runs per game in 1930, averaging one RBI every three times he took an official time at bat.

Only a year later, Wilson's day was over. His hitting fell off even more drastically than the rest of the league's, to only 13 home runs and a .261 batting average. By 1934, he was out of baseball.

Opposite page: Hack Wilson became a celebrity after his big 1930 season, but his stardom was short-lived.

PEPPER POWERS REDBIRDS TO CHAMPIONSHIP

◆

The 1931 World Series pitting the Cardinals against the Athletics powerhouse—Al Simmons, Jimmie Foxx, Mickey Cochrane, and Lefty Grove—was supposed to crown the Athletics for the third successive year. It, instead, became a showcase for the 27-year-old Cardinals center fielder, Pepper Martin.

John Leonard Roosevelt Martin starred in the minor leagues for seven seasons before crack- ing the Cardinals' lineup in '31. A writer once described him as "a chunky, unshaven hobo who ran the bases like a berserk locomotive, slept in the raw, and swore at pitchers in his sleep." Mak- ing up in effort what he lacked in ability, Mar- tin batted .300 his first season, becoming an inspiration to Depression-era fans with his fear- less outfield play and headfirst slides.

Pepper also fired up the underdog Cardinals in the Series. The Athletics won the first game 6-2 behind Grove, but Martin went 3-for-4 and stole a base. Pepper almost single-handedly won game two, creating both runs with daring baserunning in the 2-0 victory. In the second inning, he stretched a single into a double, stole third, and scored on a sacrifice fly. In the sev-

Rambunctious Cardinals star Pepper Martin led the NL three times in stolen bases.

enth, he singled, stole second, went to third on a ground out, and scored on a squeeze bunt. In game three, Martin led the Cardinals to a 5-2 win, going 2-for-4 and scoring two runs against Grove. Although the Athletics tied the Series in game four behind George Earnshaw's two-hit shutout, Pepper remained hot, knocking both Cardinal hits.

Martin really put on a show in the fifth game. He drove in a run with a sacrifice fly in the first inning, beat out a bunt in the fourth, knocked a two-run homer in the sixth, and delivered an RBI single in the eighth. Martin's four RBI led the Cardinals to a 5-1 victory and a 3-2 lead in the Series. After five games, Pepper had a .667 batting average (12-for-18), five runs scored, four doubles, one homer, five RBI, and four stolen bases.

Philadelphia tied the Series, winning game six 8-1, but that couldn't sap the momentum that Martin gave the Cardinals. St. Louis won game seven 4-2 at home. Though Pepper went hitless in the last two games, he halted a ninth-inning Athletics rally in the final game with a sprinting shoestring catch of a line drive.

Called "The Wild Horse of the Osage," Martin became a World Series hero again in 1934. With 11 hits in that seven-game Series victory over the Detroit Tigers, Martin ended his career with a record .418 World Series batting average. He will, however, be remembered for the '31 Series—what the legendary baseball writer Red Smith called "the greatest one-man show the baseball world has ever known."

RUTH CALLS HIS SHOT IN '32 SERIES

◆

The 1932 World Series seized a place in history for a single incident: Babe Ruth's "called shot" home run off Cubs pitcher Charlie Root. Like so many other Ruth anecdotes, this one grows blurrier upon closer inspection. Regardless of its veracity, the story does reflect a broader truth—that the myth of the mighty Babe transcends baseball.

Ruth had a good year in 1932, hitting .341 with 41 home runs. Although Philadelphia's Jimmie Foxx led the American League in

Babe Ruth in the 1920s.

homers—the first time that someone other than the Babe had won the homer crown since he had stomach problems in 1925—the Bronx Bombers still had the most powerful offense in baseball. They scored 1,002 runs, won 107 games, and left Foxx and the A's 13 games in the dust. In the Series, the Yankees steamed over the Cubs in four straight, outscoring them 37-19; none of the games was closer than two runs.

Ruth's disputed feat came at one of the few close moments in the World Series—with the score tied 4-4 in the fifth inning of game three. This was the first game in Chicago, and the fans, smelling disaster, were in an ugly mood. So were the players, although for different reasons. The Yankees felt that their skipper, Joe McCarthy, had been badly treated when he was fired by Chicago two years before, and they said so publicly. They also resented the Cubs for voting only a half-share in the Series money to former Yankee Mark Koenig, who had been traded to Chicago for the stretch drive and hit .353.

When Ruth came to bat, then, all kinds of abuse rained down on him from the stands. The Cubs bench jockeys hurled insults and Ruth answered back as he stepped in and took Root's first pitch for a strike; some said they then saw him hold up one finger. Two balls later, he looked at strike two and again appeared to make some kind of gesture. Finally, Ruth swung and knocked a loud two-run homer into the center-field bleachers.

These are more or less the facts. There are,

Babe Ruth, shown celebrating with a fine cigar, hit his famous "called shot" in the 1932 fall classic, his final Series. It was the last of his 15 World Series homers, a total that ranks second on the all-time list.

however, as many different accounts as witnesses. Root always fiercely denied that any "call" had taken place. If it had, he insisted, Ruth would have been digging ball three out of his ear. Ruth himself was just as adamant in refusing to confirm or deny a thing. On-deck hitter Lou Gehrig and at least one sportswriter, however, said that they were sure they saw Babe point out where and when he was going to hit a home run and then proceed to deliver. Every time there is someone who has some proof that he did, someone else comes back with proof that he did not. Fact or fabrication, the myth lives on.

HUBBELL Ks FIVE STRAIGHT HALL OF FAMERS

◆

The midsummer classic between the AL and NL in 1934 was titled "The Game of the Century." The All-Star Game had been inaugurated the year before as a gimmick to hype Chicago's World's Fair and to build circulation for the *Chicago Tribune*, whose sports editor, Arch Ward, conceived the idea. Babe Ruth's two-run homer had won the first "exhibition" for the American League, 4-2, and the NL sought to avenge the loss in the second game, held at New York's Polo Grounds.

New York Giants manager Bill Terry selected his ace pitcher, "King Carl" Hubbell, as the NL's starter in front of his home fans. The left-handed Hubbell had won the Most Valuable Player Award in 1933, leading the league in wins, ERA, and shutouts. Hubbell's "out" pitch was his screwball, which broke away from right-handed hitters and broke in on lefties.

"The Meal Ticket," as Hubbell was also called, would need all his pitches working when facing the AL's power-laden lineup, which

Giants left-hander Carl Hubbell, pitching game one of the 1936 World Series, threw a puzzling "screwball" that broke away from left-handed hitters.

looked more like a future Hall of Fame ballot—Charlie Gehringer, Heinie Manush, Babe Ruth, Lou Gehrig, Jimmie Foxx, Al Simmons, Joe Cronin, and Bill Dickey.

Before the game, Hubbell huddled with his catcher, Gabby Hartnett of the Chicago Cubs. "They've never seen a screwball like you have before," Hartnett told Hubbell. "We'll waste everything except the screwball."

It initially appeared as if the strategy would backfire, as Hubbell got into trouble before many of the 48,363 fans could get comfortable. Gehringer lined the first pitch into center for a single, and after Hubbell got ahead of Manush 0-2, he walked him on the next four pitches—not what a pitcher wants to do with Ruth, Gehrig, and Foxx next in line.

Hubbell fell behind Ruth, 1-0, then broke three straight screwballs over the heart of the plate—none of which the Bambino could touch. Next up was Gehrig, the most feared RBI man in the game. On one and two, the "Iron Horse" swung so hard missing a screwball that he almost screwed himself into the ground. The powerful right-handed-hitting Foxx didn't fare any better. After two frustrating screwballs at the knees, his immense swing at the third almost caused him to fall down.

In the second inning, with his team up 1-0, Hubbell faced the tough Al Simmons, who was known to talk himself into a hitting frenzy. A few Hubbell scroogies later, Simmons was talking to himself as he walked back to the bench. When the Washington Senator player-manag-

Above: Giant ace "King Carl" Hubbell. *Opposite page:* Hubbell's consecutive strikeouts of five Hall of Famers in the 1934 All-Star Game still ranks as one of the midsummer classic's greatest moments.

er Joe Cronin also went down on strikes, Hubbell had whiffed five of the game's greatest hitters in succession. Yankee catcher Bill Dickey ended the streak with a single.

The American League eventually won the contest, 9-7, scoring all their runs in the three innings after Hubbell departed. The outcome mattered little, however; this game belonged to King Carl Hubbell.

TREASURY OF BASEBALL

DIZZY DELIVERS 30 DECISIONS

◆

*I*n his first two seasons pitching for the St. Louis Cardinals, 1931 and 1932, Jay Hannah "Dizzy" Dean won 38 games. With his younger brother, Paul (also known as "Daffy"), joining the team in 1934, the colorful Dizzy boldly predicted that "Me and Paul will probably win 40 games." As it turned out, Dizzy was a better pitcher than prognosticator. The brother act won almost 50 games. Diz became the premier pitcher in baseball, leading the Cardinals to the National League pennant with 30 victories, and Paul produced 19 wins.

Dizzy featured an explosive fastball, a tight-breaking curve, and excellent command of both pitches. He was as aggressive on the mound as he was fun-loving off it, and he would intimidate hitters by throwing his fastball high and inside. Sometimes he would tell hitters that the heater was coming and still throw it by them.

In '34, Dean's superb pitching kept the "Gashouse Gang" Cardinals on the heels of the New York Giants, who led the league for most of the year. Dizzy then sparked a 21-4 September spurt that enabled the Cards to tie the Giants on the 28th. While the Brooklyn Dodgers were beating the Giants, the Cardinals won their last three games—two on shutouts by Dean—to take the pennant. Dizzy was named the Most Valuable Player, with his 30 victories (against only seven losses) for a .811 winning percentage. Dizzy also led the league in shutouts (seven) and strikeouts (196). He placed second in ERA (2.65), complete games (24), and games pitched (50). He even kicked in with seven saves out of the bullpen, tying him for second in the NL. Opponents had a .241 batting average and a .286 on-base percentage against Dean, third best in the league. The Cardinal offense also helped Dean. The Redbirds were the highest-scoring team in the loop, with 799 runs that year.

Before the World Series against the Detroit Tigers, Dizzy characteristically insisted that "Me 'n' Paul will win two games each." Though Detroit beat Dizzy 3-1 in game five, his victories in games one and seven and Paul's wins in games three and six gave St. Louis its second championship in four years. To those who chided his boastfulness, Dizzy pitched one of his immortal lines: "If you say you're going to do it, and you go out and do it, it ain't bragging."

Dizzy Dean, second from left.

VANDER MEER HURLS CONSECUTIVE NO-NOs IN 1938

◆

Perhaps the most unlikely thing about Johnny "Dutch Master" Vander Meer's feat of throwing two successive no-hit games in June of 1938 is that it was Vander Meer who pitched them. First scouted in a New Jersey Sunday School League (where he pitched three consecutive no-hitters), the erratic, fire-balling Vander Meer bounced around the Dodgers' and Braves' minor-league systems before landing with the Reds' Durham, North Carolina, farm club. There he struck out 295 batters in 214 innings. Cincinnati called him up for the 1937 season, putting him under the guidance of manager Bill McKechnie, who worked on developing a more consistent delivery of his impressive fastball. After a 6-10 start in 1938, Vander Meer settled into a winning groove. On June 11, he no-hit the Braves 3-0 at home. He set down the first nine Boston batters in order and then the final 13.

His next start, June 15, 1938, was a sellout, as Brooklyn's Ebbets Field became the second big-league park to host a game of night baseball. How much the brand-new, untested lights con-

Fireballing Reds lefty Johnny Vander Meer hurled back-to-back no-hitters in June 1938.

tributed to Vander Meer's second no-hitter will never be known. In any case, by the middle innings, the 40,000-strong Brooklyn crowd began to root for Vander Meer, who held the Dodgers to a pair of walks in the seventh inning and breezed along with a 6-0 lead until the ninth. All of a sudden, his wildness returned. He threw three off-target pitches before retiring the leadoff man, Buddy Hassett, on a dribbler. Eighteen pitches later, Babe Phelps, Cookie Lavagetto, and Dolph Camilli had loaded the bases on free passes, and slugging outfielder Ernie Koy was up. But Vander Meer escaped danger as Koy grounded to third baseman Lew Riggs, who threw very carefully to home for the force; the next batter, Leo Durocher, flied out to short center field.

Even though Vander Meer remained overpowering—he led the NL in strikeouts from 1941 to 1943—he never again pitched as well as he had in the second half of 1938, when he reeled off nine straight wins to finish 15-10 with a 3.12 ERA.

Vander Meer's feat hasn't been matched. Four pitchers—Allie Reynolds, Virgil Trucks, Jim Maloney, and Nolan Ryan—have thrown two no-hitters in the same season. Two pitchers have come within one hit of equaling him. In 1923, Howard Ehmke's bid for a second straight no-hitter was ruined by an infield hit that easily could have been ruled an error. Ewell Blackwell came even closer to the record in 1947, giving up a hit in the ninth inning of what would have been his second no-hitter.

HARTNETT HOMERS IN THE GLOAMIN'

◆

On Sept. 9, 1938, Chicago Cubs catcher Gabby Hartnett found himself living everyone's baseball fantasy: It's the bottom of the ninth in the year's most important game, the score is tied, there are two outs, and it's been announced that the game will be called for darkness after one more batter. Down in the count 0-2, Hartnett swats a curveball deep into the dusk to win the game.

Hartnett's blow was the culmination of a series of improbabilities. He was a veteran catch-

Hall of Famer Gabby Hartnett spent 19 of his 20 major-league seasons with the Chicago Cubs. Most feel he was the best catcher of the NL's first 90 years.

Happy Cub fans and teammates escort 38-year-old player-manager Gabby Hartnett across the plate after his famous "Homer in the Gloamin.'" It was by far the most famous of Hartnett's 236 major-league home runs.

er near the end of a career that included an MVP Award, a cumulative batting average of .297, and the then records for overall games caught with 1,790 and home runs by a catcher with 236. He was also Cubs owner Philip K. Wrigley's surprise choice to succeed Charlie Grimm as manager in midseason 1938. The move seemed to have no effect on the Cubs, who continued to bring up the rear of a four-team pennant race with the Pirates, Giants, and Reds. The Cubs then began to climb until, after sweeping a Labor Day twin-bill from first-place Pittsburgh, Chicago moved into second place at three and one-half games back. The NL sched-

ule was thrown into chaos by the arrival of a hurricane on the Eastern seaboard. Both teams lost important games to heavy rains, but Pittsburgh was most hurt; the Pirates were washed out of four games against last-place Philadelphia and penultimate Brooklyn. With a week left in the season and its lead down to a game and one-half, Pittsburgh faced Chicago in a decisive three-game showdown. In the first game of the series, a sore-armed Dizzy Dean somehow lasted into the ninth inning and won it 2-1.

Game two was a seesaw affair. The Cubs scored one in the first inning, then Pittsburgh's Johnny Rizzo hit a solo homer to tie it in the sixth. In the eighth, the Cubs again fell behind by two runs and again rallied in the bottom of the inning. With the tying runs across and two out, Pirates right fielder Paul Waner cut down the go-ahead run at the plate. The score remained five-all after Charlie Root retired the Pirates in the ninth in increasing darkness. Pittsburgh's Mace Brown got Phil Cavaretta on a fly and Carl Reynolds on a ground out, setting the stage for one of the most storied shots in baseball history. Thanks to some forgotten headline writer's search for another way to say "twilight," the word "gloamin'" has been forever linked to Hartnett.

The Pirates never recovered from Hartnett's homer, losing 10-1 the next day. For the Cubs, the series-sweep capped a 10-game winning streak and a 20-3 pennant stretch drive. In the World Series, however, the Yankees knocked the gloamin' out of Chicago 4-0.

THE IRON HORSE'S CONSECUTIVE-GAME STREAK CONCLUDES

◆

*L*ou Gehrig wore many nicknames during his 15-year career with the New York Yankees between 1925 and 1939, but none fit him better than "The Iron Horse."

From the day he became the Yankees starting first baseman on June 2, 1925 (replacing the injured Wally Pipp), until he removed himself from the lineup on May 2, 1939, Gehrig played in every game, despite illness or injury. He once played the day after being hit so hard on the head with a pitch, it was thought his skull was fractured. On those few occasions during road trips when Gehrig felt he would hurt the team by playing, manager Joe McCarthy would put Lou first in the line-up as the shortstop, then replace him in the bottom of the first with Frank Crosetti.

During his 15 years of nonstop playing, Gehrig was a superstar of the era, second only to teammate Babe Ruth. Gehrig won the Most Valuable Player Award as a member of the fabled "Murderers' Row" in 1927; won a batting title

Lou Gehrig officially retires from baseball on "Lou Gehrig Appreciation Day" at Yankee Stadium.

and Triple Crown in 1934; took the American League home run titles in 1931, '34, and '36; and drove in over 150 runs seven times, still a major-league record. He had an AL-record 184 RBI in 1931. Gehrig helped lead the Yankees to six world championships and ranks in the top 10 in 10 World Series hitting departments. Only Ruth had more career home runs than did Gehrig in the late 1930s.

But it was during the 1938 Series, when he batted just .286, that Gehrig's skills showed signs of eroding. In spring training the following year, the 36-year-old Yankee captain's hitting reflexes seemed slow, and he didn't move around first base with his usual grace. On May 1, Gehrig was batting under .150, and the day before he had left five men on base. He told McCarthy to scratch him from the lineup for the team's May 2 game in Detroit. When the Yankees were announced without Gehrig's name and Tigers fans were told Lou had voluntarily removed himself from the lineup, Detroit fans gave Gehrig a standing ovation. His streak of 2,130 consecutive games played was over.

"It's tough to see your mates on base," Gehrig explained, "have a chance to win a game, and not be able to do anything about it."

A few weeks later the world discovered why Gehrig couldn't do anything about it. He had

Above: Lou Gehrig scores one of his 1,888 career runs.
Top: Gehrig hit .340 lifetime.

contracted the rare muscle disease amyotrophic lateral sclerosis, a fatal illness now called "Lou Gehrig's Disease." When it was discovered in May 1939 that he was dying, the team announced that July Fourth would also be "Lou Gehrig Appreciation Day." With two generations of Bronx Bombers and nearly 62,000 fans present to honor "The Pride of the Yankees," Gehrig made the most emotional and memorable speech in baseball history.

"I may have been given a bad break," Gehrig told the crowd, "but I have an awful lot to live for. Today, I consider myself the luckiest man on the face of the earth."

Two years later, Gehrig died just two weeks short of his 38th birthday.

DiMAGGIO HITS IN 56 STRAIGHT GAMES

◆

To those who saw him play, Joe DiMaggio had a mystical grace about him that transcended his statistics, great as they were. It is perhaps fitting then that he had a predilection for streaks. DiMaggio earned his major-league record 56-game hitting streak in 1941; immediately afterward, he started in on a 16-game streak. When he was 18 years old and playing in the Pacific Coast League, he put together a 61-game streak.

It wasn't news when Joe started his streak with a scratch single off the White Sox' Edgar Smith on May 15. Things got interesting around game 30, when the newspapers began to dust off old hitting-streak marks, like George McQuinn's 34-game streak, which DiMaggio equaled on June 21. By the time he surpassed Ty Cobb's 1911 40-game streak and George Sisler's 1922 American League record 41, the "Yankee Clipper" was a national sensation. Pressure was building not only on Joe but on official scorers, fielders, and especially pitchers, who wanted to end the streak but not to cheat posterity by pitching around him. On July 2, DiMaggio homered off Boston's Dick Newsome to move past the major-league record of 44 games set by Baltimore's Wee Willie Keeler back in 1897 (before foul balls counted as strikes).

Joe DiMaggio won two batting titles, two slugging crowns, and two home run championships. His 56-game hitting streak in 1941 led to a .357 average.

"The Yankee Clipper" still symbolizes the Yankees' glory years of the 1930s and 1940s. DiMaggio was a great hitter, a fast runner, and a fine outfielder with a strong throwing arm who starred in 10 World Series.

Two weeks later, 67,468 Cleveland fans saw the streak come to an end. Twice, third baseman Ken Keltner made sparkling plays on DiMaggio drives down the line. In the eighth inning, DiMaggio hit a hard grounder up the middle that appeared to take a sudden hop toward the glove of shortstop Lou Boudreau, who started a 6-4-3 double play.

Looking at the statistical summary, DiMaggio's streak becomes even more miraculous. Overall, he batted .408 (relatively low considering that he had to distribute only 91 hits over the 56 games). He made four hits in a game only four times and 34 times kept the streak alive with a single hit. On several occasions the streak hung by the slenderest of threads—many of them, curiously, coming against the White Sox. In games 30 and 31, DiMaggio got bad-hop singles off the body of White Sox shortstop Luke Appling; in No. 54, his only hit was a dribbler that Chicago third baseman Bob Kennedy couldn't handle. Facing his great pitching nemesis, Sox righty Johnny Rigney, four times during the streak, DiMaggio barely managed to squeak by, going 1-3, 1-5, 1-4, and 1-3 for a .267 average.

DiMaggio's streak carried the Yankees from a .500 record to first place by a good margin. Far from shortening his swing for the sake of a record, Joe produced runs in abundance; in 223 at bats, he scored 56 runs, drove in 55, and hit half of his season total of 30 homers. This, and not the streak, is why DiMaggio was voted MVP over the .406-hitting Ted Williams.

WILLIAMS IS LAST TO BETTER .400 BARRIER

◆

Ted Williams and Joe DiMaggio were two of the greatest hitters in history. Both contemporaries and rivals, the Red Sox slugger and the Yankees center fielder were as different from each other as two players could be. No season illustrates this better than 1941, when both performed marvels,

since unequaled, with different results. DiMaggio had "The Streak," batted .357, and helped the Yankees take the pennant. Williams was the last batter to hit over .400, led DiMaggio in on-base average .551 to .440 and in slugging .735 to .643, and finished second by 17 games.

Williams was a lifetime .344 hitter who won the Triple Crown in 1942 and '47. He hit over .320 in 13 seasons and won seven batting titles. Williams was a good candidate to bat .400, primarily because of his terrific strike-zone judgment. His batting eye may have been the best of

Ted Williams looked up to few, but he respected Red Sox coach Hugh Duffy, who won the Triple Crown in 1894 with a .440 batting average, 18 homers, and 145 RBI.

"The Splendid Splinter"

all time; 11 times he drew more than 100 walks in a season and three times he drew more than 160. Besides the fact that this put opposing pitchers under pressure to throw strikes, Williams's ability to draw bases on balls meant that in his full seasons he averaged only 490 at bats—and many people feel that it's a lot easier to reach a .400 average in 500 at bats than it is in 600.

As Williams freely admitted, there were a few additional factors working in his favor in 1941. The first was Fenway Park, which helped him so much throughout his career that DiMaggio, who played in an extreme pitchers' park, actually outhit Williams on the road (.333 lifetime to .328). Anoth-

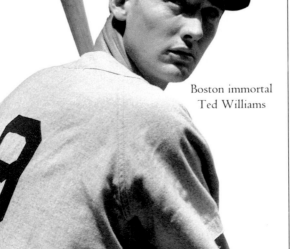

Boston immortal
Ted Williams

er was a minor leg injury that reduced Williams's at bats further, to 456, and spared him two weeks of playing in the cold, windy Boston April weather. A Red Sox pitcher named Joe "Burrhead" Dobson helped Ted hone his skills during that time by playing daily simulated games. Dobson liked to bear down hard and use his whole pitching repertoire, giving Williams what he called "the most batting practice of my life, and the best."

All this, combined with the "good luck" presence of Red Sox coach Hugh Duffy (who in 1894 hit for the highest batting average in major-league history, .440), helped Williams reach as high as .436 in June. He then began a long, steady slide, going down to .413 in September, then falling to .3995 with a doubleheader against Philadelphia left to play on the last day of the season (by contemporary baseball rules, this would round out to an official .400). Red Sox manager Joe Cronin urged him to sit the games out; Williams refused. That day, Williams went 6-for-8 with a home run to hit .406 the hard way.

OWEN'S PASSED BALL UNDERMINES BUMS

◆

Joe DiMaggio's 56-game hitting streak and Ted Williams's .406 batting average may have been the top individual baseball stories of 1941, but the best team story was the Brooklyn Dodgers. The fabled "Bums" won the NL flag for the first time in 21 years.

Brooklyn general manager Larry MacPhail was the architect of that Dodgers team, trading for players like second baseman Billy Herman from the Chicago Cubs and outfielder Joe Medwick from the St. Louis Cardinals. Another player MacPhail grabbed from the Cards was catcher Mickey Owen, who would figure prominently in one of the most memorable strikeouts in World Series history.

The 1941 Series between the Dodgers and the New York Yankees would be the first of many between the crosstown rivals, and the Yankees were heavily favored. But the Bums played hard under 35-year-old manager Leo Durocher, winning game two 3-2 and losing games one and three by one run each, 3-2 and 2-1.

Game four was a must-win for Brooklyn, but they fell behind 3-2 after four innings. In the top

Much of the action in the 1941 series revolved around Dodger catcher Mickey Owen.
Here he loses his glove but retires Yankee Joe Gordon.

Mickey Owen played 13 years in the majors but is best remembered for a passed ball. Owen stayed in the bigs until age 38, and he was a fine contact hitter.

of the fifth, the Yankees loaded the bases with two out, but colorful Dodgers reliever Hugh Casey stopped the threat. Casey then pitched three scoreless innings while his team went ahead, 4-3.

In the top of the ninth, Casey retired the first two batters. He then went to a 3-2 count on Tommy Henrich. The next pitch (which some claimed was a spitball) sunk out of the strike zone, but Henrich couldn't stop his swing, and the game appeared to be over. But as Dodger fans cheered and Casey began walking off the mound in triumph, catcher Mickey Owen was racing for the ball, which had hit his mitt and bounced in foul ground behind the plate. Henrich instinctively ran for first base. The inning—

and the Yanks—were still alive, but almost 34,000 Dodgers fans went silent, fearful that the mighty Bronx Bombers would take advantage of the miscue.

Sure enough, against a tiring Casey, DiMaggio followed with a single, Charlie Keller doubled in two runs, Bill Dickey walked, and Joe Gordon doubled in two more runs, putting the Yankees ahead, 7-4. The Dodgers would go down quietly in the ninth, and then in game five, 3-1. Thus began a new tradition that would last until 1955: the Dodgers losing the World Series to the Yankees and Brooklyn fans crying, "Wait 'Til Next Year."

A dropped strike-three pitch turned a fine catcher into one of the game's all-time goats. As *The New York Times* wrote the day after the fateful fourth game, Mickey Owen's passed ball "doubtless will live through the ages of baseball like the Snodgrass muff and the Merkel [boner]."

Yankee slugger Tommy Henrich led the AL twice in triples and hit .282 in an 11-year career.

ST. LOUIS BROWNS WIN FIRST PENNANT

◆

The St. Louis teams in both the NL and AL were the last original franchises to win a pennant. It took 51 years, but such talents as Rogers Hornsby and Jim Bottomley finally brought National League pennant-winning-caliber play to the Cardinals in 1926. Rather than improving their club, the St. Louis Browns waited for World War II and the military draft to bring the rest of the American League down to their level.

The Brownies epitomized the ragged state of wartime baseball. They had nine players age 34 or older and history's first-ever all-4F infield.

The Browns had a dismal history before 1944. The franchise bottomed out in 1939, when the team lost 111 games and came in 64 ½ games in back of New York. In the years between 1940 and 1943, they averaged 25 games out and fifth place in the standings. Even counting the pennant season of 1944, they drew a total of just 3,330,861 fans for the entire decade; in 1941, fewer than 200,000 fans saw the Browns play. They weren't much better after 1944, finishing sixth or seventh seven times before giving up and moving to Baltimore for the 1954 season.

But in 1944, St. Louis had its moment of glory. Led by 23-year-old slugging shortstop Vern Stephens (who hit .293 with 20 home runs and a league-high 109 RBI), .295-hitting Milt Byrnes, and Mike Kreevich (the only member of the team to bat over .300—at .301), the Browns offense scored a respectable 684 runs. Their pitching was solid as well. Old Nels Potter and young Jack Kramer won 19 and 17

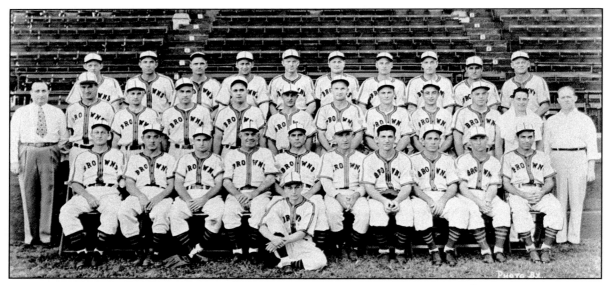

The 1944 American League champion St. Louis Browns featured no Hall of Famers, but their gritty style made them the best, if only for one season.

The Browns celebrate after clinching the 1944 AL pennant on the season's last day. Winning pitcher Sig Jakucki is front row center, and Vern Stephens and Chet Laabs, who both homered in the game, surround him.

games; the staff was rounded out by Bob Muncrief, Denny Galehouse, and the 34-year-old Sig Jakucki. Jakucki was a classic product of a time when teams had to advertise for ballplayers in the help-wanted sections of newspapers. An 0-3 lifetime pitcher who had retired in 1939, Jakucki was re-discovered in a Houston factory league and given a spot in the Browns rotation. He went 13-9 with a 3.55 ERA.

Jakucki's 13th victory gave St. Louis the pennant after a tense, three-team September dogfight. On Sept. 29, St. Louis knocked the New York Yankees out of contention with a doubleheader sweep, followed by another win the next day. The Detroit Tigers won two of three from Washington to drop into a tie for first place with the Browns. Then, on the final day of the season, Tigers 27-game winner and AL ERA-leader

Dizzy Trout lost to the Senators while two homers by Chet Laabs and one by Stephens gave the Browns the victory over New York to clinch the pennant, by one game, over Detroit. The Brownies' .578 winning percentage tied a then record for the lowest by a pennant-winner—set in 1926 by the Cardinals.

The 1944 Cardinals won their third-straight NL pennant to make that year's World Series a one-city affair. It was baseball's only all-St. Louis Series. It was a homey event: The Browns were the Cardinals' landlords at Sportsman's Park. Managers Billy Southworth (Cards) and Luke Sewell (Browns), accustomed to one team always being on the road, found their shared apartment suddenly cramped.

The Cardinals took the six-game Series in six days, but the underdog Browns put up a fight. They outpitched the Cardinals but were let down by their hitting and fielding. Don Gutteridge and Vern Stephens made three errors apiece, and the Browns committed 10 to the Cards' one.

George McQuinn scores after hitting the only World Series home run in Browns history.

GREENBERG'S GRAND SLAM WINS CROWN

◆

By late summer of 1945, the American League race looked like a near repeat of 1944, with Washington, New York, St. Louis, and Detroit all in the hunt. That year, however, former major leaguers began to return from military service. The returnee with the biggest impact on the season was slugger Hank Greenberg, who came in to pick up a Tigers team that was barely holding on, thanks to the pitching of Hal New-houser (who went 25-9 with a 1.81 ERA and won the MVP Award).

It wasn't the first time that Greenberg's heroics had made the difference for the Tigers. In 1934, he batted .339 with 63 doubles as Detroit won the pennant. The next year, he had 36 homers, 170 RBI, a .328 average, and was voted the unanimous MVP; Detroit won again. After losing 1936 to injury, he upped his home run total in 1937 to 40, hit .337, and knocked in 183 runs—the third-highest RBI count in history. In '38, he scored and drove in a combined 290 runs while confronting Babe Ruth's homer record, falling two short at 58. In 1940, Greenberg won the MVP for the second time as his

Hank Greenberg's smooth, powerful stroke produced 331 major-league home runs. One of them won the 1945 pennant for the Detroit Tigers.

50 doubles, 41 homers, and 150 RBI paced Detroit to another pennant.

One of the first big leaguers to enter the service, Greenberg left Detroit 19 games into the 1941 campaign, not to return until July 1, 1945. He homered in his first game back, against Philadelphia, and then began to play himself back into shape. By mid-September, Detroit had a one and one-half game lead after taking three of five from second-place Washington.

The pennant race in 1945, as it did the year before, came down to a crucial series between Detroit and St. Louis; the Senators would gain a tie if the Browns could manage a doubleheader sweep on the final day of the season. Virgil Trucks started for Detroit in game one against the 15-11 Nels Potter for St. Louis. With the Tigers up 2-1, Newhouser relieved Trucks in the sixth inning and narrowly escaped a bases-loaded, one-out situation. In the seventh, though, he allowed Gene Moore and Pete Gray to score the tying and go-ahead runs. The score remained 3-2 in the ninth, when leadoff man Hub Walker, pinch-hitting for Newhouser, walked, and Skeeter Webb bunted his way on. After another bunt moved both runners into scoring position, Potter walked Doc Cramer to load the bases and go for the double-play with Greenberg. Greenberg clouted his 11th career grand slam to win the game and another pennant for Detroit. In 270 at-bats, less than a half-season, the 34-year-old Greenberg had scored 47 runs and driven in 60 on 35 extra-base hits to finish with a .311 batting average.

MVP Hal Newhouser led the 1945 Detroit Tigers to a world championship.

SLAUGHTER'S DASH HOME WINS SERIES

◆

Stan Musial and Ted Williams returned home from the war in 1946 to lead their respective teams to pennants. Musial batted .365 with 50 doubles and 124 runs scored. Williams hit .342 with 38 homers, as Boston finished 12 games up. Both were MVPs.

As has happened so many times in postseason history, the stars fizzled in the 1946 World Series—Musial hit .222 and Williams hit .200—and vacated center stage in favor of such lesser lights as Rudy York, Harry Brecheen, and Enos "Country" Slaughter. Even rookie catcher Joe Garagiola had a four-hit game.

In the second-most dramatic game of the seven-game Series, York's 10th-inning home run beat Cardinals 21-game winner Howie Pollet 3-2 in game one. The next day, Brecheen, the lefty who had gone only 15-15 on the season, shut down Boston on four hits to win 3-0 and evened the Series. Boston ace Boo Ferriss then unevened it 4-0 with an equally masterful six-hitter; York contributed a three-run homer off

Enos "Country" Slaughter is captured in a rare inactive moment. His mad dash around the base paths won the 1946 World Series for St. Louis.

Enos Slaughter had 2,383 hits.

In the Cardinal half of the eighth, Slaughter singled to lead off. Two quick outs later, left-handed slap-hitter Harry Walker followed with a liner over the shortstop into left-center field, and, somehow, Slaughter scored from first base. Brecheen got his third win, and St. Louis won the Series 4-3. This play is still being debated today: Did Pesky hesitate before relaying the center fielder's throw home? Was it the fault of second baseman Bobby Doerr or third baseman Mike Higgins for not warning Pesky? Should Walker's hit have been scored a single instead of a double? Or did Boston do everything more or less right, but Slaughter, with two outs and World Series money on the line, simply ran three base-lengths faster than two men could throw a baseball roughly the same distance?

loser Murry Dickson. The two teams traded victories again in games four and five. St. Louis brought back Brecheen for game six; his second Series win, by a 4-1 score, set up a Dickson-Ferriss confrontation to decide the championship.

The score was 3-1 Cardinals after seven; Dickson had held Boston to three hits—and had doubled in the second run and scored the third. Then, in the top of the eighth, Red Sox Rip Russell singled and George Metkovich doubled to put the tying runs in scoring position with none out. Card skipper Eddie Dyer signaled to the bullpen for Brecheen to pitch to left-handers Wally Moses and Johnny Pesky, only one day after having gone nine innings. Moses struck out and Pesky lined out, but Dom DiMaggio doubled both runs in to tie the game at 3-3. The pop-up by Ted Williams let the go-ahead run die on second.

Boston infielder
Bobby Doerr

LAVAGETTO AND GIONFRIDDO STAR IN '47 WORLD SERIES

◆

The Brooklyn Dodgers and the New York Yankees each won pennants in 1947. It had been six years since the crosstown rivals had met in the World Series, so the cast of characters on both sides was vastly different from the teams that faced each other in the 1941 Series. Oh, Joe DiMaggio was still around, but the two most prominent new faces were Dodgers rookie second baseman Jackie Robinson and Yankees rookie catcher Yogi Berra. The most memorable moments of the 1947 Series (besides the fact that it was the first fall classic to be televised), however, were not supplied by the high-profile rookies, but by two Dodgers who weren't exactly household names, even in Brooklyn.

The Yankees were leading the Series two games to one going into the pivotal game four at Ebbets Field. The Bronx Bombers starter was Bill Bevens, who was a mediocre 7-13 on the season. Bevens was wild but fast on this day, and though he was walking batters all afternoon (he

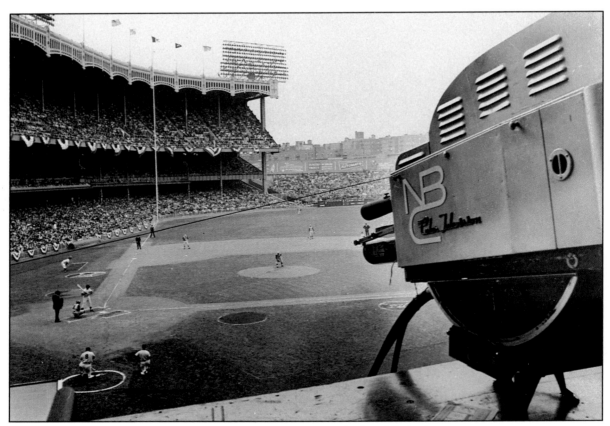

NBC televised the 1947 Series, the first fall classic shown on the small screen.

set a Series record with 10), he constantly escaped trouble. By the bottom of the ninth, the Yanks were leading 2-1 (great relief pitching by Hugh Casey had kept the game close), and Bevens was pitching a no-hitter.

Two outs away from immortality, Bevens walked Carl Furillo. After pinch-runner Al Gionfriddo stole second, Pete Reiser was intentionally walked. This was a controversial decision by Yankees manager Bucky Harris, since it's a baseball sin to put the winning run on base. Cookie Lavagetto, batting for Eddie Stanky, then blasted Bevens's second pitch off the right field wall, breaking up the no-hitter and winning the game 3-2 for the Dodgers.

The Yankees rebounded to grasp game five 2-1. The Dodgers needed two wins at Yankee Stadium. A crowd of 74,065 watched as the Dodgers went ahead 4-0 in game six, then trailed 5-4, then took the lead again with four runs in the sixth, 8-5. In the bottom of the sixth,

Dodger Cookie Lavagetto

Brooklyn outfielder Al Gionfriddo's amazing catch saved game six of the 1947 Series.

the Yankees put two runners on with two out before Joe DiMaggio stepped up. On left-hander Joe Hatten's first pitch, DiMaggio sent a fly ball to deep left field that looked like a game-tying homer. But Gionfriddo, inserted for defense that inning, raced to the 415 mark, leaped backward, and caught the ball over the bullpen fence in the webbing of his glove just before crashing into the fence. In a rare display of emotion, DiMaggio kicked the dirt at second base. Dodgers announcer Red Barber later told Gionfriddo he'd made "an impossible catch."

Unfortunately, Lavagetto's and Gionfriddo's heroics didn't help Brooklyn win the Series, as the Yankees took game seven 5-2. It didn't even help the two sudden stars keep their jobs. After the '47 Series, they (along with Bill Bevens) never played another game in the major leagues.

INDIANS CAPTURE FIRST AMERICAN LEAGUE PLAYOFF

◆

After getting his team up to fourth place in 1947, the Cleveland Indians' flamboyant owner, Bill Veeck, pulled out all the stops. He had signed Larry Doby (the AL's first black player) in 1947; added in 1948 such role players as Thurman Tucker, Allie Clark, and Russ Christopher; held promotional days for his players and the fans; and in July signed 42-year-old Negro League legend Satchel Paige. Satchel bolstered a pitching staff led by 19-game winner Bob Feller and 20-game winners Bob Lemon and rookie Gene Bearden. Such players as second baseman Joe Gordon (32 homers and 124

RBI), Doby (.301 average with 14 homers and 66 RBI), and third baseman Ken Keltner (31 homers and 119 RBI) provided the offense. It all worked for Veeck as the Indians drew more than 2.2 million fans and were in the middle of the AL's hottest pennant race in years.

The Indians had clinched a tie on the season's next to last day when Bearden beat the Tigers. Detroit's Hal Newhouser then beat Feller in the finale while the Boston Red Sox took the Yankees, leaving the Tribe and the BoSox with identical 96-58 records.

The first pennant playoff in AL history, a one-game affair, was billed as a hitting battle, mainly between Boston's Ted Williams (who batted a league-best .369) and Cleveland's 32-year-old shortstop-manager Lou Boudreau, who hit .355, scored 116 runs, drove in 106 runs, and won the AL Most Valuable Player Award. With the game at Boston's Fenway Park,

The 1948 Cleveland Indians were a veteran club who, despite leading the AL in home runs, batting average, saves, shutouts, and earned-run average, still had to win a one-game playoff with the Boston Red Sox to capture the AL flag.

Hall of Famer Lou Boudreau, the Indians' player-manager, won the 1948 AL MVP
Award. Boudreau walked 98 times that season and fanned only nine times.

Boudreau stacked his lineup with right-handed hitters to go after the huge but close "Green Monster" wall in left field. However, Boudreau shocked everyone by pitching the lefty Bearden rather than one of his righties. Still, any Indians starter would have been better than the 36-year-old journeyman the Sox were throwing—Denny Galehouse.

Boudreau, who had always hit well in Fenway, got the Indians rolling in the first inning with a homer over the 37-foot wall. Boston tied the score immediately in the bottom of the first, even though Boudreau—playing the lefty Williams up the middle—robbed the Splendid Splinter of a hit that could have led to a big inning. The game remained 1-1 until the fourth when both Boudreau and Gordon singled, and then Keltner hit a three-run blast over the Monster. When Boudreau conquered the wall again in the fifth, the score was 6-1, and it was all over for Boston. Bearden fed the Red Sox a steady diet of knuckleballs, held the great Williams to one hit on the day, and won 8-3. Cleveland went on to play another Boston team—the National League's Braves—in the World Series, which they won in six games.

PHILLIE 'WHIZ KIDS' CAPTURE THE FLAG

◆

The young 1950 Phillies, nicknamed the "Whiz Kids," are one of baseball's great Cinderella stories. After coming up 16 games short in 1949, the Phillies found that they had the NL's best pitching staff in 1950. Primarily responsible were a maturing Robin Roberts and Jim Konstanty, one of the early modern-style relief aces who appeared in a league-leading 74 games in relief. Konstanty won 16, saved 22, and was voted NL MVP. The Phils featured a diverse offense, including Eddie Waitkus (102 runs), Richie Ashburn (.303 average), and Del Ennis (.311 average, 126 RBI). They also led the majors in colorful names, including Swish Nicholson, Granny Hamner, Puddin' Head Jones, and the immortal Putsy Caballero. On Sept. 15, this group was steaming along, nine games ahead of second-place Brooklyn.

Then midnight struck. Philadelphia lost eight out of 10, including back-to-back doubleheader sweeps at the hands of the Giants, while the Dodgers were riding a seven-game winning streak. The Phillies' final two games were against Brooklyn at Ebbets Field. When the Dodgers took the first game 7-3, the Phillies had totaled seven blown games in the standings over a nine-day period. One more loss would mean that the season would end in a tie. The

The Phillies ended a 35-year drought by winning the 1950 NL pennant. Despite a mediocre attack (the Phils finished fourth in runs scored), the team had solid pitching and good defense, and were tough enough to outlast the Dodgers.

Phils came into the most important game of the season tired, and hurler Curt Simmons was lost to the Army. With few other options, manager Eddie Sawyer called on Roberts to pitch his third start in five days.

Opposing Roberts was fellow staff ace and 19 game-winner Don Newcombe. The two matched zeroes until the sixth, when the Phillies scored on Jones's RBI single. Dodger Pee Wee Reese tied it up with a homer. There was no more action until the bottom of the ninth, when Cal Abrams drew a walk and Reese singled him to second. Next, Duke Snider singled to center, sending Abrams running for home. Center fielder Richie Ashburn had collected only seven assists on the season, but this time he fired a strike to catcher Andy Seminick that put Abrams out by what Red Smith called "12 fat feet." Roberts then intentionally walked Jackie Robinson, got Carl Furillo on a pop-up, and Gil Hodges on a fly.

In the top of the 10th, Roberts and Waitkus singled, but Ashburn uncharacteristically failed to bunt the runners over. The next batter was outfielder Dick Sisler. A .276 lifetime hitter, he was an unlikely candidate for the hero's role (his father, though, was Hall of Famer George Sisler). Dick had singled three times off Newcombe that day, but his fourth hit was a high opposite-field drive that sliced into the left-field bleachers to win the game for Philadelphia, 4-1.

This was to be the Phillies' last win of 1950, however; they lost the World Series to the Yankees in four straight.

THOMSON'S 'SHOT HEARD 'ROUND THE WORLD'

◆

One of the most memorable moments in baseball history happened on Oct. 1, 1951, when New York Giants outfielder Bobby Thomson hit a ninth-inning three-run homer to beat the Brooklyn Dodgers and rip the collective heart out of fans of "Dem Bums."

It was the climax to a season known in baseball lore as "The Miracle of Coogan's Bluff," in which the Giants managed to overcome a 13½-game deficit with a little more than a month and a half left in the season. The Giants were in sec-

Ralph Branca

ond place on Aug. 12 when—with the help of a 20-year-old Willie Mays—they reeled off 16 straight wins, going 37-7 in their final 44 games. They caught the Dodgers two games from the finish line. Brooklyn had to come back from a 6-1 deficit in the season finale to beat the Phillies in 14 innings 9-8, forcing a three-game playoff between the Giants and Dodgers.

Home runs by Monte Irvin and Thomson led the Giants to a 3-1 victory in game one. The Dodgers won 10-0 in game two. For the deciding game at the Polo Grounds, Sal Maglie, a 23-game winner for the Giants, faced Dodger 20-game winner Don Newcombe. Brooklyn jumped ahead in the first inning on a Jackie Robinson single, and three runs in the eighth gave them a 4-1 lead.

But for these two teams, the ninth inning would become a microcosm of the entire season. With Newcombe tiring, Giants Al Dark and Don Mueller singled. After Monte Irvin popped out, Whitey Lockman kept the rally going with a run-scoring double. With the tying runs in scoring position, Dodgers manager Charlie Dressen brought Ralph Branca in to pitch to Thomson, who wanted to redeem himself for an earlier baserunning blunder.

Brooklyn could have walked Thomson, but that would have meant putting the winning run on base for the next batter, Willie Mays. Branca's first pitch to Thomson was a called strike. The next pitch was a fastball up and in, but Thomson hit it up and out of the park over the head of left fielder Andy Pafko. The ball landed just a few inches over the 315-mark. As Thomson circled the bases, suddenly a baseball immortal, radio broadcaster Russ Hodges screamed into his microphone: "The Giants win the pennant. The Giants win the pennant."

To the New York Giants and the rest of baseball, Thomson's blast was "The Shot Heard 'Round the World."

Bobby Thomson is mobbed following the "Shot Heard 'Round the World." It was Thomson's third homer of the year off Dodger pitcher Ralph Branca.

WILLIE MAYS MAKES, SIMPLY, 'THE CATCH'

◆

*I*n the top of the 10th inning, first game, 1954 World Series, the Cleveland Indians and New York Giants were tied 2-2. Vic Wertz, leading off for the Tribe, lashed a shot up the left-center field gap at the cavernous Polo Grounds, around 440 feet away. The ball looked like it was going to go all the way to the wall for at least a triple, but Willie Mays, the Giants speedy and superb center fielder, backhanded the ball, holding Wertz to a double. The Indians did not get the score, and the Giants eventually won the game in the bottom of the 10th 5-2.

New York wouldn't have even had a chance to win that game if not for a play Mays had made two innings earlier against Wertz—a play known simply as "The Catch."

The score was tied 2-2 in the top of the eighth with runners on first and second and none out. At the plate was Wertz, a fence buster who one season a few years earlier had 37 doubles and 27 homers. Left-hander Don Liddle was brought in for starter Sal Maglie to pitch to the left-hand-hitting Wertz. The strategy appeared to have backfired when Wertz sent Liddle's first delivery on a frozen rope to deep center field. Mays, though, got a great jump on what is the most difficult ball for a center fielder to handle. Racing full speed with his back to the plate, he came within 10 feet from the wall, stretched out his left arm, looked over his left shoulder, and stabbed the ball. He was nearly 460 feet from home plate. Then in one continuous motion, he pivoted toward the field, launched a perfect throw to the infield, and held baserunner Larry Doby from scoring from second base and Al Rosen from advancing from first. The Giants eventually got out of the inning unscathed. Many observers think that Mays's throw was as astonishing as his catch.

Right after the play, Giants radio announcer Russ Hodges said, "Willie Mays just made a catch that must have seemed like an optical illusion to a lot of folks." Dodgers general manager Branch Rickey sent Mays a note that read,

Willie Mays cemented his reputation as the finest defensive outfielder of his day with this catch against Cleveland's Vic Wertz in the 1954 Series.

AMOROS'S CATCH CROWNS 'DEM BUMS'

◆

Besides being a fine outfielder with a strong arm, a dynamic runner, and a great personality, Willie Mays could hit. He is third all-time in homers, and might rank higher had he not spent two seasons in the Army.

"That was the finest catch I've ever seen, and the finest catch I ever hope to see." If Rickey did see similar catches over the next several years, they were probably made by Mays.

The "Say Hey Kid" wasn't through for the day. In the 10th—after making the second spectacular play on Wertz (which Mays himself thought was a tougher play than The Catch)—Willie walked, stole second, and scored the winning run on Monte Irvin's three-run homer. Inspired by Mays, the Giants went on to upset the favored Indians in a four-game sweep.

With rare exceptions, it was always the other guys and never the Brooklyn Dodgers who got the big hit or made the great play in postseason competition. Even when "Dem Bums" did special things, they couldn't convert them into championships. Finally, in 1955, the situation would change, thanks to a hustling little left fielder named Sandy Amoros.

It certainly didn't seem very different in the first two games of the Series against the Yankees, the fifth such matchup between the crosstown rivals (Brooklyn lost the previous four) since 1947. The Yankees—led by Yogi Berra, Mickey Mantle, Billy Martin, and manager Casey Stengel—took the games at Yankee Stadium 6-5 and 4-2. Cries of "Wait Till Next Year" were already echoing throughout Brooklyn, especially since no team had ever turned around a 2-0 deficit in the Series.

The Bums, though, bounced back in Brooklyn, winning all three games played at Ebbets Field—8-3, 8-5, and 5-3. Amoros slugged a two-run homer in game five to help the Dodgers win. Whitey Ford's masterful four-hitter tied the Series at three games apiece, setting the stage for the Dodgers faithful to be heartbroken again.

A crowd of 63,000 watched young Brooklyn left-hander Johnny Podres (the game-three win-

"Next year" became more than a dream for Brooklyn fans in 1955 as the Dodgers finally won the World Series. The team's fans had little time to savor their triumph, however, as the Bums moved west to Los Angeles following the 1957 season.

ner) match zeros with the Yankee Tommy Byrne for three innings. The Dodgers squeezed across single runs in the fourth and sixth for a 2-0 lead going into the bottom of the sixth. Dodger manager Walter Alston inserted Amoros as a defensive replacement in left field. It would prove to be the key strategic move of the Series. Amoros replaced Junior Gilliam, who in turn moved to second base replacing Don Zimmer.

With nobody out, Billy Martin walked and Gil McDougald beat out a bunt. Berra, Hank Bauer, and Moose Skowron were next up, and Dodgers fans held their collective breath.

Brooklyn's outfield shifted toward right field for the left-handed hitting Berra, but Yogi crossed them up, hitting a long drive down the left field line. The blast looked like a sure hit, but Amoros raced toward the line, and at the last instant, reached out and speared the ball about knee high. It was fortunate that Amoros was left-handed so he didn't have to backhand the ball. Amoros abruptly stopped, whirled, and fired the ball to shortstop Pee Wee Reese, who in turn relayed to Gil Hodges, doubling McDougald off first base. McDougald, sure that the ball would drop (as did everyone else in Ebbets Field), had already passed second base before reversing his direction.

It would prove to be the last Yankees threat of the game as Podres allowed only three singles over the next three and a third innings. Next year had finally arrived for the fans of Brooklyn.

LARSEN TWIRLS PERFECT GAME IN 1956 FALL CLASSIC

◆

What made the 1956 World Series different from the one played in 1955 was that the Yankees beat Brooklyn in seven. What made the two similar was that another unknown player stole the spotlight and is now an immortal.

Going into the Series, 27-year-old Don Larsen was a lifetime 30-40 pitcher. In the second game of the '56 Series, he couldn't even make it past the second inning. But for one magical moment, Larsen pitched the only perfect game in Series history.

The Series was tied at two wins apiece when Larsen, an 11-7 pitcher on the season, started game five at Yankee Stadium. Employing an unusual no-windup delivery that he instituted late in the season, Larsen struck out two Dodgers in the first inning. One was Pee Wee Reese, who he fanned on a 3-2 count. It would be the only time Larsen would throw three balls to a hitter the entire game. In fact, in throwing just 97 pitches for the game, Larsen never hurled more than 15 pitches in any inning.

Dodgers hurler Sal "The Barber" Maglie matched Larsen out for out, retiring 11 Yankees

Above: Don Larsen and Yogi Berra. *Opposite page:* Don Larsen.

in a row. The 12th batter, Mickey Mantle, homered in the fourth. When the Bombers picked up another run in the sixth, all eyes turned to Larsen.

Larsen's defense saved his perfecto with dazzling plays. In the second inning, Jackie Robinson hit a line drive off third baseman Andy Carey's glove, but shortstop Gil McDougald grabbed the ball in time to nail Robby. In the fifth, Gil Hodges hit a ball to deep left-center field that was turned into an out by Mantle's spectacular backhand catch. In the seventh and eighth, McDougald and Carey both made excellent grabs of line drives. Dodger Sandy Amoros also hit a liner that was just foul but would have been a double.

By the top of the ninth, the crowd of 65,000 was cheering with every pitch Larsen threw. After the game, Larsen said: "I was so weak in the knees out there in the ninth, I thought I was going to faint. My fingers didn't feel like they were on my hand."

Carl Furillo flied to right for the first out. Roy Campanella sent the first pitch deep to left that veered foul by inches. Left-handed batter Dale Mitchell batted for Maglie. The first pitch was a ball. Then Larsen got a called strike and a swinging strike. Mitchell fouled off the next pitch before taking one on the corner that umpire Babe Pinelli called strike three. Larsen pitched into baseball history.

TREASURY OF BASEBALL

HADDIX HURLS PERFECTO BUT LOSES IN THE UNLUCKY 13th

◆

When 35-year-old Pittsburgh Pirates pitcher Harvey Haddix woke up on the morning of May 26, 1959, his head was aching from a bad cold. When Haddix went to sleep that night, it was his heart that was aching. He had just produced one of the greatest pitching performances in baseball history—and lost.

Despite the cold and a cough, Haddix made his scheduled start against the Braves at Milwaukee, and showed no effects of the illness. It was the Braves hitters who looked sick. Haddix used his fastball and slider to turn back the fearsome Hank Aaron, Eddie Mathews, Joe Adcock, and the rest of the Milwaukee lineup inning after inning.

Though Haddix later said that he was unaware of it, the crafty left-hander was pitching a perfect game going into the ninth inning. He thought for sure he had walked a couple of hitters. The only problem for Harvey was that the Pirates weren't scoring any runs off Braves starter Lew Burdette. Bill Virdon got to third base for the Bucs in the top of the ninth, but did not score, so even Haddix knew that a nine-inning perfecto wouldn't be enough to win. He got the first two outs that inning before Burdette, batting for himself, yelled out, "I'll break

Harvey Haddix poses for the camera before game five of the 1960 World Series. Haddix enjoyed a fine career as a starter and reliever.

up your no-hitter." Burdette struck out, and Haddix had pitched only the eighth perfect game since 1876. When he retired Johnny O'Brien in the 10th, Haddix became the first pitcher ever to retire 28 batters in a row.

Haddix made even more history thanks to his team's inability to score a run off Burdette. After keeping the Braves hitless through the 10th, 11th, and 12th innings, Haddix became the first pitcher to hurl a no-hitter for more than 11 frames. The Pirates, meanwhile, got their 12th hit off Burdette in the top of the 13th, but did not score. When Bucs manager Danny Murtaugh suggested Haddix call it a night, the pitcher refused to quit, saying, "I want to win this thing."

In the bottom of the 13th, Braves second baseman Felix Mantilla hit a grounder to third and reached on a throwing error, the first of 37 batters to get on base. Then Mathews sacrificed Mantilla to second, and Aaron was walked intentionally. Big Joe Adcock then sent Haddix's second pitch—"my only bad one all game"—

over the left field fence for a game-winning homer. Haddix's masterpiece, which became more famous than most no-hitters, was lost.

A bizarre ending to the game, Aaron, who thought that the ball had dropped in front of the fence, headed back to the dugout after touching second. Adcock was called out when he reached third base, and the official score of the game was 1-0.

Joe Adcock (sliding into home), a key player in Harvey Haddix's near-perfect game, was one of the big offensive guns for the Milwaukee Braves in the late 1950s. Adcock, a 6'4" first baseman, hit .277 lifetime with 336 major-league home runs.

MAZEROSKI'S TATER GIVES BUCS TITLE

◆

The 1960 World Series between the New York Yankees and Pittsburgh Pirates was a rematch of the 1927 Series, the last time the Bucs had been to the fall classic. Thirty-three years later, the Pirates must have felt they were facing "Murderer's Row" all over again. With Mickey Mantle and Roger Maris leading the way, the Yankees set World Series records for batting (.338) and home runs (10). They also set marks in outhitting the Pirates 91 to 60 and outscoring them 55 to 27. But one swing of Pirates second baseman Bill Mazeroski's bat made all those records footnotes in history.

The Series was tied 3-3 after six games because the Yankees scored most of their runs in their three victories, 16-3, 10-0, and 12-0. The Pirates won their three games by more reasonable scores of 6-4, 3-2, and 5-2.

In game seven, at Pittsburgh's Forbes Field, however, Pittsburgh took a page out of the Bombers' book, scoring four runs in the first two innings. Pirates first baseman Rocky Nelson smashed a two-run shot in the first inning. Yankees reliever Bobby Shantz held the Bucs at bay through the middle frames, while his team unlimbered its attack. Home runs by Bill Skowron and Yogi Berra in the fifth and sixth, respectively, made it 5-4 Yankees, and two more runs in the

eighth gave New York a three-run edge. The Pirates, though, were able to fight back in the bottom of the eighth, helped by some luck. A Bill Virdon grounder, which looked like a sure double play, took a bad hop and hit shortstop Tony Kubek in the throat. Then a Dick Groat single drove in one run. Roberto Clemente beat out an infield hit that scored Virdon. The next man up, catcher Hal Smith, blasted a three-run homer to put Pittsburgh up 9-7.

Bill Mazeroski trots home after hitting the Series-winning homer in 1960, bringing the Steel City its first world championship since 1925. From 1950 to 1959, the Pirates finished last six times.

1960 Yankee Ralph Terry (pictured) served up Bill Mazeroski's series-winning homer in 1960.

Buc pitcher Bob Friend couldn't hold the lead in the ninth. Bobby Richardson and Dale Long each singled. Pittsburgh hurler Harvey Haddix came on, but surrendered a single to Mantle, scoring Richardson. Yogi Berra grounded to Nelson, who made a nice play and stepped on first. When Nelson fired to second to double Mantle, Gil McDougald (pinch-running for Long) waltzed in from third to tie it at 9-9.

Mazeroski led off the bottom of the ninth for the Pirates. Maz, who was known as a great-fielding second baseman, was having a fine offensive Series. His two-run homer in game one

proved to be the winning hit. He had smacked six other hits, including two doubles. Now he was facing right-hander Ralph Terry; Maz smacked the reliever's second pitch over left fielder Berra's head and into the seats to win the game and the Series. The more than 36,000 fans erupted, and it seemed like half of them went to greet baseball's newest legend at home plate.

The Pirates celebrate Hal Smith's homer in the eighth inning of game seven of the 1960 Series. Smith, a catcher, hit 58 homers in a 10-year big-league career.

MARIS PASSES BABE WITH 61 HOMERS

When Roger Maris began to close in on Babe Ruth's record for the number of home runs in a single season in 1961, he was fighting more than history. In the 34 years since Ruth had hit his 60 homers in 1927, he had come to be regarded as a baseball icon. Most fans were horrified at the idea of a mere mortal challenging the Babe's holiest record. By season's end, commissioner Ford Frick had a pronouncement that an asterisk would be placed next to Maris's record if it took him more than 154 games—the length of a season in Ruth's time—to reach 60.

The years that have passed since 1961 haven't helped Maris's reputation. For one thing, Maris may have been an excellent right fielder, good enough to win two MVP Awards on Yankee teams that featured Whitey Ford, Yogi Berra, and Mickey Mantle—but any comparison of Maris to Ruth is inappropriate. Ruth batted .356 in 1927, 87 points higher than Maris's 1961 average. Maris's career-high in batting was .283; Ruth didn't hit as low as the .280s until his last full season, when he was 40. The colorless Maris also failed to measure up to the Bambino in press rela-

Above: Roger Maris cranks out homer No. 61 to break Babe Ruth's single-season record. Maris' 275 career home runs include 133 in a three-year span. *Opposite page:* Mickey Mantle (left) and Maris valiantly raced for Ruth's record in '61.

The early 1960s Yankees featured (from left) Roger Maris, Yogi Berra, Mickey Mantle, Elston Howard, Moose Skowron, and Johnny Blanchard.

tions. While Ruth was outrageous, charming, and an endless source of newspaper copy, Maris was brusque and testy, or worse. As the march toward the record progressed, his relationship with the press deteriorated.

Maris had another problem: Mickey Mantle. The popular Mantle also made a run at Ruth's record in the expansion year of 1961. The Yankee fans added to the mounting pressure on Maris by rooting vigorously for Mantle. In mid-July, Maris narrowly led Mantle, who batted behind him in the cleanup position, 35 homers to 33. By Sept. 13, Maris was up 56 to 53. Mantle then fell off the pace because of an injury and ended the season with 54. Maris was still four homers short of tying Ruth by game No. 154, which was only a week away. Unable to escape from an oppressive barrage of media and public

attention and with his hair falling out from nerves, Maris nevertheless continued to hit home runs. In game No. 154, he came within one long foul ball off Orioles pitcher Dick Hall of tying Ruth in the Babe's Baltimore hometown.

Six days later, Maris hit his 60th in New York off of Baltimore's Jack Fisher. The next day, implausibly, Maris took a day off to regroup emotionally. The next two games Roger was stopped short of hitting a circuit clout. But, on the last day of the season, he hit No. 61 into the right field seats at Yankee Stadium off Boston's Tracy Stallard. Finally showing some joy, Maris danced and celebrated his way around the bases, and for once, the Stadium crowd cheered him.

Today, Frick's asterisk has been forgotten. Maris's career may be underrated, but his record no longer is.

MAURY WILLS STEALS 104 BASES

◆

*I*n 1961 Roger Maris topped Babe Ruth's single-season home run record, upsetting those who didn't want to see one of baseball's most venerable records from one of baseball's icons come crashing down. Another sign that many of the venerable records were going to fall came the very next season when in 1962 Dodger shortstop Maury Wills stole 104 bases to break Ty Cobb's single-season milestone of 96 stolen bases.

Originally a pitcher, Wills was rejected by a Giants scout who said, "There's no such thing as a 155-pound pitcher." Signed by the Dodgers as a shortstop, Wills lacked consistent hitting ability. Major-league teams had little use for his speed because of the static offensive philosophy of the 1950s. Wills spent eight years in the minors before playing his first full season with the Dodgers in 1960 at age 27. Two years later, the baseball world began to notice that Wills was a serious threat to Cobb's record. In just 100

Maury Wills steals his 97th base in 1962 to break Ty Cobb's 1915 record. For the season, Wills stole 104 sacks and was caught just 13 times. In 1915, Cobb stole 96 and was caught 38 times.

Maury Wills spent eight years in the minors before a mid-1959 call-up to Los Angeles. The speedy shortstop sparked the Dodgers to four pennants and introduced the basestealing offense of the 1960s and 1970s.

games, he equaled the club record of 58 steals. On Aug. 26, Wills stole his 72nd; suddenly, much like Maris the previous year, Wills came under tremendous mental and physical strain. He played through foot injuries, hitting slumps, and a bad right hamstring to reach 95 steals in 154 games. Commissioner Ford Frick chose that moment to revive his ridiculous asterisk idea (putting an asterisk next to a record to show that there was a different number of games played), which posterity has fortunately ignored.

Wills passed Cobb in game 156—actually the number of games Cobb played in 1915 because of two replayed ties. Wills added No. 101 to No. 104 in the three-game pennant playoff against the Giants. Even though the Dodgers lost the pennant, Wills was voted MVP over Willie Mays (who hit 49 homers) and Dodger teammate Tommy Davis (who had 153 RBI).

In a historical sense, Wills's record was probably a more significant achievement than that of Maris, who was a power hitter in a power-hitting era. By reviving the art of basestealing, Wills helped to change the face of the game. The stolen base had lain dormant as an offensive tactic since 1920, when Ruth showed how to score runs in bunches with one swing of the bat. It bottomed out in the NL in 1938, when Stan Hack led with only 18 swipes. Wills led the league in 1960 and 1961 with only 50 and 35 stolen bases, respectively. Set in 1915, Cobb's mark had stood for 57 years, 23 years longer than Ruth's, before 1962.

Wills led the NL in stolen bases three more times after 1961 and stole 94 in 1965. He retired in 1972 with 586 career stolen bases, then good for fifth on the all-time list, behind dead-ball stars Cobb, Eddie Collins, Max Carey, and Honus Wagner. In the succeeding two decades, Wills has been pushed down on the list by his followers: Lou Brock (who broke Wills's season record with 118 steals in 1974), Rickey Henderson (who broke Brock's record with 130 in 1982), and others. It is clear that Wills's brand of baseball is here to stay.

CARDS PASS PHILLIES, SNATCH '64 FLAG

◆

The collapse of the Philadelphia Phillies in 1964 was one of the most memorable fiascoes in baseball. The National League yielded one of the most turbulent pennant races in history. With Philadelphia in front of the pack by six and one-half games and only 12 games left to play, the residents of "the City of Brotherly Love" geared up for the World Series.

Philadelphia's squad was led by Rookie of the Year third baseman Dick Allen (29 homers and 91 RBI), outfielder Johnny Callison (31 homers and 104 RBI), and the keystone combination of second baseman Tony Taylor and shortstop

Ken Boyer of St. Louis won the 1964 NL MVP Award, hitting .295 with a league-best 119 RBI.

Bobby Wine. The pitching staff had 19-game winner Jim Bunning (who threw a perfect game against the Mets), 17-game winner Chris Short, and 12-game winners Art Mahaffey and Dennis Bennett. The Phillies, indeed, appeared to be sitting pretty.

Then Philadelphia started losing ugly, as their hitting and pitching fell apart. Beginning on Sept. 18, the Phillies lost 12 of 15 games, including 10 straight. To make matters worse, two games were lost on steals of home, and another was given away on a dropped fly ball. Even manager Gene Mauch was not immune to choking. As the slide took hold, Mauch began pitching his aces Bunning and Short on two days rest. Each lost the three games he pitched on the new schedule.

Gene Mauch managed mostly poor teams for 26 years, never reaching the World Series.

Richie Allen smashed 29 homers and batted .318 to win 1964 NL Rookie of the Year honors.

In the meantime, the Phillies' competition took full advantage of the opportunity. With a lineup that featured Frank Robinson, Vada Pinson, and Deron Johnson, the Cincinnati Reds won nine in a row. The St. Louis Cardinals won eight in succession to make it a three-team race to the wire. The Phils pulled themselves together enough to win their last two games, but the Cards, who had already clinched a tie with Cincinnati two days earlier, beat the New York Mets 11-5 on the final day to seize the flag. Philadelphia beat the Reds on the final day to finish in a tie for second with Cincinnati at 92-70, one game out of first.

The Cardinals added rookie Lou Brock to their roster during the season, and he respond-ed by hitting .348 for St. Louis. Third baseman Ken Boyer led the league with 119 RBI. He also batted .295 with 24 homers and 100 runs scored while winning MVP honors. St. Louis' lineup included first baseman Bill White (.303 average and 102 RBI), center fielder Curt Flood (NL-leading 211 base hits), and shortstop Dick Groat (35 doubles and 70 RBI). The Cardinals rotation included Ray Sadecki (20-11), Bob Gibson (19-12), and Curt Simmons (18-9). The Cardinals beat the Yankees in the World Series four games to three, making St. Louis a champion for the first time since 1946. The Phillies had never won a World Series. To this day, many heartbroken Phillies fanatics still blame Mauch for blowing the pennant.

Lou Brock, acquired by St. Louis early in 1964, helped the Cardinals rally to win the NL flag.

ROBINSON IS MVP IN BOTH LEAGUES

◆

Frank Robinson began his illustrious career with the Cincinnati Reds in 1956 by hitting 38 home runs (tying a rookie record set by Wally Berger in 1930), scoring an NL-leading 122 runs, and taking the Rookie of the Year Award. Even then, even in a league that boasted such players as Willie Mays and Hank Aaron, it seemed possible that Robinson could be an MVP.

Over his next four seasons in Cincy, Robby was one of the game's most consistent run producers, averaging 32 home runs, 92 RBI, and 95 runs scored, and batting over .300 in 1957 and '59. He didn't fully explode until 1961, however, when he led the Reds to an NL pennant and won the MVP on the strength of 37 homers, 124 RBI, 117 runs scored, a .323 batting average, and a .611 slugging percentage (he also stole 22 bases).

Vada Pinson (left) and Frank Robinson were stars of the Cincinnati outfield. Pinson led the NL in hits twice and batted .286 in an 18-year career. Robinson scored over 100 runs six times while a member of the Reds.

Robinson sustained that solid pace over the next four seasons, racking up the kind of numbers that today would earn a player millions. His best year, statistically, was in 1962. That season, he drove in 39 homers, had 136 RBI (third best in the NL), and posted a .342 average.

In 1965 Frank hit .296 with 33 homers and 113 RBI. The Reds rewarded Robby—the team's best hitter—by trading him to the Baltimore Orioles for pitcher Milt Pappas (the '65 AL All-Star Game starter), hurler Jack Baldschun, and outfielder Dick Simpson before the 1966 season. Reds general manager Bill DeWitt called Robinson "an old 30." Depending on what side it is viewed from, it was either one of

Frank Robinson's 586 home runs rank fourth on the all-time major-league list. He hit 30 or more homers in 11 seasons but won only one home run crown.

Oriole Frank Robinson enjoyed a banner year in 1966, winning the Triple Crown and the Most Valuable Player Award and was also the World Series MVP. A 12-time All-Star, Robinson played in five fall classics.

the best or worst trades in baseball history. The Orioles were a solid team in the early 1960s, but the acquisition of Robinson, a team leader who they needed, made them unstoppable. A man of great pride, Robby wanted to prove the Reds had made a mistake in dealing him, and prove them wrong he did. He led the American League in home runs (49), RBI (122), and batting average (.316) to take the coveted Triple Crown. He also topped the junior circuit in runs scored (122), on-base percentage (.415), total bases (367), and slugging percentage (.637). He was in the top five in base hits (182), doubles (34), and walks (87). Robinson's tremendous season and his considerable leadership earned him the league's Most Valuable Player Award, the first player to win that honor in both leagues.

The Orioles, with great pitching, staunch defense, and Robinson's power, won the pennant—their first since moving from St. Louis (they were the Browns) in 1954.

Robinson didn't stop there. In the Orioles' four-game World Series sweep of the Dodgers, he hit two homers. His first was a two-run blast off Don Drysdale in the first inning of game one. His second, again off Drysdale, in game four proved to be the only run of the contest. Robinson was named the World Series MVP.

Above: Robinson and a bat was one of baseball's most fearsome combinations during the 1960s. He helped push the O's over the top. *Opposite page:* Robinson was not only a star player but was also the majors' first African-American manager, taking the reins for Cleveland in 1975.

KOUFAX WINS FIFTH STRAIGHT ERA TITLE

◆

In 1966, Sandy Koufax won 27 games, lost nine, and won the National League's earned run average title for the fifth straight year with a 1.73 ERA. In 1967, Koufax was out of baseball.

At what seemed to be the height of his reign, the overpowering left-hander of the Los Angeles Dodgers was forced to retire at 31 after pitching—and winning big—with an arthritic left elbow for nearly three seasons. His departure concluded one of the most extraordinary pitching careers ever.

Koufax signed with his hometown Brooklyn Dodgers in 1954 at age 19. His record over his first seven years in the majors—he never played minor-league ball—was just 54-53. He could throw a fastball through a wall, but couldn't hit a spot drawn on that wall. He was the epitome of wildness in a pitcher. After a

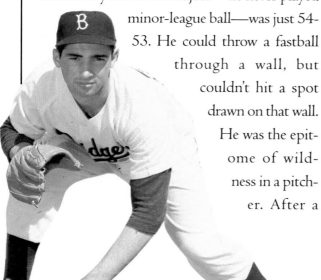

Sandy Koufax

dismal 8-13 season in 1960, Koufax almost quit the game. Then, Dodgers catcher Norm Sherry spotted a flaw in Koufax's delivery. Like magic, Sandy became a dominant hurler with an explosive fastball and sharply breaking curve.

For the next five years, Koufax was arguably the greatest pitcher baseball has ever seen. His record over that period was 111 wins and 34 losses, for an incredible .761 winning percentage, and a 1.98 ERA. Koufax also led the NL in shutouts three times, averaged 289 Ks per year (including an NL-record 382 in 1965), and threw a record four no-hitters (broken by Nolan Ryan in 1981). Koufax's last no-hitter, in '65, was a perfect game.

"Trying to hit Sandy Koufax in those years," said Pittsburgh slugger Willie Stargell, "was like trying to drink coffee with a fork."

Koufax's first good year came in 1961, when he was 18-13 and led the league in strikeouts. In 1962, he was 14-7 with a 2.54 ERA, his first earned run average crown. His best season, however, was 1963. He went 25-5 to win his first of three Cy Young Awards and his only Most Valuable Player Award. In the Dodgers' 1963 World Series sweep against the New York Yan-

Sandy Koufax (top center) with Dodger teammates, including Don Drysdale (top left), Duke Snider (bottom right), and Jim Gilliam (bottom left). Before coming to Los Angeles, Koufax struggled. However, spacious Chavez Ravine and good advice from catcher Norm Sherry helped Sandy become a great pitcher.

kees, Koufax set a record (since broken) for strikeouts in one game (15). He also set or tied four-game Series marks in starts, complete games, innings (18), and strikeouts (23).

Koufax kept up his awesome pace in 1964, winning 19, losing five, and notching a 1.74 ERA. In 1965, he went 26-8, had a career-high 382 Ks, and a 2.04 earned run average. He won his five ERA titles by 0.26, 0.23, 0.44, 0.09, and 0.49 points over the runner-up.

Arthritis began afflicting his left shoulder as early as 1962. His last three seasons, Koufax often had to pack his arm in ice for a half hour after a game and quit throwing between starts. After the 1966 season he retired to save his arm from permanent damage.

No pitcher since has produced a string of seasons to equal his dominant years. For one brief shining half-decade, Koufax may have been the greatest pitcher of all time.

YASTRZEMSKI LEADS RED SOX TO SERIES

◆

The Boston Red Sox were already looking more like a second-division team during the late 1950s, and the retirement of Ted Williams after the 1960 season only accelerated the process. From 1960—when they were 32 games out of first—until 1967, the BoSox never won over 76 games.

Boston finished in ninth place in 1966, 26 games out of first place. The BoSox' hope for the future, though, was in the person of young Carl Yastrzemski, who came up in 1961 heralded as "the next Ted Williams." While Yaz wasn't as splendid a splinter as Williams, he was no slouch. Yaz led the league in batting his third season and hit over .300 again in 1965. Other than this left-handed-hitting right fielder, the Red Sox offered their fans little excitement.

Little excitement until 1967, that is. The Red Sox hired the tough Dick Williams as manager before the season got underway. The team—which already had a solid young nucleus with Yaz, first baseman George Scott, third baseman Rico Petrocelli, and outfielder Tony Conigliaro—started rookies Mike Andrews at second base and Reggie Smith in center field

Above: Carl Yastrzemski was heir to Ted Williams in Boston. *Opposite page:* Yaz collected 3,419 hits.

and made right-hander Jim Lonborg the ace of the pitching staff. Andrews helped anchor the infield, Smith hit 15 homers, and Lonborg won 22 games and the AL Cy Young Award.

But the real story of the '67 Red Sox was Yastrzemski, who produced one of the most glorious seasons ever. Yaz not only led the AL in batting average (.326), home runs (44), and RBI (121) to win the coveted Triple Crown—he also led the league in hits, total bases, on-base percentage, and slugging average to capture Most Valuable Player honors. "For that one season," said Dick Williams, "there could not have been a better baseball player." Shouldered by Yaz and his productive bat, the Red Sox did the near impossible: They went from next-to-last place all the way to first in one season.

Not that the pennant race was easy. It was, in fact, a dogfight to the wire. Boston ultimately took the crown by just one game, thanks to Yaz, who in the last two weeks of a four-team battle batted .523 with five home runs and 15 RBI. In the final two games of the regular season, Yaz went 7-for-9 and made countless superb defensive plays.

Unfortunately for Boston fans, their team couldn't get a championship. They lost to St. Louis in seven. Yaz continued his career year in the fall classic, batting .400 with three homers (two in game two) and five RBI.

TREASURY OF BASEBALL

McLAIN WINS 31, GIBSON EXCELS IN 1968 HURLER'S YEAR

The 1968 season will always be known as "The Year of the Pitcher." It was a year in which one hurler (Bob Gibson) produced a microscopic ERA of 1.12, another (Don Drysdale) set a record with 58 consecutive scoreless innings, and a third won 30 games for the first time in 34 years (Denny McLain). It was also a season in which an AL batting title was won with an average just over .300 (.301 by Carl Yastrzemski).

When the confident and colorful Dizzy Dean won 30 games for the Cardinals in 1934, four of those were in relief (as were four of the 31 games that Lefty Grove won three years earlier). When the confident and colorful 24-year-old McLain won 31 in leading the Tigers to a pennant, all the victories came as a starter.

Ironically, the Tigers tried to trade the hard-throwing right-hander when he went 17-16 in 1967, after posting a 20-win season in '66. It was one of those proverbial "the best trades are the ones not made." Although McLain went 0-2 in his first two starts, he had won his 15th game by July 3. Pitching every fourth day, McLain notched his 20th victory on July 27, becoming the first pitcher since Grove to win 20 by Aug. 1. Overall, McLain won 23 of his next 26 decisions.

Above: Denny McLain's 1.96 ERA and 336 innings pitched led to an amazing 31 wins in 1968. *Opposite page:* McLain never could match his 1968 performance but won 24 more games in 1969 before falling on hard times.

McLain's unusual success in 1968 was twofold. He added a slider to his sidearm fastball and curve, making him especially tough on right-handed hitters. Also, he had terrific offensive support. With a lineup of such hitters as Al Kaline, Norm Cash, and others, the Tigers led the league in runs.

McLain went for win 30 in the Sept. 14 game against Oakland. Although Dizzy Dean was in the stands and the game was nationally televised, McLain didn't seem up to the task. Going into the bottom of the ninth, two Reggie Jackson homers had put the A's up 4-3. The Tigers, however, were not surrendering. Kaline, pinch-hitting for McLain, walked, and Mickey Stanley singled, putting the winning run on. An

TREASURY OF BASEBALL

Above: Bob Gibson's 1.12 ERA in 1968 was baseball's lowest in 54 years—but he still lost nine games that season. *Opposite page:* Gibson won 20 games five out of six years between 1965 and 1970. He also went 7-2 in World Series play with a 1.89 ERA.

infield error tied the game, and Willie Horton won it with a blast to left field.

McLain won his next start for No. 31, securing, in the process, the Cy Young and MVP Awards. He ended the season by leading the AL with 28 complete games, 336 innings pitched, and a .838 winning percentage. He was in the top five in the league with a 1.96 ERA and 280 strikeouts.

Although McLain's 31 victories were outstanding, it wasn't 1968's most dominating pitching performance. Bob Gibson's phenomenal 1.12 earned run average is the lowest for a pitcher with more than 300 innings in history and the lowest since Dutch Leonard's 0.96 set in 1914.

In leading the St. Louis Cardinals to the World Series, Gibson won 22 games while losing only nine for a .710 winning percentage. He completed 28 of the 34 games he started. He won the NL Cy Young Award hands down, adding league-leading totals of 268 strikeouts and 13 shutouts. He was in the top five in wins, complete games, and innings (305). He held NL opponents to a collective .184 batting average and a .233 on-base average, both lowest in the circuit. Gibson also set a World Series record for Ks in a game (17) and in a Series (35).

LOLICH KEYS TIGERS IN '68 WORLD SERIES

◆

The 1968 World Series between the Detroit Tigers and the St. Louis Cardinals was billed as a battle of baseball's two best pitchers, Cy Young Award-winners Denny McLain and Bob Gibson. In the end, however, it was a portly left-hander named Mickey Lolich who stole the spotlight in Detroit's tremendous comeback from a three-games-to-one deficit in the Series.

Game one was all Gibson, as the speedballing right-hander shut out the Tigers on five hits and set a World Series record for strikeouts with 17. Detroit bounced back in game two behind the 17-game winner Lolich, who pitched a six-hitter in an 8-1 victory. St. Louis won the next two games in Detroit, 7-3 and 10-1, the latter

Detroit lefty Mickey Lolich

behind Gibson's second straight complete game (McLain lasted only two and two-thirds innings). It seemed as if a second straight title was in the Cards, since it seemed like an overwhelming task for the Bengals to win three straight sudden-death games.

Lolich again came through in the clutch for the beleaguered Tigers, this time with a 5-3

Al Kaline

complete-game win. The turning point of the Series may have occurred in the fifth inning, when outfielder Willie Horton nailed Lou Brock at the plate on Brock's failure to slide.

Detroit manager Mayo Smith made a critical decision for game six. He brought back his ace McLain, who had barely broken loose in game four before he was knocked out, on two days rest—and the 31-game winner delivered. McLain's complete game in a 13-1 win gave the team momentum. The Tigers scored 10 runs in the third; the highlight was Jim Northrup's grand slam.

Game seven pitted Gibson against Lolich, and the two hurlers engaged in a superb scoreless pitching duel for the first six innings. Gibson struck out Lolich in the third, racking up his 32nd strikeout of the Series and, in the process, breaking his own record set in 1964; he ended with 35 Ks. In the sixth, the Cardinals threatened, but Brock (who tied a Series record with 13 hits and batted .464) and Curt Flood were both picked off first by Lolich's deceptive left-handed move.

Those baserunning blunders would come to haunt the Cardinals in the next inning. With two outs in the seventh, Norm Cash and Willie Horton singled off Gibson. Then Northrup tripled and Bill Freehan doubled to put Detroit

up 3-0 and stun the 55,000-strong home crowd. While Detroit added a single run in the ninth, only Mike Shannon's two-out homer touched Lolich. Lolich's three victories earned him the Series MVP. Al Kaline and Northrup each smacked two homers and drove in eight runs. Norm Cash added five RBI. Detroit's first title since 1945 made the Tigers the third team in history to overcome a 3-1 deficit and win the World Series.

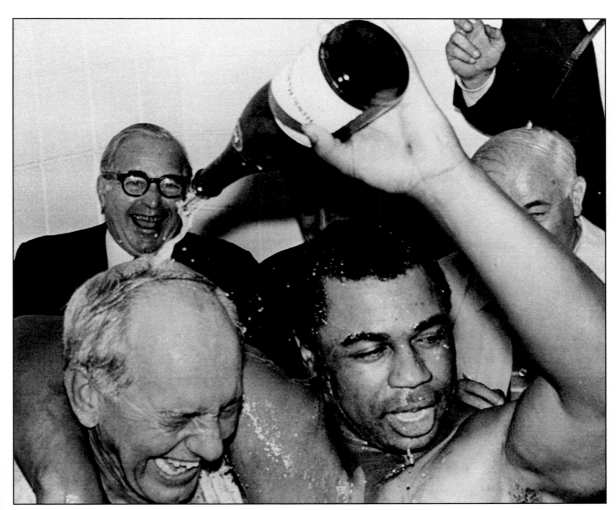

Willie Horton pours champagne over Tigers manager Mayo Smith as Detroit celebrates their 1968 World Series victory. Horton, who played 18 years in the majors, hit .304 in the Series after slugging 36 home runs during the regular season.

MIRACLE METS ASCEND TO REACH CHAMPIONSHIP

◆

Tom Seaver pitches for the Miracle Mets in 1969. After a 25-7 regular season record, "Tom Terrific" won game one of the NLCS over Atlanta and made two starts in the Series, including a 10-inning 2-1 win in game four.

*I*n 1969, New York was being tagged the "Miracle Mets" even before the start of the World Series against the Orioles. Perennial losers, the Mets' best season in their seven-year history had been in 1968 when they were 73-89 and finished ninth. In '69, the Mets parlayed great pitching—led by young Tom Seaver and Jerry Koosman—tight defense, timely hitting, and curious luck into 100 wins and one of the biggest transformations in baseball.

In winning the 1969 NL East, the Mets were pretty good and very lucky. One day, they won a doubleheader against the Pittsburgh Pirates by identical scores of 1-0; and in each game, the Mets pitcher—Jerry Koosman and Don Cardwell—drove in the winning run. Al Weis hit two homers all season, and each won a game against the Cubs—at Wrigley Field. During their mid-September march to the pennant, they faced Steve Carlton of the St. Louis Cardinals and struck out 19 times for a new record. Then Mets outfielder Ron Swoboda hit two two-run homers to give the Mets a 4-3 victory; he struck out the other two times he batted. The Cubs held a comfortable lead into late August, but in September Chicago dropped eight games in a row while the Mets reeled off 10 straight wins. New York won the title by eight games.

The Mets knew that beating the Braves three straight in the NLCS was one thing, but beating Baltimore was another. It appeared the Orioles would make short work of the Series when they topped Mets ace and 25-game winner Tom Seaver 4-1 in game one.

The Mets, however, spent all season finding ways to win. In game two, Koosman no-hit the Orioles for six innings while trying to make a Donn Clendenon solo homer stand up. The O's scored a run in the bottom of the seventh, but the Mets grabbed the game in the ninth on an RBI single by utility infielder Al Weis.

In game three, rookie right-hander Gary Gentry and young Nolan Ryan hurled a shutout at the Birds, thanks to a couple of spectacular catches by center fielder Tommie Agee. With the Mets up 3-0 in the fourth, the Orioles put two on with two out. Elrod Hendricks then belted a Gentry pitch up the left-center field gap, and Agee, going full speed toward the wall, nixed the apparent extra-base hit when he backhanded the ball in the webbing of his glove. Then the Orioles loaded the bases in the seventh. Paul Blair hit Ryan's first fastball deep to right-center field. Agee made a diving catch on the warning track. The two great defensive plays prevented five Orioles runs.

Game four was a pitching duel between Seaver and Baltimore lefty Mike Cuellar. The Mets were leading 1-0 in the top of the ninth when right fielder Ron Swoboda made his own

Left-hander Jerry Koosman won games two and five of the 1969 World Series. In 18 Series innings, he allowed just four runs and seven hits. Koosman won 222 games in a 19-year career and fashioned a 3.36 lifetime ERA.

incredible catch. With runners at first and third and one out, Brooks Robinson hit a drive to short right-center field. Swoboda dove and stretched his arm across his body. The ball landed in his glove before he hit the turf. In the bottom of the 10th, the Mets winning run scored after J.C. Martin laid down a sacrifice bunt and was hit by the ball as he ran to first.

The seemingly inevitable came the next day. The Mets wiped out a 3-0 Orioles lead on a Clendenon two-run homer in the sixth (his third of the Series, which earned him the MVP) and an unlikely second Series homer by Weis in the seventh, a solo shot. In the eighth, two doubles and an Orioles error led to two runs and made the Mets champions.

Above, top: One of Tommie Agee's two great catches in game three. *Above, bottom:* Ron Swoboda robs Brooks Robinson in game four. *Opposite page:* (From left) Cleon Jones, Agee, and Swoboda, the Mets' outfield in 1969. Jones hit .340 with 75 RBI, Agee swatted 26 homers and batted .271, and Swoboda drove in 52 runs on just 77 hits.

'HOOVER' ROBINSON CLEANS UP IN SERIES

◆

*I*n the long history of the World Series, nobody had ever turned it into a defensive showcase the way Brooks Robinson did in 1970. The Baltimore Orioles Gold Glove third baseman already had a reputation for being one of the greatest ever at his position. In the five games against the Reds, he proved his supremacy to the world.

The Orioles, who desperately wanted to avenge their previous year's loss to the New York Mets, won game one at Cincy 4-3, but the out-

Lee May, who hit .389 with two homers, was almost the Reds' entire offense in the 1970 Series. Tony Perez congratulates May after his homer in game one.

In the 1970 Series, Boog Powell (left) scored six runs, and Brooks Robinson (right) hit .429, notched two homers, and excelled on defense.

come would have been different if not for the "Human Vacuum Cleaner." With no outs and the score tied in the bottom of the sixth, Reds first baseman Lee May hit a smash down the third base line. Robinson, who was a slow runner but incredibly quick at third, backhanded the ball as it appeared to go past him into foul territory. In one motion, he turned and threw off-balance to first, nailing May by a step. In the seventh, Robinson hit the game-winning homer.

Robinson continued his human highlight film act in game two. He dove toward shortstop to turn one potential hit into a force play and backhanded another May grounder that he converted into a double play. Although the Reds

The unstoppable 1970 Baltimore Orioles steamrolled everyone in sight. First, they won
the AL East by 15 games, leading the league in both runs scored and fewest allowed.
Then, they stomped a good Minnesota team in three straight to take the ALCS. Finally,
they disposed of the NL champion Reds in five games in the World Series.

scored four runs in those innings, Robinson's plays kept the game close enough for the Orioles to launch a comeback and a 6-5 victory.

His fielding clinic continued in game three as he continued to show how a third baseman makes every possible play. In the first inning, he made a leaping grab of a Tony Perez shot and turned it into two outs. In the second, "Hoover" backhanded Tommy Helms's swinging roller and threw him out by a step. Robinson also continued his great hitting in the Series, going 2-for-4 with two RBI in a 9-3 victory.

The Robinson hitting show was in the spotlight again in game four as Brooks smacked four hits (tying a Series record), including a homer. The Reds, however, went on to take the game 6-5. In game five, Cincinnati jumped to a 3-0 first-inning lead, but the Orioles responded with two runs in each of their first three frames. They were leading 9-3 in the ninth when Robinson provided one last glimpse of his magic at the hot corner—something for the fans to remember him by. He made a diving catch of a Johnny Bench line drive. He also batted .429 with nine hits in five games (tying a record). After the Series, Bench marveled, "I never saw Pie Traynor play, but if he was better at playing third than Brooks Robinson, he had to be inhuman."

CLEMENTE PROVES WORTH IN CLASSIC

◆

*I*n the field, there was no purer competitor than Pittsburgh Pirate Roberto Clemente. He was a great right fielder with perhaps the best arm among history's outfielders. He regularly collected 20 assists a season, and won 12 Gold Gloves. With his exquisite quickness and timing at the plate—and a slashing, inside-out swing that produced line drives—he was a perennial contender for the bat ing title. It was only off the field, with management, the fans, and the media, that Clemente sometimes seemed out of sync.

From 1961 to 1967, Clemente won four batting titles and drove in or scored 100 runs five times. He won an MVP Award in 1966. But with Pittsburgh never managing to win a pennant, Clemente's status as a star somehow remained shaky.

In 1971, the Pirates won the NL East and defeated San Francisco 3-1 in the NLCS. Clemente hit .341 for the season but played only 132 games as the effects of age, a chronic bad back, and years of playing baseball year-round began to catch up with him. It took his outstanding play in the 1971 World Series

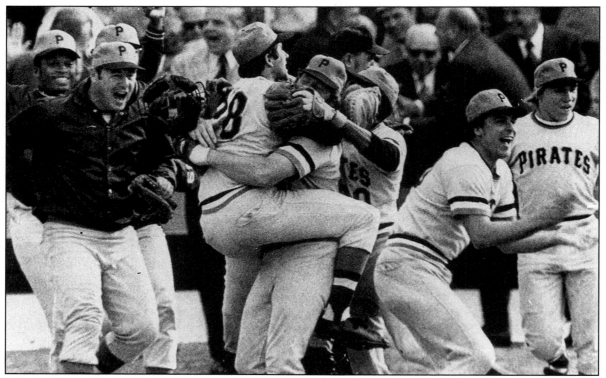

Above: The victorious Pirates celebrate winning the 1971 Series over the heavily favored Orioles. Even with stars like Roberto Clemente and Willie Stargell, the Bucs were lightly regarded. *Opposite page:* Clemente was a force at bat.

against Baltimore for Clemente to finally gain the respect he deserved.

Playing with his usual furious hustle, Clemente made impossible diving catches, froze baserunners with his rifle of an arm, and hit .414. Covering the 1971 Series, Roger Angell wrote: "Clemente was playing to win, but also playing the game almost as if it were a form of punishment for everyone else on the field."

With their offense and staff of four 20-game winners, the defending champion Orioles were strong favorites; after four games, however, the Series was tied two-all. Continuing a streak he had started in the first game of the 1960 World Series, Clemente had at least one hit in each game. In game five, Nellie Briles two-hit the Orioles and put the Pirates up in the Series again; Clemente had a hit. He came close to

The donations pour in for the Roberto Clemente Fund after his death in 1973.

eliminating the Orioles in game six. His first-inning triple narrowly missed clearing the left-center field wall, and his third-inning home run put the Pirates up 2-0. But Baltimore came back to win 3-2. In the fourth inning of the seventh game, Clemente struck again, launching a solo homer to left. Steve Blass limited the Orioles to four hits and won 2-1. Clemente's 12 hits and five extra-base hits in the Series led all hitters; he didn't record a single assist as no Oriole dared try to take an extra base on him. He was the overwhelming choice as Series MVP.

Clemente played only one more season. Killed in a plane crash on his way to bring relief to earthquake-stricken Nicaragua on the last day of 1972, he left behind a .317 career batting average on exactly 3,000 hits. The Hall of Fame inducted Clemente in 1973.

The best defensive outfielder of his time, Roberto Clemente also collected 3,000 hits, won four batting titles, and scored 100 runs three times.

CARLTON WINS 27 FOR PHILLIES

For four years the St. Louis Cardinals had waited for Steve Carlton to develop into the dominant left-handed pitcher they thought he'd be when he came up in 1967. He'd constantly tease the Cardinals management with games like that 19-strikeout classic he threw against the Mets in 1969. But the Cards also knew they had to be patient, considering the baseball axiom that says left-handers take longer in developing than right-handers. Finally, in 1971, after a 10-19 '70 season, Carlton blossomed and went 20-9.

But when Carlton hassled with Cardinal owner Gussie Busch over his contract, the beer baron traded Carlton to the Philadelphia Phillies for their ace right-hander Rick Wise. Nobody had to wait three to five years to see who would get the better of this deal. In one year it was called one of the worst trades ever made.

The 1972 Phillies were a terrible team. They won just 59 games and lost 97; only the four-year-old expansion Padres were as bad. The Phillies would have been even worse without Carlton and his 27 victories. On the days he pitched, Philadelphia played almost like pennant contenders. His victories represented 46 percent of the total wins that Philly earned that year. With him, they played .378 baseball; subtract Carlton's decisions, the Phillies were a .270 team.

"It was really hard to explain," shortstop Larry Bowa, who played behind Carlton that year, once recalled, "but when 'Lefty' was on the mound, we always felt confident we would win. We felt like a different team because he always kept us in the game. I guess we were trying to live up to his excellence."

In winning his first of a record four Cy Young Awards in 1972, Carlton also won pitching's triple crown, adding NL leads in ERA (1.97) and strikeouts (310) to his league-leading 27 victories, becoming just the 23rd pitcher since 1900 to accomplish the feat. It was one of the greatest pitching seasons in baseball history. He

During Steve Carlton's spectacular 1972 season, he held opponents to a .206 average.

Steve Carlton debuted with St. Louis in 1965 and won 77 games for them. In 1971, his final year with the Redbirds, he was 20-9 with a 3.56 ERA.

also added league leads in innings pitched (346) and complete games (30)—and he threw eight shutouts and had a .730 winning percentage, second in the league in those categories. He also had a 15-game winning streak. In 1972, and most of his career, Carlton possessed an excellent fastball and curve. But his out pitch was a devastating slider that was especially tough on right-handed hitters.

The media couldn't get much from Carlton to explain his phenomenal success in '72. Notoriously inaccessible to the press, Carlton eventually stopped talking to reporters altogether by 1978 and was nicknamed "Silent Steve." But he did plenty of talking on the mound. He continued being unhittable for the next 16 years, accumulating 329 lifetime victories and 4,136 strikeouts.

AARON BREAKS BABE'S CAREER HOMER RECORD

◆

During a career that spanned from 1954 through 1976, Hank Aaron was never known as just a home run hitter. He could hit homers, to be sure, leading the NL in four different seasons and belting 44 homers in four seasons. Aaron never hit more than 47 in any season, but the silent superstar was methodical and consistent. "Hammerin' Hank" had a quick, efficient swing, which derived its power from strong, sinewy wrists.

Aaron walked away with the MVP crown in 1957 (during which he hit a late September home run to give Milwaukee the pennant), batting titles in 1956 and 1959, and a lifetime .364 average in 14 World Series games. It was not until June 10, 1972, however—when Aaron hit his 649th homer to pass Willie Mays and take second place on the all-time list—that his power exploits drew national attention.

Suddenly, there was great interest in the 38-year-old Aaron and in the possibility of his hitting another 66 homers—the number needed to break the lifetime record of 714 round-trippers set by Babe Ruth. "Even if I'm lucky enough to hit 715 homer runs," Aaron said modestly, "Babe Ruth will still be regarded as the greatest home-run hitter who ever lived."

Hank Aaron hits his 714th career home run off Jack Billingham to tie Babe Ruth's all-time record. Aaron, who played 21 years with the Braves before finishing his career back in Milwaukee with the Brewers, led the NL four times in four-baggers, four times in doubles, and four times in RBI. He drove in more runs (2,297) than anyone in history.

Above, left: Hank Aaron hits homer No. 715 to claim the all-time crown. *Above, right:* Hank Aaron and his associate with the ball that Hank broke the record with. *Opposite page:* Aaron's powerful swing produced two batting championships.

Going into the 1973 season needing only 42 homers to pass Ruth, Aaron was bombarded by pressure from all sides. "It should have been an enjoyable time," he once recalled, "but instead, everywhere I went people were talking about home runs. And I had no privacy."

Aaron hit No. 713 on the next to the last day of the 1973 season. When the Braves' 1974 season began on the road, the team's owners tried to sit Aaron out. Commissioner Bowie Kuhn ruled that the club would have to play him during its first three games. On April 4, Aaron tied Ruth—on his first swing of the season off Cincinnati Reds pitcher Jack Billingham into left-center field. It had taken Aaron 2,890 more at bats than the Babe to hit 714 homers.

Four days later, the Braves played a nationally televised game against the Los Angeles Dodgers. There were 53,000 people in the stands at Atlanta Stadium and another 35 million viewers, all hoping to witness history. And Hammerin' Hank didn't let them down. Al Downing walked Aaron on five balls in the second inning. Then, on his first official at bat of the game in the fourth inning, he knocked a fastball over the fence in left field for the monumental homer. Aaron had conquered what he called "the Cadillac of baseball records."

Aaron traveled around the bases a few more times before he was through, accumulating 755 homers upon his retirement two years later (as a member of the Milwaukee Brewers).

TREASURY OF BASEBALL

MARSHALL MAKES 106 TRIPS TO MOUND

◆

The Los Angeles Dodgers had led the NL West by as many as 11 games in July of 1973, only to be overtaken by Cincinnati. With the primary factor in the slide being a weak bullpen, the Dodgers pushed to strengthen their pitching attack for '74; they traded with the Expos, exchanging outfielder Willie Davis for the right-handed screwballing relief pitcher Mike Marshall.

Marshall was a bit of a screwball personality. A doctor of physiology, he engaged in his own training regimen and intimidated coaches and managers who wouldn't let him maintain his independence. After struggling early in his career, he developed as a reliever under Gene Mauch at Montreal.

After three seasons with the Expos, Marshall had won 33 games, saved 70 (leading the league in 1973), and appeared in 223, setting a record for games with 92 in '73. The closest thing to an every-day player a pitcher could be, Marshall established, once and for all, the importance of the short reliever in modern baseball.

The Dodgers started fast in 1974, racking up a 36-14 record by the end of May. Then from the middle of June until early July, Marshall pitched in a record 13 straight games, winning six in relief. "A lot of guys can probably go out there 13 days in a row," said Jim Brewer, Mar-

Rubber-armed Mike Marshall is the only pitcher ever to appear in 100 games in a season. He owns three of the top seven single-season appearance totals.

shall's bullpen mate, "but I can't think of anyone who could be as effective as Mike was."

The Reds tightened the gap in the pennant race in the West, closing to within one and one-half games as late as Sept. 14. Marshall kept the Dodgers from collapsing as they had the year before. His excellent relief work stopped a six-game losing streak in mid-August, and his victories in two games in the last week held off the

Reds. "A lot of guys were key to us winning that year," said Dodgers starter Don Sutton, "but Mike was unbelievable."

Marshall ended up breaking his own record for appearances with an astounding 106, relief innings with 208, and games finished with 83. Overall, he saved 21 games, won 15, struck out 143 batters, walked only 56, and compiled a 2.43 ERA. He was voted both Fireman of the Year and the league's Cy Young Award winner (the first ever won by a reliever).

The Dodgers defeated the Pirates for the 1974 NL pennant, with Marshall appearing in two games. Los Angeles lost to Oakland in five games in the World Series. Marshall saved the Dodgers' sole victory, only to yield the winning run in the seventh inning of game five after Los Angeles had tied it the previous frame. He pitched in all five games, giving up only one run and striking out 10 in nine innings. Marshall's 1974 will go down as one of the greatest seasons ever by a relief pitcher.

Sal Bando has just been thrown out by right fielder Joe Ferguson on a close play at the plate in game one of the 1974 World Series. The Dodgers won just one game from Oakland as the Athletics captured their third straight world championship.

FISK'S HOMER WINS 1975 GAME SIX

◆

Simply say the words "game six," and many baseball fans will know what you're talking about. The sixth game of the 1975 World Series between the Cincinnati Reds and the Boston Red Sox is considered by many as the most exciting World Series game ever played—and the Series is regarded as one of the best.

The Reds were leading the Series three games to two going into Boston's Fenway Park on Oct. 21, a contest that had been postponed by rain for three days. The Red Sox jumped in front in the first inning on a three-run homer by AL MVP and Rookie of the Year Fred Lynn. Cagey Cuban right-hander Luis Tiant made it hold up until the top of the fifth when the Reds rallied to tie it up. George Foster of the Reds then drove in two runs in the seventh, and Cesar Geronimo smacked a solo shot in the eighth to take a 6-3 lead and pin the BoSox to the ropes.

The Beantowners bounced back in the bottom of the eighth. After the first two batters reached base, Reds manager Sparky Anderson summoned reliever Rawly Eastwick, the sixth Cincy pitcher of the game (they would tie a Series record with eight). Eastwick retired the first two batters and had a 3-2 count on left-handed pinch hitter Bernie Carbo—a former Red who was the first player Cincinnati select-

Carlton Fisk holds the all-time record for games caught, with 2,229. In his 24-year major league career, Fisk belted 376 home runs. A native New Englander, Fisk debuted with the Red Sox in 1969 and was the AL Rookie of the Year in 1972. In 1975, he helped bring Boston a pennant with a .331 average despite missing two months with injuries. After the 1980 season, he joined the Chicago White Sox as a free agent.

Fisk's homer in game six of the 1975 World Series changed baseball. His attempt to
wave the ball fair was the first televised "reaction shot."

ed in the initial draft in 1965, one pick ahead of Johnny Bench. Bernie fouled off one pitch, then blasted a fastball over the center field fence to tie the game.

In the bottom of the ninth, the Sox loaded the bases with none out. Will McEnaney got Lynn to hit a shallow fly ball to left field. George Foster made the catch and nailed Denny Doyle at the plate trying to score. The game went into extra innings.

The Red Sox turned on its own defensive power in the 11th inning. With one out and one on, Joe Morgan belted the ball to deep right field, but Dwight Evans snared it with a leaping one-handed catch. Evans then threw to first baseman Carl Yastrzemski, doubling off Ken Griffey to end the threat.

It was past midnight and reliever Pat Darcy was working his third inning when Red Sox catcher Carlton Fisk led off the 12th. He swung at Darcy's first delivery and hit a high fly ball down the left field line. As the ball traveled on its arc, the television cameras showed Fisk dancing down the line and waving his arms, practically willing the ball to stay fair. The ball hit the foul pole to give Boston a 7-6 victory.

In the seventh game, the Red Sox blew a 3-0 lead and lost to the Reds 4-3 on a run in the ninth inning. Boston had won the game six battle, but Cincinnati had won the war.

CHAMBLISS'S BLAST WINS THE PENNANT

◆

*P*arity may be good for football; in baseball, however, the natural order of things seemed to include a New York Yankees dynasty. Starting with Babe Ruth and continuing through the days of Mickey Mantle, baseball fans always had great Yankees teams to love or to hate. Then, in 1965, the Yankees fell to sixth, and in 1966, New York finished dead last, marking the beginning of a decade-long pennant drought.

In December 1975, arbitrator Peter Seitz released Dave McNally and Andy Messersmith from their contracts, a decision that brought about a new era of free agency. And in 1976, the Yankees returned to postseason play. In many minds, these two events are related. In fact—Catfish Hunter notwithstanding—this new Yankees dynasty was built on trades, not on free-agent signings. In addition to home-grown products outfielder Roy White and catcher Thurman Munson, the 1976 club featured first baseman Chris Chambliss, third baseman Graig Nettles, and outfielder Oscar Gamble (traded from Cleveland), outfielder Mickey Rivers and hurler Ed Figueroa (from California), second baseman Willie Randolph and pitcher Dock Ellis (from Pittsburgh), outfielder Lou Piniella (from Kansas City), and reliever Sparky Lyle (from Boston).

Back in Yankee Stadium after a two-year exile to Shea and under the management of Stengel-protégé Billy Martin, this Bronx Bomber team stormed past defending division-winner Boston and a fading Orioles dynasty to take the AL East by 10½ games. Facing George Brett, Hal McRae, and the Royals in a five-game ALCS, the two teams alternated wins through game four.

It was Dennis Leonard versus Figueroa in a fifth-game thriller that established the pattern for three straight years worth of epic New York-Kansas City postseason wars. John Mayberry's homer gave the Royals a 2-0 lead in the first frame. The Yankees tied the score in the bot-

Chris Chambliss's 1976 blast gave the Yankees their first AL championship since 1964. In the ensuing World Series, Chambliss hit .313 in a losing cause.

Yankee catcher Thurman Munson had a .292 lifetime average in an 11-year career.

tom of the inning with a Rivers triple and a White single. Chambliss (who had hit .293 with 17 home runs and 96 RBI on the season) then sacrificed White home. The Yankees then scored two each in the third and sixth to build a 6-3 lead after seven.

In the top of the eighth, Brett tied the score with a three-run shot off of Grant Jackson. Then, in the bottom of the ninth, Chambliss faced journeyman right-hander Mark Littell and drove the first pitch of the inning into the right-center field seats, over the outstretched arm of McRae. Yankee Stadium erupted, and Chambliss had to fight the crowd to circle the bases. Later, after the crowd had left the field, Chambliss came back on the field and touched home plate, secretly ensuring the home run. In the World Series, the Yankees didn't fare so well. New York was humiliated in a four-game sweep by the Big Red Machine.

REGGIE HITS BACK-TO-BACK-TO-BACK HOMERS IN SERIES

◆

There were two Reggie Jacksons. One is the Reggie that hit 563 home runs and led the league in homers four times; he also struck out 2,597 times—the most in history—and batted .262 lifetime. The other Reggie was "Reggie the Show," and that one had to be seen to be appreciated.

In October, the two Reggies became one. Jackson played in 11 League Championship Series (batting .227) and five World Series (72 games in all), and his postseason record shows why he was called "Mr. October." He hit 10 career World Series homers—fifth-best of all time—and batted .357, ninth-best. At .755, he is the greatest slugger in World Series history. Jackson homered and drove in six runs for Oakland to become the MVP of the 1973 Series—nothing compared with his 1977 performance, in which he swatted five home runs in six games.

Coming to New York in 1977, Jackson signed one of the first big free-agent deals ($2.96 million over five years). "I didn't come to New York to be a star," he announced. "I brought my star with me." Self-described as "the

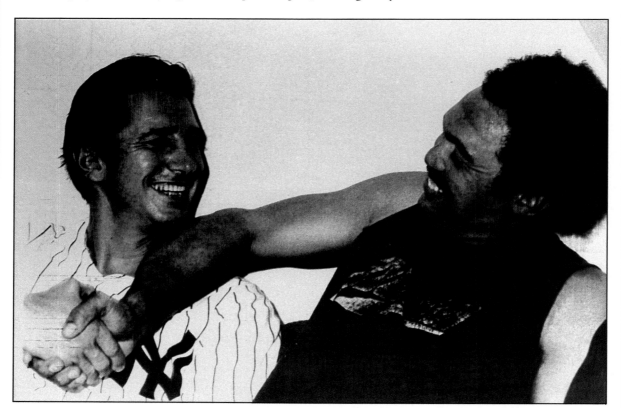

Above: Reggie Jackson (right) shakes hands with Billy Martin. *Opposite page:* Jackson hits back-to-back-to-back homers in the 1977 Series.

Reggie Jackson, "Mr. October," still ranks in the top 10 in eight World Series offensive categories. He played in five fall classics.

straw that stirs the drink," his ego ruffled the feathers of veterans like Thurman Munson and Graig Nettles, who had led the Yankees to the 1976 flag. As it turned out, it was Jackson's 32 home runs and 110 RBI that proved to be critical in a tight 1977 pennant race.

In the World Series, Jackson started slowly, going 1-for-6, as the Yankees and Dodgers split the first two games. He contributed an RBI single in the victory of Mike Torrez over Dodger Tommy John in game three. Jackson was just getting started. In the second inning of game four, his double started a three-run rally and his sixth-inning, opposite-field home run capped a 4-2 New York win. The Dodgers took the next game 10-4, but in the eighth inning Jackson homered again.

The thunder came early in game six. Facing Burt Hooton his first time up, Jackson walked on four pitches. With a 3-2 lead in the fourth, Hooton made the mistake of throwing a first-pitch strike, and Reggie hit it out of the park. The next inning, Reggie homered off reliever Elias Sosa's first pitch to put the Yankees up 7-3. Not even Charlie Hough's knuckleball could stop Reggie in the eighth as he homered again on the first pitch; the Yankees won the game 8-4 and the Series 4-2. Jackson matched Babe Ruth's record of three homers in a World Series game (in both the 1926 and 1928 Series), but not even Ruth had accomplished the feat with only three swings. Counting the last at bat of game five, Jackson had hit home runs in four at bats on only four swings.

DENT'S BLAST WINS EAST FOR YANKEES

◆

For the first half of the 1978 AL East pennant race, the Boston Red Sox led comfortably while the defending champion New York Yankees were in disarray. On July 17, New York bottomed out in fourth place, 14 games behind Boston. It would have been worse if not for Ron Guidry, who was winning nearly every start on his way to a 25-3 record. Catfish Hunter's sore arm wouldn't heal, Goose Gossage was ineffective, and Thurman Munson's bad knees prevented him from catching every day. Overshadowing all of this was Billy Martin's running feud with

Yankee third baseman Graig Nettles starred both at the plate and in the field in the 1970s.

Yankee hurlers Ron Guidry and Goose Gossage in 1978 combined for 35 of New York's 100 wins.

Reggie Jackson, which culminated in Martin's firing on July 24.

Under new manager Bob Lemon's calming presence, the Yankees' luck began to change. Hunter rebounded and started to win, and the bats came alive; the Yankees won 10 of 12 and, later, 16 of 18. In September, the Red Sox lead was down to four games before a four-game home series against New York. With Fred Lynn and Carl Yastrzemski hurt, Boston suffered a second massacre, losing each of the four games in a rout. Boston, however, refused to die. After slipping to three and one-half games behind in mid-September, the BoSox battled back to regain a tie on the last day of the season, forcing a one-game pennant playoff at Fenway.

Guidry took the mound to face 16-game winner Mike Torrez. In the second inning, Yaz hit a home run off Guidry. Boston was up 2-0 in the seventh when Bucky Dent came up with two on and two out. The Yankees shortstop had only 16 extra-base hits on the season. Dent broke his bat on Torrez's second pitch and fouled the ball off his instep; he continued only after having it numbed with ethyl chloride. Dent swung at the next pitch and poked a harmless-looking fly that carried over Fenway's Green Monster to give New York a 3-2 lead.

That's where the highlight film ends, but the game went on. In the eighth, Jackson hit a two-run shot. It turned out to be the margin of vic-tory, as the Red Sox scored twice off a shaky Gossage in the bottom of the inning. Down 5-4 in the bottom of the ninth with one out and Rick Burleson on first, Jerry Remy hit a liner to right that Lou Piniella lost in the sun. The quick-thinking Piniella acted as though he had it, and by sheer luck, the ball came right to him on a bounce. Piniella's decoy prevented Burleson from going to third, where he would have scored when Jim Rice hit a fly for the second out. Instead, Boston's season ended when Yastrzem-ski popped up to Graig Nettles.

Bucky Dent celebrates his pennant-winning three-run homer against the Red Sox in 1978.

STARGELL, PIRATES PLUNDER 1979 SERIES

◆

The 1979 World Series was a rematch of the 1971 Series between the Pittsburgh Pirates and the Baltimore Orioles. The Orioles were seeking to avenge the defeat they suffered after being up in that Series 2-0. This time, however, they would have to do it against "The Family," led by team father-figure, co-NL MVP Award winner (with Keith Hernandez), and inspirational leader Willie "Pops" Stargell. The disco craze was at its zenith in 1979, and one of the top hits that

John Candelaria was 14-9 for the 1979 Pirates and won game six of the World Series. "The Candy Man" captured 177 wins in a 19-year big-league career.

summer was "We Are Family" by Sister Sledge. The Pirates adopted the song as their theme.

The Pirates danced over the favored Cincinnati Reds in the National League Championship Series, beating them in three straight games on the strength of Stargell's MVP performance. The 38-year-old captain won game one with a three-run 11th-inning homer, hit a single and a double in the Pirates' 10-inning game-two victory, and belted a homer and a double in the 7-1 game-three triumph.

The slogan-less Orioles, on the other hand, stuck to the business of baseball, concentrating on giving solid pitching performances and racking up home runs. In the first game of the World Series, lefty Mike Flanagan made five first-inning runs—highlighted by a two-run homer from Doug DeCinces—stand up in a 5-4 vic-

Sidewinding reliever Kent Tekulve still ranks second on the all-time games pitched list. He appeared in an NL-leading 94 games for the 1979 Pirates.

tory. Although Pittsburgh won game two, the Orioles thumped the Bucs in a pair of scoring outbursts, 8-4 and 9-6 (winning the latter game after being down 6-3).

Stargell had gone 5-for-9 in the last two games, and the Pirates refused to think negatively. In game five, the Pirates bombarded Baltimore for seven runs in the last three innings. The Orioles were confident going into game six, however. They were returning home, and they had the great veteran righty Jim Palmer starting the contest. Although Palmer pitched well, John Candelaria and Kent Tekulve were better, combining for a seven-hit shutout in a 4-0 Pittsburgh victory.

Baltimore jumped out to an early 1-0 lead in game seven; Stargell, however, wasn't about to see his family denied. The man who gave out "Stargell Stars" to his teammates during the sea-

Willie Stargell boosted the Bucs in 1979. Not only did "Pops" lead the Pirates by inspiration, he also led on the field, slugging 32 homers and batting .281.

son for making big plays deserved one of his own in the sixth after he belted a two-run homer off Scott McGregor, his third of the Series. Meanwhile, Pirates relievers Don Robinson, Grant Jackson, and Tekulve stifled the Orioles, as the Pittsburgh offense (which batted .323 for the seven games) tacked on two more runs in the ninth to take the crown.

Stargell finished the seven games with a .400 batting average, an .833 slugging average, three homers, seven runs scored, and seven RBI. This offensive output earned him the Series MVP Award. In the Steel City that evening, they were dancing in the streets.

Oriole third sacker Doug DeCinces slides into Pirate Phil Garner in the 1979 Series. DeCinces hit 237 homers, and Garner later managed in the majors.

PHILLIES CAPTURE THEIR FIRST TITLE

◆

As the 1980s broke open, there remained one of the 16 major-league teams from 1901 that had yet to win a World Series. The closest the Philadelphia Phillies had come to the crown in their 97-year history was in 1915 and 1950, when they won pennants, and in 1964, when they lost the pennant in the season's last week.

In the late 1970s, however, the Phillies evolved into an NL power, having played in (and lost) the Championship Series in 1976, 1977, and 1978. After winning the 1980 NL East pennant (they beat Montreal by a game), the Phils hoped that their momentum would carry them to a title. Their opponent in the NLCS was the pitching-plentiful Astros.

Houston gave Philadelphia's Pete Rose, Mike Schmidt, Tug McGraw, & Co. all they could handle. After the Phillies won game one, Houston pulled out two extra-inning games, the second one on a combined 11-inning shutout by Joe Niekro and Dave Smith. The Astros had the Phillies on the brink of defeat in game four, leading 2-0 going into the eighth, but Philadelphia fought back to make it 3-2. Houston tied it in the bottom of the ninth, but the Phillies won the third straight extra-inning game of the NLCS with two runs in the 10th.

One of the most exciting Championship

Former 1970s "Big Red Machine" teammates Pete Rose of the Phillies (back) and the Astros' Joe Morgan sprawl over second base during the 1980 NLCS.

Tug McGraw celebrates after saving game four of the 1980 NLCS against the Astros.

Royals at bay, his teammates scored two runs in the ninth to go ahead 4-3. McGraw, who always had a flair for the dramatic, gave Phillies fans a scare when he walked the bases loaded in the bottom of the ninth before finally saving the game. In game six, Phillies ace left-hander Steve Carlton held the Royals to one run for seven innings, while Philadelphia scored four. In came McGraw again, walking the bases loaded three times in the last two innings. Each time, however, he managed to get the big out, including a foul pop-up that bounced out of catcher Bob Boone's mitt and into Pete Rose's glove. When Willie Wilson of the Royals struck out for a record 12th time to end the game, the City of Brotherly Love boasted a world champion.

Series ever gained more intensity in game five. The lead changed hands four times until, after nine innings, it was seven-all. The Phillies squeezed across a run in the 10th for the win.

After the NLCS, the World Series seemed almost anticlimactic. The Phillies kept up their momentum, however, winning the first two games in Philadelphia after being down 4-0 (to win 7-6) and 4-2 (to win 6-4). Kansas City bounced back in their home park, taking the next two games 4-3 (in 10 innings) and 5-3.

In the pivotal fifth game, Kansas City led 3-2 after six innings, and the Phillies brought in McGraw, the veteran reliever. While he kept

Above: Mike Schmidt was the main power source of the 1980 Phillies' championship drive, slugging 48 home runs. *Opposite page:* Catcher Bob Boone directed the Philadelphia pitching staff.

RICKEY HENDERSON SWIPES 130 BASES

◆

There was a time when stolen-base records could be neatly divided into pre-Maury Wills and post-Maury Wills records. Before Wills, the NL record-holder for stolen bases in a season was Cincinnati's Bob Bescher, who swiped 81 in 1911. Bescher was still the NL leader 51 years later when Wills stole 104. It was the same story in the AL, where the pre-Wills major-league record of 96 was set by Ty Cobb in 1915. New major-league marks were set in 1974 by Lou Brock and in 1982 by Rickey Henderson.

Henderson's career as a basestealer began when Billy Martin introduced "Billy Ball" in order to stimulate a powerless Oakland offense. As Martin put it: "I managed around him. If Rickey got on base, we scored runs." Henderson's stolen-base total jumped from 33 to 100 in 1980, and the A's moved from last place to second. Billy Ball took the A's to the strike-year playoffs in 1981, but they lapsed to 94 losses in 1982.

It was the lost 1982 season that enabled Martin to turn Henderson completely loose on the base paths. With the team going nowhere, he stole second and third with abandon, regardless of game situations. Although his success rate fell to 75 percent (excellent, but about five points below his career percentage) and he set a new major-league record with 42 times caught stealing, Henderson's 130 steals smashed Brock's major-league record by a dozen.

Henderson stole his 100th base early in August. When he went against Brewer pitcher Mike Caldwell on Aug. 26, Henderson had 117 steals (and Brock was in attendance). He opened the game with a single. Caldwell attempted to keep Henderson close to the bag, but on the fourth pitch he took off and was safe at second, tying Brock's record. Henderson was unable to break Brock's record the rest of the game. The next night off of Doc Medich, Henderson walked his first time up. After Medich threw several times to first to lessen Henderson's lead, the pitcher brought the pitch home. Henderson flew toward second and got his 119th steal. The game was stopped for a short ceremony. When the contest continued, the new record-holder went on to steal three more bases.

What really set Henderson apart is that for the most part of his career basestealing was not the strongest part of his game. The main thing he did was score runs—around 100 a year. Many consider him the model leadoff hitter. He also delivered about a .290 batting average, a .400 on-base average, and power (he holds the major-league record for most home runs leading off a game). But in one year, 1982, Henderson was all about basestealing.

Opposite page: Rickey Henderson ran wild in 1982, stealing 130 bases to shatter Maury Wills' 20-year-old mark. Rickey swiped 100 sacks three times.

RYAN BEATS CARLTON TO STRIKEOUT MARK

◆

Walter Johnson's all-time record of 3,508 career strikeouts was once considered as unbreakable as Babe Ruth's 714 home runs. Once Hank Aaron busted Ruth's mark, however, no career record seemed safe. By the start of the 1980s, six hurlers—Gaylord Perry, Nolan Ryan, Tom Seaver, Steve Carlton, Don Sutton, and Phil Niekro—had reached or were gaining on 3,000 lifetime Ks.

By 1983, Ryan and Carlton were not only in a position to pass Johnson easily, they were on track to post more than 4,000 lifetime strikeouts. There was only one question: Who would break Johnson's record first?

It was fitting that the man who threw a fastball nicknamed "Ryan's Express" would be the one to overtake a pitcher nicknamed "The Big Train." Ryan started the 1983 season 60 Ks ahead of Carlton (3,494 to 3,434). Ryan needed just five strikeouts to break Johnson's record when he started against the Montreal Expos on April 27. Without his usually explosive fastball, it took Ryan until the eighth inning to make history. He struck out Brad Mills looking at a curveball for the 3,509th.

Almost a month later, Carlton got his 3,509th K when he struck out San Diego's Garry Templeton. The race was on for Carlton

Steve Carlton acknowledges the cheers after breaking Walter Johnson's career strikeout mark. "Lefty's" 4,136 Ks rank second on the all-time list.

to catch Ryan for the career lead. Ryan injured his thigh in early May and missed a month. On June 7, Carlton topped Ryan with 3,522 strikeouts. That night, Ryan fanned three to remain in second place, but in his next start, he whiffed 12—and the two artists were tied at 3,535.

Baseball fans were excited at the prospect of watching this duel all summer long. Carlton, however, pulled away in August and ultimately led the league with 277 Ks (Ryan had 183). That June, *The New York Times* had said, "Despite his being two years older than Ryan at 38, Carlton is likely to be around longer." In October, *The Sporting News* wrote, "With over 3,700 strikeouts, Carlton's record is as out of reach as DiMaggio's 56-game hitting streak or Hack Wilson's 190 RBI."

How wrong those venerable papers of record were. Ryan went ahead of Carlton by two at the end of 1984 and pulled away in '85, ultimately reaching the amazing total of 5,000 strikeouts in 1989.

Carlton retired after the 1987 season with 4,136 lifetime strikeouts and is still second behind Ryan on the all-time list. Gaylord Perry also passed Johnson by the end of 1983.

The New York Times assessed Ryan's lifetime achievement by saying that if a player had passed Ruth's homer record by the same percentage that Ryan was ahead of Johnson, he would have 980 homers. Ryan's response was "guess I'm going for 1,000 homers."

Nolan Ryan won 11 strikeout crowns and ranks first on the all-time K list with 5,714.

GOODEN SHATTERS ROOKIE K RECORD

◆

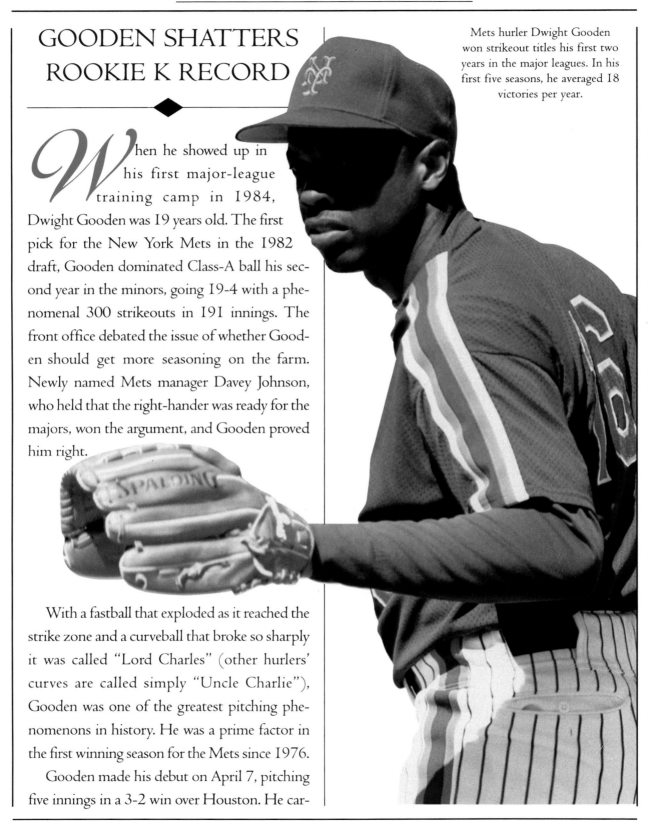

Mets hurler Dwight Gooden won strikeout titles his first two years in the major leagues. In his first five seasons, he averaged 18 victories per year.

When he showed up in his first major-league training camp in 1984, Dwight Gooden was 19 years old. The first pick for the New York Mets in the 1982 draft, Gooden dominated Class-A ball his second year in the minors, going 19-4 with a phenomenal 300 strikeouts in 191 innings. The front office debated the issue of whether Gooden should get more seasoning on the farm. Newly named Mets manager Davey Johnson, who held that the right-hander was ready for the majors, won the argument, and Gooden proved him right.

With a fastball that exploded as it reached the strike zone and a curveball that broke so sharply it was called "Lord Charles" (other hurlers' curves are called simply "Uncle Charlie"), Gooden was one of the greatest pitching phenomenons in history. He was a prime factor in the first winning season for the Mets since 1976.

Gooden made his debut on April 7, pitching five innings in a 3-2 win over Houston. He carried a no-hitter into the eighth inning against Pittsburgh two months later, winning 2-1. In July he became the youngest player ever selected to the All-Star Game, and in the first of his two shutout innings, he struck out the side.

As the season reached into September, an avalanche of rookie strikeout records fell. On Aug. 27, Gooden broke Gary Nolan's record for Ks by a teenage rookie (206). During a one-hitter against the Chicago Cubs on Sept. 7, Gooden's 11 Ks shattered Grover Alexander's NL rookie record of 227 strikeouts. In his next start, Gooden struck out 16 Pirates to break Herb Score's rookie record of 245 Ks set in 1955.

Gooden followed that pitching performance with another 16 strikeouts against Philadelphia, setting an NL record for Ks in two consecutive games with 32 (shattering the record held by the great Sandy Koufax) and a modern major-league record of 43 Ks in three consecutive games. As Gooden's legend grew, Shea Stadium fans started hanging "K" signs for each strikeout that "Doc" notched.

Overall, Gooden went 17-9, was second in the league in ERA with a 2.60 mark, and set the rookie strikeout record with an astounding 276 Ks, 36 more than the loop's runner-up. He also established a major-league record with an average of 11.39 strikeouts per nine innings and led the league in allowing the fewest hits per game, 6.65. In the Rookie of the Year election, Gooden received 23 out of a possible 24 first-place votes, becoming the youngest player to win the honor.

Dwight Gooden broke Herb Score's rookie strikeout record in 1984, and did it pitching fewer innings than Score had. Gooden was the Mets' first-round pick in the June 1982 draft and spent less than two full seasons in the minor leagues. His 300 strikeouts in 191 innings at Class-A Lynchburg in 1983 led the Mets to summon him.

ROSE GETS HIT 4,192 TO SURPASS COBB

◆

When 22-year-old Pete Rose showed up at the Cincinnati Reds training camp in 1963, few of the team's veterans thought he had a chance to make the cut. His skills seemed average at best. He did, however, have a strong point—hustling. During his career, he developed another specialty—accumulating base hits.

Two years after winning the NL Rookie of the Year Award, the switch-hitting Rose led the league in hits with 209. He had 1,000 hits at the midway point of 1968, and just five years later he was up to 2,000. "My goal," he had said in 1972, "is 3,000. If I can play 150 games for the next five years, I'll reach 3,000 on July 16, 1977 . . . no, make that 1978."

Rose was as clairvoyant as he was cocky. On May 5, 1978, he became only the 13th man to pass the 3,000 hit mark; he had also tied the NL record for hits in 44 consecutive games. And Rose, just 36 years old, was showing no signs of letting up.

Not only did it appear possible that Rose could get 4,000 hits, it also seemed that Ty Cobb's all-time record of 4,191 hits might be in jeopardy.

After the 1978 season, Rose signed as a free agent with the Phillies and promptly had his 10th 200-hit season, a record. He led the Phillies to the World Series in 1980, and his 185 hits that year put him at the 3,547 mark, fourth all-time behind Stan Musial, Hank Aaron, and Ty Cobb.

The years looked as if they were catching up with Rose when in 1983, at age 42, he knocked only 121 hits. Just 201 hits away from the record going into '84, he signed with the Montreal Expos, then returned later in the season to his hometown Reds as player-manager. Rose was only 94 hits behind Cobb by year's end, and the nationwide countdown was on.

Playing as the Reds part-time first baseman in 1985, Rose posted 90 hits by the weekend of Sept. 6. The Reds were in Chicago and, as manager, Rose could have kept himself out of the lineup to ensure breaking the record in Cincinnati. He felt he needed to play for the team to win, however, and he went on to tie Cobb at 4,191 hits on Sunday, Sept. 8.

Three days later, 47,237 fans packed Riverfront Stadium, only a few miles from where Rose grew up. In the first inning, Rose faced Padres right-hander Eric Show. With the count 2-1, Show threw a slider inside. Rose fought the pitch off and drove it to left-center field for a single. The game was halted. As the crowd gave Rose a standing ovation, his son ran out to first base. Never one to show any emotion on a baseball field other than grit and hustle, Rose hugged his son and cried.

Opposite page: Pete Rose acknowledges the crowd after shattering Ty Cobb's all-time hit record. *Above:* Rose led the National League in hits seven times, runs four times, and won three batting titles. He also batted .381 in NLCS play.

BUCKNER BOOTS METS TO 1986 TITLE

◆

Eleven years after the Boston Red Sox had been in one of the most memorable sixth games of the World Series, they found themselves in another one. Unlike 1975, when the Red Sox triumphed over the Cincinnati Reds on a Carlton Fisk home run, the Boston ballclub came up on the short end this time, and largely because of an easily playable ground ball.

The New York Mets, who had won 108 games during the regular season and took the NL East by 21½ games, were favorites to win the championship. Boston was 95-66 on the season. Both teams won closely contested League Championship Series that were among the best LCSs of all time.

The Mets dropped their first two home games against Boston 1-0 and 9-3. The New York bats did wake up in Fenway Park, where they won the first two games 7-1 and 6-2. Bruce Hurst, who had shut out the Mets in game one, then pitched a 4-2 contest, putting the BoSox one game from an upset Series title.

Tied three-all after nine innings, game six appeared in the bag for Beantown when Sox outfielder Dave Henderson homered to lead off the 10th. Then a Wade Boggs double and a

Mookie Wilson in his at bat during game six of the 1986 World Series. In his wildest dreams, he probably couldn't have imagined that such a bizarre string of events would make him the cause of one of the most exciting games of all time.

Marty Barrett single gave Boston what seemed to be an important insurance run. As Mets Wally Backman and Keith Hernandez went down against Red Sox reliever Calvin Schiraldi, fans prepared to celebrate their first Series title since 1918, when Babe Ruth pitched for Boston. Gary Carter kept the Mets alive with a single to center. Then Kevin Mitchell, batting for reliever Rick Aguilera, knocked a single to center. Although Schiraldi got two strikes on Ray Knight, the third baseman fought off a fastball and blooped a single to center, driving in one run and putting the tying one on third.

Bob Stanley relieved Schiraldi and faced Mookie Wilson. With the count 2-2, Wilson fouled off three pitches. Stanley's next delivery, low and inside, hit off catcher Rich Gedman's glove; Mitchell danced down the line with the run that tied it. With Knight now in scoring position, Wilson hit two more pitches foul. "I just wasn't going to strike out in that spot," he said. Wilson tapped Stanley's next pitch down the first-base line for an apparent third out. As Boston first baseman Bill Buckner bent down to field the ball, however, it skipped through his legs. Knight brought home the winning run.

The Red Sox went up in game seven 3-0 before the Mets exploded with eight runs between the sixth and eighth innings. The New York team went on to win the game 8-5. Another championship had slipped beyond Boston's— and Billy Buckner's—grasp.

Buckner's boot is now recorded in baseball history as one of the great Series blunders.

Despite being an excellent player, Bill Buckner will be remembered for booting Mookie Wilson's easy grounder and costing Boston the championship.

McGWIRE BLASTS ROOKIE-RECORD 49 ROUND-TRIPPERS

◆

The 1987 season was a bonanza year for offense in general and the home run in particular. Among the many hitting milestones from that year included a new major-league record for total home runs with 4,458; 20 or more homers hit by a record 51 AL players; three teams (Detroit, Toronto, and Baltimore) hit over 200; Toronto hit a record 10 homers in one game.

Amid all this excitement and controversy, it's not hard to see how the Oakland Athletics Mark McGwire's total obliteration of the rookie home run record got somewhat lost in the shuffle. McGwire actually broke a number of rookie slugging records, many of which had stood for a long time. Cleveland's Al Rosen set the AL mark in 1950 with 37. The NL record had been set by Wally Berger, who hit 38 in 1930, and matched by Frank Robinson in 1956.

Great things were not predicted for McGwire in 1987. In fact, he came into spring training as a long shot to unseat Carney Lansford at third; the A's plan was to give first base to Rob Nelson, who had swatted 52 home runs over the previous two minor-league seasons. But McGwire looked so good in camp that he was given Nelson's job in spite of a .167 spring-training batting average. Teammate Jose Canseco pre-

dicted: "[McGwire is] going to hit 30 homers and drive in more than 100 runs."

McGwire made half a prophet out of Canseco by hitting 33 homers before the All-Star break. Inevitably, speculation started about the rookie's chances of breaking Roger Maris's record. Of course, there are reasons why many more than 100 men have hit 40-plus home runs in a season and only 17 have reached 50, and McGwire was much too level-headed to put that kind of pressure on himself. Things were tough enough already with American League pitchers being a little more careful with him in the second half; he hit only three home runs (with only 12 RBI) in August. He had the flu so severely during that time that he lost 10 pounds. McGwire, though, came back healthy, laid off bad pitches, and rebounded with a nine-homer September to break the rookie home run record with 49, a margin of almost 30 percent.

McGwire ended the season with the rookie-season records not only for home runs but for total bases with 344, for slugging percentage with .618, and for most extra-base hits in a season with 183. He tied the team RBI mark of 118. Against Cleveland in June, he hit five home runs in two games, and he scored nine runs in nine consecutive plate appearances, tying another AL record. For the season, 17 of McGwire's home runs came on first pitches, while 20 homers came when he was leading off the inning. McGwire became the first unanimous Rookie of the Year selection since Carlton Fisk in 1972.

Mark McGwire hits one of his 49 homers in his rookie year.

HERSHISER SETS SCORELESS INNINGS RECORD WITH 59

◆

*I*t is referred to as "a career year," that one amazing season when a baseball player puts it all together and plays better than anyone, including himself, ever deemed he could. Orel Leonard Hershiser IV had one of those career years in 1988, the season in which he shattered one of the game's most unbreakable of records—Don Drysdale's streak of 58 consecutive scoreless innings.

The long and lean Los Angeles Dodgers right-hander had been one of the NL's best pitchers since coming up in 1984. Nicknamed "Bulldog" by Dodgers manager Tommy Lasorda, Hershiser featured an above-average fastball, an outstanding curve, a great sinker—and the control to throw them anywhere in the strike zone. After four years in the league, he had become an intelligent hurler, studying hitters and pitching to their weaknesses.

Hershiser was in the midst of dissecting the NL's batters when the streak originated on Aug. 30. Going 17-8 and pitching the Dodgers to the NL West pennant, the 29-year-old just then seemed to shift into high gear. One team after another fell under his shutout spell—Atlanta (3-0), Cincinnati (5-0), Atlanta (1-0), Houston (1-0), and San Francisco (3-0)—until Sept. 28, when Hershiser

The year 1988 will always be special to Orel Hershiser. During his last start of that season, Bulldog was able to break Don Drysdale's record of 58 scoreless innings. He bested the record by one inning, pitching 10 scoreless innings in that game.

was just nine shutout innings shy from tying the benchmark set by Don Drysdale, another great Dodger right-hander. Hershiser matched the 20-year-old record during that game, putting up nine goose eggs against the Padres. The Dodger offense, however, also failed to score, giving Hershiser a chance to pitch another inning and break the record. "It was the best I'd ever seen [Hershiser] pitch," said Padre Tony Gwynn, one of the game's best hitters. "I grounded out four times on a sinker, and he set me up differently each time."

The only question that remained was whether or not the pitching sensation would last through a 10th inning. Lasorda and pitching coach Ron Perranowski persuaded Hershiser, who said he would be satisfied sharing the record with Drysdale, to go for the break. "If he

Orel Hershiser

hadn't," said Drysdale at a press conference after the game, "I would have gone out there and kicked him in the rear." Hershiser took the mound and retired the Padres in order, pitching 59 consecutive scoreless innings.

Hershiser extended his career year into postseason play, claiming both the NLCS and World Series MVP Awards in leading the Dodgers to a world championship. By opening the NLCS against the Mets with eight shutout innings, Hershiser racked up 67 straight innings in which he was not scored upon; he then closed the series with a shutout in game seven. He went on to keep the Oakland A's scoreless in one of the World Series games. He finished the season with a 23-8 record and a 2.26 ERA.

In 1988, Orel was an All-Star and won a Gold Glove.

GIBSON DELIVERS CLASSIC FALL SHOT

◆

*I*n the climactic scene of the film *The Natural*, damaged baseball player Roy Hobbs wins the championship by hitting a game-ending home run so prodigious it destroys a light tower. In game one of the 1988 World Series, life imitated art.

The Los Angeles Dodgers and the Oakland Athletics met by virtue of beating the Mets and Red Sox. The A's—with sluggers Jose Canseco and Mark McGwire and a fine pitching staff headed by Dave Stewart and Dennis Eckersley—had won 104 games during the season and were favored to beat the Dodgers. The Dodgers, however, had two points in their favor: Cy Young Award winner Orel Hershiser and league MVP Kirk Gibson.

Above and opposite page: After hitting the game-winning homer in his only at bat in game one of the '88 World Series, a happy Kirk Gibson meets the media.

As the Series got underway, however, it appeared that Gibson's inspirational leadership would be coming more from the bench than the field. He had strained his left hamstring in game five of the playoffs, and he hadn't swung at a pitch since injuring his right knee in game seven.

Los Angeles got power early from Mickey Hatcher, who homered in the bottom of the first. The A's answered with Canseco's grand slam in the next inning. A Dodger run in the sixth made it 4-3. When the game reached the eighth, Gibson picked his body off the trainer's table, put an ice bag on his knee, suited up, took some practice swings off a batting tee, and told manager Tommy Lasorda he was able to hit if he was needed. Gibson hadn't been able to swing a bat that morning.

Eckersley walked Mike Davis leading off the last of the ninth. Light-hitting Dave Anderson had been put on deck as a decoy. Gibson emerged from the dugout, hobbled to the plate, and looked completely overwhelmed as he fouled off two pitches. When he hit the next slider foul, he almost fell out of the batter's box. A few pitches later, Davis stole second. All Gibson needed to bring him home to tie the game was a hit.

On a 3-2 count, Eckersley appeared to throw a slider down and away. Gibson, however, reached out with his powerful arms and got enough wrist action into the swing to, amazingly, send the ball far into right field and out of the park for a game-winning home run.

As Gibson limped slowly around the bases, his arm raised in the air, Hall of Fame broadcaster Jack Buck probably echoed the feelings of a nation when he said, "I don't believe what I just saw." Neither did the A's, who won only game three and lost the Series four games to one.

TREASURY OF BASEBALL

RYAN COLLECTS SEVEN NO-HITTERS

◆

As a member of the Angels, Nolan Ryan threw four no-hitters in the three seasons between 1973 and 1975. His first was on May 15, 1973, against the Royals. Two months later, he struck out 17 Tigers and walked four to record his second. On Sept. 28, 1974, Ryan walked eight Twins while striking out 15 for his third career no-hitter. He tied Sandy Koufax's

career record of four by shutting down the Orioles on June 15, 1975.

By 1981, however, Ryan still stood tied with Koufax for the record. The 34-year-old right-hander had one of his best seasons, for the Astros, going 11-5 with a league-leading 1.69 ERA. On Sept. 26, Ryan broke the tie. Starting against the Dodgers at the Astrodome on national TV, Ryan struggled with his control the first three innings, walking three batters and throwing a wild pitch. Although he had 10 strikeouts over those first six innings, he let up in the final three to give him better control of his pitches. The strategy worked. Reggie Smith

Above and opposite: Nolan Ryan, strikeout king, puts his body through the mill as he twirls magic on the mound.

TREASURY OF BASEBALL

led off the ninth, and Ryan threw three strikes by him. Ken Landreaux then grounded to first for the second out. On a 2-0 pitch, Ryan threw a big curve that Dusty Baker bounced to third base for an easy out. Ryan had his first no-hitter in six years and a record.

In 1989, Ryan jumped to the Rangers and led the AL that year with 301 strikeouts. On June 11, 1990, he was making his second start since coming off the 15-day disabled list with a stress fracture in his lower vertebrae. He was 4-3 at the time with a 5.11 ERA and was facing the defending world champion Oakland A's. Ryan's son Reese sat on the bench with his pop, giving him encouragement. In the ninth inning,

Roberto Alomar was Ryan's final victim in No. 7.

Ryan struck out leadoff batter Ken Phelps, got Rickey Henderson to ground out, and got Willie Randolph to foul out. When the final out was made, Ryan struck out 14 and walked only two, becoming the oldest pitcher to ever hurl a no-hitter.

He wasn't finished. On May 1, 1991—the same day that Rickey Henderson broke Lou Brock's record for stolen bases—Nolan, in Arlington, retired 27 of 29 Toronto Blue Jays, who went on that year to become world champs. He walked only two batters while striking out 16, and had one K every inning. Gary Pettis, a five-time Gold Glover in center field, hustled in to catch a blooper hit by Manny Lee for Ryan's closest call. When Ryan pitched his first no-hitter, Sandy Alomar Sr. was a teammate. When Ryan struck out the final batter for his seventh no-hitter, that batter was Roberto Alomar, Sandy's son.

Nolan Ryan seemed to defy the aging process. In 1991, The Express is congratulated by teammates after throwing his seventh no-hitter.

TWINS HOME IN, OUTLAST BRAVES

David Justice tags one in the 12th inning of game three for the win over the Twins.

NFL commissioner Pete Rozelle dreamt that his league would achieve parity during the 1970s. Baseball in the '90s achieved parity as the Twins and the Braves, both last-place teams in their divisions in 1990, won pennants in 1991. Atlanta in 1990 had the poorest record in the majors with a 65-97 mark, but the Braves rebounded in one year to a 94-68 record in 1991 on the strength of a young rotation, headed by Cy Young recipient Tom Glavine and Steve Avery. In the NLCS, the Braves prevailed four games to two over the powerhouse Pirates, with Avery gaining shutouts in games two and six.

The Twins knew how to put the "home" in "Homerdome"—the nickname for Minneapolis's Hubert H. Humphrey Metrodome— as they had the best home record in baseball in 1991 (51-30) on their way to a 95-67 record. Scott Erickson won 20 games, Rick Aguilera saved 42, and Kirby Puckett led the offense. Minnesota beat Toronto 4-2 in the ALCS.

The Twins continued their domination at the Metrodome with a 5-2 victory in game one of the fall classic against the Braves, as Jack Morris pitched seven innings, giving up five hits and two runs. Chili Davis hammered a three-run homer to give the Twins a 3-2 game-two victory. Ron Gant singled in a run in the third, but

after he returned to the bag at first, Kent Hrbek applied a hard tag that literally lifted Gant off of the bag, and umpire Drew Coble called Gant out.

In Atlanta for game three, Mark Lemke singled home Dave Justice in the bottom of the 12th inning for a 5-4 win. A record 42 players were used during the game, along with 12 pinch hitters—including Aguilera, who was the first pitcher to pinch hit in a fall classic since Don Drysdale in 1965. Morris pitched six strong innings in game four, but the Twins could not win because Lemke again came up big at the plate. With the score tied 2-2 in the bottom of the ninth and one out, Lemke tripled, then scored on a Jerry Willard sac fly—just beating the tag of Twins catcher Brian Harper. Harper was trying to recover from being run over by

Lonnie Smith in the fifth inning—one of the hardest collisions in Series play. Lemke tripled twice in Atlanta's 14-5 game-five trouncing.

The Twins were thrilled to get home for game six, as Puckett pasted an 11th-inning solo shot off of Charlie Leibrandt for a 4-3 Twins victory. Morris came back for game seven, pitched 10 innings of seven-hit shutout baseball, and waited for a Gene Larkin single in the 10th to deliver to Minnesota a second world championship in five years. In 1991, as in 1987, all the Twins' victories came in the Homerdome.

An exalted Kirby Puckett touches all four to win game six.

CARTER'S CLOBBER CHEERS BLUE JAYS

◆

The Toronto Blue Jays may have been defending world champions in 1993, but a group of rag-tag rogues from Philadelphia captured the hearts of fans everywhere.

Led by Lenny Dykstra, John Kruk, Tommy Greene, Curt Schilling, a host of platoon players, and the "Wild Thing," Mitch Williams, the Phillies improved from a 70-92 record in 1992 to a 97-65 mark in '93, winning the NL East. In the NLCS, the Phillies unexpectedly upended the Atlanta Braves—owners of baseball's best rotation and best record (104-58).

In the AL, the Blue Jays boasted a solid organization and the top-three batters in the loop—John Olerud, Paul Molitor, and Robby Alomar. While Toronto's pitching wasn't stellar, it was good enough to support the fine offense. The Jays went past the White Sox in the ALCS to vie for the first back-to-back championships since the Yankees in 1977 and '78.

Blue Jays' ace Juan Guzman and NLCS MVP Curt Schilling both struggled in game one, but Olerud provided the pop that the Jays needed to win 8-5. Jim Eisenreich, a platoon

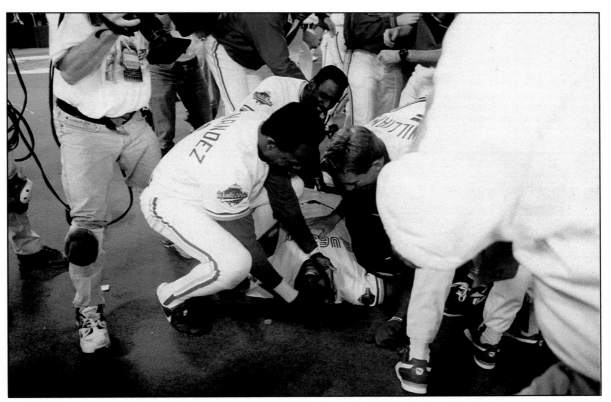

Joe Carter is mobbed by his mates after his bases-loaded blast. It was the second series-ending homer in the history of the Fall Classic.

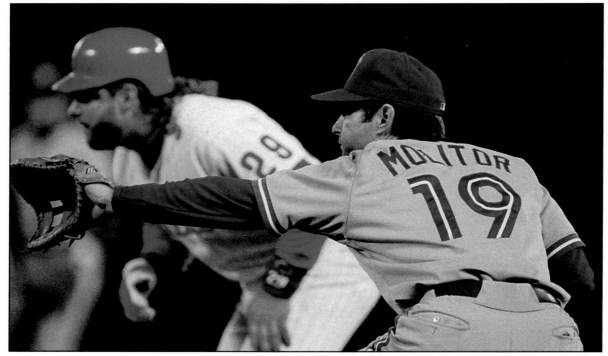

Above: Paul Molitor and Phillie John Kruk. *Opposite page:* Paul Molitor homered in the 1993 World Series and was named MVP.

outfielder for the Phils, in game two crushed a three-run homer during a five-run third frame for a 6-4 Phillies win. The Jays rebounded to pound Philadelphia 10-3 in game three.

Game four was the highest-scoring and perhaps the most chaotic affair in Series history. The Blue Jays came back from 6-3, 12-7, and 14-9 deficits in the contest to win 15-14. Schilling came back in game five to shut Toronto out on five hits to win 2-0. In game six, the Phillies rebounded from a 5-0 deficit to take a 6-5 lead through eight innings.

As the Phillies had done all season, they turned to Williams to shut the door. Toronto leadoff man Rickey Henderson stood and watched Williams throw four straight balls.

After Devon White flew out, Molitor singled, and Henderson stopped at second. Joe Carter stepped to the plate.

Carter watched Williams deliver two straight balls to him. Mitch was famous for walking the bases loaded yet getting out of the inning unscathed. Carter looked at a strike and swung and missed a slider. Williams tried busting Carter inside with a fastball to ring up a K, but Carter turned on it and sent it over the left-field fence. It was the second Series-ending homer in fall-classic history (after Bill Mazeroski's homer in 1960) and the first to ever bring a team from behind to win a Series. Molitor was named the Series MVP for 12 hits and eight RBI, but the hero's role forever would be Joe Carter's.

Incidents of Baseball

THE GAME'S WATERSHED MOMENTS

Baseball follows America, sometimes literally, as when the Braves moved out of Boston to pursue bigger audiences where the population was burgeoning—West. Babe Ruth helped draw more supporters, but broadcasting also enlarged the fan base across the land.

This subsequent diamond manifest destiny led to rival leagues, not only the American League but the Federal League and the Mexican League. Another potential rival league, the Continental League, helped to expedite expansion. There are times, nevertheless, that baseball has been in front of America; this was never more evident than in 1947 when Jackie Robinson broke the color bar in the major leagues.

BIRTH OF THE AMERICAN LEAGUE

★

When Ban Johnson saw an opportunity to challenge the preeminence of the National League, he jumped at the chance. Johnson, a former college baseball player and ex-sportswriter, almost single-handedly created the American League and broke the stranglehold the National League held on professional baseball.

In 1893, Johnson became president of the moribund Western League, a Midwestern minor league. Under his stewardship the newly renamed Western League was a huge success, but Johnson had a larger goal.

The National League cut back from 12 to eight teams in 1899; Johnson sensed an opportunity. He renamed the Western League "The American League." He stocked the league with recent NL castoffs, and convinced St. Paul owner Charles Comiskey to move his franchise to Chicago and go into head-to-head competition with the NL Cubs.

The NL didn't take Johnson seriously until it was too late. His new league was highly successful in 1900, as the new Chicago White Sox won the first American League pennant. Emboldened by the league's success, Johnson declared war.

In 1901, he proclaimed the American League a "major" league. He moved franchises into several cities abandoned by the NL, and others into cities that already sported an NL franchise. The AL raided the senior circuit of over 100 players, including such stars as Cy Young, Jimmy Collins, and Napoleon Lajoie.

Fans turned out in force for the new league. The 1901 pennant race went down to the

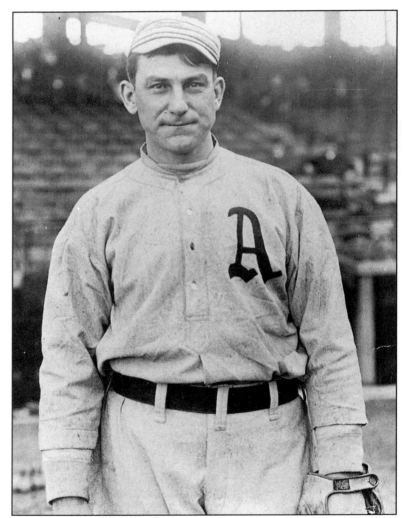

Nap Lajoie was one of the stars raided from the existing National League to help the upstart American League gain footing.

The 1900 New York Giants pose with owner Andrew Freedman (center).
After experiencing mediocre results (and many managerial changes), Freedman sold the
team to John Brush in 1903. With manager John McGraw, the team regained success.

wire before the White Sox edged Boston by four games.

No one in the National League had the authority to respond effectively to Johnson's challenge. The AL completed another successful campaign, and even more players jumped to the new circuit. With the National Agreement governing player contracts due to expire, the National League sued for peace in the fall of 1902.

The two leagues agreed to compete as separate but equal entities. Johnson, NL president John Pulliam, and Cincinnati president August Hermann (an old Johnson crony) formed the National Commission, which was given the authority by both leagues to run baseball. Johnson dominated the triumvirate.

Each league soon recognized it could be more successful in tandem than either could alone.

That reality was made obvious at the end of the 1903 season. Owner Barney Dreyfuss of NL champion Pittsburgh challenged William Killea, owner of pennant-winning Boston of the AL, to a postseason "world's series." The National Commission approved of the challenge, Dreyfuss and Killea worked out the specifics of the best-of-nine game series, and on Oct. 1, 1903, the two clubs met in Boston for the first game of the modern World Series.

While Pittsburgh was a slight favorite, due primarily to the presence of star shortstop Honus Wagner, the Pirates' pitching staff was riddled with illness and injury. Pitcher Deacon Phillippe performed yeoman-like duty in the Series, eventually pitching five of the eight games played. Boston, on the other hand, featured hurlers Cy Young and Bill Dinneen, and was paced by third baseman Jimmy Collins.

The Series was marked by controversy, lack of crowd con-

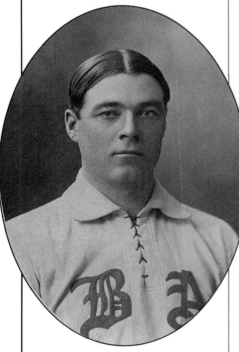

Big Bill Dinneen (pictured here in his Boston days), threw two shutouts in the 1903 World Series.

trol, and a popular song called "Tessie." Pittsburgh was able to take advantage of overflow crowds in the first three games in Boston to bang out a string of ground-rule doubles and triples and jump to the Series lead. Some thought Boston was on the take. When the games reached Pittsburgh, the Pirates continued to dominate and took a three-games-to-one advantage.

Enter a Boston bartender and raconteur with the unlikely name of Michael "'Nuf 'Ced" McGreevey, leader of a group of Boston fans called the Royal Rooters. Under McGreevey's leadership, the Rooters began the incessant singing of an innocuous ditty named "Tessie."

Their vocal pyrotechnics drove Pittsburgh to distraction, and Boston stormed back to win four straight and take the Series in eight games. Each club made money, fans loved it, and it looked as if the Series would be an annual occurrence.

But the wounds of the war between the National and American Leagues took a bit longer to heal. In 1904, owner John T. Brush of the National League champion Giants announced he had no intention

Ban Johnson was many things to many people. His crowning achievement was as the formation of the American League.

of playing the AL pennant winner. Brush and AL president Ban Johnson had been adversaries for more than a decade, and Brush, opposed to the truce, was in no mood to help Johnson. The New York Highlanders also appeared likely to win the American League pennant, and Brush didn't want to risk losing to his crosstown rivals.

When Boston overtook New York on the last day of the season, Boston's new owner, John Taylor, pleaded with Brush to play. Brush still refused, but later stated that if the Giants won the pennant in

RIVAL LEAGUES DEFY MAJORS

★

Since the early days of baseball, certain wealthy men have dreamed of owning a baseball team. But the fraternity of club owners has always been an exclusive group. The demand for owning a baseball team has always outstripped the supply of available franchises. On a number of occasions, this situation has spawned the creation of rival leagues.

In the 19th century, a number of leagues battled for supremacy before the National League and the American League consolidated their relationship in 1903. While the two leagues have existed in har-

mony, they have had to fight off a number of challenges.

"The Federal League of Baseball Clubs" was formed in 1913. Following the example set by Ban Johnson in the creation of the American League, the Midwest-based Federal League began as a minor league. After successfully completing the 1913 season, the league declared itself a major league, shifted several franchises into cities already occupied by NL and AL clubs, and began raiding each league of stars. Another baseball war was on.

The battle was short and violent. After initial peace talks broke down, in 1915 the Feds filed an antitrust suit against organized baseball. The NL and AL responded by upping

Cy Young as he appeared in his days with the AL Boston team.

1905, they would agree to a similar challenge.

In the off-season, Brush wrote up a series of conditions under which World Series play could resume. The National Commission approved of Brush's plan. The World Series has been played every season since, the embodiment of peace, and peaceful competition, between the two leagues.

While the Federal League wasn't around long, it provides an interesting footnote for baseball history. Pictured here is the 1914 Buffalo Feds of the Federal League. The strength of the two existing major leagues made the war waged by the Federal League little more than a short-lived skirmish.

The NL and AL failed to acquire Benny Kauff from the Feds.

the stakes and trying to raid the Federal League of its best players, such as Benny Kauff, known as the Ty Cobb of the Federal League. The battle proved costly for the Feds, although Kauff stayed. Attendance dropped in 1915, and several clubs lost money.

On Dec. 22, 1915, the Federal League made peace with organized baseball. Several owners were allowed to buy into existing major-league franchises, and all players, some of whom had been banned after jumping leagues, were reinstated. While the existence of the league is now just a footnote in baseball history, one monument to its existence still stands:

Wrigley Field, home of the Chicago Cubs, was the original home of the Federal League Chicago Whales.

The Mexican League posed the next challenge to major-league baseball's status quo. In 1946, Mexican millionaire Jorge Pasquel tried to bolster the six-team Mexican League with an influx of highly paid major leaguers. Although Pasquel had no intention of going in head-to-head competition with organized baseball in the United States, he offered some of baseball's biggest stars huge sums of money to play south of the border. The Cardinals' Stan Musial, who earned only $13,500 with St. Louis, was offered $175,000.

Only a handful of players took Pasquel up on his offer,

Stan Musial was the No. 1 target of Mexico's Jorge Pasquel.

among them such established major leaguers as Giant pitcher Sal Maglie, Cardinal pitcher Max Lanier, and Dodger catcher Mickey Owen. Baseball commissioner Happy Chandler frightened most players into remaining in the major leagues

Weeghman Field, now Wrigley Field, was built in 1914 to house the Federal League's Chicago Whales. It is the lone visual reminder of the Federal League's futile attempt to give the NL and AL some competition.

baseball had sent the players a strong message: The reserve clause was sacrosanct.

The Continental League was created, on paper anyway, on July 27, 1959. The new league hoped to take advantage of the absence of baseball in locations recently abandoned by the big leagues, such as New York. Branch Rickey was appointed league president. At the same time, organized baseball was facing yet another legislative challenge to its unique antitrust exemption. Hoping to thwart the effort, they agreed to accept the new league. Franchises were awarded, and the league made plans to start operation in 1960.

The transition from paper to reality was difficult, however. The bill to remove baseball's antitrust exemption failed in the U.S. Senate. Major-league baseball now felt no pressure to cooperate with the new league. In August 1960, the major leagues voted to expand by at least two clubs. One Continental League backer, William Shea, was allowed to buy a franchise. Within two years, baseball placed teams in Washington, Los Angeles, Houston, and New York. The Continental League was history.

Happy Chandler sent a strong message to the players who might be considering jumping to the Mexican League: If you go, you can't come back. Although a few players took their chances, not many were willing to risk permanent blacklisting to leave the established organization, despite the promise of quite a bit more money. After just a few years, the Mexican League collapsed.

by blacklisting those players who jumped from ever playing major-league baseball.

But Pasquel's money ran out in 1948, and most grew disenchanted with Mexican baseball. Chandler eventually allowed the players to return. But organized

THE BLACK SOX SCANDAL UPENDS THE GAME

★

In the best-of-nine game 1919 World Series, the Chicago White Sox were heavy favorites to defeat the Cincinnati Reds. But in the opening game, White Sox pitcher Eddie Cicotte was uncharacteristically wild and was hit hard in a 9-1 defeat. The next day, White Sox pitcher Lefty Williams suffered similar problems, and Chicago lost again. Dickie Kerr pitched a shutout for Chicago in game three, but in game four Cicotte made a critical error and lost for the second time. In game five, Williams pitched better, but he still lost 5-0 as a walk and an error, by outfielder Happy Felsch, gave the Reds four runs in the sixth inning. Behind Kerr and Cicotte, the Sox bounced back to win the next two games, but fell to the Reds in game eight as Williams lost his third game. The Reds won the Series 5-3.

Even before the Series started, there were rumors that the White Sox were going to throw the Series. Chicago

Black Sox player Lefty Williams

owner Charles Comiskey was notoriously cheap, and his players amenable to the idea of supplementing their salaries by other means. After Chicago lost, a number of sportswriters and baseball officials began to take those rumors seriously. At several key moments in the Series, it had appeared as if some members of the White Sox were playing to lose.

The rumors of 1919 grew into a full-blown investigation in 1920. A grand jury in 1920 indicted eight players—pitchers Ed Cicotte and Lefty Williams; outfielders Happy Felsch and

Joe Jackson; infielders Chick Gandil, Swede Risberg, and Buck Weaver; and utility man Fred McMullin. Chick Gandil emerged as the ringleader of the plot. He had been approached by gamblers backed by gangster Arnold Rothstein and offered $80,000 to throw the Series. Gandil brought other players into the fold. He eventually pocketed $35,000, Cicotte received $10,000, while Joe Jackson, Happy Felsch, and Lefty Williams made off with $5,000. The other players received nothing, but had "guilty knowledge" of the fix. The press dubbed the men "the Black Sox," for darkening the integrity of the game. Chicago

Due to poor decision making, Eddie Cicotte was banned from the game.

sportswriter Hugh Fullerton wrote a column that told the story of a child approaching Jackson on the courthouse steps and asking "It ain't so Joe, is it?" History has since remembered the phrase incorrectly as "Say it ain't so, Joe."

The scandal rocked baseball. The three-man National Commission of Ban Johnson, John Heydler, and August Hermann were under fire for a series of controversial decisions throughout the 1919 season. The Series fix was the last straw. The public was losing faith in the game. Baseball owners first stripped the Commission of much of its power, then scrapped the triumvirate. Shortly after the grand jury met, U.S. Judge Kenesaw Mountain Landis was named the commissioner of baseball.

The flamboyant Landis, a trusted public figure, was given a free hand to run baseball as he saw fit. He took office in January 1921.

The players went on trial for conspiracy in June. The trial itself was one of the low points in the history of

Kenesaw Mountain Landis, second from the left.

American jurisprudence, compromised by missing evidence, perjury, and other irregularities. None of the gamblers ever faced charges, while the players were acquitted for lack of evidence.

One day later, armed with his extraordinary power, Landis used the full authority of his office and announced that no player in-

volved in gambling "will ever play professional baseball." He banned the eight players for life.

Landis's decision was hailed at the time and helped restore public trust in the game. The "Commissioner System" took the business of baseball away from the leagues and gave the commissioner

Purported ringleader Chick Gandil

new authority to rule in baseball's "best interests." The new system made interleague squabbles insignificant and allowed organized baseball to operate as a single unit.

The fallout from Landis's decision was long-lasting. The eight players were indeed banned for life, and most lived out their lives in disgrace. Some protested their innocence, and many later historians have taken up their cause. Jackson, a virtual illiterate and one of the best players in the game at the time, is a somewhat sympathetic figure. He didn't throw a game; in fact, Jackson was the leading hitter in the Series. But he did accept money. Had he not done so, Jackson would certainly be in the Hall of Fame. His cause has since been argued in a number of books and movies.

As late as 1989, commissioner A. Bartlett Giamatti turned down a resolution from the legislature of Jackson's home state of South Carolina that requested his exoneration.

Jackson had one of his finest seasons in 1920. He had a .392 batting average and 121 RBI. Despite hitting .375 in World Series play, the fact remains that Joe had agreed to accept money to fix the games.

THE GAME ERUPTS IN 1920

★

Baseball changed in 1920, and the main reason was Babe Ruth. Before 1920, teams still played so-called "scientific baseball." In the scientific game, the stolen base, the hit-and-run, and the sacrifice bunt epitomized play. Ty Cobb was the embodiment of this style and the era's best player. But in 1920, Ruth smashed 54 home runs, more than anyone thought possible. The game was never the same.

The "Dead-Ball Era" was over starting in the 1920 season. In fact, while the game did change, the actual ball had little to do with it. In 1910, a cork-center ball was developed to replace the rubber-center ball. The new ball was "livelier," yet it led to no dramatic upsurge in home runs. While batting averages did rise, teams still used the same few baseballs over and over and still played in the scientific style. After a few innings, the new cork ball was only a little more lively than its predecessor.

While the lively ball did help Ruth to hit home runs, a series of other factors also came

A young George Herman Ruth swings a bat. After the debacle that threatened to ruin the public's confidence in the game, along came salvation in the guise of the Babe. He literally changed the rules by swinging for the fences.

into play. In 1920, baseball manufacturers changed the wool yarn used to wrap the ball, making it more resilient and more uniform. Baseball also banned the use of the spit-ball and other trick pitches. The ball was easier to hit and easier to hit farther. All baseball needed was a catalyst.

Ruth was the man. Swinging a 48-ounce bat with a thin handle, he generated tremendous bat speed and swung for the fences, a heretical concept in "scientific" baseball. He succeeded grandly, and others soon adopted his style. The home run rendered scientific baseball obsolete. The outcome of the game now hinged on one mighty swing of the bat. Fans loved it.

One other event in 1920 contributes to the popular notion that the season marked a change in the game. On Aug. 16, in the fifth inning of a game between the New York Yankees and the Cleveland Indians at the Polo Grounds, Cleveland shortstop Ray Chapman faced submarine pitcher Carl Mays. Chapman started to square to bunt and push the ball down the first base line. Mays saw Chapman move, and, following common pitching strategy, threw the ball up and in, trying to induce a pop-up.

The ball came bounding out to Mays, who fielded it and

Carl Mays felt that the Chapman incident kept Mays out of the Hall of Fame, even though he won 207 games and won 20 or more games in five seasons.

On Aug. 16, 1920, Ray Chapman was struck in the head by a submarine pitch. He perished 12 hours later.

threw to first. Only then did he notice Chapman on the ground. The ball had struck him on the side of the head. While Chapman walked off the field under his own power, he was soon rushed to a hospital. He died the next morning after surgery, the first and only major-league player to be killed by a pitch.

Mays was vilified by some fans and members of the press, who accused him of intentionally beaning Chapman. In fact, the pitch was an accident, and Mays felt badly about the incident. He was no more at fault than Chapman.

Chapman's death led to a decision by baseball to use only new, clean baseballs, providing the final factor that led to the death of the Dead-Ball Era.

BROADCASTING SWELLS BASEBALL'S AUDIENCE

★

*B*efore 1921, the only way to know what happened at the ballpark was to be there. Except for newspaper accounts, fans had no real alternative to attending the game in person. That was fine if one lived near the ballpark in a city with major-league baseball. If not, major-league baseball was simply a story in the morning newspaper, and nothing more.

On Aug. 5, 1921, that changed. Westinghouse radio station KDKA broadcast the first major-league baseball game, from Forbes Field in Pittsburgh between the Pirates and the Phillies. Sitting in a ground-level box seat at Forbes Field, 26-year-old Harold Arlin broadcast the Pirates' 8-5 win against the Phillies to a few thousand listeners. Arlin would later admit he considered his initial broadcast over a converted telephone as a "one-shot project," but two months later, the World Series was broadcast on the East Coast. A year later,

Harold Arlin was the first person to call a baseball game, on Aug. 5, 1921.

the Series drew a radio audience of more than 5 million people. It didn't matter that in the beginning many broadcasts were, in fact, studio re-creations from teletype reports. It

sounded like baseball and was just as exciting.

Radio swept America in the 1920s, and baseball rode the wave. By the 1930s, nearly every major-league game was broadcast. Radio broadcasting served major-league baseball well, bringing in much needed revenue through advertising and promoting the game. All across the nation, baseball fans huddled before the radio as the voices of broadcasting pioneers Red Barber, Graham Mac-Namee, Harry Heilmann, and Arch McDonald regaled fans of the exploits of their favorite heroes. When Babe Ruth faced Pitcher Charlie Root in the 1932 World Series, fans heard the voice of Tom Manning say,

The Dean of American Sportswriters, Grantland Rice, at the NBC microphone with broadcasting pioneer Graham MacNamee (left) during the early days of baseball on radio.

Leo "The Lip" Durocher (left at mike) and Red Barber at the first telecast baseball game. Now, through the miracle of modern technology, baseball would come into homes across America. It took very little time for those involved to realize the marketing potential of this new medium.

"He points again to center field! And here's the pitch. . . . It's going! Babe Ruth connects and here it goes. The ball is going, going, going, high into the center field stands, into the scoreboard. It's a home run, it's gone! Whoo! Listen to that crowd." In an instant, everyone was part of history. The "called shot" went directly from the bat of Ruth and landed in the front parlor.

The success of baseball on the radio led naturally to its technological successor: television. On Aug. 26, 1939, NBC station W2XBS televised the first game. Announcer Red Barber described the action between the Reds and Dodgers in Ebbets Field, as shadowy fig-

ures danced across a cathode-ray tube into the future.

While World War II slowed the advance of television, the medium exploded after the war. While more than 40,000 fans poured into Braves Field to watch Boston play host to Cleveland in the 1948 World Series, another 50,000 fans watched the game crowded around 100 televisions set up in the Boston Common. Soon, every bar in every big-league city in the country sported a television set. On Oct. 3, 1951, the Dodger-Giant playoff was the first game to be nationally broadcast. When Bobby Thomson's ninth-inning home run beat Brooklyn, and radio broadcaster Russ Hodges screamed "The Giants win the pennant!" over and over, millions more watched the action on television and heard Ernie Harwell's less histrionic description. Within the decade, nearly every American home had a television. The future of baseball was on TV.

By the mid-1950s, television usurped radio as baseball's preferred method of broadcast. Since that time, television has sent baseball around the world and delivered millions to the coffers of major-league teams.

Incidents of Baseball

Television proved to be a necessary, if sometimes demanding, partner in the success of the game. The medium made broadcaster Joe Garagiola, a journeyman ballplayer, and Bob Uecker, who wasn't even a journeyman, household names. It has delivered magic moments such as Don Larsen's no-hitter, Roger Maris's 61st home run, and Hank Aaron's 715th home run into millions of American homes. Television made Phil Rizzuto's "Holy Cow!", Mel Allen's "How about that!", and Harry Caray's "It could be, it might be, it is!" part of the American vernacular. Television provided the money that led to expansion, which has fueled the era of free agency. In a day and age when it is not always possible, or affordable, to go to the ballpark, television has brought the ballpark home.

On-air personality Mel Allen (right). His voice, via radio transmission, brought baseball alive for those who followed the game at home. In 1978, Allen and Red Barber were the first broadcasters inducted into baseball's Hall of Fame.

JACKIE ROBINSON BREAKS THE COLOR BAR

★

On April 15, 1947, Jackie Robinson of the Los Angeles Dodgers became the first African-American baseball player to appear in a major-league game since Moses Walker appeared in 42 games for Toledo in the American Association in 1884. While Dodger president Branch Rickey received most of the credit for breaking baseball's "color" line, the process was actually more complicated.

While baseball flourished in the first half of the 20th century, most fans didn't even notice that the National Pastime failed to include a substantial portion of the nation's citizens. Americans of African descent were banned from organized baseball due to an unspoken agreement between owners. But, like everyone else, blacks loved baseball. A number of all-black teams barnstormed the nation, sometimes facing teams made up of white big leaguers. The Negro National League functioned as the black counterpart

to the major leagues. Fans, both black and white, knew of the exploits of catcher Josh Gibson, pitcher Satchel Paige, and infielder Oscar Charleston. But few were willing or able to challenge the status quo.

Men and women of vision and courage, however, were well aware of the discrepancy. Many thought that if America was to ever progress beyond segregation, it was imperative that African Americans play major-league baseball. In the early 1930s, a number of black sports editors formed the "All-American Society of Negro Sports Editors." Their one goal was to make white America

aware of the black ballplayer and to break the color line.

Long before Branch Rickey ever heard of Jackie Robinson, he was well-known to readers of the black press, who openly campaigned to place Robinson in the major leagues. They knew the college-educated Robinson, a military veteran and an All-American running back while at UCLA, possessed all the necessary personal qualities to break the color line. He was intelligent, strong, proud, and very talented.

Branch Rickey was named Dodger president in 1942. He was determined to break the color line. He believed it was

Above: Jackie Robinson signs his groundbreaking contract as Branch Rickey (right) and Dodger manager Burt Shotton look on. *Opposite page:* An all-around athlete, Jackie Robinson withstood the abuse and discrimination to became one of the finest players of the game of baseball. He was elected to the Hall of Fame in 1962, his first year of eligibility.

His unique place in history and play on the field gave Brooklyn fans a lot to cheer about. They could show support by wearing a Jackie Robinson button and could read all about their brightest star on the pages of magazines like *Sports Stars.*

wrong, thought World War II made its eventual breakdown inevitable, and hoped by integrating the Dodgers first to gain an advantage over other clubs. He sent his scouts out to find black players under the smoke screen of scouting for a new franchise in the Negro National League.

By no accident he found Robinson, who starred for the Kansas City Monarchs in the Negro Leagues. On Oct. 23, 1945, Rickey signed Robinson to a contract to play for the Dodgers' Triple-A farm club in Montreal. In an incident that has since become legend, Rickey warned Robinson that he could expect abuse from other fans and players, and Rickey expected Robinson to turn the other cheek. Robinson asked Rickey if he wanted a ballplayer who lacked the courage to fight back, and Rickey responded, "No. I want a ballplayer who has the courage *not* to fight back."

Robinson succeeded on all counts. In his first game, on April 18, 1946, he had four hits, including a home run, and stole three bases. He hit .349 for Montreal and led the International League in hitting. Rickey installed him at first base for the Dodgers in 1947.

Robinson had a difficult time. Several of his own teammates refused to play with him and demanded trades. Several NL teams tried to enact boycotts, and he took intense abuse from both fans and opposing players. But Robinson took Rickey's advice. Jackie turned the other cheek and simply played harder.

The door to the major leagues was open, and the color line was gone. By the end of the season, four other African Americans appeared in the major leagues, and a number of clubs signed more black players to minor-league contracts. Most players and fans supported Robinson. He was named the Rookie of the Year in 1947 and helped lead Brooklyn to the pennant, though the Yankees lost the Series.

The play of Robinson and the black stars that followed in his wake revolutionized baseball. Robinson's accomplishments made efforts to end segregation in other areas of American society easier. Robinson himself led the Dodgers to a decade of success, was named to six All-Star teams, appeared in six World Series, and was named NL MVP in 1949. By the time Robinson was elected to the Hall of Fame in 1962, every team in the major leagues was integrated. Robinson's courage as the first African American to play major-league baseball provided inspiration to a generation of Americans.

Pee Wee Reese (second from left) and Jackie Robinson (far right) teamed up to give the Dodgers one of the most lethal double-play combinations. In his first game, Jackie had four hits, including a home run, and three stolen bases.

THE BRAVES MOVE TO MILWAUKEE

★

At the end of the 1902 season, American League president Ban Johnson moved the Baltimore franchise to New York City. For the next 49 years, the same 16 teams played in the same cities. That was major-league baseball, and most fans naively assumed it would stay that way forever.

On March 18, 1953, while the Boston Braves played the New York Yankees in an exhibition game, all that changed. By the time New York rallied to win 3-2, the Boston Braves were obsolete. The team had moved to Milwaukee.

People were stunned. In Boston the next day, newspapers were published edged in funereal black. A joke spread around town that while Boston was the land of the free, it was no longer the home of the Braves. Vandals slipped into Braves Field and stole home plate. In an instant, baseball changed. The shift of the Braves to Milwaukee heralded a new era in major-league baseball. For the first time, most fans realized that baseball was a business. The era of expansion was around the corner.

Lou Perini (left), then-President of the Boston Braves, and 1953's National League president, Warren Giles, discuss the possibility of moving the franchise to Milwaukee. The move made fans realize that baseball was a business.

After the Braves succeeded following their move, other teams wanted to move. Walter O'Malley, Nelson Rockefeller, and New York Mayor Robert Wagner discuss the future of the Brooklyn Dodgers.

In Boston, the perennially underfinanced Braves had long played second fiddle to the wealthier Red Sox. But in 1948 they won the National League pennant and drew nearly 1.5 million fans to Braves Field. The future looked bright.

It wasn't. Within five seasons, a series of bad trades, poor performances, and management mistakes wrecked the Braves. In 1952 attendance tumbled to less than 300,000. Boston Owner Lou Perini finally had enough.

Meanwhile, in Milwaukee, Wisconsin, county government built a ballpark to house the Triple-A Brewers, the Braves' farm club. The team drew well, and the local officials hoped to convince a major-league team to move there. Owner Bill Veeck of the St. Louis Browns was tempted by Milwaukee's offer. Perini hoped to stay in Boston, and originally planned to play there in 1953, but he couldn't risk losing the Milwaukee market. Veeck's interest forced his hand, and Perini made his move.

The Braves were wildly successful in Milwaukee in 1953. Other owners quickly took notice. Some cities were desperate for baseball, and local governments were willing to build new stadiums for free. Even if a team was already making money, there was more to be made in a new location. The temptation was too great.

The Braves' move in 1953 was the first trickle in what soon became a flood. Franchise transfers, and then expansion, became the rule. Veeck moved the Browns to Baltimore in 1954. The Athletics left Philadelphia for Kansas City in 1955. Both the Dodgers and Giants abandoned New York for California in 1958. Washington moved to Minnesota in 1961. New teams appeared in California and Washington in 1961, New York and Houston in 1962, and Seattle, Montreal, San Diego, and Kansas City in 1969.

With expansion came new teams, new ballparks, diluted talent, and a series of changes that forced baseball abruptly into the 20th century.

But in a perpetually evolving game like baseball, change is the only constant. After a period of uncertainty, the game righted itself. New teams spawned new traditions. Only 40 years since the Braves' move sparked the era of expansion, baseball's earlier configuration seems like a quaint reminder of another time. And the Braves? In a little over a decade, they grew disenchanted with Milwaukee. In 1966, they moved to Atlanta.

THE ASTRODOME IS LAUNCHED

★

During a visit to Rome, Houston Judge Roy Hofheinz visited the Coliseum and learned that it had once been covered with a huge awning to keep the sun off spectators. The lightbulb went off, and the idea of the Astrodome was born.

Heralded as the Eighth Wonder of the World, the Astrodome opened on April 12, 1965. The building included many features previously unavailable in ballparks. The seats were padded, the building was air-conditioned, and luxury private boxes were available to corporations. The building itself became Houston's biggest tourist attraction. In one way or another, every major-league stadium built since the Astrodome has responded to this new concept.

Yet the most pronounced influence of the Astrodome on the game wasn't apparent when the building first opened. In 1965, the Astrodome had real grass. The roof was made of 4,796 clear glass panels which let in sunlight, allowing a specially selected grass to grow.

There were problems with the arrangement from the outset. Glare from the panels made it nearly impossible for outfielders to follow the flight of the ball, and grass didn't exactly flourish in the artificial greenhouse. In the winter of 1965, the grass died.

By 1966, Hofheinz installed "Astroturf," an artificial grass named after the stadium. While players complained about hardness of the surface and the way the ball bounced, Astroturf offered major-league owners one distinct advantage. After installation, it was nearly maintenance-free. In outdoor stadiums, Astroturf drained quickly and made rainouts rare.

A splurge of new stadiums built in the early 1970s followed the model of the Astrodome. Most were planned as domes only to be scaled back to open-air facilities due to costs. But artificial turf still carried the day. Busch Stadium installed the surface in 1970, and by 1971 new stadiums in Cincinnati, Pittsburgh, and Philadelphia had followed suit. Others replaced natural grass

The interior of the Houston Astrodome held surprises for all. For fans, the cushioned seats, air-conditioning, and no rainouts were delightful changes. Other aspects weren't quite as favorable. This photo, before the first game in 1965, shows the short-lived attempt of indoor grass.

The Houston Astrodome. Called the Eighth Wonder of the World, the Dome created changes that still affect the game today, such as making speed a priority. Gabe Paul had a slightly different take on the innovation: "It will revolutionize baseball; it will open a new area of alibis for the players."

surfaces in existing parks with an artificial surface.

The effect on the game was profound. The new surface turned simple ground balls into singles. Soft line drives now careened past outfielders and bounced off the fence for extra bases. Many teams turned to speed and defense to best take advantage of the new surface. Baseball was becoming a different game. Certain players became successful major-league ballplayers solely because their skills were enhanced by the new surface.

But in recent years, the trend appears to be reversing itself. Artificial surfaces have been removed in a number of open-air parks. Complaints from high-priced stars about damage to their knees and backs were taken seriously. Fans, initially intrigued by the novelty of the ersatz grass, began to express their preference for real grass.

Except for the domed stadiums, the era of Astroturf appears to be ending. The surface has recently been replaced by real grass in several ballparks, other teams are considering the change, and new open-air ballparks have been built using real grass. Dick Allen once said, "if horses won't eat it, I don't want to play on it."

MESSERSMITH, McNALLY USHER FREE AGENCY

★

Since the reserve clause—which binds a player for life to the team that holds his contract—was first created, players have resisted its constraints. The clause has worked to create league stability and resolve possible contractual conflicts between owners. But that peace has been gained at the expense of the players' freedom of movement and right to earn the highest possible salary through competitive bidding.

Not until the 1970s did players finally loosen the chains of the reserve clause. In 1969 outfielder Curt Flood of the St. Louis Cardinals was traded by St. Louis to the Philadelphia Phillies. Flood protested the move. In a letter to Baseball commissioner Bowie Kuhn, Flood asked to be declared a free agent, writing, "After 12 years of being in the major leagues, I do not feel I am a piece of property to be bought and sold irrespective of my wishes." Kuhn refused Flood's request, and Flood filed suit.

Despite former Supreme Court Justice Arthur Goldberg championing his cause, Curt Flood (above) lost his appeal for free agency. All was not lost, however, as his case set the groundwork for other players' rights.

After two years of litigation, Flood's suit was dismissed, and the sanctity of baseball's reserve system was upheld. The Supreme Court ruled that baseball, due to historical precedence, was exempt from the antitrust legislation that otherwise made the reserve system illegal. But Flood's battle proved to be a lightning rod for player discontent.

During the 1974 winter meetings, the Baltimore Orioles traded star pitcher Dave McNally to the Montreal Expos. Under the existing "Basic Agreement" governing player contracts, McNally, as a player with 10 years experience, including five with his current club, had the right to approve the trade. It was known as "The Curt Flood Rule."

McNally reached a tentative contract agreement with the Expos and approved the trade. Then Montreal reneged. When McNally refused to sign a new contract, Montreal invoked a provision in the standard player's contract and renewed McNally's contract at a reduction of 20 percent.

In Los Angeles, 20-game winner Andy Messersmith faced an analogous situation. Messersmith and the Dodgers failed to agree on a new contract, and the Dodgers invoked a similar renewal. Marvin Miller, head of the Major League Baseball Players Association, filed a class action suit on behalf of both players challenging the provision.

Both McNally and Messersmith played the 1975 season under the renewals, but neither had signed a contract binding him to his team. After the season, arbiter Peter Seitz declared that both players had fulfilled their contractual obligations by playing under the renewal year, and Seitz declared them free

Dave McNally used what was known as "The Curt Flood Rule" to gain free agency. He and Andy Messersmith were the first two to achieve this goal.

Opposite page: Andy Messersmith (pictured) and Dave McNally have affected all players.
Above: A young Messersmith has no idea he will make such a mark.

agents. The owners fired Seitz and appealed his finding. The decision was upheld in federal court. Following the lockout of players from spring training in 1976, a new Basic Agreement was signed that provided for free agency. While the reserve clause was retained, it was dramatically weakened. Players won the right of free agency.

The dynamics of the game changed rapidly. With only a few restrictions, players were allowed to sell their services to the highest bidder. The result-

ing bidding wars for players increased salaries dramatically. Wealthy owners such as the Yankees' George Steinbrenner used free agency to fuel championship teams.

While the effects of the McNally-Messersmith decision has since benefitted all players, what became of McNally and Messersmith? For each, the victory was bittersweet. McNally immediately suffered shoulder trouble and retired after the 1975 season. Messersmith was one of the first free agents to

cash in, and in 1975 signed a three-year, $1.75-million contract with the Atlanta Braves. But after one productive season, Messersmith also hurt his arm. He went on to pitch ineffectively for both the New York Yankees and the Los Angeles Dodgers, and retired following the 1979 season. Today, probably only a few players would recognize the names of Curt Flood, Dave McNally, and Andy Messersmith as the agents of change that have since made so many millionaires.

Baseball Life

SUNUP TO SUNDOWN
IN THE BIG LEAGUES

Tranquil, the ballpark slowly rouses with the arrival of players, ushers, and vendors. The stadium swings into full gear as early fans bustle through the turnstiles, get their scorecards and hot dogs, and emerge in their seats. TV broadcasters and sportswriters interview the stars of yesterday's game before the umpire yells, "Play ball!" Behind-the-scenes members of the team, from the general manager to the ticket taker, work to make these nine innings enjoyable.

At game's end, the concession stands close, the crowd thins, and the grounds crew prepares the field for another day of baseball.

A DAY IN THE LIFE OF A BALLPARK

★

This is the story of a midsummer day and night at a typical major-league ballpark in a midsized city. The characters are composites, based on what the people who hold those jobs do in similar situations every day. The home team is playing .500 ball, less than expected, but it is still only six games out of first. The pitching staff has looked especially good. The team isn't scoring enough runs, and it is rumored the team may deal their No. 2 starter, 25-year-old lefty Ted Beecher, for right-handed power hitter Luis Jimenez.

Players come and go: Brooklyn skipper Max Carey (left) greets the newly acquired George Kelly in 1932.

8:15 A.M.

★

Sherry Cardwell, the receptionist, had her nose deep in the sports page when media relations director Will Minshall walked in the ballpark's office doors. He wiped the sleep from his eyes; last night's game had been a long one, with a rain delay just as the 10th inning was getting started. But he couldn't be late this morning. There was still a chance the deal would happen today. Two weeks ago the GM had asked him for a complete stat breakdown on Jimenez, that Yankee outfielder, with particular interest in his ability to hit righties as well as southpaws, and how much more power he showed on the road as opposed to playing in the Stadium. Just to be ready, he thought to look up the number of the Yankee PR rep, to coordinate the announcement if it did happen. Minshall's phone was ringing as soon as he stepped into his office. Its double ring notified him it was an outside call. "Media relations."

It was the voice he knew from dozens of similar calls. Nasal, intelligent, pleading for

Pine tar is sticky stuff to help the batter keep a grip. As George Brett knows, 18 inches is the limit.

inside information. "Is it true you guys are going to trade Beecher for Jimenez and Sammy Tyler and put Tommy Siglin on the DL? That would leave my fantasy team stuck without a catcher."

"There have been rumors to that effect, but nothing has been announced." How do these guys get their information?

"When would you be making the announcement if there is a deal?"

"Shortly after we know about it."

In the next office, Will's assistant, Pat Hinton, was listening to a fan gush about how wonderful Arch Conroy had been signing autographs for her son's little-league team after a recent game. Well, that's one out of four, Hinton thought. The last three calls about Conroy complained that he rudely ignored kids waving scorecards in his face. His mind wandered as he glanced down at the latest stat sheet. Hmmm. Conroy's batting average for autograph signing is the same as his real batting average.

Back in the other office, the fantasy owner was begging.

"C'mon, Will. You can tell me. I'm your pal."

"Yes, Dave, I know you are. You're one of my best pals. And you'll know as soon as we make the announcement."

"So there *is* a deal today!"

"I didn't say that."

8:50 A.M.

★

General Manager Art Renko hung up the phone and glanced at his assistant, Brian Tate, with a sour look.

Tate read his mind. "Tyler wants his contract extended two more years?"

"We'd give him one, but there's no way we can do two. Cripes, he's 34 now."

"A lot of good catchers hang around a long time."

"And for every one that does, two more have knees blow out. We'll also need that

The grounds crew chalks the lines, creating what for many is paradise. "Ninety feet between home plate and first base may be the closest man has ever come to perfection," sports columnist Red Smith once wrote.

dough next year when Swanson and McFarlane are eligible for arbitration."

"Maybe we should ask for a couple of their young pitchers. McGarrison? Stumpf?"

The GM rattled his fingers on his desk. "We need an experienced catcher. We've got

young pitchers. Oh, well, I'll let Mark know." He knew manager Mark Woolf liked Jimenez as a hitter; Woolf had coached him in the low minors. Renko reached for the phone, then replaced it on the cradle. That 10-inning loss last night was a long one. Let Mark sleep.

9:17 A.M.

★

The daylight grounds crew had already been on the job an hour, removing the field's tarp, doing cleanup work, when the supervisor sent seven of them up to the right-field stands. Tom Luce left his post after repairing his third broken seat. Last night's rain had been just bad enough to cause the leaky roof out there to douse a couple dozen seats. There was no forecast for wet weather today, so they were going to try and recaulk several roof sections. But they had to do it in a hurry; their regular jobs of cleanup and field preparation wouldn't wait. The crew who tended to the field during the game expected everything to be ready to go when they arrived at four o'clock.

9:28 A.M.

★

About a week before each homestand, there was a regular meeting that included the ticket manager, representatives of the promotions department, stadium authority, the concessionaire, public relations, and security to plan for

Above: The grounds crew rakes and prepares the infield. *Opposite page:* Ty Cobb poses at the end of his career, with the Athletics. He once said, "The great American game should be an unrelenting war of nerves."

what would be needed. The ticket manager's projections of sales were the key to everybody else's plans: everything from how many hot dogs and programs would be needed to how many ushers would be on hand to who would hand out the T-shirts on T-shirt night to who would take charge of the busload of wheelchair-bound young fans due in Saturday. The list of people singing the National Anthem and first-ball throwers was also announced at the meeting. The ticket manager bases his judgments on a dozen factors: pre-sales, how much giveaway days added to the crowd, what the long-range weather forecast said, traditions of certain teams drawing more, how many out-of-town fans

might show up, and group sales, for example.

But if this trade went through, it could knock his projections off the mark. If Beecher was gone by Friday, someone else would take his Friday start. Beecher had always drawn well, particularly on Fridays. A lot of fans like him, so they often decide on the day of the game to go, resulting in several thousand walk-up sales that day. Many of the fans sit in general admission, so the ticket manager had planned to open two more sections that night, and staff the two concession stands nearby. But with Beecher gone, the manager would probably give Maggert a start out of the bullpen. Maggert was definitely no gate

attraction. Not that many walk-up sales were going to happen to see him. The ticket manager made a note to call the concessionaire and security if the trade happened.

9:55 A.M.

★

Chamber of Commerce commissioner Walt Crandall was a little early for his 10 o'clock meeting with the team's president.

"Hello, Sherry," he greeted the receptionist. "Did we get Jimenez?"

"Not yet."

"Too bad. Is Tom ready?"

Walt bustled down the carpeted hall to the president's office, ignoring the team portraits hanging on the walls on both sides. The two men shook hands like old friends. Crandall liked Tom Rhines. The president never used bluster to make a point; he always was totally under control. Everything about him, from the neatness of his tie's knot to the clean organization of his desk, looked professional.

"Are we getting Jimenez, Tom?"

Stretching helps players to relax. As Yogi Berra (without the cap) said, "Baseball is 90 percent mental. The other half is physical."

The sigh was familiar. "It comes down to money. Money we don't have. Tyler wants his contract extended further than we can. But we do need some punch in the lineup."

"Would you bat him third?"

"And move Chip? I don't think so. But. . . ."

Crandall finished his sentence for him. ". . . on-the-field decisions are not your job."

"Walt," Tom started the business, "We are going to expand our community work with our baseball clinics. We need to push for more inner-city activities. I'd like to get inner-city churches involved."

"And you want me to kick open the right doors for you."

"Right. You understand better than I the political situations that go on with some

One of the great pleasures of baseball has always been getting to the game early enough to watch batting practice. The first great manager, Harry Wright, established BP instead of just tossing the ball to loosen up.

The bullpen pitchers of the 1993 Philadelphia Phillies (who won the NL pennant), led by closer Mitch Williams (third from right, with the white bandanna), go through their pregame paces before the ivy-covered walls of Wrigley Field.

of our community leaders. There are egos and turf battles going on there. We want to make sure we get everyone involved who can help, but we don't want to create problems for ourselves. All I'm asking is for some guidance. Then we'll have a planning meeting with everyone involved—parks and recreation, the mayor's department, everybody—and then hold a press conference to kick it off."

"Isn't there a major-league baseball initiative on that order already?"

"Yes. The RBI program, they call it. We'll get them in on it, too. But we want to make it work from within, not rely on them. You know how I feel about the idea of baseball players as role models. . . ."

"They're just professionals, doing their jobs," Walt quoted the president's words.

"Right. But when we see a chance as a team to help, and the players are willing to, we must take advantage of that opportunity."

"Speaking of players who want to help, don't you think

Spriggs is getting a nasty knock on the talk shows? You listen to the talk shows, don't you?"

"Every one, when I'm in town. I agree about Spriggs. He's not a bad guy; he just has a bad temper, and it looks bad. I've had Will talk to him about the way he deals with the press, but the kid is such an intense person. I don't want to put a damper on that."

"He refused to talk to the press after that game last week."

"He was angry at Martinez. Thought he didn't hustle on the double-play ball. Spriggs told Will afterwards that he didn't want to talk because he was afraid he'd say something he might regret."

"So he was trying to protect a teammate, and the press took it out on him."

"Exactly."

11:05 A.M.

★

Cris Harvey, the financial manager repeated himself. "It just seems to me that we could help cash flow substantially if we cut back on that heavy advertising buy the two weeks before the All-Star Game. Use a few spot announcements during the games, fine, but don't throw away money until after the break."

The advertising manager, Carol Joyner, asserted: "We planned that buy in February to take advantage of those two weekend-long promotions. Early July is when there are the most other choices for people instead of baseball games. Summer is in full swing, picnics, vacations are starting. We *have* to remind folks that baseball is here."

Harvey was precise in his tone of voice. "We could use the dollars now."

Ted Williams, famous curmudgeon and great hitter, said in one of his most famous quotes: "Baseball is the only field of endeavor where a man can succeed three times out of 10 and be considered a good performer."

President Rhines spoke. "It seems to me this advertising investment will pay off later in the season. The numbers show that people who come to a game for the first time before the All-Star break are more likely to return than those who don't make their first appearance till later. Let's leave it as it is."

They stood up to leave the meeting.

"We could sure use that cash," Harvey said.

The president's smile was barely visible. "I'll tell Art to sell a pitcher."

12:15 P.M.
★

Curt Smith, the concessionaire manager, double-checked his "kill sheet." It was the map of stadium seating indicating which sections would be closed for the night's game. With that information, he knew which concession stands to staff and stock. When the house was full, he needed nearly 600 concession workers to man the four-dozen stands. Tonight would be a good night, but not an overflow crowd. He circled the needed items in red and had

the data sent to his assistant, so that the event supervisors could call the people they needed to work that night. Concession folks showed up an hour to an hour and a half before the gates opened, two and a half hours before game time.

Having the right amount of people to work the concession stands for a particular game was one of the most important jobs he had to do. Too few people, and the fans wouldn't get their hot dogs and nachos fast enough, and complaints would pour in. Baseball fans hollered about poor service much faster than football fans or rodeo fans. Having the TV

screens so that the folks in line could watch the game while they waited was not really much help. They wanted to be in their seats with their beer and popcorn, watching the game in person. On the other hand, if there were too many concession personnel for the attendance, his operation was wasting money.

He double-checked the sales figures for the souvenir stands. The expansion teams' caps were selling even faster than he had expected; he made a notation to order more. The Triple-A team had changed its colors this year. It wasn't mimicking the big club, as had

A Colorado Rockie provides a pregame interview that has added significance because it is before the first-ever ball game played by the Rockies, on April 5, 1993, at Shea Stadium against the New York Mets.

Cincinnati Reds outfielder Frank Robinson reads fan mail and enjoys an ice cream bar in the clubhouse. About winning he said: "Close don't count in baseball. Close only counts in horseshoes and grenades."

been the tradition for years. Since anything with a baseball logo on it had become big money, it was important to be different, not the same. The new logo and colors for Triple-A were selling fast.

12:25 P.M.
★

Will took a call from a local TV station. They were asking for press credentials to visit the clubhouse, which would normally have

been an automatic okay, but the credentials were for Jack Rodman, an *investigative* journalist.

"Is Rodman doing baseball now?" Will asked.

"Kind of," the producer answered. "He found out that John Menefee has filed for personal bankruptcy, tax problems, stuff like that, and he wanted to . . ."

Will was firm. "No. We will credential the press to cover baseball, but prying into players' personal lives is not something we'll help you do."

The producer was polite, then pushy, but Will repeated his answer. The other line rang. "Sorry, but we just won't," Will said, and hung up.

3:30 P.M.
★

Manager Woolf took his time getting dressed. He had been putting on a baseball uniform every day, six months a year or more, for a long time, but there was still a personal and tactile pleasure in donning the garb. He liked the feel of the clean white uniform, and he remembered how many times he had been forced to wear a uniform that wasn't clean, back in the days of minor-league bus travel, when each man's gear was his own responsibility, and there were no clubhouse men around to handle the details. With everything

Above: Frank Cashen, GM of the Mets, chats with Cub skipper Gene Michael. *Opposite page:* Mickey Mantle.

TREASURY OF BASEBALL

on but his shoes and shirt he moved out to his office. Waiting there, as they always were, were his coaching staff.

Buttoning his shirt and tying his shoes would take 20 minutes or more, because with each movement he made he asked a question of his panel. "They've got Biende going for them. He throws high and outside. Is that a good enough reason to start Boehler?"

Fred Pfeiffer, the youngest coach and the one with the most to prove, answered first. Mark liked the fact that Fred always had an opinion, but it was an opinion he seldom valued highly. "Boehler looked awful against Fernandez last week. Same sort of stuff."

The program vendors' motto: You can't tell the players without a scorecard—especially in spring.

The autograph seeker gets his reward, as Brian Fisher of the Yankees delivers with his John Hancock. Roger Angell wrote that Tommy Lasorda says to rookies: "Always give an autograph when somebody asks you."

Doc Maul, whose ancient face looked like a pair of dirty baseball cleats, spoke next. "No comparison, the way I see it. Fernandez's ball was moving. A lot. Nobody couldn't have hit it. Against Biende, Boehler'll have a better chance."

Doc had been a minor-league catcher, as had a couple of other members of the coaching staff. Mark, formerly a pitcher, had a lot of respect for what catchers knew.

"I was talking to Flip Tibbs the other day," offered Wash Dorsey, "and he said that Biende's pitching coach is after him to give up that three-seam fastball, the one that sails outside like that to righties."

"And almost takes the nose off lefties," Pfeiffer injected.

"Has he pitched since then?" Woolf asked.

"Dunno."

"No starts. Might have used him in relief," Pfeiffer replied.

"Fred, call upstairs." The young coach contacted the media department. "No appearances," he said as he hung up the phone.

"Guess Boehler'll sit. If Biende hasn't changed his stuff, Boehler might get in as an early pinch hitter. MacFarlane's been walking a lot lately. Is he just seeing the ball good, or is he scared of something?"

"The beaning happened more than three weeks ago," answered Dorsey.

"Talk to him, Wash. If he's playing better and walking a lot I might move him up in the lineup. If he's playing scared and walking a lot, I might move him down." No one else could quietly ask a player a question and get an honest answer as easily as Wash could.

"Any word on Jimenez, Skipper?"

Woolf waved away the question with a snarl, paused for a second, then almost shouted his answer. "Damn Tyler wants two more years guaranteed on his contract. Cripes, when I was playing I just waited every Christmas for a contract and hoped to God it wasn't a cut notice."

A loud noise from the locker room caused the group of men to go quiet.

"Yee-hah!" Art Swanson, the team's regular second baseman, was waving a piece of paper. "You're looking at the world's spokesman for Auto-Clean spark plugs! Ladies and gentlemen, if you want a spark plug that'll last for 72 years, get Auto-whatchamacallit spark plugs! Best the world has ever seen. I'll be on billboards! I'll be on TV! And I'll be making a mint for doing it."

Mark Woolf looked around his desk at his coaching staff.

The managers deliver the lineups to the umpires and the announcer (the chap with the megaphone). The home-plate arbiter (with the face mask) will then proceed to go over the ground rules with the managers.

Pfeiffer was giggling, the rest were sullen. After trying to change things single-handedly for several years, Woolf had realized it was impossible to keep today's wealthy ballplayers from talking about money in the clubhouse.

Bo Sharpe quit rooting through his locker looking for a deck of cards and mumbled to himself about getting a new agent. He took the soup bone a friend had given him years ago and began to work over his bats. Severely.

The three beat reporters were milling around the clubhouse cubicles, chatting with different players, digging for background information that could serve as a feature later in the season, or provide a unique angle for a regular game report. One spoke to Dave Ritz, who was oiling his glove as though it were a dear friend, even though Ritz hadn't played in the field since the first week of the season.

One surprising face was there. Winston Kazak, the columnist. Whereas the beat reporters traveled with the team, got to know the guys, and almost became part of the organization, the columnists stayed aloof. Their stock-in-

Tom Seaver (right) gets comments from San Francisco Giants manager Roger Craig. The two former Mets pitchers took divergent career paths—managing and broadcasting—after their playing days were done.

trade was opinion, always offered with pontifical certainty. "The team won't make it to the Fourth of July unless they trade for power . . .They will lose the left fielder to free agency. . . .They'll never beat the Giants." Luckily for them their columns ended up at the bottom of bird cages, and few people remembered their absolute certainty when some facts proved them wrong later.

Kazak stopped by Sharpe's cubicle where the muscular (Continued on page 459)

Left: Mile High Stadium in Denver, home of the Colorado Rockies, housed minor-league baseball since 1948, as well as the Denver Broncos of the NFL. *Below:* An aerial view of Riverfront Stadium in Cincinnati, which was opened in 1970. It is just south of Pete Rose Way. Riverfront's home plate is from Crosley Field, home of the Reds from 1912 to 1970.

Left: The House that Ruth Built, Yankee Stadium has the classic feel of a ballpark yet with somewhat standard dimensions. It was not that way before the 1974 to '75 renovation, when it had a 295-foot right-field porch and a 460-foot center-field wall.

Right: Before the Yankee Stadium renovation in 1974 and '75, monuments to Lou Gehrig, Miller Huggins, and Babe Ruth that were in center field were in play. Foul territory is roomy for catchers but negligible for fielders down the line.

Opposite page: The second ballpark in St. Louis to be called Busch Stadium, Busch II opened in 1966 as an early example of the various-use structures that would house major-league teams. *Left:* Mile High Stadium in Denver, originally called "Bears Stadium" for the American Association Denver Bears. With the thin air, Mile High has been home to some prodigious shots, notably by Joey Meyer in 1987, who launched a seat-seeking missile 582 feet into the upper deck.

Right: Kansas City's Royals Stadium was opened in 1973, yet it was a baseball-only facility, unlike the multipurpose facilities opened around the country at that time. The fountains in center field are not traditional, but the structure was designed, as was Dodger Stadium 11 years earlier, in the tradition of a classic ballpark.

Left: Baltimore's Oriole Park at Camden Yards, opened in 1992, was a return to the asymmetrical outfield of yesteryear. The Baltimore & Ohio warehouse cuts into the right-field, giving the ballpark a wonderful backdrop and a mature feel.

Right: Pittsburgh's Three Rivers Stadium is beautifully situated where the Allegheny and Monongahela Rivers meet to form the Ohio River.

Above: Wrigley Field didn't start hosting night games until 1988, 53 years after the first night game in the major leagues. Philip Wrigley, owner of the Cubs, had lights ready to install in the spring of 1942 but instead donated the lights to the war effort after Pearl Harbor.

Left: Oakland-Alameda County Coliseum was built in 1965, and it is a simple circular stadium that was in vogue in that time period. Although the large foul territory hinders batters, management has improved the ambiance, for example adding a hand-operated scoreboard in the late 1980s that shows the major-league linescores to further the nostalgic impact.

Former players have found it relatively easy and lucrative in the broadcast booth from the days of Waite Hoyt on. Reggie Jackson, never afraid of speaking out when he was a player, here interviews Dave Stewart.

outfielder was in a state of near-meditative silence. "Say, Bo, I wanted to ask you about O'Farrell. Was he really trying to knock you down last Thursday? Or is he just wild?"

Sharpe's only answer was an icy glare. Kazak had his next column: "When the players are going well, they're eager to talk to the press. When they're slumping, their massive egos get in the way."

5:10 P.M.

★

There was something different that happened to the park about this time every day. Tom Rhines enjoyed taking a stroll around the place

early on game nights. It gave him a chance to look things over firsthand. He wanted to double-check the rain damage in the right-field stands. Sometimes he'd stop by the clubhouse for a few words with

Mark and the players. Always casual, never anything important, just to let them know he was there.

He checked his watch. Two other owners from smaller cities were flying in for tonight's game. They'd have dinner in the Club and talk about finances before going to the team's box for the game. Tom preferred to have other team representatives sit in the field box rather than in the team booth. Appearances.

Several things about the park indicated it was coming to life at this time. There was the noise: the hollers of the players on the field, talking trash as they took batting practice; the shouts of the concession staff as they stocked the stands for

Trying to get ballplayers to do the pregame interview—whether you are a baseball beat writer or national sportscaster—usually is a tough assignment. Guys like Ryne Sandberg are usually agreeable, however.

that night's crowd. And there were the smells: ballpark smells of hot dogs and popcorn, scents that could be found in any park, from the biggest major-league stadium to the most ancient Class-A ball venue, odors that linked them all together, saying, This is baseball. Stopping by a walkway to the field, Rhines could see the grounds crew finishing up the foul lines.

Around the batting cage, the players were discussing how much they charged for autograph-signing sessions. Card shows were the best, it was agreed, although store openings were also good. Swanson said, "Any time someone will be making money because you're there, you have to charge more. If they're getting some, so should you." The other players nodded.

6:10 P.M.
★

As the home team finished batting practice, Will left the field for dinner in the press lounge. He checked off his mental notepad: The three players he wanted to attend a church athletic picnic next month all agreed. He had left word for the umpires to call about clarification of the eighth-inning confusion last night, when a player seemed to have batted out of order. The press would be asking him about it soon. Sometimes the umpires would speak to the press, sometimes not.

Two managers, Tom Kelly of the Twins (left) and Buck Showalter of the Yankees, talk shop before commencing battle.

Four different reporters asked him about the trade for Jimenez. He told them all he knew: Talks were ongoing. Will noticed that three asked the same question of Art Renko. Over dinner Will and his assistant, Pat Hinton, looked over the final edition of the notes they would provide to all the members of the press.

During his time in the press lounge, Will kept his eyes and ears open. He heard what reporters were saying to each other. Some of their conversation was exactly the same as you would hear from a set of fans discussing last night's TV highlights: Did you see the catch Chapman made? Who

Get 'em while they're hot.

A knight of the keyboard puts the finishing touches on that day's game story and sends it through the ticker. While many think that the baseball beat isn't enticing, others agree with Red Smith when he said, "Sportswriting is the most pleasant way of making a living that man has yet devised."

would have thought Symons would be one of the league leaders in wins after that shoulder surgery? Even sportswriters belonged to fantasy leagues, Will noted.

6:25 P.M.
★

The radio booth was in a joyous mood. Everyone was smoking a cigar except for Big Bill Dyer, whose doctor had told him tobacco had cut short his big-league career by five years. Big Bill had a chocolate cigar to chomp on, courtesy of Mark Ross, the sound engineer, whose wife had given birth the night before.

"Hey Mark, did she go into extra innings, too?" someone asked.

Big Bill spoke with deep-voiced authority. "I told you she should have bunted for that early run."

6:35 P.M.
★

Smiley Williams was on his way to work. Armed with $80 and a handful of tickets, he liked to get himself an early post between the stadium and the two biggest sports bars in the area. Fans coming out of there often had tickets to sell, or wanted some to buy. The fact that they had had a few beers before they reached Smiley only made it easier for him to get tickets for less and sell them for more.

6:55 P.M.
★

Becky Lizotte, an associate in stadium operations, met Rico Vincenzo

One of the primary lessons baseball fans learn is patience. This applies whether waiting until the bottom of the ninth to see if the home team can rally to waiting for your favorite player to emerge from the clubhouse.

at the press gate. Rico was a stocky tenor with no hair who sang an impressive national anthem, although his day job was as a bartender. He would bend his chunky torso back at the waist and wave his arms as though he were conducting a symphony orchestra as he belted out the high notes. The fans loved him.

7:15 P.M.
★

The lineups were announced and then posted in the press box. Joe Boehler was starting at short. The press experts began offering their opinions. "He always hits Biende." "He's only in there to bunt; Biende always keeps the ball down."

7:32 P.M.
★

Rico ended his anthem with a flourish that had the medium-sized crowd cheering. He strutted off the field as though he were Caruso. A youngster wearing a red T-shirt with the words "Say NO to drugs" threw out the first pitch, which backup catcher Tommy Siglin fielded

Above: After a hot dog, nothing goes down better than some ice cream.
Opposite page: The National Anthem was played only on special occasions before games until World War II.

neatly on one hop and handed back to him as he ran off the field pounding his mitt. The home plate umpire bellowed "Play Ball." The starting pitcher, Glenn Cox, fired the first pitch—a fastball strike at the knees. In the press box, Will announced, "Tonight's game began at 7:36 P.M."

Even though he did this job 81 times a year, every game began with a little rush of excitement for Will. He knew Pat felt the same way, although he was kept a little busier tracking down stats and entering each play into the computer, where it became part of the league's official stats

as soon as the game was over. Being here was being a part of history, Will thought. He liked to think he was being paid to watch the game for the people who weren't there. Of course, that was the media's job, too. But by giving them accurate information and helping them put things in historical perspective, his role was a little larger. He remembered the triple play last season that happened so fast some of the writers didn't even notice it.

7:58 P.M.
★

Smiley Williams was waving tickets at the last stragglers headed for the park. "Last chance! Great deals! Box seats—I got two together, I got four—just 10 bucks apiece."

8:02 P.M.
★

Big Bill Dyer announced: "This is our Super Foods Grocery Giveaway Inning, fans. If we hit a homer this inning, Tom McNulty of Effordburg will win $800 in Super Foods groceries."

On the first pitch, cleanup

Hugh Duffy leans on the dugout rail during his tenure as the manager of the Boston Red Sox in the 1920s. While he wasn't a highly successful manager, Duffy was well regarded as an informal batting coach for many years.

hitter Wilbur Robinson lofted a fly ball over the left-center field wall.

Big Bill Dyer grunted. "Isn't it great to be lucky, Tom? Eight hundred bucks will buy a lot of frozen pizza and potato chips."

Will announced, "That was Robinson's fourth home run of the season and 14th RBI. Three of his homers have been solos. It was his second leading off an inning and his first on the first pitch. All have been against right-handed pitching."

8:03 P.M.

★

In the third inning, with first baseman Jim Robataille on first and two fly outs, Boehler reached out for a Biende fastball and slapped it down the right-field line.

"Way to go, Joe! Way to *go!*" Woolf clapped his hands. His intuition had proven right. But Robataille wasn't stopping at second. He took a wide turn and headed for third. Woolf turned his head so he could see both the runner and the throw. The right fielder, Sammy DeSalis, picked the ball up smoothly and unleashed a super toss. Third baseman Joey Formo brought his glove down on Robataille's leg with the tag, but Robataille's trailing right foot kicked the ball loose. Boehler steamed into second.

"Error, Formo. Assist, DeSalis," the official scorer announced over the press box intercom, and the scoreboard operator flashed the sign. "That was Formo's 17th error, DeSalis's fifth assist," Will added.

Woolf gave his sign. Even though the pitcher was up with two outs, he ordered a bunt. Cox handled the bat well, and Woolf wanted him to bunt to third. Sometimes after a guy makes a bad play he'll hurry his throw. Could use another run right now.

The first pitch to Cox was high and away. The next was also high, but he got the bunt

California Angels catcher Bob Boone remains in disagreement with home-plate umpire Tim Tschida about the strike zone and exactly where it should be located in that evening. Tschida, however, while letting Boone have his say, is uninterested in Bob's opinion, having already given Boone the old heave-ho.

down. However, he poked it too hard and Formo's throw to first was routine.

"Nice try, Coxie," Wash Dorsey shouted.

8:18 P.M.

★

"More dogs! We got a hungry crowd tonight!" Jim Mattox shouted back to the grill in Concession Stand No. 23.

Formo took a 3-2 pitch from Cox for ball four to lead off the fourth. "That was Cox's first walk in $11\frac{2}{3}$ innings," Will announced over the loudspeaker. "But it was his third three-and-two count this game," beat reporter Sam Boyland noted out loud.

A double play started neatly by Boehler and a called third strike to Biende ended the inning.

Art Swanson led off the last of the fourth with a homer to right on a two-and-one pitch. Bill Dyer made the call, then was handed a sheet of paper. "That's an Auto-Clean Spark Plug Homer for Art Swanson," he glumly read. "Auto-Clean: Your Spark Plug that always

Some Yankees make a wish: Baseball's free-agent mascot, the Famous Chicken, is about to take in today's game on a wing and a prayer.

makes a hit." The engineer saw the look on Dyer's face and laughed aloud.

The press box announcement was brief. "That's Swanson's first homer of the year and 26th RBI."

"Will," someone asked, "do you think the new endorsement deal is going to turn Swanson into a power hitter?"

"No, just a power investor."

Bad baserunning showed up again in the bottom of the fifth. With one out, Robinson singled down the left-field line but was a goner trying to stretch the hit into a double.

Coach Pfeiffer cracked, "We got two leadfoots who think they're Jesse Owens."

Sitting alone in his booth, General Manager Renko wondered if he could get some speed to go along with Jimenez instead of the catcher Tyler. He also wondered where Tom Rhines was. A quick look through the binoculars spotted him with two other owners down in the field-level seats.

8:42 P.M.

★

"That Robinson always tries to do too much," Smiley Williams grumbled into his beer.

"How'd you do tonight?" the bartender, Willie Mack, asked him.

"Not bad. Fifty-two bucks. Gimme another beer."

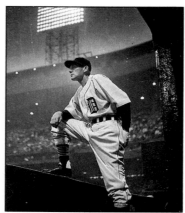

Manager Red Rolfe looks on. "There are only two kinds of managers: winning managers and ex-managers," said Gil Hodges.

Peanuts, Cracker Jack®, and all the accessories make a trip to the ballpark a success.

9:38 P.M.

★

"Hey Will," Boyland called. "Did the umpires talk about that call last night?"

"Said that the batter never reached the box."

"Sounds sensible enough. Some of the rules get too tangled when you think about them too much."

9:51 P.M.

★

"Last call for beer! No more beer after the seventh-inning stretch!"

Dodger Stadium, opened in 1962, was built with team money in Chavez Ravine, overlooking Los Angeles and surrounded by the San Gabriel Mountains. Designed by architect Emil Praeger, Dodger Stadium retained the feel of the classic ballparks of the 1910s as well as any structure had until Oriole Park at Camden Yards opened.

The vendors were looking forward to getting home early.

Still a fast game, Boyland thought. He had to file his first story for the early edition at 10:15. He relaxed, sat back and stretched. With some luck, it might be his final, too.

Cox disposed of the first two batters in the seventh without difficulty. But catcher Bill Georges, the No. 8 hitter in the lineup, cracked his second double of the game, a one-hopper off the left-field wall.

Cox hurried a pitch home that skipped past his catcher. Georges was on third.

Pinch-hitter Juan Rotendo came up, swinging many more bats than someone his size should. Woolf thought, If I bring in the lefty now, we'll just see Tommy Underwood, a much better hitter. I'd rather have a tired Cox facing a .200 hitter than anybody facing Underwood.

But Cox left a fastball up in the strike zone, and Rotendo blooped a single to left. The game was tied. Woolf went to the mound. Cox offered no excuses. Reliever Antonio Olivo entered the game.

As Olivo warmed up, Will called out his stats over the loudspeaker. He would give Cox's game stats after the inning was over, or after the men who Cox's responsibility had been retired or scored.

Olivo's first man was Chuck Rogers, the switch-hitting leadoff man. Rogers rapped a single to left, and Rotendo stopped at second. The next batter, DeSalis, rolled an easy grounder to short, but Boehler tried to pick it up off his right foot and kicked it into the outfield. Rotendo was able to

scamper in with the lead run. A fly out ended the inning.

Woolf's mind was spinning. Maybe Boehler isn't a shortstop, maybe he should be moved to the outfield. Show patience with him as a hitter

and he responds, but. . . . And why was Olivo trying to pitch Rogers inside anyway?

"The line on Cox: six and two-thirds innings, five hits, three runs, two earned," Will announced. "He struck out seven and walked three."

10:58 P.M.

★

In the bottom of the ninth inning, Woolf decided to send Dave Ritz out to face closer Mark Shackleford. The fans gave a lusty cheer when Ritz was announced. His career would probably last only through the season, but he was a borderline Hall-of-Famer and a crowd favorite. He began his career as a slugger, then cut down on his swing and hit .300 four times. When his legs got old he reverted to belting the ball and delivered a few clutch pinch-hit blasts, but he had hit none this year, and was batting near .170.

The crowd chanted and clapped, trying to conjure up some ancient magic. But Shackleford was as sharp as ever. Formo bobbled Ritz's grounder for an instant, but still had plenty of time to catch the aging runner. Boehler flied weakly to

Tommy Lasorda conducts a manager's meeting on the mound. He once said, "I believe managing is like holding a dove in your hand. If you hold it to tightly, you kill it, but if you hold it too loosely, you lose it."

Yankee Stadium's celebrated deep center field and left field were each amazingly endless
before the renovation of 1974 and '75. Yogi Berra once explained why the shadows
made playing left field in Yankee Stadium difficult during afternoon games late in the
season by saying, "It gets late early out there."

Players, broadcasters, and fans make the best out of the dreaded rain delay. For those viewing at home, 1975 World Series highlights or an interview with the bench coach fill the minutes that at times turn to hours before the game resumes.

center. Pinch hitter Tom Spriggs slapped a two-hopper that shortstop Shuertz backhanded, and tossed him out.

11:10 P.M.
★

"Time of tonight's game, three hours and thirty-four minutes. Winning pitcher, Biende, now six and two. Save Shackleford. Loser was Cox. He is now eight

and seven. Attendance 28,541. Home runs: Robinson, his fourth; Swanson, his first; De-Salis, his second."

The printer quickly spat out the game summaries and stats, and Will handed a set of each to the writers as they left for the clubhouses.

The fans straggled out. A few remembered the days when a ninth-inning appearance by Dave Ritz meant some excitement.

11:20 P.M.
★

The postgame activity took place with an efficient suddenness. As the clubhouse doors opened for the press, the gates on the concession stands banged shut and were locked. Most of the cleanup work had been done in the final innings, but the stand managers made sure everything was in order for the next night's game. The grounds crew removed the bases and began bringing out the tarp to cover the infield. Art Renko said goodnight to his boss as the two entered their cars, always parked next to each other in the office lot.

Manager Woolf answered the questions civilly, but the hot breath of the three-game losing streak was on his neck. "I figured Boehler could swing the bat against Biende, and he did. He had two hits. Yes, I thought he was rushing his throw in the seventh. I tried to get another inning from Coxie, but he was shot. We used a lot of pitchers last night."

Bo Sharpe didn't want to talk about his seventh-inning strikeout. The out-of-town writer asked Will if he could interview Dave Ritz before the game tomorrow for a story on the former star's career.

"Dave'll be here at four," Will said. "He always is."

11:40 P.M.

★

here was no one left in the park that Sam Boyland could see except the other writers in the press box, filing their stories. He re-read his

twice, twice more than many of the other guys usually did, and pressed the key that electronically sent it off to the paper. He went into the back to get another diet soda, then he walked out with Will and Pat Hinton, the last folks out

of the park.

"Think the trade will go through tomorrow, Will?"

"We'll see. But I can guarantee you I'll be ready."

"He wants Jimenez even more than Woolf does," Hinton cracked.

Postgame nowadays is a time for providing media interviews, reflecting on that day's work, and deciding where to go to dinner. Stan Musial here (in 1954) holds three bats signifying the three round-trippers he hit that day, the first game of a doubleheader. He went out and blasted two more in the nightcap.

Landscape of Baseball

THE PEOPLE'S GAME

Baseball has always been a kids' game.
It is throwing and running, hitting and catching. Yet while "you gotta have a lot of little boy in you" to treasure the game, according to Roy Campanella, baseball—and cousins stickball, softball, whiffle ball, and the like—has been played for generations by the old as well as the young. Across the map, from T-ball to the Over-50 leagues, from the minor leagues to the backyard pickup game, millions have grabbed a bat and stepped up to the plate, finding that their moment in the sun exists between the lines.

Above: Batting a pitched ball is the hardest single task to accomplish in sports, according to Ted Williams. The best way to learn how to hit is to start young and practice quite often for many years. *Left:* This young man winds up to pitch. While in the beginning it seems that all you have to do is rear back and throw the ball to be a pitcher, there is more to it than that. "Hitting is timing. Pitching is upsetting timing," Warren Spahn said. The pitcher-to-batter conflict has always been central to baseball. Ken "Hawk" Harrelson once observed, "baseball is the only sport I know that when you're on offense, the other team controls the ball." It is up to the defense, more specifically the pitcher, to deliver the ball, thus controlling the tempo and the strategy of the game. Charles Peverelly in *The Book of American Pastimes*, published in 1866, wrote, "it is a game which is peculiarly suited to the American temperament and disposition. . . . From the moment the first striker takes his position, and his bat poises, it has an excitement and *vim* about it, until the last hand is put out in the ninth inning."

Above: One of the greatest players to ever don a uniform, Stan Musial, slides across home plate. Players like Musial are, of course, ideals. But you don't need Musial's skills to play with Musial's heart. *Right:* All you really need is the desire to keep playing. While the long climb from an amateur player to being a major leaguer is part of the country's, and the world's, lure to the game, in the end, it is baseball itself that is the draw. Pete Rose once said, "I'd walk through hell in a gasoline suit to keep playing baseball," and the millions who play, every chance they get, feel the same way. Roger Angell wrote, "Baseball's time is seamless and invisible, a bubble within which players move at exactly the same pace and rhythms as all their predecessors. This is the way the game was played in our youth and in our fathers' youth, and even back then—back in country days—there must have been the same feeling that time could be stopped. Since baseball time is measured only in outs, all you have to do is succeed utterly; keep hitting, keep the rally alive, and you have defeated time. You remain forever young."

Above: The traditional postgame handshake signifies that each team tried its best and the best qualities of sportsmanship prevailed. *Right:* T-ball is where it all begins.

Above: The fundamentals are passed from generation to generation. All it takes is practice. *Left:* The fun part of baseball is the actual game.

Above: You're never too young to start swinging the lumber. *Right:* Juan Marichal had nothing on this youngster's leg kick.

It doesn't take much more than desire (and knickers) to step up to the plate
and take your cuts.

Youth baseball, like its adult counterpart, went from sandlot pickup games to a more organized article. This is a scene from the 1962 Little League World Series.

Little League was created in 1939 in Williamsport, Pennsylvania, by Carl Stotz. Joey Jay of the Cincinnati Reds was the first major leaguer to have been involved in Little League. The Little League World Series is broadcast every year on network television.

Right: It's always good to put another one in the "W" column.
Below: This high school hurler brings the heater.

Left: The team is nine players advancing together toward the common goal of winning.

Above: Able to foul the ball back, the batter was able to at least get a piece of it. The catcher was truly the backstop. *Left:* The batter gets ready to put some aluminum on it.

Above: It's a close play at the plate. *Right:* At the Pan American Games, the hitter knocks it back through the box.

Left: It's a sacrifice, but sometimes you gotta square around and lay one down.

Above: This underhander puts some mustard on it. *Left:* The second sacker is about to complete the potential twin killing.

Right: Playing first base requires that you stare down the batter, protect the line, and still cover the bag. *Below:* Sometimes being a crusher is no picnic.

Left: There are days that you just swing the hammer. *Above:* Sometimes it takes an iron man to play the game.

There's no way to win an argument with the man in blue, although you know it was here, but the umpire insists that it was over there.

Top left: You can try to show him the glove. *Middle left:* You can try to show him the ball. *Bottom left:* And you can even try to show him the base, for crying out loud. But will he listen? Will he listen to reason?

Opposite page: The leadoff man goes for it during a game at the University of Arizona. *Left and bottom:* The right way to do it and the left way to do it are put on display during college baseball action.

Amateur international competition may be the most satisfying aspect of the game, especially when you bring home the gold.

Left: Pitching in to represent your country. *Above:* The United States Olympic Baseball Team in 1988 won the gold medal in Seoul, South Korea.

Team USA celebrates in Seoul in 1988.

Left: A baserunner goes for it during the 1990 Goodwill Games. *Above:* Jim Abbott was a hero in the '88 Olympics, pitching a seven-hitter in the finale to bring home the gold.

Above: Baseball has certainly become a passion with many countries throughout the world. Japan and Taiwan are pictured ready to play in the 1984 Olympics. *Right:* Anywhere home happens to be, once you step to the plate, you still have to take your cuts. Baseball, or *beisu boru* is huge in Japan, rivaling sumo.

Left: Japan's first all-professional team was formed in 1920, and the country's first professional league was started in 1936. Suspended toward the end of World War II, the league was revived by General Douglas MacArthur.

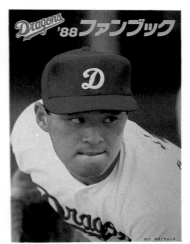

Above: The Dragons' yearbook for 1988. Japan has seven sports-only daily newspapers that concentrate mainly on baseball.

Left: A batter gives the ball a ride, just like the two most famous hitters in Japanese history: Sadaharu Oh and Shigeo Nagashima. Oh is celebrated as a home run king (868 in his career), while Nagashima was perhaps Japan's most popular player.

Opposite page: The lessons of the game can cut across cultural barriers. As in America, baseball in Japan teaches youngsters teamwork and discipline.

Left: Dickie Thon of Puerto Rico tags out William Suero of the Dominican Republic during the 1993 Caribbean World Series. *Below:* The members of the Puerto Rican team celebrate after winning the game in the *Serie de Caribe.* Winners of the Caribbean's various leagues have met in the *Serie de Caribe* since 1949.

The Caribbean has been a fantastic source of young players for the major leagues for 80 or 90 years. One of the major reasons that such places as the Dominican Republic or Venezuela are so rich with ballplayers is that *beisbol* is for many countries in the Caribbean more than a National Pastime; it is more a regional passion.

You don't need much more than a ball, a bat, and a passion for the game to play baseball.

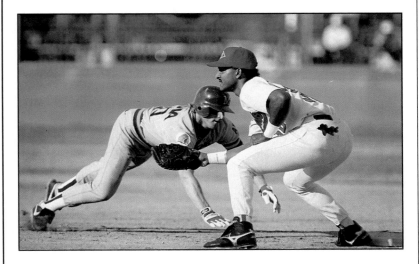

A baserunner dives back to first on a pickoff attempt during a game in the Mexican League.

A stolen base is foiled in the Mexican League. The league is a Triple-A circuit and is part of the National Agreement.

Days of Baseball

Days of Baseball

TAKE ME OUT
TO THE BALLGAME

*A fan's relationship to baseball remains essentially personal.
Most follow one team, whether in the big leagues or in the minors.
Some fans delve into the game's history through its memorabilia or a
trip to Cooperstown. Still others find pleasure in rushing to the
newspaper every morning to follow "fantasy" teams. Many are emphatic
devotees of one particular player. Busing to a game with like-minded
compatriots or meeting them in the same spot in the bleachers or the
skybox, fans communally express their passion for baseball, yet they can
still relate to the game in their own unique way.*

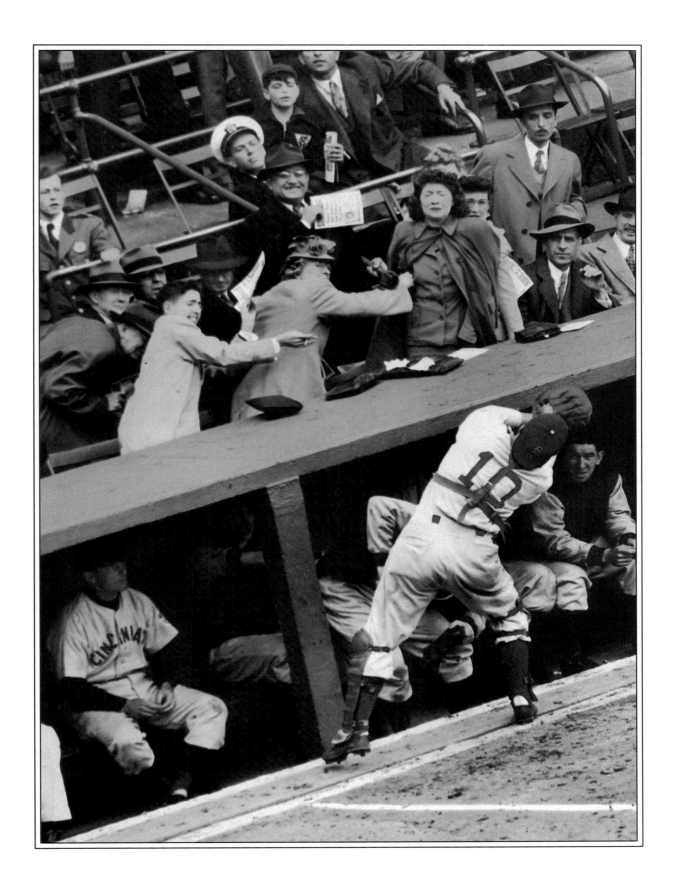

ANOTHER COUNTRY

★

Baseball is a tapestry of researchable incidents, patterns, and personalities. It is a richly textured past, with its history beginning in 1876. It is reborn every spring, and it lives in memory. We visit this world first as players, card collectors, hero-worshipers, and glove-soakers. We are transported to it by television, taken to ballparks, then find newspapers and books. We go to ballparks ourselves, and always we visit this realm in dreams, television, movies, until it's only memory. We go to this place our whole lives. Baseball is part of the great circle from childhood to old age.

Baseball starts officially, in 1876, with the birth of the National League. On a Sunday in June of that year—the league didn't play on Sunday then—George Armstrong Custer lost his men and his scalp. That year the telephone was invented, Mark Twain published *Tom Sawyer*—the other great celebration of American boyhood. America, that new idea, was 100 years old. Baseball, in continuous and recognizable form, flows from that summer, through our childhoods, dreams, into the collective American memory. One NL franchise is still in the city where it started: the Chicago Cubs.

Baseball is as durable as a creation of the imagination. The child and the game dwell where time doesn't exist. For those who make a living at baseball—playing, owning, and beat-writing—it was and is money. But for us, fans, who remember and dream, who collect and root, who travel to and from this place in imagination—this place that hasn't moved out of Brooklyn, can't expand, and won't be cheapened no matter how much money it makes. For us, who sit by televisions and know the stories—baseball is wonderful.

Baseball is a level American playing field of the heart. What goes on in our heads— the telling, remembering, imagining—is what Roger Angell calls the "inner game" and "the interior stadium." This other place, this American Eden, is as essential as Twain's river.

From the beginnings of baseball, there exists a thread that extends into our present day. Those who were present at the 1903 World Series (*above*) felt the passion, much like those who follow their favorite team today (*opposite page*). A rich and full legacy awaits all those who become entranced by its magic.

TRIVIA

★

Roger Angell's notion of inner games in interior stadiums perfectly describes baseball trivia. This "inner game" is between fans and their memories, their memories and other memories, their present and baseball's past.

Some trivia questions are just "look-'em-ups." They can be answered by consulting MacMillan's *Baseball Encyclopedia.* Others are so obscure they can't even be found in the arcane fields of MacMillan. The last are divine, Socractic probes that reveal more than baseball. They require research, association, and deduction, while opening the imagination.

"Look-'em-ups" are not necessarily obtuse. They add knowledge, if not wisdom. Who are all the players who hit 30 or more home runs in a season in each league? This is a mildly interesting question. When you have spent the requisite hours with the *Encyclopedia,* or the necessary milliseconds at a computer, you get the correct 14 names. This is interesting and can pass time in the bleachers, or on an airplane, or at a party where a

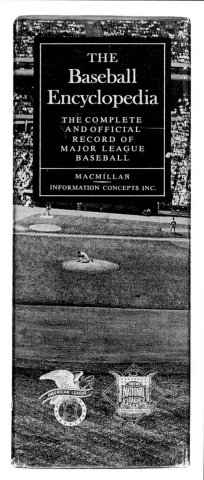

Above: The Baseball Encyclopedia. Opposite page: Darryl Strawberry signs autographs.

know-it-all is talking baseball. The question may send the know-it-all to the bathroom to think, or at least to shut up. This is fun and socially useful, but not profound. The answer, by the way, is Frank Robinson, Frank Howard, Dick Stuart, Jeff Burroughs, Dick Allen, Bobby Bonds, Reggie Smith, Fred McGriff, Larry Parrish, Jason Thompson, Darrell

Evans, Dave Winfield, Dave Kingman, and Greg Luzinski.

Because a question can be looked up in MacMillan or found on a database, doesn't make it a candidate for the sublime. At the trivia contest at the Society for American Baseball Research national convention a few years ago, this question was asked: "Who was the Russian-born pitcher who won more than 300 games in the Japanese League?" Amazingly, one of the SABRites got the answer. This is world-class trivia, and at a SABR convention you can meet world-class trivia players. Some won't even go to a game because they prefer to study. The trivia-meisters constantly practice, look for challengers, and seek new questions. For them no piece of baseball is trivial. They have defined themselves as knowers of baseball, though trivia is not a way to better understand the game. The answer is Victor Starffin.

The best questions reach the sublime. They are the shortest questions with the longest answers. This Q-and-A resonates beyond baseball into the heart of mysteries—America's and our own. Who

was the first man of color to have an impact on major-league baseball? This isn't 14 players who hit 30 homers in each league. This is where baseball and America speak to each other.

Baseball is sometimes a mirror, and this question shows our darkest reflection. Jacques Barzun's famous dictum—he who would know the mindset of America should know baseball—ought to be reversed. He who would know baseball should know America. America provides raw material for baseball.

The answer is Louis Sockalexis, and his story is tragic. Sockalexis played 66 games for the NL Cleveland Spiders in 1897, 21 games in 1898, and seven in '99, yet the Cleveland AL club is named for him. A Penobscot Indian from Old Town, Maine, Sockalexis was not the first man of color to play in the major leagues. African Americans Moses Fleetwood Walker and his brother, Welday, played in 1884 in the American Association, which was then a major league. The Walkers were driven out of baseball by Cap Anson, who boasted of this in his autobiography.

Louis Sockalexis can stake a unique claim in baseball history. It may surprise some to find out that Sockalexis, the first Native-American star in the game, is paid homage to by way of the Cleveland Indians.

Sockalexis wasn't the first Native American to play major-league baseball. James Madison Toy, who played for Cleveland Forest Cities of the American Association, in 1886 and '87, was the first Native American to play big-league ball. These men are important, but Sockalexis was the first man of color who was a star. John McGraw said that Sockalexis had the most talent of any man he ever saw, although he played only 94 career games. In 1915, when a contest was held to name the Cleveland club, it was named in his honor. The first man of color to be a star ultimately destroyed himself with drink.

Sockalexis's story is ascertainable only against the background of 1890s America. The census of 1890—the year incidentally of the last "Indian Battle," the slaughter at Wounded Knee—declared the frontier officially closed, and intellectuals worried about the American character with the frontier gone. Cities teemed

This photograph of the Sioux baseball team was taken around 1910. Thanks in part to the extraordinary play of Louis Sockalexis, the door to professional ball was opened a tiny bit farther, although inequities still exist today.

with crime. The Jeffersonian vision of a citizenry of enlightened farmers was now a nostalgic dream. Trusts ruled the economy, and immigrants were swelling the cities. Against this background, a Native American appeared in the enclosed frontiers of major-league ballfields who could play the game better than anyone had seen it played. Fans, "kranks" as they were called, were wild to see him. They came in record numbers, some wearing war paint and feathers; many whooped and howled. Newspapers in every NL city ballyhooed the arrival of the "Ball-playing Indian" who could run so fast, throw so far, and hit so hard. He made a phenomenal catch in St. Louis, an unbelievable throw in Louisville, and homered his first time up in New York. In three months, drink had ruined Sockalexis's career. The devils that pursued him were stronger than his desire to play the "national pastime."

A trivia question leaves us with the image of the first celebrated player of color, playing out the game in the Eden-like sanctuaries of the National League, seven years after the frontier closed, seven years after the final slaughter of his people, and destroying himself before his first season was half over.

FANTASY LEAGUE BASEBALL

★

The Baby Boomers were indulged by Spock-reading parents; blessed by Willie, Mickey, and the Duke; spoiled by Elvis and the Beatles; made too much of themselves in the '60s; had too much sex in the '70s; made too much money in the '80s; and, not surprisingly, are leaving their mark on fandom in the '90s with a pastime indulged in by 2 million Americans—Rotisserie[R], or fantasy, baseball. Fantasy league baseball is another extension of Roger Angell's interior stadium. Fantasy players develop a roster that they draft or purchase at auction. All the players in either the AL or the NL are available (some fantasy leagues use players from both, but that is infrequent). Then, as the season progresses, what your players do is where your team stands. These offensive categories include home runs, batting average, RBI, and maybe runs or stolen bases. The pitching categories may be wins, Ks, ERA, a ratio of walks and hits over innings pitched, and maybe saves. If there are 10 teams in your league, and

Imagine Sandy Alomar Jr. is at your beck and call. The reality of fantasy leagues is, on paper at least, he could be your star.

your players have amassed the most home runs, you get 10 points in that category. If your team has the second-most runs, you get nine points, and so on. A stat service provides weekly and final rankings. At the end of the season, the total point winner gets a pot, which in some leagues where each transaction costs money can be as high as $5,000.

What makes fantasy baseball a marriage-destroying, get-a-life enterprise is that trades can be made, and any player not on a roster (these teams usually have 23 players, plus three on a supplementary list who can be called up any time) can be drafted from a pool of available players. Minor-league players can be taken as a gamble and placed on the supplementary list. The worry of fantasy owners, like all GMs and managers, is injuries. When a player is hurt or benched, he must be replaced. Fantasy-league baseball can become all-consuming. How many people at their desks are actually calculating stats, making trades, or reading *Baseball America* to learn about college and minor-league players? Fantasy baseball rewards knowledge, and knowlege is infinite.

If trivia is a way to learn, compete, to play against the past, then fantasy baseball is full-contact trivia. Fantasy owners can lose interest in baseball except for numbers in box scores. They call "900" numbers late at night about games in progress. They call each other any time. They devour the newspaper before saying good morning to their children.

Rotisserie® was invented in New York City by Glen Waggoner and others. They formed a league before stat services exsisted: They had to figure their own weekly statistics. It must have taken hours. Those fantasy pioneers truly crossed into another level

You can't tell the players without a scorecard. Stats are the mainstay of a fantasy-league diet. Before services were formed to provide statistical information, it was up to the individual to figure their own—a time-consuming task.

of participation. Waggoner writes the annual *Rotisserie® League Baseball: The Official Rule Book and Draft Day Guide*, which is the bible for most leagues. Fantasy league books were the best-selling baseball books of the 1980s. The need for information, rankings of players at each position, predictions based on their last three years, and dope on rookies has spawned books, magazines, newsletters, and a cottage industry of stats. *USA TODAY's Baseball Weekly* is the weekly bible because it prints games played at each position. If Carlos Baerga plays one inning at shortstop, you can dump your shortstop, play Baerga, and use someone else at second base, like Kirby Puckett, who has played a few innings at second. Fantasy league is not real baseball. It's a numbers

game. It's a mind game. Glen Waggoner says it's "The Greatest Game Since The Great Game Was Invented," and if you can no longer run and throw, he is right.

It's not surprising fantasy baseball was invented by and caught on so thoroughly with Baby Boomers. The generation that explored activism and consciousness in college needed to expand the frontiers of rooting in midlife. For many in their 30s and 40s, fantasy baseball revived a dying interest. Having grown up with Willie, Mickey, and the Duke, the Astroturf, free-agent world of the Bonfire '80s was a turnoff. Fantasy baseball, where you have control, where you win the players, where what they do, they do for you, revitalized interest in baseball.

To be a winner, you have to have your head in the game. Baseball fanatics love all aspects of the sport. Fantasy leagues have necessitated that a wealth of information be available on established players and rookies.

For some, participation in a fantasy league takes them back to a simpler time. Although there's no Joe DiMaggio, the essence of the game is still present.

Fantasy baseball has similarities to Strat-O-Matic Baseball, a game where you pick teams and play a whole season, if you have the patience. Fantasy baseball is infinitely more sophisticated because what the players do is not based on a spinner or dice but on what they *actually* do. This is the first game where your knowledge, your hunches, and your sense of who is good and when he'll cool off are the game. There's immense satisfaction in getting a favorite player and watching him the whole season. He is *yours!* This is like getting the best baseball cards, except they come to life. Fantasy returns some of the innocence players had when we were kids. It doesn't matter how much money they make, how many teams they have left, how rude and arrogant they are, they are yours in a safe place. And the safe place is not non-PVC plastic sheets or memory. It is a league, with standings, trades, bragging rights, and the satisfaction of reading the box scores every day to chart the progress of your team.

Fantasy baseball is a testament to the hold baseball has on the imagination, and a testament to imagination itself. No matter how baseball is changed, someone finds a way to get to its essence. Fantasy baseball is a triumph over the establishment. Neither the owners, the players, nor the media profit by it.

THE HALL OF FAME

★

*L*ike all activities involving reverence, baseball has its pilgrimages and sacred places. Almost every fan makes the hajj to Cooperstown once in their life—with a parent or their own children. The green, pleasantly commercialized village in upstate New York—convenient to nothing, accessible to no major airport, and, like Mecca, surrounded by sparsely inhabited country—is wholly satisfying.

Any semi-informed fan knows baseball wasn't invented in Cooperstown by Abner Doubleday on a June day in 1893 (when Doubleday was

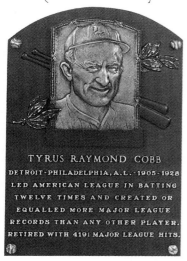

TYRUS RAYMOND COBB
DETROIT-PHILADELPHIA, A.L.·1905-1928
LED AMERICAN LEAGUE IN BATTING
TWELVE TIMES AND CREATED OR
EQUALLED MORE MAJOR LEAGUE
RECORDS THAN ANY OTHER PLAYER.
RETIRED WITH 4191 MAJOR LEAGUE HITS.

Ty Cobb was one of the first five inductees into the Hall. This plaque commemorates his contributions.

From left: Ford Frick, Kenesaw Mountain Landis, William Harridge, and William Bramham take part in the 1939 ribbon-cutting ceremony for the Hall of Fame dedication in Cooperstown.

actually a plebe at West Point), but the town is beautiful, and the Hall of Fame is impressive, though the area with the plaques themselves is smaller than the swelling immortality conjured by the phrase "in the Hall of Fame." Indeed, one expects what is actually a wing of a moderately sized museum to have the grandeur of Westminster Abbey. But the museum is terrific, and the town—with its green meadows and top-dollar memorabilia shops—looks like the place where baseball should have been invented.

Stephen Jay Gould has written eloquently of the appeal of creation myths as opposed to less dramatic, unheroic processes of evolution, which produced baseball and human beings. Creation myths simplify and humanize, and in the early part of the century, baseball needed a non-British Eden, but Cooperstown is more than a tourist attraction based on a fairy tale. No other sport's hall of fame is like Cooperstown, because the past dwells in baseball as it does in no other sport.

Because a baseball game is seven minutes of action spread over three hours, fans, like announcers, fill the spaces in action with anecdotes, comparisons, and numbers. The spaces are filled with the past—the story that starts in 1876—which is found in Cooperstown. The presence of the past makes baseball different. Baseball is a narrative, and each fan a narrator.

The Hall of Fame is a small wing off the best museum in the world. From Armand La Montagne's statues of Ted Williams and Babe Ruth to baseballs from Nolan Ryan's no-hitters to Cy Young's pipe, the museum has artifacts from this world where we spend so much of our lives. Here are Ty Cobb's sliding pads, Wee Willie Keeler's bat, and Lou Gehrig's locker. Here, too, is a photo of Joe DiMaggio in an Army uniform during World War II where Joe radiates the easy and handsome vitality that translated to a kind of perfec-

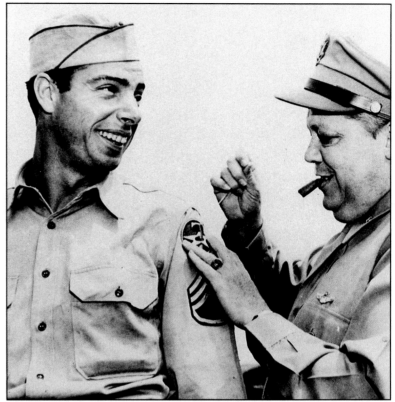

A hero in any uniform. Through pictures like this one and other memorabilia, the Hall of Fame let s us do more than idly reminisce. For many, it may evoke a feeling of actually being a part of this magnificent legacy.

This signed baseball by Honus Wagner at Cooperstown brings a certain reality to one's inner game.

tion on the field those of us who never saw him don't understand—not until you see this picture, anyway. The photo makes Joe DiMaggio, icon, come alive; that is the spirit of the museum. Other cultures worship ancestors and feel their presence in daily life. We do this in baseball. We don't go to Cooperstown because we need a kitschy version of a baseball Eden, and we don't go as city dwellers who need a dose of pastoral creation myth. We go

because Cooperstown, like baseball, is a work of imagination. The imagination manifests itself in works of art, such as statues, photos, and displays of uniforms. It manifests itself in objects that make our inner lives visible. All museums are art museums. Whether they celebrate the history of painting or the history of baseball, they celebrate the human need to make significant and beautiful objects.

BALLPARKS

★

There are other pilgrimages on the fans' hajj. Writers from Roger Angell to John Updike have written elegantly of stadiums. One of the most interesting developments of the 1980s, with the boom in baseball consciousness, was fan effort to influence stadium construction. A generation of ballparks was replaced in the 1960s and 1970s with phoney-turfed, multipurpose mediocrities that housed NFL teams, rock concerts, and tractor pulls. In celebrating old parks, it isn't necessary to confuse them with places of worship; they were not cathedrals. Ballparks are places where we engage in a cultural activity, which involves a sense of the past, as well as a good seat, and are conduits of tradition. Oriole Park at Camden Yards is a better conduit than Three Rivers Stadium. Fan opinion helped make Camden Yards look and feel like a portal to the past rather than a television studio that offers a half-time show.

Ballparks are not churches any more than baseball is a religion, but they are wonderful. They are the present and the past. Only three—Tiger Stadium, Fenway Park, and Wrigley Field—look enough like they did when Babe Ruth strode to the plate or took that large body out to right on mincing steps. The new

From Forbes Field in 1909 (*above*) to Candlestick Park (*below*) memories abound at the Hall.

Yankee Stadium is a compromise. The dimensions are shorter, the seats are plastic, and the grand facade is gone. The place where Mantle, Maris, DiMaggio, Ruth, and Gehrig played has been tampered with, but it's worth a trip. The park that has the overhanging and over-awing feel of old Yankee Stadium is Tiger Stadium, which is a mighty place built with old genius. It has a huge center field for great plays and a pennant

porch within easy reach for slugging. In old Yankee Stadium, Joe DiMaggio had room to work his magic on fly balls, and fans saw 60 and 61 home run seasons. That combination could not be beat. Tiger Stadium will be replaced by the next century. All fans should see it before it's gone.

Fenway and Wrigley are pretty. They are small and are good places to hit, so games are unpredictable and fun, and most seats offer a good view. If Tiger and old Yankee were like the Roman Colosseum, then Fenway and Wrigley are the Globe Theater. In both, the present and the past coexist so

naturally, one wonders what other old parks, such as Forbes or Crosley or Shibe, would be like had they been preserved rather than destroyed.

There is nothing like watching a game in a park where baseball has been played for 80 years. It is taking a place with your ancestors.

The facade of old Yankee Stadium. It was ballparks like this that saw the greats like the Bambino, Joltin' Joe, the Mick, and others work their magic and forever claim a place in our hearts and minds. While few modern ballparks can conjure the same intense sense of the past, things have been improving thanks in part to input from the fans.

THE SHAPE OF MEMORY ★

The shape of baseball's past changed in the last 15 years. The 1980s saw an explosion of baseball information. More and better baseball books were published. Prose improved in the wake of Roger Angell. Daniel Okrent and Harris Lewine's *The Ultimate Baseball Book*, published in 1979, raised standards for design and photo research. The Society for American Baseball Research (SABR) became nationally known, giving anyone the chance to become part of a re-search network, meet researchers, and publish serious work. Excellent baseball histories—by such writers as Mike Sowell, Kevin Kerrane, and Robert Creamer—were published by major houses, while more arcane matters were published by SABR and such small presses as Meckler and McFarlane. Bill James became an industry by making statistics more meaningful, creating new numbers, and turning his brilliant methods to the past. ESPN brought humor and intelligence to the dreary province of sports reporting. Memorabilia became big business, and *The Wall Street Journal* rated base-

The indefatigable Ty Cobb may have proven less palatable had he been subject to the constant barrage of media like many of today's stars.

ball cards as one of the best investments of the 1980s. By 1989, there were three baseball encyclopedias, and information was available on an ever-increasing number of databases.

Some of this revolution has been almost satirical. The fantasy camp, where aging fans pay to play aging heroes, may in fact resemble a fat camp more than the games we remember. But active nostalgia coupled with the explosion in

While studying about the game's heritage helps you to become a well-rounded fan, no amount of reading can replace the enriching experience of actually attending a game.

information makes this the richest time to be a baseball fan.

The self-defined "sports bar" is an invention of the 1980s. Bars have always been hubs for rooting, gambling, and sports talk. The sports bar, however, is a place that caters to those who define themselves as fans; it is a place where you can strut your fanhood. Sports bars offer many games on many screens, courtesy of a satellite dish or cable, and the walls are decorated with sports photos and memorabilia. They are a commercial attempt to create the interior stadium and are the Hard Rock Cafes of sports, not the neighborhood tavern. Like a fantasy baseball camp, the sports bar combines activity and nostalgia—the photos, the memorabilia, the "instant nostalgia" of the big game—in a place fans can be secure in their identities.

A more scholarly way to improve the interior stadium is knowledge. In the 1980s, the Society for American Baseball Research grew from a 1,200-member group of specialists to a nationally known organization of 6,000. Anyone can join SABR. It's not MENSA; there is no entrance examination. Anyone can learn the

Above: Unlike so many milestones from days gone by, Hammerin' Hank's record-setting blast was watched by many via TV. *Opposite page:* At Wrigley Field, great seats are often just outside of the Friendly Confines.

San Francisco fans pleaded with then-president Fay Vincent to keep the Giants in town. Other cities have not been as fortuitous and have had to bid their teams a fond farewell.

basic techniques of baseball research—SABR has published a book about how to research—and give a presentation at a regional meeting or the National Convention, and publish their work in either SABR's *Research Journal* or *The National Pastime.* Serious fans are no longer isolated.

SABR was founded in 1972 by a scholarly federal employee, L. Robert Davids, and 15 aficianados in Cooperstown. The first SABR *Research Journal* was published in 1973, and one has appeared every

every year since. Davids edited the *Journal* until 1983—after which it grew bigger, became slicker, and added photos. No baseball researcher is more respected. The dedication to *The Bill James Historical Baseball Abstract* reads: "This book is dedicated to the man who has done more for baseball research than anyone else living—L. Robert Davids."

The Society for American Baseball Research is the best communal path to baseball's past. SABR is an open network of serious fans, researchers, book collectors, and writers. The research has revealed such matters in the past as the correction of Walter Johnson's shutout total from 113 to 110 (he was relieved in three games), and the discovery of a second minor-league hitting streak of 69 straight games (in 1887), which is the second-longest in baseball history. SABR is an excellent way to meet people who love baseball.

Even with the explosion of knowledge, the best place to find baseball's past is still in the sports sections of old newspapers. Any city library has newspapers on microfilm, and there you can search and regain lost time.

By the time Preacher Roe took the field, stats were well documented. For many of the early years, one must almost be a detective to put together the facts.

VIRTUAL BASEBALL

★

Baseball rooting, like every form of entertainment, stands on the threshold of a revolution. Virtual reality, the computer-generated simulation of reality, will change rooting. With goggles that surround the face, and a glove to provide sensation, the viewers are no longer spectators. They are in an electronically created "reality," and they play. Instead of watching Babe Ruth, you can pitch to him. Or you can play right field in old Yankee Stadium while Roger Maris bats. If you don't want to play, you can watch the 1927 American League season, or program the machine to observe the '27 Yankees play the '63 Dodgers. If you want single combat, what about pitting the 1911 Ty Cobb against the 1963 Sandy Koufax, or the 1948 Stan Musial against the 1930 Lefty Grove? The entire history of baseball is data, and you can watch, enter, or combine any of it. Current and past seasons are not obsolete. They are necessary to increase the database. And this data presents endless possibilities.

Could virtual reality ever replace the sights and sounds of the ballpark?

The next great baseball question is reality or fantasy? Do you want to watch the real Barry Bonds or virtually play against a virtual Barry Bonds? The future will offer a choice of alternative "realities." Fantasy or reality? This will be the "to be or not to be" of the next century.

Virtual baseball will not replace real baseball any more than artificial turf replaced grass, but like turf and grass, the two will exist side by side. Unlike turf or grass, however, we will be able to choose. We can join the 150-year tapestry of baseball as spectators and players. It will be quite a choice.

Virtual reality will come to all cultures. No one will be better prepared than baseball fans. As researchers, fantasy-league general managers, trivia buffs, spectators, and dreamers, we have known other worlds our whole lives.

Through virtual reality, you can don your fedora and claim a seat for spectacular events or even participate in them.

Baseball and Culture

GRAND SLAM MOVIES, LITERATURE, ART, CARDS, MUSIC, AND MORE

Baseball is a staple of American popular culture, and it is integral to our modern national identity. Poets write diamond verse, artists paint portraits of players, and songwriters compose ballads celebrating the old game. The drama of the game is recounted every day in the local newspaper and every year in a multitude of books. In movies and in literature, baseball inspires both romantic portrayals of a simple past and exacting scrutiny at the world today. The riches encompassing the game, in everything from bubble-gum cards to Warhols, confirm that baseball is truly a work of art.

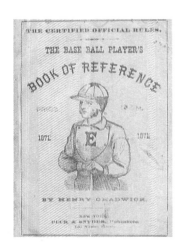

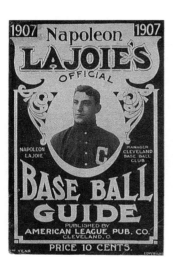

Above and below: Chadwick's 1871 *Base Ball Player's Book of Reference*, an early rules guide, and Cleveland second baseman Napoleon Lajoie's *Base Ball Guide*, published in 1907.

The culture of baseball, indeed its very status as the National Pastime, was established through the popular press. No game has ever received more comprehensive coverage and been better served by writers. Pulitzer Prize-winner Red Smith was once quoted as saying that the quality of writing about any given sport was in inverse proportion to the size of the ball used in that sport. Hence, golf and baseball were afforded an exalted status compared to the relatively thin prose documenting the exploits of their counterparts on the gridiron and gymnasium floor.

Baseball's popular press has existed nearly as long as the game itself. Publications such as *The Sporting News* trace their roots back well over a century, and contemporary writers such as Peter Gammons and Tom Boswell are members of a fraternity that once included such literary figures as Walt Whitman, Ring Lardner, and Damon Runyon. Yesterday's wood engravings and roto-gravure sections have given way to color laser photos and computer graphics. If anything, the coverage of baseball in the popular press is more diverse and colorful than ever before.

Baseball writing and sportswriting in America began with Henry Chadwick in the late 1850s. As a boy in England, Chadwick had played rounders and cricket, baseball's old-world ancestors. After viewing his first baseball game in 1856, the then cricket correspondent of *The New York Times* fell in love with the game he believed could become as significant to America as cricket was to his homeland.

Chadwick became obsessed with the game both as a writer and as the game's chief advocate. He saw in baseball a game where the moral virtues of his newly adopted nation were served by clean living and vigorous exercise. In time he would be known as "Father

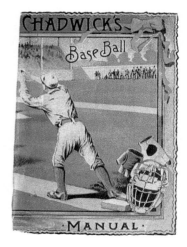

Chadwick's Base Ball Manual, just one of the many books published in the 19th century bearing the imprimatur of "Father Chadwick." Note where the first baseman is standing.

Chadwick." In 50 years, he did more than anyone to promote the best interests of baseball.

Among other things, he developed the box score; chaired the National Association Rules Committee; edited baseball's first annual guide, *Beadles Dime Baseball Player,* and later DeWitt's and Spalding's baseball guides; and continued to write baseball for the *Brooklyn Eagle, New York Clipper,* and *New York Times,* among other newspapers. He was a staunch supporter of umpires in an age where the press was swift to bait them and subject them to public ridicule. Perhaps most importantly, Chadwick remained independent enough to stand up to the game's vested interests when it came time to note "suspicious play" and "queer games" in the gambling-rife world of 19th-century sport. Baseball became the purest of popular professional sports through his vigilance.

Right: The masthead of *The Base Ball Player's Chronicle*, the first paper devoted exclusively to baseball. The publication, edited by Henry Chadwick, was instituted in 1867.

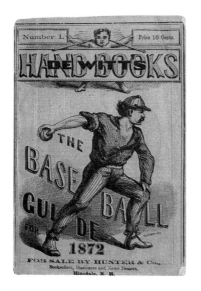

Yet another early baseball publication edited by Henry Chadwick, this edition of *DeWitt's Base Ball Guide* dates from 1872. By the 1870s, literature concerning "The National Game" had become a lucrative business.

It was Father Chadwick who created the unbroken chain of statistical and anecdotal material that forms the bedrock of baseball culture. He died in 1908 at age 83 after serving the game for over half a century. His death came as the result of a cold that began after he refused to wear an overcoat to the home opener of the Brooklyn Dodgers. It is ironic that the Baseball Writers Association of America was started in the same year that their tribal patriarch died. Chadwick remains to this day the only writer to be selected to the main wing of Baseball's Hall of Fame.

The 19th century saw a great proliferation of baseball writing other than that penned by Chadwick. Newspapers began to cover the game in the 1850s, and coverage increased greatly following the conclusion of the Civil War. The game grew during this period as a reaction to the war's end and became a vehicle through which the country could heal its wounds. Periodicals such as *The Ball Players' Chronicle*, started in 1867, and *The New England Baseballist*, started in 1868, were the first exclusively devoted to baseball. Baseball had reached the threshold of the cultural mainstream.

Baseball in its infancy had shared space in the sports section with such gentlemanly pursuits as chess, sailing, yachting, and racing. Soon it began to dominate the sports page. Town nines begot professional teams such as the Red Stockings, and such teams became part of the National Association and National League. Big-time baseball was born and, with it, the baseball beat.

Shortly after the formation of the National League in 1876, the landscape of America's sporting press began to change dramatically. Writers such as Oliver Perry Caylor of *The Cincinnati Enquirer* soon became as big in the public arena as the players they covered. In 1885 and 1886 Caylor took an unprecedented sabbatical and managed the Reds of the American Association to second-place and fifth-place finishes. He would also manage the New York Metropolitans in 1887, a season in which he continued to write while also serving as part owner of the team.

In 1882, Joseph Pulitzer realized that sports, and baseball in particular, was helping to sell his newspapers. He subsequently started the nation's first multipage sports section in the *New York Daily Graphic*. It soon started a national trend. Before long newspapers were assigning more talent to cover the growth of America's leisure industry led by baseball.

It was also during this era that baseball coverage took on an added dimension with the emergence of the first baseball cartoonist. The great baseball cartoonists are baseball's least-appreciated journalists. In many instances their work is the best documentation of the players and games of the eras before motion pictures.

Baseball cartooning began in 1877 with Christopher "Christo" Smith of Buffalo, who ironically never published a baseball cartoon in his life. Despite this fact his work stands today as the first example of the once-familiar genre. Like fellow graphic (and political) satirist Thomas Nast of *Harper's Weekly* fame, Smith was born in Germany, as Christoff Schmidt. Smith emigrated with his brothers to New York. Unlike his counterpart Nast, however,

Like political cartoons of the 1870s, Christo Smith's cartoons concerning the International League's Buffalo club were topical, precisely drawn, and bitingly funny.

Another Christo Smith 1877 International League cartoon. Both of these comics concern the daily doings of the Buffalo team and feature "Pud" Galvin.

Smith took up pen and brush purely as a sideline to his work in the family sign and paint shop.

During the 1877 season, Smith served the Buffalo club that played games in the National League and International Association as an inning-by-inning scorer for a large on-field scoreboard. Not only did he record the score, but he also was inspired to create cartoons depicting his interpretation of the afternoon's action. These drawings were displayed on a daily basis in the front window of Garson's Clothing Store in downtown Buffalo.

Historian Joseph Overfield has uncovered 34 of Smith's original drawings, which may comprise the total oeuvre of his baseball work. Because Buffalo only played an abbreviated 40-game schedule and Smith only made cartoons for one season, this portfolio is all that remains of the work of this baseball pioneer. Within half a century his craft would grace the sports pages of America.

In the age before the electronic media of film, radio, and television, the baseball cartoon played a vital role in the everyday life of the fan. Not only did these cartoons document the action of the games themselves, paying particular attention to the outstanding hits, tags, and catches of a given afternoon, but they also served as the only vehicle of baseball information for the legions of illiterate and semiliterate fans. For such fans the baseball cartoon became a hieroglyphic. The compact batting stance of a favorite star or the glowering visage of an opposing pitcher was readily imparted through these pictures

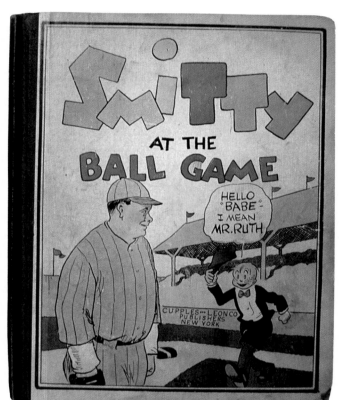

"Smitty at the Ball Game" features a portrait of Babe Ruth. Early baseball fans got much of their information on the game from comics.

Left: A cartoon of bespectacled 1930s Red Sox hurler Danny MacFayden, drawn by the great Gene Mack. Baseball cartoonists had an important place during the pre-television era.

Above both: In 1938, the Goudey Company issued a series of cards featuring photographs of players' heads placed on caricatures of their bodies, which emphasized the strength of the players. Joe Medwick is at the top and Joe DiMaggio bats below.

in the penny press. It is no exaggeration to speculate that much of America's sporting folklore was conveyed through these images to the multitude of immigrants who arrived on these shores at the turn of the century. In a short time, the children of these immigrants would dot the rosters of major-league teams.

These cartoons also served as an editorial vehicle for the creation of heroes and goats. They became a forum more powerful than mere still photographs. Bill Gallo, the esteemed sports cartoonist of the *New York Daily News,* still chooses to include a hero and goat in his World Series game cartoons. The images within these cartoons were immediate and often more powerful than the written words they were meant to supplement.

Among the greatest of the cartoonists that depicted baseball's "Golden Age" from the 1920s through the 1940s was Gene Mack of *The Boston Globe.* A distant relative of Connie Mack, Gene was a rarity among artists in that he was also skilled as both a writer and historian. Among his talents was an uncanny knack for capturing the movement and image of a player using only a few spare lines. Long before videotape, Mack would provide the

Baseball and Culture

Right: Great baseball rivalries, such as the Yankee/Red Sox clashes of the 1940s, were often spoofed in cartoons. Historical or comic characterizations of the Red Sox as "Pilgrims," or the Brooklyn Dodgers as "Bums," dominated the cartoons of the time.

An all-too-rare example of modern baseball cartooning by Bill Gallo of the *New York Daily News*, featuring the 1986 World Champion Mets.

graphic equivalent of a game highlight reel within several square inches of column space. Many of these cartoons were started, finished, and restarted in the confines of the press box. Like most sports journalists of his day, Mack was expected to crank out copy nearly every day. The fact that Boston was a two-team baseball town during his career ensured that the press box was his home away from home for most of his five-decade career.

Historians and baseball collectors remember Mack as the ingenious talent behind one of baseball publishing's true gems, a slim volume issued by *The Sporting News* in 1947 entitled *Gene Mack's Hall of Fame Cartoons of Major League Ballparks.* The cartoons in this booklet not only depicted the architecture and design of each park in perfect detail but also included an incredibly intricate anecdotal history of each park. For example, in his Fenway Park portrait he included more than incidental drawings that depict the people and events that comprise the history of the park. It was here that Mack's skills as a historian more than matched his artistic prowess.

On the other hand, fellow *Sporting News* contributor and longtime *New York World-Telegram* cartoonist Willard Mullin worked in a completely different style from Mack. However, like his Boston counterpart, he was considered a journalist by his peers, and his work was one of baseball's visual signatures in the era before television. Mullin's work was characterized by his ability to either create an exact likeness of his subject or witty caricatures. Mullin created a multitude of cartoons depicting the mascots of teams in all sports. His most memorable mascots are the Brooklyn Bum for the Dodgers and the lumbering thick-necked Giant for the New York and San Francisco Giants. Many authorities consider Mullin to be the greatest sports cartoonist of all time.

In the era before television, there was barely a daily in the country that didn't employ a full-time sports cartoonist, who invariably spent most of his time chronicling baseball. The names of many of the great artists have been obscured by the passage of time; however, there are literally hundreds who deserve to be listed for the significant documentation of baseball. Among that legion were draftsmen such as Bob Coyne, Pap, TAD Dorgan, Vic Johnson, Bill Gallo, Eddie Germano, Phil Bissell, Burris Jenkins, Wallace Goldsmith Jr., and Allan Maver. The profession of the full-time sports cartoonist is one of the few in baseball that have

Cartoons were also used for commercial purposes. This 1939 Wheaties ad features Chicago Cubs catcher Gabby Hartnett and his 1938 pennant-winning "Homer in the Gloamin."

Right: New York Giants hurler Christy Mathewson, featured on a 1913 *Police Gazette* front cover. Although the *Gazette* didn't make its mark publishing baseball stories, the popular, handsome Christy Mathewson could always sell a few papers in New York.

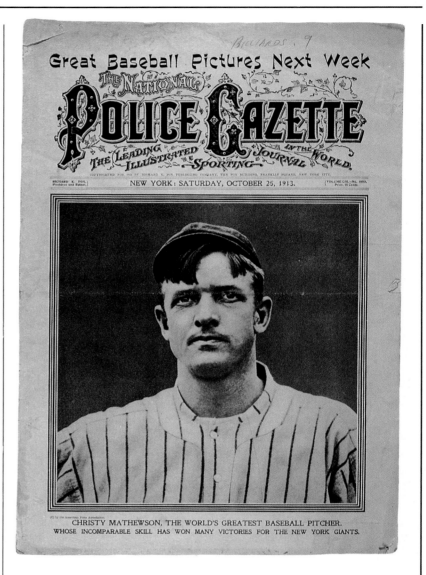

CHRISTY MATHEWSON, THE WORLD'S GREATEST BASEBALL PITCHER.
WHOSE INCOMPARABLE SKILL HAS WON MANY VICTORIES FOR THE NEW YORK GIANTS.

Giants hurler Rube Marquard graces this cover of *Sporting Life* dating from 1917, its last year of publication. Once a top seller, it was eventually surpassed by *The Sporting News.*

literally disappeared, with fans, historians and the sporting press left that much poorer.

In 1883 another lasting baseball tradition was started, as Francis C. Richter started a journal that would be the bellwether for all subsequent national sporting weeklies. His journal, devoted to baseball and popular pastimes such as shooting, was dubbed *Sporting Life.* It competed with the brash *Police Gazette.* The *Police Gazette,* through publisher Richard Fox, was primarily concerned with the promotion of events such as heavyweight prizefights to

THE DIAMOND FIELD.

HOW THE BASEBALL SEASON OPENED AT THE POLO GROUNDS, N.Y. CITY—SCENES AND EPISODES OF THE GAMES, WITH PORTRAIT OF THE MANAGER OF THE NEW YORK TEAM.

I—In the Field. II—A Short-stop. III—A Home Run. IV—Fair Admirers. V—Waiting for a Ball. VI—An Unpopular Referee. VII—James Lyman Price, Manager.

Left: This 1884 edition of *The National Police Gazette* featured a cartoon entitled "The Diamond Field," which illustrated a day at the ballpark. The cartoon mainly focuses on umpire-baiting, the then-novelty of female fans, and the grand spectacle of the event itself.

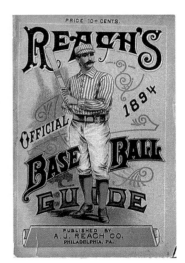

The 1894 *Reach Base Ball Guide*, published by Albert J. Reach of Philadelphia. Most annuals of the time included cartoons and photos as well as statistics, rules, and stories.

supplement its ample coverage of popular theater and vaudeville. In its day the *Police Gazette* was a combination of today's *National Enquirer* and a tabloid sports section.

Because Fox was new to baseball, he treated the game as trivial and left the door open for Richter and, later, Alfred H. Spink of *The Sporting News* to capture baseball-hungry readers.

It was through these weeklies that baseball journalists not only chronicled the game but shaped its future. Richter not only

After beginning publication in 1886, *The Sporting News* soon became America's top sports weekly—a position *TSN* still holds, although it no longer focuses primarily on baseball.

Alfred Spink, co-founder of *The Sporting News*. The paper began and is still published in St. Louis.

founded *Sporting Life* in 1883 but also helped start the Philadelphia Phillies in the same year. In 1907 he was even offered the presidency of the National League but turned it down. Although *Sporting Life* was baseball's oldest weekly, it went out of business in 1917, in large part due to a greatly successful competitor from St. Louis, *The Sporting News,* which would become known to all as "The Bible of Baseball."

Baseball's oldest continually published journal, *The Sporting News* started in 1886 in St. Louis. Founded by Alfred Henry Spink and brother Charles, the weekly would soon grow to become baseball's most authoritative journal. Within two years of its founding, it would achieve a circulation of nearly 40,000.

The individual who did the most to establish the reputation of the paper was J.G. Taylor Spink, son of Charles Spink and editor in chief for five decades. Known for his changing moods and profane tirades, he was also a tireless advocate for the improvement of the game. Working seven days a week, Spink drove his writers and editors to drink, with his late-night phone calls and forceful manner.

Under his stewardship, *The Sporting News* not only helped to uncover the Black Sox scandal by informing baseball authorities of leads in the case, but also continued to expose any and all stories of corruption in the game. The paper led the way in promoting the game to fans by establishing highly promoted annual awards for rookies, pitchers, and Most Valuable Players. *The Sporting News* also supported the baseball establishment on issues such as expansion. Among the multitude of writers to work for the paper was Ring Lardner, who penned a column entitled "Pullman Tales." It was this work that led the multitalented author to write about fictional rookie Jack Keefe, who became the protagonist in his classic book, *You Know Me Al.* Other writers and columnists have comprised a

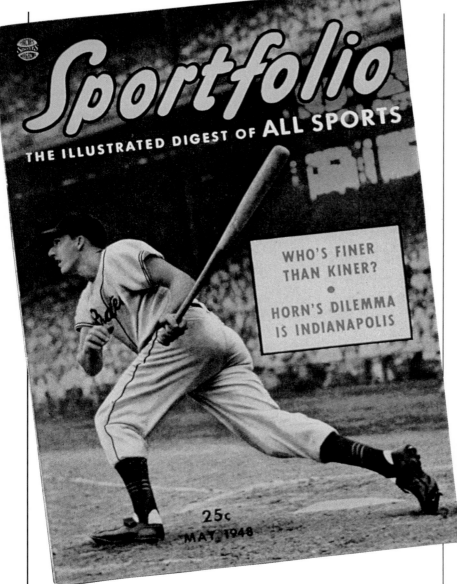

Left: Home run king Ralph Kiner is pictured on the cover of *Sportfolio*'s May 1948 issue. Splashy photo magazines became a staple of publishing in the 1940s, as technology made glossy photo reproduction less expensive.

Jackie Robinson's face graced many magazine covers in the 1940s and 1950s, and this "baseball preview" issue of *Sport Life* is no exception.

Sport Magazine, a glossy monthly still in publication, featured Milwaukee Braves star Eddie Mathews on the cover of their April 1957 issue.

who's who of baseball writers, including Dan Daniel, Fred Lieb, Shirley Povich, Bob Addie, Jim Murray, Wells Twombley, Joe Falls, Lee Allen, Harold Kaese, Bill Conlin, Leonard Koppett, and Peter Gammons.

In recent years the paper has changed dramatically, much to the chagrin of some longtime subscribers. Not only did it drop the subtitle of "The Bible of Baseball," it also began carrying more coverage of sports, such as football, basketball, and hockey. In the

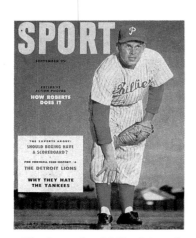

The September 1953 edition of *Sport Magazine* featured Philadelphia Phillies righthanded pitching star Robin Roberts on its cover.

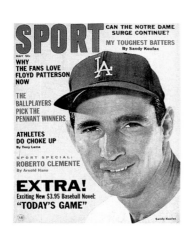

early 1990s the unthinkable occurred: The paper stopped carrying box scores of major-league games. Despite these changes the paper still is a major player in baseball journalism, with the publication of its annual guide, record book, and register. They, along with their many other publications, have been staples of baseball libraries for nearly a century.

Although not published as a weekly, *Baseball America* was founded in 1981 in British Columbia by Allan Simpson, in his garage. It was founded both in reaction to the fact that *The Sporting News* had abdicated its former position as baseball's bible and as a vehicle to chronicle the extensive world of minor-league and collegiate baseball, which had hitherto been largely ignored by the mainstream press.

At present *Baseball America* has greatly expanded its coverage of major-league baseball as well, and it has included the work of columnists, such as Peter Gammons. The Durham, North Carolina, newspaper was purchased by former Durham Bulls owner Miles Wolff, who has coordinated the publication's expansion. It is now regarded as the rightful heir to the baseball preeminence once enjoyed by *The Sporting News*.

In 1991, the baseball world greeted another newcomer and contender for the title of "Bible of Baseball" with the publication of *USA Today Baseball Weekly*. In many ways this would be known as the publication built for the growing legion of fantasy-league baseball fanatics. Hence the distinguishing feature of this weekly is an almost fanatical devotion to statistics.

It would take an MIT-trained scientist to edit baseball's most informative and stylish monthly: Ferdinand C. Lane became the founding editor of *Baseball Magazine* in 1908. Although it would last for 50 years, the magazine was especially well produced in the period before and during World War I. Included in the magazine were extensive feature and player profiles, as well as poetry and baseball cartoons. The graphic design, especially the color paintings used for early covers, has made the magazine a rare collector's item. Likewise the scope of information presented in each issue makes *Baseball Magazine* a significant research tool.

Baseball Magazine was joined in 1942 by another monthly called *Baseball Digest,* which continues today. It was a forum for both established baseball writers and the sort of amateur historians who would later make up the membership of the Society for American Baseball Research. Both current and historical topics are covered in *Baseball Digest.*

With the founding of the Society for American Baseball Research in 1972, baseball historians and scholars finally created a vehicle for both the discussion and publication of hitherto undocumented baseball history, lore, and statistics. The Society publishes two annual journals, *The Baseball Research Journal* and *The National Pastime,* as well as a monthly bulletin for nearly 7,000 members.

A lively array of small magazines has also sprung up within the past few years and comprises what might be termed as baseball's alternative press. Chief among these publications are *Spitball, Fan, The Cooperstown Review,* and *The Minneapolis Baseball Review,* also known as *Elysian Fields.* Each of these includes poetry, interviews, reviews, and coverage of the fine arts as they relate to baseball.

The future of baseball's popular press would delight the likes of Father Chadwick and J.G. Taylor Spink as coverage of the game remains as comprehensive and lively as ever. A new dimension will be added to this world with the proliferation of sophisticated electronic information during the coming age of the information superhighway.

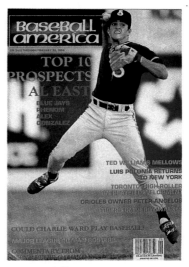

Baseball America, a biweekly magazine, made its mark in the 1980s by focusing on up-and-coming minor league prospects. Toronto's young shortstop Alex Gonzalez is featured on the cover of a February 1994 issue.

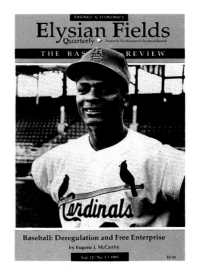

Elysian Fields featured Curt Flood on the cover of its first 1993 issue, which discussed the economics of modern baseball. Flood's challenge of the reserve clause helped changed baseball for good.

The National Pastime has inspired countless authors to pen nearly as many books about the game as there have been players who ever toiled in the major leagues. Perhaps this is a slight exaggeration, as more than 10,000 men have enjoyed at least a cup of coffee in "the show." Nevertheless, many pundits agree that baseball possesses the greatest literary tradition of any sport. Search the sports section of any bookstore and you will find that baseball occupies nearly half to two-thirds of the shelf space. Even Sportspages bookshop in London carries nearly 500 baseball titles.

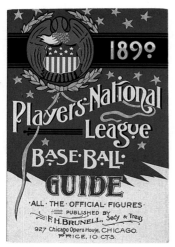

The 1890 *Players' National League Base Ball Guide.*

The origin of baseball literature extends back to ancient Egypt, where hieroglyphics depicting ball games were found on the walls of tombs and other shrines. Similar ball games using a bat or other striking object are also seen in Mayan and Pre-Columbian art. There are even figures shown playing ball in medieval illuminated manuscripts. Such ball games and their variations have seemingly been a constant component of the human experience. Is there any doubt that there were also ancient variations of the "Hot Stove League" as well? For surely wherever ball games have been played there have also been fans and students of these games, whose roles have also included the duties of chronicler and storyteller.

All literature comes from the oral tradition of storytelling. This is best typified by Homer, who told the stories of the *Odyssey* and *Iliad* to listeners where he held court. Baseball and most sports remain as some of the last vestiges of the oral tradition left in Western society. The common experience of viewing games invariably lead to the communal discussion of these events. These discussions can take place in the company cafeteria or within the pages of a book. These discussions form the basis for the creation of literature, and baseball has been inspiring American literature for nearly two centuries.

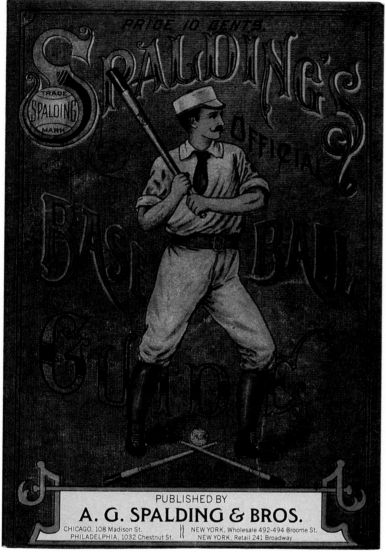

PUBLISHED BY
A. G. SPALDING & BROS.
CHICAGO, 108 Madison St.　　NEW YORK, Wholesale 492-494 Broome St.
PHILADELPHIA, 1032 Chestnut St.　　NEW YORK, Retail 241 Broadway

Left: Albert Spaulding's *Official Base Ball Guide.* Spaulding was a star pitcher for Chicago in the 1870s before retiring to build his lucrative sporting goods business.

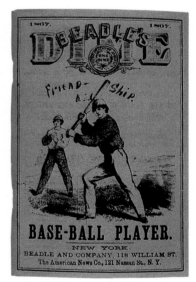

Beadle's Dime Base-Ball Player, the first annual baseball guide, was edited by Henry Chadwick. This issue dates from 1867, nine years before the founding of the National League.

It is difficult to pin down an exact year or point to one single work that begins modern baseball literature. Much of the earliest work pertaining to baseball, rounders, and other ballgames is found in children's literature. Occasional game accounts would also surface in the press in the era before the Civil War. Indeed, the first description of a game called "base or goal ball" to be printed in the United States was included in the *Boy's and Girl's Book of Sports* published in Providence, Rhode Island, in 1835. Despite the name affixed to the text, it described nothing more than the rules for rounders. Glenn Stout has argued that baseball literature begins with the publication of Ernest L. Thayer's masterpiece *Casey at the Bat* in 1888. He wrote in the 1988 *SABR Review* that, "while Ernest L. Thayer's classic verse is neither the first poem to utilize baseball as its subject, nor the first to capture the game under the guise of literature, *Casey at the Bat,* 100 years after its first appearance, remains the most memorable piece of baseball writing ever produced. No subsequent poem, column, short story, or novel approaches *Casey* for its ability to delineate our attraction toward the game."

Although largely ignored by academia and mysteriously absent from most anthologies of American poetry, *Casey,* subtitled by Thayer "A Ballad of The Republic," is one of the great American poems. It is a work that remains as fresh today as when it first appeared in the *San Francisco Examiner* on June 3, 1888.

Not only is Thayer's poem an accurate portrayal of the socio-economic status of the game in the 1880s, with teams comprised of Irish and Scotch-Irish players, but his anonymous cheering throng of 5,000 souls have only just started to enjoy the leisure time created by the burgeoning industrial society in which they live. Such a scene would have been impossible only two decades earlier, when the game was still relegated to local meadows and the fields of schools and social clubs.

Casey is reflective of the Gilded Age, with its slate of urban pastimes born of industry and a shifting population. It also depicts the assimilation of first-generation and second-generation immigrants, such as Casey and Cooney.

However, the basic truth of the poem lies in the fact that failure is more common to the human condition than success. Baseball provides the perfect landscape in which to document failure

Baseball has always had a literary bent, and players often were subjects of novels such as Lester Chadwick's *Baseball Joe, Home Run King.*

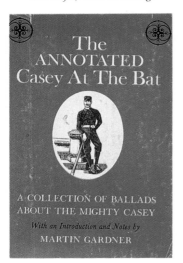

Martin Gardner's *The Annotated Casey at the Bat* discusses the place of the classic ode in both baseball's and America's history.

JUNE   15 CENTS
READ BAN JOHNSON

PUBLISHED BY THE BASEBALL MAGAZINE COMPANY, 65 Fifth Ave., N. Y.
Sold at all leading News-stands in the United States and Canada.

Left: An essay by AL president Ban Johnson graces this edition of *Baseball Magazine* from the early 1900s. Images of handsome, airbrushed baseball heroes were common at the time.

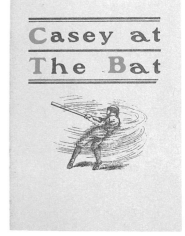

A first edition of Ernest Laurence Thayer's classic ode *Casey at the Bat*. From its earliest appearance in 1888, the dramatic poem became a centerpiece of American culture.

through the game's most basic and primal confrontation, batter versus pitcher. Because nearly every American has either played baseball or has swung a bat or thrown a ball, the poem is central to our common heritage. Like Casey we all hope for another turn at bat.

Two entire volumes are devoted to the poem: *The Annotated Casey at the Bat* by Martin Gardner and *Mighty Casey* by Eugene Murdock. Both include the work of many imitators who have concocted alternative versions of the verse. Invariably Casey is depicted as stroking a dramatic hit to win the day. Even Mrs.

Munro's *1877 Our Boys Baseball Rules*. As baseball grew in the late 19th century, the need to present codified rules became more apparent, and books like this were common.

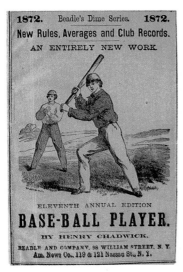

Beadle's Dime Baseball Player, which was published from 1860 to 1881. By 1872, it expanded to include new statistics, updated rules, and records of big-league clubs.

Casey is depicted as striking out, with the result being "So Casey eats cold beans tonight."

Sportswriting great Grantland Rice wrote at least five such versions, with such titles as *Casey's Revenge* and *Mudville's Fate*. Twenty-four such ballads comprise much of Gardner's book, including a hilarious version from *Mad Magazine* entitled *Cool Casey at the Bat*. Murdock chips in with several more imitations and parodies and also writes a substantial text detailing both Thayer's career and a controversy between Thayer and George Whitfield D'Vys over the true authorship of the poem.

Actor and forensic speaker De Wolf Hopper made a career out of giving readings of the poem. By his own estimation he had given at least 10,000 performances of the poem during his career. Even the Disney Studios were compelled to make a wonderful animated short of the poem. Casey will forever remain as a national treasure and the bedrock upon which an entire genre of literature has been built.

Over the years there have been many surveys of baseball literature that have attempted to determine the best baseball books in several categories. Among these surveys were those conducted separately by *Spitball* editor Mike Shannon and Paul Adomites, founder of both the *SABR Review* and *Cooperstown Review*. A review of these surveys and several baseball libraries resulted in the following baseball book list.

Among the first baseball books ever were statistical and narrative guides such as *Beadle's Dime Baseball Player*, issued from 1860 to 1881, and the *DeWitt Baseball Guide*, issued from 1868 to 1885. Both were edited by Henry Chadwick and both contained a wealth of information regarding the early game. Apart from containing mere statistics and descriptions of teams, these books were instrumental in increasing the popularity of the game. One can imagine these books in the duffles of settlers heading West in covered wagons or in the hands of the children of newly arrived immigrants.

The 1867 *Beadle's Guide* contains a lengthy position-by-position description of player selection and strategy. The description of right field will warm the heart of anyone who has been selected last in a pick-up game and is proof that the game has changed little in over a century.

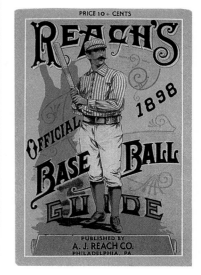

Al Reach, a sporting-goods magnate and former left-handed second baseman in the National Association, was publisher of the *Reach Guide.*

> *Right Field*
>
> *This is the position that the poorest player of the nine—if there be any such—should occupy; not that the position does not require as good a player to occupy it as the others, but that it is only occasionally, in comparison to the other portions of the field, that balls are sent in this direction.*

In 1876 a baseball publishing watershed was established with the publication of the first annual *Spalding Baseball Guide*. This guide, also edited by Henry Chadwick, would become the official yearly record of organized baseball until 1941.

In 1884 *Reach Baseball Guide* was first issued under the editorship of Francis Richter of *Sporting Life* magazine. Although less comprehensive in its overall coverage than the *Spalding Guide*, *Reach* could be counted on to include such wonderful tidbits of information as detailed obituaries of significant baseball figures and a chronological listing and account of on-field brawls.

Among the other important annual guides to be published were the *Player's National League Baseball Guide for 1890*, which appeared for the one season of Players' League action; *Sol White's 1908 Baseball Guide* (documenting early African-American baseball); *Nap Lajoie's Baseball Guide*, which appeared from 1906 to 1908; the *Wright and Ditson Guide*, which appeared off and on

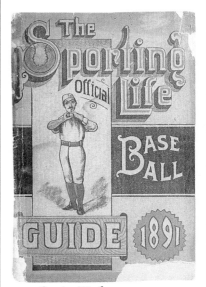

Sporting Life, for many years baseball's top magazine, published an annual in 1891, but could not compete with the *Reach* and *Spaldling* guides.

Right: The front cover of the second and final *Bull Durham Baseball Guide*, published in 1911. Smaller magazines could not crack the market.

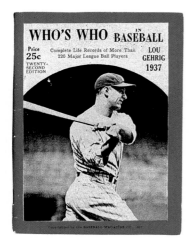

Above: Who's Who In Baseball, a compendium of player statistics, has been available every year since 1916 and is still published in a nearly-identical format each season.

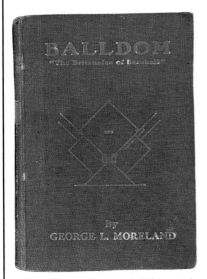

One of the earliest baseball historical and statstical encyclopedias, George L. Moreland's *Balldom: The Britannica of Baseball* dates from 1914 and is still used today.

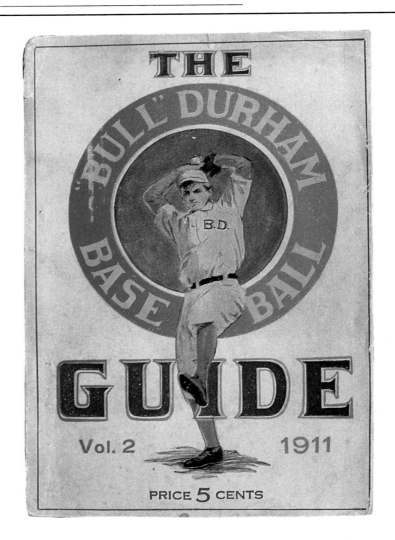

from 1874 to 1912; the *Victor Guide,* from 1896 and 1897; the *Universal Guide* from 1890; the *Sporting Life Guide,* from 1891; and the *Bull Durham Guides,* 1910 and 1911.

In 1942 *The Sporting News* picked up the mantle from Spalding and Reach and began publishing its own yearbook as baseball's official annual record. And though they would face competition from *The Commissioner's Guide* in 1943 and *The Barnes Guide* in 1945 and 1946, *The Sporting News Guides* were finally recognized as major-league baseball's one and only official annual following the death of commissioner Kenesaw Mountain Landis in 1944.

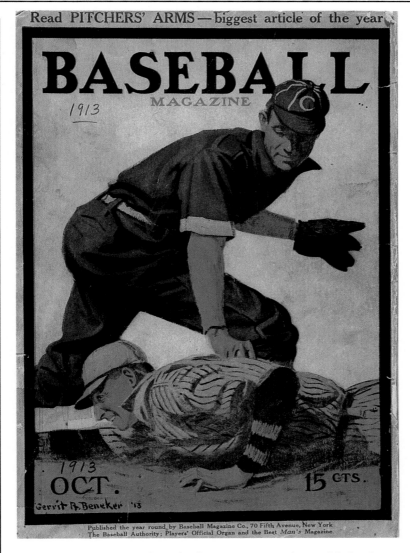

Read PITCHERS' ARMS — biggest article of the year

BASEBALL
MAGAZINE

1913

1913
OCT.   15 CTS.

Gerrit R. Beneker '13

Published the year round by Baseball Magazine Co., 70 Fifth Avenue, New York
The Baseball Authority; Players' Official Organ and the Best *Man's* Magazine.

Left: The monthly *Baseball Magazine,* "the Baseball Authority," published well into the 1950s. This issue, dating from 1913, features the typically fine art of the era.

719
JOE DiMAGGIO'S GREAT BOOK!

BASEBALL FOR EVERYONE

by Joe DiMaggio

A SIGNET BOOK

THE INSIDE STORY OF OUR NATIONAL PASTIME!
LIVELY ANECDOTES OF BIG LEAGUES AND BIG LEAGUERS;
GAME-WISE TIPS FOR FANS AND PLAYERS, YOUNG AND OLD

Player-written books (usually penned by sportswriters) have always marked the baseball literary landscape. Joe DiMaggio's *Baseball for Everyone* is part of the tradition.

The Sporting News Guides, which continue to be published, are known for their informative text, comprehensive listing of major-league and minor-league statistics, and for their in-depth "year in review" segments. For many years the guides also included a team picture of every major-league team.

The Sporting News also continues to publish *The Baseball Register*, which it first issued in 1941. These volumes were comprised of a player-by-player listing of major-league and minor-league statistics, and information such as players' wives' maiden names, wedding dates, college attendance, hobbies, and all transactions

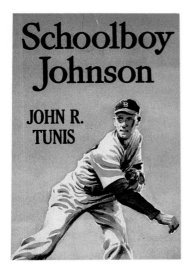

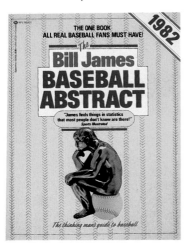

Above and below: Two very different baseball books. Novelist John Tunis's *Schoolboy Johnson* charted the career of a young fireballer, and *The Bill James Baseball Abstract* defined baseball analysis in the 1980s.

involving the player. For many years the *Register* also included a player photograph. Special sections were devoted to managers, coaches, and umpires. For nearly 25 years each edition would begin with an illustrated profile of a player or team.

Who's Who in Baseball is another staple of baseball publishing that has stood the test of time for nearly a century. It still remains as baseball publishing's biggest bargain. It is a pulp masterpiece of comprehensive player stats and photos for less than the price of a bleacher seat.

The decade of the 1980s saw a boom in the publication of statistical annuals with the birth of the *Bill James Baseball Abstract* (and later *The Bill James Baseball Book*), *The Elias Baseball Annual*, and others. Bill James would become as familiar a name as many star players, because his vast baseball knowledge and frank opinions would delight fans and nonfans alike. In many ways, James is the modern equivalent of such honored baseball savants as number-cruncher extraordinaire Ernest J. Lanigan and former Hall of Fame historian Lee Allen. James's special talent is combining both words and numbers to make his often seamless arguments. His lively writing style and biting wit make him one of the most significant baseball authors of his generation.

Although a comprehensive baseball encyclopedia was many years away, there were several books that appeared in the first part of the century that attempted to chronicle baseball's narrative and statistical history. The first of these was *Balldom, The Brittanica of Baseball* by George Moreland. First published in 1914, *Balldom* is still a valuable research tool, as it chronicles the game from city to city and franchise to franchise.

The task of assembling the first encyclopedia of baseball fell to former *Sporting News* editor Ernest J. Lanigan, who published his volume entitled *The Baseball Cyclopedia* in 1922. This 216-

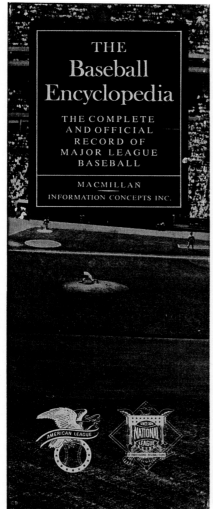

Left: The outer box and spine of the first *Baseball Encyclopedia*, published by MacMillan in late 1969. The "Big Mac" revolutionized the exploration of baseball records.

Both above: Boston Braves scorecards, sold at Braves Field, dating from 1951 and 1952. After the 1953 season, the Braves moved to Milwaukee, where they won the World Series in 1957.

page paperback, while not a comprehensive encyclopedic treatment of the game, did include features, such as a listing of 3,500 players who had played in the majors since 1901, a profile of every major-league franchise from 1871, and a multitude of stories and statistics detailing such events as the major leagues' first perfect game, pitched by J. Lee Richmond in 1880, to accounts of every no-hit game ever pitched.

It would take until 1951 before a comprehensive baseball encyclopedia would be issued. Written by the team of Hy Turkin and S.C. Thompson and published by A.S. Barnes, *The*

Official Encyclopedia of Baseball would sell 50,000 copies and establish itself as baseball's official record for nearly two decades.

The centennial of professional baseball in 1969 was seen as the perfect time for the Macmillan Publishing Company to publish an encyclopedia that would forever end all baseball arguments and set the standard of excellence for the most quantified game on the planet. *The Baseball Encyclopedia* by Macmillan was made possible both by an incredibly astute team of researchers and through the use of sophisticated computers. It is still considered a masterpiece and the standard work for early baseball information.

In 1974 the team of David S. Neft and Richard M. Cohen, both of whom had performed instrumental work on the Macmillan *Encyclopedia*, published their own work, *The Sports Encyclopedia, Baseball*. This work differs from all other encyclopedias in that it treats baseball in a seasonal fashion and is the best single source for research on the subject.

Twenty years after the publication of the first Macmillan encyclopedia, fans witnessed the impossible as yet another encyclopedia emerged to claim the top spot as baseball's best stat and fact book. *Total Baseball* was the brainchild of John Thorn and Pete Palmer, and weighed in at an impressive seven pounds. Containing nearly 700 pages of narrative history divided into 38 chapters, this volume also included the complete record of every major leaguer in history.

Much of what sets this volume apart from its predecessors is its broad scope of interest as well as the new categories added to each player's career statistical record. Pete Palmer has concocted such information as total average, runs created, stolen base runs, batting runs, fielding runs, park factors, and stolen base average to join the more standard stats such as runs

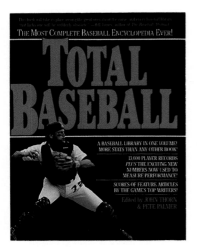

Total Baseball, John Thorn and Pete Palmer's revolutionary work of the 1980s. It was the first book to combine fascinating new statistics with informative and well-researched historical essays in one volume.

batted in and batting average. A CD-ROM version of this masterpiece could include photos and action footage of the game's great moments.

Baseball is again blessed with several key works documenting its long history. Professor Harold Seymour of Finch College wrote the first serious history of the game. His rewritten Cornell doctoral thesis was entitled *Baseball—The Early Years* and was published in 1960. It was followed by two more volumes: *Baseball—The Golden Age* and *Baseball—The People's Game.* In these works Seymour, a former Brooklyn Dodger batboy, documents the history of the game while giving insight into the people who made the game into both a national and international treasure.

Likewise, the histories of baseball by David Quentin Voigt, professor of history at Albright College, are equal to Seymour's works. Voigt wrote *American Baseball: From Gentleman's Sport to the Commissioner System* in 1966 and *American Baseball: From the Commissioners to Continental Expansion* in 1970, among others. Their appeal lies in their readability, as they are not only scholarly in content but also accessible to a general audience. In 1987 Voigt penned a superb one-volume illustrated compilation of his work, *Baseball, An Illustrated History.*

Perhaps the most entertaining baseball history book ever written is *The Bill James Historical Baseball Abstract.* James covers the history of the game from 1870 to the mid-1980s in comprehensive decade-by-decade chapters. Included therein are player evaluations as well as a wonderful compendium of information such as lists of the best baseball books and movies of each decade. James also expounds on the way in which the game changed in each decade and treats readers to essays on subjects such as the origins of platooning and the concept of Most Valuable Players. James again proves he is the heir of great baseball men like Chadwick and Lee Allen in both his

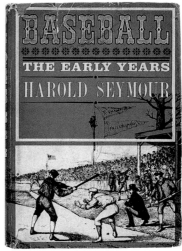

Historian Harold Seymour published a three-part history of baseball. The first volume, from 1960, was *Baseball—The Early Years*, one of the first scholarly baseball works about baseball.

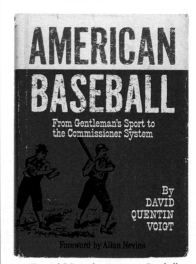

David Voigt's *American Baseball: From Gentleman's Sport to the Commissioner System*, dating from 1966, is another in a fine series of academic-based baseball histories.

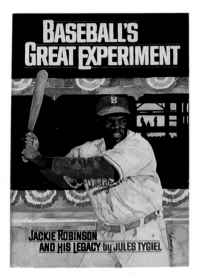

Jules Tygiel's *Baseball's Great Experiment* discusses the history of African-American baseball, racism in the sport, and Jackie Robinson's career with the Dodgers.

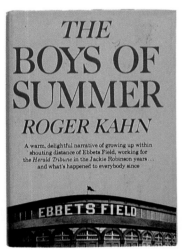

Roger Kahn's *The Boys of Summer* is a nostalgic ode to the Brooklyn Dodger teams of the 1940s and 1950s. Kahn has written several well-regarded books.

enthusiasm for the game and his desire to share his knowledge and understanding of the game.

In the realm of specialized histories there is a handful of truly distinguished volumes. Among them is *Eight Men Out*, the gritty account of the plot and the players behind the 1919 Black Sox scandal. Eliot Asinof's book reads like a novel, as original source material such as court records, eyewitness accounts, and news stories are woven into a tragic tale.

Another bittersweet story is that of Jackie Robinson as told by Jules Tygiel in his book entitled *Baseball's Great Experiment, Jackie Robinson and His Legacy*. Robinson is shown to be both a man of passion and sorrow as he undertakes the incredible burden of being the first black to perform in the major leagues. Tygiel is another scholar with writing talent who crafts a fine, readable story from an intricate array of sources. Fred Lieb covered baseball from the days of Ty Cobb to those of Pete Rose, and his reminiscences entitled *Baseball As I Have Known It* is a first-person account of the game's great moments and personalities. Like Woody Allen's *Zelig*, Lieb is seemingly everywhere in the game, hobnobbing with a who's who of Hall of Famers and characters.

No compilation of baseball histories would be complete without mention of the two greatest oral histories of the game, namely Larry Ritter's landmark *The Glory of Their Times* and Roger Kahn's *The Boys of Summer*. When Ritter's book came out in 1966, it helped spur a renewed interest in the history of baseball. In interviewing many of baseball's turn-of-the-century heroes, Ritter captured the essence of his subjects in a manner similar to that used by Allan Lomax, who interviewed and recorded such American musical treasures as Jelly Roll Morton for the Library of Congress. One can almost hear the voices of these players as Ritter captures the flavor of their youth and the youth of our National Pastime. In a similar vein, Kahn revisited his own youth, where as both a fan and young reporter he followed the Brooklyn Dodgers in their glory years. He also revisited the players he originally rooted for and reported on. Each player is sensitively portrayed by Kahn, who devoted individual chapters to the likes of Preacher Roe, Carl Erskine, Clem Labine, Jackie Robinson, Pee Wee Reese, and Carl Furillo, among others. This book is both about precious memories and the havoc time reaps upon us all.

Among the great illustrated books on baseball stands *The Ultimate Baseball Book* by Daniel Okrent and Harris Lewine, with fine historical text by David Nemec. The design and presentation of this volume is flawless, and the book has enjoyed a long life in three separate editions. Likewise, historian Donald Honig has made his reputation as both one of baseball's most prolific authors as well as the author of two marvelous compilations of player photographs, which document hundreds of National and American League players from 1900 to the present. Another indispensable illustrated history is *The Negro Baseball Leagues, A Photographic History* by Phil Dixon and Patrick J. Hannigan. This mammoth tome includes mostly never before published photographs and documents the history of the Negro Leagues unlike any book since Robert Peterson's *Only the Ball Was White*.

The genre of team history was created with the publication of the Putnam series of team histories in the late 1940s. Penned by such writers as Fred Lieb, Frank Graham, and Harold Kaese, these volumes stand as landmarks in the history of the game. Only the obscure yet fabulous volume entitled *The San Francisco Giants: An Oral History* by Mike Mandel and the comprehensive illustrated histories of the Red Sox and Yankees by George Sullivan have shone among recent efforts.

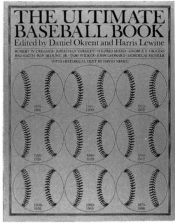

The Ultimate Baseball Book by Dan Okrent and Harris Lewine. Beautifully illustrated and featuring interesting, personal text by several noted authors, including Tom Wicker, Robert Creamer, and Red Smith, the book has seen several reprintings.

Although relatively new, Phil Dixon's *The Negro Baseball Leagues*, featuring fine text and photography, is taking its place with the best African-American baseball work.

Above and right: New York Giants yearbooks from 1954 and 1955. A cartoon behemoth was the Giants' symbol for many years, and New York won several NL crowns in the 1950s. However, in 1957, the Giants would leave Coogan's Bluff and move to the sunnier climes of San Francisco.

Starting with the publication of Cap Anson's *A Ball Player's Career* in 1900, the genre of baseball biographies has grown to almost the status of a cottage industry within the game. Each season seems to produce a bevy of "as told to" biographies of superstars du jour. And while most are dreadful examples of the quick-buck school of literature, there have been an almost equal number of thoughtfully written baseball biographies.

Among the best of the genre are any of the books by Robert Creamer, including his wonderful books on Babe Ruth (*Babe:*

The Legend Comes to Life) and Casey Stengel (*Stengel: His Life and Times*). As a former editor of *Sports Illustrated*, Creamer possesses a fluid writing style, and his research is impeccable. Likewise, Ed Linn, formerly of *Sport* magazine, is the master of the "as told to" genre with baseball books such as *Veeck as in Wreck*, *The Hustler's Handbook* (also with Bill Veeck), and *Nice Guys Finish Last* (with Leo Durocher) to his credit. In these books, Linn makes himself invisible while crafting and articulating the thoughts and experiences of his raucous subjects.

The best first-hand player accounts written to date have been by pitchers Jim Brosnan and Jim Bouton. Brosnan, a bookish bespectacled reliever, broke new literary ground with the publishing of *The Long Season* and *Pennant Race*. Although these were hardly kiss-and-tell stories, the pitcher's wry observations and sardonic wit were not appreciated by baseball officials who decried his hobby. On the other hand, Jim Bouton, with the help of sportswriter Leonard Shecter, shocked the baseball world and had fans laughing out loud with *Ball Four*, a diary of Bouton's life with the Seattle Pilots and other teams. This was the first book to violate the sacred code of the clubhouse that called for players to respect the privacy of their peers and not tell of their sundry indiscretions and alleged misdeeds. Rumor has it that former teammate Mickey Mantle still won't talk to Bouton, over two decades after the release of the book.

Among the scholars who have written great baseball biographies are Eugene Murdock, with his landmark biography of American League President Ban Johnson, and Charles Alexander, with his biographies of Ty Cobb and John McGraw.

Donald Honig emulates Larry Ritter in his two oral histories entitled *Baseball When the Grass Was Real* and *Baseball Between the Lines*. Both books chronicle baseball between the wars and convey much of the same magic and wonder of Ritter's seminal work.

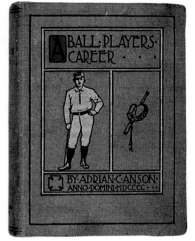

Cantankerous Hall of Famer Adrian "Cap" Anson's *A Ball Player's Career*, one of the first baseball biographies, was published in 1900.

Jim Brosnan's *Pennant Race* documented the 1961 NL title drive. It was his second book. *The Long Season* explored 1959.

Above: The Society for American Baseball Research publishes an annual *Baseball Research Journal*, full of interesting facts and valuable research by the Society's members. *Above, middle:* Robert Creamer's biography of Babe Ruth, *Babe: The Legend Comes to Life*, pulled no punches in its frank depiction of the "Sultan of Swat"'s life with the Yankees. *Above, far right:* Jim Bouton's updated version of *Ball Four*, entitled *Ball Four Plus Ball Five*, included discussion of his 1970s pitching comeback with the Atlanta Braves.

Both contain fine mini-biographies of many of the players who toiled in baseball's golden age. In Luke Salisbury's classic fan account entitled *The Answer is Baseball*, the author ruminates on the great questions of the game while sharing his witty observations on life, literature, and his favorite sport.

The Fireside Book of Baseball, a series that contains four volumes, are the best-edited anthologies in all of sport. Editor Charles Einstein has plumbed the depths of baseball literature and reportage to assemble a quirky, informative, and ingenious patchwork quilt that captures the soul of the game through great writing.

Two anthologies that match the *Fireside* series for originality are *Baseball I Gave You All the Best Years of My Life* and *Baseball Diamonds*, both edited by the formidable team of Richard Grossinger and Kevin Kerrane. These books are a fresh assortment of poems, parodies, interviews, stories, and nostalgia mostly taken from the small press literary world. Other anthologies include John Thorn's excellent two-volume *The Armchair Book of Baseball* series and the anthologies of work from the Society of American Baseball Research entitled *Insiders Baseball*, *The National Pastime*, and

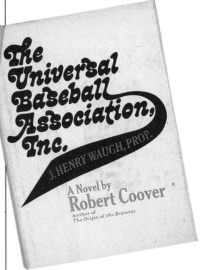

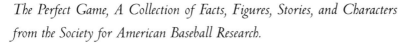

The Perfect Game, A Collection of Facts, Figures, Stories, and Characters from the Society for American Baseball Research.

The collections assembled from the works of writers Roger Angell and Tom Boswell also sit at the top of baseball's required reading list. Angell, a writer and editor at *The New Yorker*, has made baseball writing a fine art in his five decades of writing essays about the game. Boswell, a sportswriter for *The Washington Post*, has evoked comparisons to Angell with his equally insightful and evocative work.

Baseball fiction is a genre all to itself, like the detective novel or the harlequin romance. In fact, baseball fiction is the oldest component of baseball literature with children's novels about the national pastime dating well back into the 19th century.

From Frank Merriwell and his chums at Yale to Roy Hobbs, Joe Hardy, and "Shoeless Joe," baseball's fictional heroes have sold novels. Among the great works of baseball fiction are Bernard Malamud's *The Natural*, a dark tale of baseball as primeval myth. Likewise Robert Coover creates a fantastic world with baseball as its core in *The Universal Baseball Association,*

Above: The Universal Baseball Association, Inc., by Robert Coover, was published in 1968 and has become a classic piece of modern baseball fiction. *Above, middle:* Donald Honig's *Baseball Between the Lines.* Honig ranks as one of baseball's best current historians and has continued the fine tradition of the oral history. *Above, far left:* Master showman Bill Veeck told his story (with help from Ed Linn) with *Veeck as in Wreck.* This reprinting dates from Veeck's return to the game in the 1970s.

Right: Perhaps the finest novel ever written about baseball, Ring Lardner's *You Know Me Al.* The book's lead character, Jack Keefe, was drawn from Lardner's observations of star Chicago White Sox pitcher Ed Walsh.

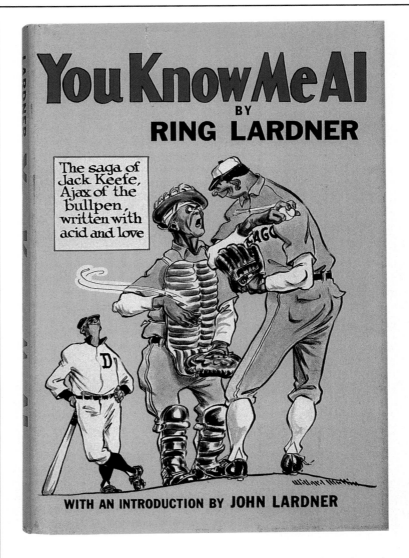

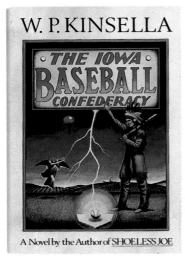

W.P. Kinsella's wild baseball fiction, *The Iowa Baseball Confederacy.* Kinsella's *Shoeless Joe* later became the film *Field of Dreams.*

Inc., J. Henry Waugh, Prop. Here a man plays God with a dice baseball game that becomes a world unto itself.

Canadian writer W.P. Kinsella creates a looking-glass world similar to that of Alice in Wonderland when he takes us through the fields of dreams that exist in his baseball novels entitled *Shoeless Joe* and *The Iowa Baseball Confederacy.* Where else would Leonardo da Vinci and Ty Cobb share the same diamond? Although most baseball fiction cannot hold a candle to the wonder and color of the real thing, it is a growing genre. There is even a subgenre that has arisen of baseball murder mysteries.

The combination of baseball and the cinema, two of America's greatest institutions, has never been the source of particularly memorable entertainment. With a few notable exceptions, the majority of baseball films have been poorly written and acted by performers who seemed to forget even the most rudimentary aspects of hitting, throwing, and fielding. Despite these problems, baseball films are still an important record of our National Pastime. These films tell us of the role baseball played in society as a sort of national mythology, not unlike the more successful genres of westerns and true-crime dramas.

In Gary Dickerson's book, *The Cinema of Baseball,* he discusses the importance of film as a vehicle of cultural instruction. For generations, the movies have been a chief vehicle by which Americans have learned and acquired "American" values and culture. The films of any given nation reflect the mentality of that nation in a more direct way than through other artistic forms. Critic Andrew Bergman has stated that "every movie is a cultural artifact and as such reflects the fears, values, myths, and assumptions of the culture that produces it. Films are neither viewed nor created in a void." In America, especially in the years before television, movies were the center of communication and cultural diffusion.

In the first half of the 20th century, the cinema and baseball were particularly important to immigrants. Not only did both institutions entertain these newcomers, but both also served as a primer on the manners, rules, morals, and customs of their new home. Before long the children and grandchildren of these immigrants would play and manage in the big leagues as well as grace the credits of many a Hollywood production.

Like other American film genres, the baseball film conveys many national values, including fair play, the work ethic, the promise of

Released shortly before his death in 1947, *The Babe Ruth Story* starred William Bendix as the Babe and featured Claire Trevor and Charles Bickford. Like many baseball films, it hardly told the truth about Ruth's life or career but appealed to sentimental audiences.

fame and wealth, and the value of comraderie and friendship. For many, baseball films provided the first glimpse of the magical spectacle called the big leagues. In countless picture shows in rural America, the mystique that already enshrouded the major leagues was magnified by the flickering images of ballparks and players once only imagined.

Gary Cooper, posing with Babe Ruth, portrayed Lou Gehrig in *Pride of the Yankees,* released shortly after "The Iron Horse"'s death.

The first baseball film was shot by Thomas A. Edison in 1898, only four years after he had made history by creating the world's first motion picture, *Fred Ott's Sneeze.* His baseball film released under the title of *The Ball Game* was comprised of footage of two New Jersey amateur teams. The next year Edison released a short entitled *Casey at the Bat,* a film that bore no resemblance to the famous poem of the same name. In Edison's film, a rough comedy, the slugger beats up the umpire after striking out. It was from these humble beginnings that the genre of baseball film was started. In the century that has passed, there have been several hundred baseball films produced to join Edison's initial effort.

Baseball has remained as a staple of the American cinema. Unfortunately for fans and historians alike, many of the first baseball films have been lost forever. This is due to the fact that most of the films produced between the start of World War I and the start of World War II were shot on nitrate film. This film decomposed badly and in some instances even spontaneously combusted. Not only have many baseball titles disappeared, but many other Hollywood productions as well.

One can only read the reviews of these "lost" films and speculate about the many other productions from this era, the documentaries and newsreels that have also disappeared. For example, was there film shot of the first World Series in 1903 or the first American League games in 1901? While the chance of uncovering such footage is remote, the prospect is one that keeps researchers combing the attics and basements of archives and warehouses.

The movies, like baseball, were a product of the industrial revolution. With its newfound leisure time, the American public was happy to escape into diversions with which it could relate. The marriage between baseball and the cinema began with the game being used as a device to get heroes into funny situations. The first of these baseball comedies was Edison's

Yankee catcher Bill Dickey (left) poses alongside Gary Cooper in a promotional photograph from the 1942 film *Pride of the Yankees*.

1907 production entitled *How the Office Boy Saw the Ball Game*. In this film the office boy arrives at the ballpark only to find that he is seated next to his boss. A 1911 film, *The Baseball Bug* tells the tale of a woman who hires three major-league pitchers (Chief Bender, Rube Oldring, and Jack Coombs of the Philadelphia Athletics) to prove to her husband once and for all that he is not big-league material.

Other light cinematic fare from the period included *Baseball and Bloomers*, *Baseball's Peerless Leader* (starring Cub Hall-of-Famer Frank Chance), *The Baseball! Fans of Fanville*, *Breaking into The Big League* (with John McGraw and Christy Mathewson), *Bumptious Plays Baseball*, *Home Run Bill*, *Kill The Umpire*, *Spit Ball Sadie*, *Somewhere in Georgia* (with Ty Cobb and written by Grantland Rice), and *Strike One*.

Pitcher Monty Stratton was 30-14 for the White Sox in 1937-38 but lost a leg in a hunting accident before the next season. His return (after receiving an artificial leg) as a batting practice pitcher and then as a minor league star was the subject of *The Stratton Story*.

Historian James Mote identifies the first true baseball drama as the 1909 production *His Last Game*. In this film a team of Choctaw Indians, led by star pitcher Bill Going, are set to play a club comprised of local cowboys. Following a scene where the Native-American pitcher turns down a bribe to throw the game, he is seen drinking a tainted brew that had been drugged by the gamblers. He then shoots one of the gamblers and, following receiving the death sentence, is allowed a reprieve to pitch in the crucial ballgame. This decidedly nonpolitically correct film concludes with the victorious pitcher seated cross-legged at his open grave calmly smoking a last pipe as he awaits a firing squad. The film was released with the execution scene removed.

During this same period a time-honored tradition was started as the first major leaguer starred in his own film. The first of these players was New York Highlander Hal Chase, a native Californian, who appeared in *Hal Chase's Home Run* in 1911. In the film Chase helps a friend's love interest by hitting a dramatic homer to win the pennant for his team and the girl for his buddy.

Other players who appeared in silent films were Christy Mathewson, Giant teammate Mike Donlin, Ty Cobb, and Frank "Home Run" Baker. Donlin, a star outfielder for the Giants, had aspirations beyond that of cinematic footnote. He produced an autobiographical film entitled *Right Off the Bat* in 1915. In this film Donlin indulges in a great deal of self-mythologizing as he follows his rise from small-town slugger to major-league celebrity. The former vaudeville performer's film was well-received by critics, and this success would lead to a career in Hollywood where he would play a variety of bit and character parts. *Right Off the Bat* would, however, be his only starring role.

The rise of the movie industry and that of Babe Ruth occurred almost simultaneously. During the economic boom of the 1920s, Ruth was packing fans into ballparks as silent features with stars

Anthony Perkins starred in 1957's *Fear Strikes Out*. The film told the true story of Red Sox outfielder Jimmy Piersall, who suffered an emotional breakdown but recovered and enjoyed a lengthy major-league career. Perkins's performance received excellent notices.

Left: Jackie Robinson as himself, Minor Watson as Branch Rickey, and Richard Lane as Montreal Royals manager Clay Hopper in *The Jackie Robinson Story*, released in 1950. Ruby Dee also starred as Rachel Robinson.

such as Rudolph Valentino and Clara Bow were packing them in at the local Bijou.

The first of Ruth's feature-film roles was as the small-town slugger in *Headin' Home*, a five-reel silent movie released in 1920. In this long-forgotten film, the 24-year-old Yankee slugger goes from being a humble ice man who plays ball as a hobby to the World Series star he would become in real life. In describing his role in the film, Ruth would later write with some irony that "There never was a movie quite like *Headin' Home*. Thank God." Despite his less-than-dynamic performance in *Headin' Home*, Ruth's charisma brought him another starring role in the 1926 film *Babe Comes Home*. In what critics have described as both a delightful and dreadful performance, Ruth plays a ballplayer whose fiancée refuses to marry him unless he gives up chewing tobacco. Once he gives up the habit his team goes on a losing streak as the slugger also goes into a terrible slump. Finally his girl, played by Anna Q. Nilsson, relents, and the chaw-bound slugger leads his team to victory. Ruth also parlayed his fame into a number of bit roles, most notably in *Speedy* and *Pride of the Yankees*. Playing opposite Gary Cooper's Lou Gehrig, Ruth played himself.

Pride of the Yankees was the first baseball film to garner significant attention from the critics and film community alike. It received 10 Academy Award nominations and featured proven Hollywood performers such as Gary Cooper, Walter Brennan, and Teresa Wright. It was the first serious baseball film ever made and was also the first baseball biography ever filmed.

Gehrig is portrayed as the All-American hero who is devoted to his family while pursuing excellence as a star athlete at Columbia

Above: Featuring such show classics as "Heart," "Whatever Lola Wants, Lola Gets," and "The Game," *Damn Yankees* ran over 1,100 performances on Broadway and is still popular today. *Opposite page: Damn Yankees*, first a successful Broadway musical, became a hit film in 1958, starring Tab Hunter and Gwen Virdon. The story concerned one Washington Senators fan's attempt to sell his soul to win his team a pennant.

TREASURY OF BASEBALL

University. Determined to become an engineer to fulfill his mother's dream, he only signs to play professional baseball after she enters the hospital for an operation. He knows that the operation will require the money that she had set aside for his tuition. In the end Gehrig not only compensates for his failure to complete his degree at Columbia but becomes one of America's most recognized sportsmen, as he and Babe Ruth create the Yankee Dynasty.

This emotional film never fails to jerk a tear or two from even the most cynical viewer, as Cooper reenacts Gehrig's famous farewell at Yankee Stadium, where he says: "Some people may say that I've had a bad break, but today I consider myself the luckiest man on the face of the earth." Despite the fact that the baseball action in this film is kept to a minimum, Cooper, a natural right-hander, had to work overtime to make his movements similar to the left-handed Gehrig. For weeks Cooper was instructed by former National League batting champion Lefty O'Doul on the finer points of the game. Viewers will see that Cooper never really succeeded in imitating the "Iron Horse." In fact the filmmakers finally resorted to filming Cooper in a uniform with the number reversed. Wearing this he batted from the right side of the plate and ran from third to home in reverse of the usual path. When the film was processed it gave the illusion of a lefty batter running to first.

Although Gehrig never lived to see this film, he followed Babe Ruth to Hollywood in 1938, when Lou starred in the film *Rawhide*. In this production Gehrig plays himself in a fictitious retirement where he takes up the role of a cowboy-rancher who stands up to a corrupt cattleman's association. Somehow his New York accent made this effort far less credible than his on-the-field heroics.

Other baseball films of the Depression era were *Fireman Save My Child*, *Elmer the Great*, and *Alibi Ike*, all of which starred comedian Joe E. Brown. Each had corny, predictable plots concerning small-town

Robert Redford starred as Roy Hobbs in the screen adaptation of Bernard Malamud's novel *The Natural*. While many decried the film's complete rewriting of the novel's downbeat conclusion, the film has many charms.

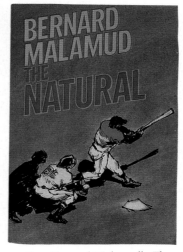

Above: Bernard Malamud's *The Natural* is still a highly regarded novel. It is based partially on the story of Phillies first baseman Eddie Waitkus. The film version had almost nothing to do with the original work.

players who are at first corrupted by and ultimately triumph over the temptations of the big city and the fame associated with big-league stardom. Brown and fellow screen comedian Buster Keaton were avid baseball fans who would often organize games on the sets of movies. Indeed, they were allowed by contract to do so. Brown's son and namesake would later become general manager of the Pittsburgh Pirates.

Following the success of *Pride of the Yankees,* there were several notable baseball biographies adapted to film. Most notable among them was *The Stratton Story,* starring James Stewart and June Allyson. Directed by Sam Wood (*Pride of the Yankees*), this film chronicled the true story of pitcher Monty Stratton, who returned to organized baseball after his leg was amputated following a hunting accident. Like most of the baseball biographies made in this era, the storyline follows a star who overcomes adversity through courage and innate decency. In each instance the hero is also supported by a strong and loving wife. Other notable Hollywood baseball biographies include *The Jackie Robinson Story* (with Jackie Robinson playing the lead), *Pride of St. Louis, The Winning Team* (with Ronald Reagan as Grover Cleveland Alexander), and *Fear Strikes Out* (with Anthony Perkins as Jimmy Piersall).

The worst of the bunch was *The Babe Ruth Story*, starring beefy character actor (and former Yankee batboy) William Bendix. In this late-show staple Bendix swings a bat like a man on roller skates swatting a fly with a rolled up newspaper. Ruth is depicted as a plaster saint who drinks milk between at bats and hospital visits, never as the earthy prodigy who plays as hard off the field as on. Bendix badly misplays Ruth as a lovable bumpkin, therefore denying his audience a glimpse at the fascinating character who used to insist that his teammates not only accompany him to the speakeasies on Saturday night but also to mass on Sunday morning. The disastrous John Goodman portrayal of Ruth nearly a half century later is no better. Here the husky sitcom star makes Ruth into a crude caricature, a corpulent pig intent only on satisfying his every primal desire. Neither the baseball nor the historical accuracy of this film is credible. The Ruth story remains fertile territory for the right filmmaker and actor.

Above: Eight Men Out, based on Eliot Asinof's book, starred Charlie Sheen as Happy Felsch, one of the Chicago "Black Sox" who conspired with gamblers to throw the 1919 World Series.

Opposite page: John Goodman, co-star of the TV series *Roseanne,* starred in *The Babe,* a 1993 movie that failed to capture any of the magic surrounding The Sultan of Swat. The film failed to garner raves, and the definitive story of Ruth's life and myth has yet to be made.

Among the best baseball films ever made was the musical *Damn Yankees,* adapted from the Broadway show of the same name. Starring Tab Hunter as Joe Hardy and Gwen Verdon as Lola, this film is a modern version of the Faust myth. Here a middle-aged Washington Senators fan named Joe Boyd sells his soul to the devil (played by Ray Walston) to become Joe Hardy, the Adonis who can lead his beloved team to victory over the hated Yankees. The plot is only made more dramatic when it is revealed that the devil is himself a Yankee fan. Hardy immediately begins leading the Senators on an extended winning streak that puts them in the thick of the pennant race. The young slugger reveals little of himself to his teammates as he boards in the same house he once lived in as Joe Boyd. Here he sees his wife as if for the first time and falls in

The All American Girls Professional Baseball League of the 1940s was the subject of the 1992 film *A League of Their Own*. The smash hit starred, among others, Rosie O'Donnell, Geena Davis, and Madonna as ballplayers.

love with her again. It is this love that leads Hardy to renounce his pact with the devil despite the advances made upon him by the sultry Lola, who attempts to persuade him to remain with Satan. In the end we see the dramatic spectacle of Boyd as his middle-aged self having to make the pennant-winning catch for the Senators.

It is interesting to note that one of the great periods of baseball, namely the late 1950s through the 1960s, yielded little in the manner of significant baseball movies. It is only in the 1970s, with the release of films such as *Bang the Drum Slowly* in 1973 and *The Bad News Bears* in 1976, that baseball once again captured the imagination of Hollywood.

In *Bang the Drum Slowly*, Robert DeNiro plays Bruce Pearson, a journeyman catcher attempting to play for one last season in the majors despite having Hodgkin's disease. The plot centers around his friendship with Henry Wiggin, his teammate and ace pitcher for the New York Mammoths. This film is very much like its football counterpart *Brian's Song*, with a focus on the men's friendship and Pearson's mortality.

On the other hand, *The Bad News Bears* became a notorious film when it was first released due to the four-letter vocabulary of its Little League protagonists. Featuring Walter Matthau as the manager and Tatum O'Neal as the precocious (and overage for Little League competition) pitcher, this film more closely documents the antics of real kids than any of its cliché-ridden predecessors.

New ground was also broken in 1976 with the release of *The Bingo Long Traveling All Stars and Motor Kings*, an adaptation of William Brashler's novel about Negro League baseball in the 1930s. A distinguished cast including James Earl Jones, Billy Dee Williams, and Richard Pryor plays a renegade troup of barnstorming ballplayers out to snub the owners who had abused them. This film was the first attempt to document baseball's separate and unequal heritage. It is a wonderful story told with humor, pathos, and wit. Pryor has a particularly funny scene where he attempts to win a spot in the white major leagues by pretending he is Cuban.

It would be nearly a decade before baseball again made a major impact at the box office, with the release of *The Natural* in 1984. This adaptation of Bernard Malamud's novel starred Robert Redford as Roy Hobbs, the mysterious outfielder who leads the New York Knights to the Holy Grail—the World Series. The plot blends elements of the King Arthur legend with old fashioned baseball clichés as the screenwriters twist the outcome of the novel nearly 180 degrees. Despite the change of plot, this film succeeds beautifully as the best-looking baseball film ever made. Purists delight in the attention to detail, which includes players leaving their gloves on the field between innings and the presence of photographers on the field during play. Everything from the uniforms, equipment, ballparks, outfield advertising, and on-field action rings true.

Tom Hanks portrayed an All American Girls Professional Baseball League manager in *A League of Their Own*. His character, who uttered the memorable "There's no crying in baseball!" was loosely based on Jimmie Foxx, who actually ran one of the league's squads.

Baseball and Culture

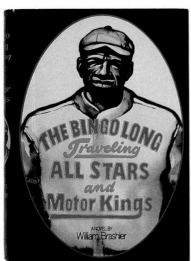

Above top and bottom: James Earl Jones portrayed star slugger Leon Carter in the 1976 film adaptation of William Brashler's novel *The Bingo Long Traveling All Stars and Motor Kings*, an account of the barnstorming black teams of the 1930s. Billy Dee Williams played pitcher Bingo Long.

Likewise, *Bull Durham* is a delight for fans as it presents an unvarnished and comical look at life in the minor leagues. Written and directed by former Oriole farmhand Ron Shelton, *Bull Durham* features a witty, literate script acted by a superb cast including Kevin Costner, Tim Robbins, and Susan Sarandon. The action centers around the relationships formed by baseball groupie Sarandon (Annie Savoy) who selects both Robbins (as pitcher Nuke Laloosh) and Costner (as veteran catcher Crash Davis) as her pupils in lovemaking, metaphysics, and literature. The result is a sexy film that chronicles two national pastimes and presents the game in human terms devoid of cliché.

Another 1988 effort that also contributed much to the genre was John Sayles's accomplished version of Eliot Asinof's classic account of the Black Sox scandal entitled *Eight Men Out*. Not only does Sayles bring the dead-ball era to life with true-to-life staging and costumes, but he also composes a script devoid of the usual baseball platitudes. While we are subjected to the inevitable spectre of the street urchin pleading "Say it ain't so" to Joe Jackson, we are treated to excellent performances by an ensemble cast. Especially good are D.B. Sweeney as Jackson, David Strathairn as Ed Cicotte, John Cusack as Buck Weaver, and John Sayles himself as Ring Lardner. Sayles has one of the best scenes in the film as he saunters through the White Sox club car following one of the more obviously "cooked" games and sings, "I'm Forever Blowing Ballgames" to the tune of "I'm Forever Blowing Bubbles." While this complicated story would have been best suited to a miniseries format, *Eight Men Out* stands as perhaps the most intelligent and informed baseball feature film to date. In typical Sayles fashion it is built with a wonderful script and talented cast on a shoestring budget.

In 1989, *Field of Dreams*, starring Kevin Costner, became the 1980s version of *Pride of the Yankees*, both from an emotional and box-office standpoint. Its almost treacly sentimentality and totally unbelievable plot struck a chord with America. Adapted from W.P. Kinsella's novel *Shoeless Joe*, the film explores the meaning of family and the relationship between a father and son through the world of baseball. The magic realism of Kinsella's book is expertly transferred to film as the ghosts of a host of great dead-ball era players, including the banished Black Sox with Shoeless Joe Jackson, visit an Iowa cornfield to play ball. Only those who believe in them can see them play. Costner's character also named Kinsella builds the field after hearing voices that tell him to: "Build it and they will come." It is a film about the role of baseball in our culture, especially as a bridge across the generations. There is not much baseball in the film, and when the ghosts begin playing they even have a clueless Joe Jackson batting right-handed.

Proof positive that baseball movies had come of age was the release of *A League of Their Own* in 1992. This tale of the All American Girls Professional Baseball League of the 1940s combined a stellar

Kevin Costner as Ray Kinsella and James Earl Jones as novelist Terence Mann in the smash hit *Field of Dreams*. Based on W.P. Kinsella's novel *Shoeless Joe*, the film explored baseball as an American institution, a healer of old family wounds, and a supernatural, mythic force.

Right: Kevin Costner with Amy Madigan, who played Costner's long-suffering wife in *Field of Dreams*. Much of the film takes place on the Iowa farm on which the Kinsellas live.

Above: Kevin Costner cemented his growing reputation as box-office star and All-American film hero for the 1980s with his performance as Ray Kinsella in 1989's *Field of Dreams*.

cast with an intelligent script, supplemented with decent action sequences. Tom Hanks is cast as manager Jimmy Dugan, a boozy former star seeking another ticket to the big leagues as a coach or manager. His charges include the likes of Madonna, Rosie O'Donnell, Lori Petty, and his star catcher, played by Geena Davis. The plot of this film hinges both on the shaky status of the league itself and the equally shaky relationship between sisters Davis and Petty. For many this film was an introduction to the very fact that the women's professional league existed at all. If anything, this film is an appropriate tribute to the hundreds of women who played in the pioneering league. Despite the corny ending where one sister defeats the other in the final championship game, the overall effect of the film is one of both discovery of a hitherto ignored part of our National Pastime and a respect for the women who made it happen.

Surely there will continue to be baseball films as long as the game is played. It will always be a suitable and particularly American framework from which to tell stories. Like other film genres, it is kept fresh with new heroes with which each generation can identify; from Elmer the Great to Nuke Laloosh, the game remains the same.

The first known artistic representations of baseball have their origins in early British and American children's literature, where crude games of baseball are shown played on the village green, very much in the tradition of cricket.

The very first image of baseball, or, more accurately, town ball, played in America is a woodcut depicting boys playing ball on Boston Common in front of the Massachusetts state house and its signature gold dome. This illustration dates back to 1834 and is from *The Boys' Book of Sports*. In this picture a pitcher and batter are shown with fielders (including two catchers) and what seems to be a basepath. The game is shown as most fans view it today, namely as a pastoral oasis in an urban society. Were it not for the dome and faint outline of several houses in the background, these boys would be children of the country. However, their presence in downtown Boston is an echo of days to come at ballparks such as Fenway Park.

Popular prints from newspapers and magazines as well as book illustrations were the first sources of baseball art. The renowned printmakers Currier and Ives made at least two baseball prints, including the monumental *The American National Game of Baseball at Elysian Fields, Hoboken, N.J.* It is this color lithograph that is the most vivid and engaging vision of early baseball.

Not only is the layout and configuration of the diamond depicted, but crowds are shown surrounding a field where order and decorum rule the nation's newly developed pastime. One of America's lasting images of the game is also formulated here. Members of the white team are shown both in the field of play

The first known image of baseball in America, a group of boys playing. This 1834 illustration is excerpted from *The Boys' Book of Sports*.

This Currier and Ives print of a famous 1865 game in Hoboken, New Jersey, between the Atlantics and the Mutuals is, for many, the strongest existing image of early baseball.

Above: The Baseball Player, Douglas Tilden's great 19th-century sculpture, graces Golden Gate Park.

and as a team unit, impeccably dressed and posed in their best daguerreotype poses on the sidelines. Even the spectators are well dressed and orderly. Surely this was a game to be played and enjoyed by gentlemen. Following the rapid growth of the game, many noteworthy American artists attempted baseball paintings with varying degrees of success. Artists such as David Gilmour Blythe, William Morris Hunt, John La Farge, George Luks, George Bellows, Charles Dana Gibson, and Thomas Eakins painted baseball subjects.

It is Eakins's 1875 painting entitled *Baseball Players Practicing* that is considered by many to be baseball's first great masterpiece. Eakins, an athlete himself, depicted many sporting scenes during his career, notably rowing and boxing. The Philadelphia resident also was a regular visitor to the Jefferson Street Grounds, where he watched the then Philadelphia Athletics of the National Association. What he found at this ramshackle ballpark were players who "were very fine in their build. They are the same stuff as bullfighters only bullfighters are older and a trifle stronger perhaps." Eakins depicts these players in classic baseball poses that seem as timeless as the figures of ancient Olympians on a Grecian urn.

Another heroic representation of 19th-century baseball is Douglas Tilden's monumental bronze sculpture entitled *The Baseball Player*. This work, which is located in San Francisco's Golden Gate Park, depicts a pitcher preparing to deliver the ball. His rigid posture and determined look give him the look of a warrior. Replace the ball with a saber and the baseball uniform with military garb and you would have a sculpture of a Zouave from the Civil War.

It is the creation of such a sculpture that marks the transition of the public attitude towards athletes. Once regarded as mere tradesmen, athletes (particularly baseball players) were now being viewed in more classical terms as ideals of American manhood. With no wars left to fight save for the last frontier skirmishes, the nation wanted heroes of a different sort.

Similar images of ballplayers are seen on a much smaller scale in the work of sculptor Isaac Broome. In his ceramic piece entitled *Baseball Vase*, Broome depicts players in a variety of heroic poses as they hit, throw, and field. This work was created for the 1876 United States International Exhibition—The Centennial—held in Philadelphia. Broome's piece was created as a national symbol depicting our love of competition. The democracy of the United States as represented by the three figures is directly related to the democracy of antiquity symbolized by the classical design of the urn. The eagle perched atop the urn is the symbol of the new nation. This is the first work that shows baseball as a symbol of American identity.

Among the many mass-produced artistic images of baseball were the woodcut illustrations included in publications such as

Issac Broome's ceramic sculptures on baseball were among the first artworks to identify baseball as part of the emerging American identity. This piece is Broome's *The Catcher*.

This *Harper's Weekly* woodcut is an excellent example of how baseball was infiltrating the way of life in America.

Harper's Weekly, Frank Leslie's Illustrated Newspaper, and *The New York Clipper.* Such images documented the growth of the game for a public eager to learn of its newfound heroes. Among the first of these images was a two-page spread from *Harper's Weekly* in 1859 showing fans viewing a game from carriages and tents upon the manicured lawns of the Elysian Fields in Hoboken, New Jersey Historians consider this to be one of the first prints depicting adults playing baseball.

In 1874 *Harper's Weekly* once again published a significant visual documentation of early baseball with an important series of prints chronicling baseball's first international tour. This tour, which featured the Boston Red Stockings and Philadelphia Athletics, took place in Great Britain and Ireland before curious and skeptical crowds of cricket enthusiasts. These prints showed ballplayers as gentlemanly archetypes and ambassadors not just of baseball but of a newly unified United States.

With the dawning of a new century, the popularity of baseball and the art that celebrated it skyrocketed. World renowned artist George Bellows—a former schoolboy all-star shortstop from Columbus, Ohio—found baseball and other sports such as boxing to be a favorite subject. He first attracted attention with such boxing paintings as *Stag at Sharkey's* and *Both Members of This Club.* In his powerful 1906 drawing entitled *Take Him Out,*

Bellows captures the raw, dark energy of an unruly crowd watching a ballgame at a key juncture in the action. The artist has probably depicted the denizens of gambler's row, a familiar haunt in many ballparks of the era. Bellows just catches a whiff of the underside of the National Pastime in this image of the "less than Elysian Fields" of early 20th-century major-league baseball.

In *Three Base Hit*, James Daugherty has combined futurist and cubist techniques to capture an especially dynamic and nonpastoral view of baseball. It is baseball as seen through a kaleidoscope. The increased speed of the game and the coming element of power hitting are depicted here. The artist also intended to make a statement regarding the lowly status of American art at the time. It was around the time of this painting that artists such as Picasso, Matisse, and Braque were making

James H. Daugherty crafted this lovely *art nouveau* piece entitled *Three Base Hit*. One can almost hear the roar of the home crowd as the graceful motion on the canvas echoes the beauty of the game. Many artists have tried to capture the essence of the sport.

Right and above: Norman Rockwell is renown for capturing bits of everyday American life and translating it into a delightful piece that evokes something in all who view it. This work, entitled *The Dugout,* was also used as a cover for *The Saturday Evening Post.*

their impact upon American artists. Daugherty is having fun with the painting while making a dramatic graphic statement about the future direction of American art (and unintentionally baseball) at the same time.

Many baseball paintings were created merely to reflect the ambience, character, and joy of the game. Among these works and among the more famous baseball paintings are the Norman Rockwell illustrations commissioned for *The Saturday Evening Post.* His painting entitled *The Dugout*—which appeared in the *Post* on Sept. 4, 1948—is a portrait of the very heart and soul of the Chicago Cubs franchise, summing up decades of frustration. Here the visitors' dugout at Braves Field serves as the setting for another typical Cubs drubbing as the players and coaching staff sit in disheveled bewilderment. The crowd seated behind the visitors' dugout delights in their inadequacy while showering them with invective and derisive laughter. In this painting the Cubs become "everyteam," therefore inviting our sympathy and reminding us that baseball is defined more by failure than success. One year after painting this illustration, Rockwell executed another *Post* commission entitled *Bottom of the Sixth*, which shows a more anecdotal image of the game. Here three umpires consider game-threatening rainfall while rival coaches argue over the possible outcome of their decision. Rockwell captures both the humor of baseball as well as our lasting image of umpires everywhere.

Claes Oldenburg's monumental 20-ton, 100-foot-tall sculpture entitled *Batcolumn*, installed in downtown Chicago, is a tribute both to baseball itself and to the storied baseball tradition of the Windy City. The sculpture, crafted of a latticework of 1,608 diamond-shaped pieces of steel, is baseball's version of the Washington Monument. Even the late Richard J. Daley,

This larger-than-life sculpture gives new meaning to the phrase, "Walk softly and carry a big stick!" Located in Chicago, Illinois, this towering work seems fitting for "The City of Big Shoulders."

Since baseball first began, artists have tried to capture the game on canvas. This holds true even in modern works. According to pop artist Andy Warhol, Tom Seaver was a worthy representation of the glorious sport.

Right: Eight years after artist Andy Warhol captured the likeness of Tom Seaver, he chose Pete Rose as a subject. One could argue that Warhol seems to think that Charlie Hustle was the epitome of the Cincinnati team.

former Chicago mayor and White Sox fanatic who was hardly known as a fan of modern art, loved the piece that stands in front of the Great Lakes Program Center.

Fellow pop artist Andy Warhol also found inspiration in baseball subjects. His portraits of ballplayers include Pete Rose and Tom Seaver. Rose is shown in true pop art fashion in an enlarged baseball card, an appropriate pose for a player who will be remembered for his mercenary instincts and for his head-first slide. On the other hand Seaver is shown in an understated pose, reflecting on his craft and career.

Vincent Scilla is an artist who combines both representational and pop elements in his work. His portrait of Warren Spahn,

Left: Artist Vincent Scilla liked to play visual tricks on viewers of his work. Here his portrait of Warren Spahn is accented by the use of the Hebrew National hot-dog billboard.

entitled *Hebrew National,* depicts the Braves southpaw against the backdrop of a Hebrew National hot-dog billboard. A similar canvas entitled *Hit the Hat and Win Five Bucks* shows an African American posed in his stance alongside a wall that includes the symbol of Cream of Wheat cereal. In both paintings the artist shows baseball in a landscape of American vernacular imagery where the players also become a part of that landscape.

Working in a more traditional style is Lance Richbourg, a painter who is the son of a former major-league outfielder of the same name. Many of Richbourg's paintings pay homage to the heroes of the game, shown usually in heroic poses or dramatic action sequences. His portrait of New York Giants manager John McGraw shows the man players feared perched atop the end of an old-fashioned iron batting cage watching his men take their licks. His pose is not unlike that of a ship's captain at the helm or a conductor surveying a symphony orchestra. Richbourg has captured both the grandeur and the rugged texture of the so-called golden age of the National Pastime. His portrait of Roy Campanella captures the awesome

Above: Another piece by Vincent Scilla. He delighted in taking the ordinary and giving it a twist, often using stadium billboard advertisements as backgrounds.

power and presence of the catcher who captured MVP Awards before becoming paralyzed as the result of an auto accident.

Also working in a representational style is Andy Jurinko. An accomplished portrait painter, he has completed more than 400 portraits of post-World War II players for a volume that will be baseball's first illuminated manuscript. He also is recognized for his mural-sized paintings of such ballparks as Fenway Park, Tiger Stadium, Yankee Stadium, Shea Stadium, Braves Field, Wrigley Field, and Ebbets Field. Jurinko is one of the game's great history painters. In the tradition of this 19th-century genre, his work celebrates the game and painstakingly portrays the players and the ballparks.

Thom Ross is a history painter who portrays baseball as part narrative, part national myth. He has created paintings and sculptures that depict many of the game's heroic players and moments. His sculpture of Willie Mays depicts the Giant superstar making his immortal catch off Vic Wertz in the 1954 World Series. Ross has created this sculpture as a five-panel work, which gives the impression of time-elapsed photography. The sculpture has been installed in venues such as Cooperstown and Yellowstone National Park.

Painter Michael Schacht also brings a strong historical perspective to his work. A distant relative of baseball's one-time clown prince Al Schacht, Michael paints in a bold colorful style

Above: With it's vivid color and rich detail, *Twilight at Shea* almost seems to be a photo. Artist Andy Jurinko is one of the game's great history painters. In the best tradition of this 19th-century genre, his work both celebrates the game and portrays the players and the ballparks.

Like poetry in motion. Thom Ross has created this sculpture of Willie Mays as a five-panel work. The images seem to bring to life the magic that was Mays. This work has been installed in a variety of venues.

that practically makes his portraits veritable pictograms of the game. His portrait of Willie Mays concentrates on the most basic of stylistic elements and is an elegant portrayal of the "Say Hey Kid."

No chronicle of baseball painters would be complete without mention of the work of Ralph Fassanella. Originally a union organizer in New York, Fassanella paints in a primitive style reminiscent of Grandma Moses. His ballplayers are as proletarian as the workers he once organized. They play in ballparks that are much like factories. He depicts players as workers in an environment where their lives seem to approximate those of the working people shown watching them from the stands.

Photography has also been a major medium of artistic expression for the National Pastime. It was the first sport in America to be extensively chronicled by photographers. The first baseball photographs date from the 1850s and are mostly studio portraits of players. With the development of better equipment, the camera moved outside to the diamond itself and began to capture the essence of the game. Baseball photography came into its own following the turn of the century, and photographers such as Francis P. Burke of Chicago and Charles M. Conlon of New York were its first great masters.

Burke specialized in portraits of teams and individuals, with some action work as equipment and working conditions allowed. His portraits are austere and beautifully composed. Burke had a tremendous rapport with players; he shows them at ease near the batting cages and dugouts, revealing the humanity of the players. Conlon also composed portraits that are still considered the standard. His work transcended that of any sports photographer of his era, and the majority of his photographs are now considered works of art. His action photos were ahead of their time in terms of composition and content. His famous shot of Ty Cobb sliding into third in a cloud of dust is considered to be one of baseball's greatest photographs.

After equipment advances allowed the camera to move to where the action was, people have been recording windows of time. Charles M. Conlon, the creator of this wonderful shot of Ty Cobb, was one of the first great masters of this medium.

His portraits of players from the first three decades of this century are the most accomplished visual record of major-league baseball extant. Not only are they valuable research tools but, like the Civil War photographs of Matthew Brady, allow the viewer to encounter the subjects as human beings. His use of extreme close-ups invite such intimacy and do away with telltale trappings such as caps or bats. Conlon knew his audience was already familiar with the accomplishments of his subjects and wanted to present his viewers with a more personal look at their heroes.

Right: Pulitzer Prize-winning photographer Dick Thompson snapped this unusual shot of Ted Williams. Like other great photographers, Thompson realized there was more to taking exceptional pictures than simply pointing a camera. He often would relax the subject by telling a joke or story and was thus able to capture on film something that transcended the ordinary.

Opposite page: With the advent of color photography in the 1930s and '40s, this medium gained quick popularity. Ozzie Sweet's work graced more covers of *Sport* than anyone else. We can see evidence of his talent in this portrait of Roberto Clemente. The somber pose of the player in his uniform also gives us a glimpse of the person inside. Hat over his heart, Clemente gave his life trying to bring relief to others. Although there is no way Sweet could have foreseen the future, this photo seems to say otherwise.

Leslie R. Jones of *The Boston Herald* was another photographer whose work transcended reportage. His portraits of Ted Williams as a rookie in 1939 capture the brash intensity of the young slugger. Jones, like all photographers of his era, relied not only on his keen eye and technical skill but also on an astute sense of public relations to get the shots he wanted. In order to get Williams (or any other player) to sit long enough for a portrait, Jones had to elicit a laugh with a joke or tell a good story while setting up the shot. These images and those of Dick Thompson, the Pulitzer Prize-winning photographer of *The Boston Herald American*, show the importance of such skills. Both men covered one of the most competitive baseball beats in the country and created many memorable baseball photographs.

With the development of color photography in the late 1930s and early 1940s, the new medium increasingly became a staple of magazine illustration. The master sports photographer of this era was Ozzie Sweet, who shot more covers for *Sport* magazine than anyone and filled the pages of that and other

Walter Iooss Jr. was able to capture the emotion of a close play at the plate in this great photo.

magazines with images that made athletes appear as glamourous as Hollywood stars. Sweet, who had appeared as an extra in several Hollywood westerns, understood how the star-making machinery worked and shot portraits with an unmistakable sense of craftsmanship and style. Unlike the portraits by Conlon and Burke, Sweet's portraits reflected the new status of athletes as superstars and marketable entities. Despite their glamour, his portraits never fail to reveal the human qualities of the subjects. If only through a faint smile or expression, they are shown enjoying their role both as Sweet's subject and as an object of public attention.

Among the photographers who share both the documentary instincts of Conlon and the aesthetic sense of Sweet are Robert Riger, Walter Iooss Jr., Scott Mlyn, John Weiss, and Henry Horenstein. Each has authored noteworthy book-length photo essays on baseball. In Riger's collaboration with Branch Rickey, *The American Diamond*, the photographer (who is also an accomplished artist) captures the great players of the 1950s and 1960s in action and portrait shots. His action photos capture the unique body language of each player.

Much in the spirit of Riger's work are the color photographs of Walter Iooss Jr. In his volume entitled simply *Baseball*, he presents a portfolio of his best baseball images culled from work from *Sports Illustrated* combined with a narrative text by the nonpareil Roger Angell. Iooss alternately deals with the quiet, reflective moments and momentous occasions of the game. Such photographs range from a shot showing a batting-practice pitcher filling a ballbag to Reggie Jackson in the Yankee clubhouse following his historic three-homer explosion in the final game of the 1977 World Series. Like many of his noteworthy predecessors, Iooss is both a reporter and an artist.

Walter Iooss Jr.'s work, which includes shots like this wonderful display of Harmon Killebrew's batting form, prove him an exceptional artist.

Scott Mlyn focuses exclusively on the behind-the-scenes workings of the game in his photo-essay entitled *Before The Game*. The photographs in this book capture the informal world of ballplayers as they prepare to play. Mlyn depicts players reading their mail in the clubhouse, taking treatment in the trainer's room, and cavorting on the field. Here is a world unknown to most fans but as familiar as the world of any playground or school locker room. Mlyn's photo-essay is a ticket to a world where the athlete's code has always been, "What you see here, what you say here, let it stay here when you leave here."

A photo-essay with an equally appropriate title is *The Face of Baseball* by John Weiss. The color portraits of Weiss share much with the extreme close-up portraits shot by Conlon over half a century before. Weiss truly gives his viewers an up close and

Photos like this one of Ted Williams with ex-teammates at Fenway Park in 1992 are the trademark of Henry Horenstein. His work spans the globe, adding a richness and depth that others miss.

personal experience as they are treated to an array of dugout portraits of players of both leagues from the 1980s. Horenstein's *Baseball Days*, written with Bill Littlefield, documents baseball as both a national and international pastime. He is one of the first photographers to travel to Latin America to document its rich baseball culture. Throughout his work Horenstein's color photographs plumb the geography, both literally and figuratively, of the game.

The landscape and architecture of baseball has been best captured by photographer Jim Dow in a series of panoramic photographs of major-league and minor-league ballparks. In most instances these parks are shown empty, a mode that forces us to focus on the form, function, and soul of the park. With his keen eye and penchant for shooting parks from interesting and unpredictable perspectives, Dow reminds us why we treasure ballparks.

Music has always played a major role in sports, from the playing of national anthems to the fight songs resounding at college sporting events. Music is as much a part of the ritual of most sporting events as the pregame warm-up or television timeout.

Baseball has a rich and varied musical heritage that goes far beyond the well-known standard "Take Me Out to the Ballgame." The first sheet music devoted to the game dates back to the 1840s. The game would emerge as a true national pastime partially through the efforts of Tin Pan Alley.

In his monumental work *Everything Baseball*, author James Mote lists hundreds of baseball song sheets, both recorded and unrecorded. Mote notes that "in the 19th century, published sheet music enjoyed a prominence in the American marketplace that is all but forgotten today. In the years before the phonograph was invented, the parlor piano was virtually a standard piece of furniture in the American home. Nightly sing-alongs were a ritual in many families of those days, and sheet music, which sold for pennies each, was accumulated for all occasions and tastes."

From waltzes and two-steps to ballads, the variety of early baseball music was astounding. Baseball even had a budding composer (and dentist) in Chicago White Sox pitcher Doc White, who composed several nonbaseball songs that appeared in sheet music. His composition "Little Puff of Smoke" was written with the help of Chicago sportswriter Ring Lardner.

Former Detroit Tiger infielder and manager George Moriarty would become the first major leaguer to earn membership in the American Society of Composers, Authors and Publishers. Among

In days gone by, sheet music like "Oh You Babe" was all the rage.

Fans could pay homage to the Babe, a favorite musical topic, by singing his song.

Babe Ruth was the subject of several popular songs in his playing days.

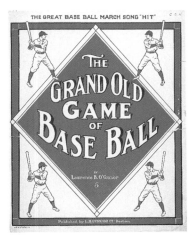

"The Grand Old Game of Base Ball" was written by Lawrence O'Connor in 1912.

his credits were "I Can't Miss That Ball Game," "Little Alligator Bait," and "Remember Me to My Old Gal." Moriarty became a major-league umpire, serving for many years.

Many songs assumed the role of team anthem. In the instance of the 1903 Boston Pilgrims—who became the Red Sox—a popular tune of the day entitled "Tessie" was sung by their fans at every game. Often lyrics were changed to taunt the opposition, as was the case in the first World Series, also in 1903, where Pirate shortstop Honus Wagner was derisively serenaded on a constant basis. Wagner batted over one hundred points under his career average for the Series with a .222 average, and his Pirates lost by five games to three in the best-of-nine Series.

In 1908 vaudeville performer Jack Norworth composed the song that is probably the best known in America after "Happy Birthday" and "The Star-Spangled Banner." While riding on a subway, he noticed a sign advertising a Giants game at the Polo Grounds. Immediately he began writing down a draft of "Take Me Out to the Ballgame," and after nearly half an hour he had composed a classic. Ironically Norworth had never been to a baseball game or the Polo Grounds. Norworth's song begot a host of imitators, including a song by George M. Cohan entitled "Take Your Girl to the Ballgame." The yellow scraps of paper upon which Norworth wrote his song are among the treasures at the National Baseball Hall of Fame. It was 34 years after composing baseball's standard song that Norworth finally attended a game at Ebbets Field.

Among baseball's other great hits are those that have been collected by broadcaster and baseball music buff, Warner Fusselle, for his two recorded collections entitled *Baseball's Greatest Hits, Volume 1 & 2*. In these collections, he has assembled a playlist that includes, among others, "Joltin' Joe DiMaggio," "Say Hey (The Willie Mays Song)," "Move Over Babe (Here Comes Henry)," and " I Love

Mickey." The first collections also include the classic reading of *Casey at the Bat* by actor DeWolf Hopper and the classic "Who's On First" dialogue between Bud Abbott and Lou Costello.

Joe Raposa's sentimental ballad "There Used to Be a Ballpark Here" was recorded by Frank Sinatra, and it became one of baseball's great nostalgic paeans. In a similar vein, the song "Heart" from the musical "Damn Yankees" became baseball's great inspirational anthem.

Among contemporary baseball tunes, the songs of Terry Cashman, Steve Goodman, John Fogarty, and Bruce Springsteen have made lasting impressions. Cashman's series of "Talkin' Baseball" songs have become standards second only to the venerable "Take Me Out to the Ballgame" in terms of fan recognition. Cub diehard Goodman penned his "Dying Cub Fan's Last Request" shortly before both the Cubs 1984 division championship and his own premature death of cancer. Creedence Clearwater Revival veteran Fogarty scored a hit in 1985 with "Centerfield," a song still played in most every major-league and minor-league park before every game. Springsteen's "Glory Days," while not a traditional baseball song, is about a former star pitcher and the passage and toll of time. Even several classical composers such as Charles Ives and William Schuman adopted baseball themes in their work. Ives penned a piano composition based on variations of the old baseball tune "Over the Fence is Out," and Schuman wrote the score for an opera based on the poem *Casey at the Bat.*

Among the more musically inclined major leaguers who have plied their hobby "professionally" are slugger-doo-wop singer Lee Arthur Maye, pitcher-organist Denny McLain, outfielder-crooner Tony Conigliaro, basestealer-singer Maury Wills, and Hall of Famer-country musician Dizzy Dean. This hardball quintet would be backed up by either the Gashouse Gang Cardinals with Stan

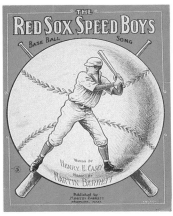

"The Red Sox Speed Boys," a satire of the perpetually slow-footed Boston Red Sox, was written by Massachusetts natives Henry Casey and Martin Barrett and published in 1907.

Lou Gehrig starred in a 1938 musical western entitled *Rawhide.*

Musial on harmonica, the Brooklyn Dodger Sym-Phony led by fan extraordinaire Hilda Chester, the Boston Braves troubadours, or ex-Oakland Athletics vice president—as a teenager under owner Charlie Finley—(formerly M.C.) Hammer.

Baseball's theatrical history is also extensive but without much distinction, save for notable hits such as "Damn Yankees" and "Bleacher Bums." Although there have been more than 50 plays devoted to the National Pastime, only those mentioned above and several others have made it out of theater's "minor leagues," namely the Off Broadway and dinner-club circuit. The reason for this failure lies in the fact that baseball talk alone cannot hold a mainstream audience for very long. Also, baseball by its very nature requires space, preferably the expanse of a ballpark, to aid in telling the story. The game is still waiting for a monologue production, a genre in keeping with the game's oral tradition. It is not hard to imagine a show starring Casey Stengel in the style of the successful Mark Twain and Harry Truman Broadway productions.

For many years, starting at the end of the 19th century, players would supplement their incomes by acting in vaudeville. Stars such as Christy Mathewson and Babe Ruth were lured by the promise of easy money to the stages of the home cities. In more recent times, players such as Don Drysdale and Willie Mays have appeared on network sitcoms, and the voices of stars such as Wade Boggs and Don Mattingly were even used on an episode of *The Simpsons*.

Not only have former players made it as part-time actors, but they have nearly taken over the broadcasting of the game on television, beginning with former Cleveland player Jack Graney. Among the most renowned of the player-broadcasters have been Dizzy Dean, Bob Uecker, Joe Garagiola, Phil Rizzuto, Bill White, Ralph Kiner, Lou Boudreau, Ken Harrelson, Herb Score, Duke Snider, Jim Kaat, Steve Blass, and Tim McCarver.

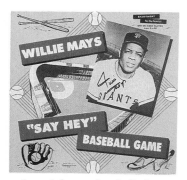

Several famous baseball players have had baseball board games marketed bearing their names, and Hall of Famer Willie Mays was one of them.

The film box for *Babe Ruth: King of Swat*, one of many films made about or featuring the oft-photographed Ruth during his playing days.

On one evening in 1989 the famed international auction house of Sotheby's sold an astonishing $269.5 million worth of art at their New York gallery. Within a month of that sale, the same auction house would bring the gavel down on items such as Bobby Bragan's 1943 Brooklyn Dodger uniform, Charlie Dressen's 1952 Dodger jersey, and a bevy of baseball cards and other assorted hard-ball memorabilia. In the space of less than two decades, the hobby of baseball-card and memorabilia collecting had left the flea markets and yard sales of America to become big business.

The appearances of baseball demigods such as Ted Williams and Johnny Bench on the Home Shopping Network and QVC, once unthinkable, is now routine. When Simon and Garfunkle asked, "Where have you gone, Joe DiMaggio," it is hard to believe they imagined the Yankee Clipper seated amidst accountants and memorabilia show promoters signing a single autograph for the equivalent of a week's wage for a school teacher.

Baseball cards such as the famed Honus Wagner T-206 tobacco card have sold for prices normally reserved for Old Master paintings. When Los Angeles Kings owner Bruce McNall and Kings superstar Wayne Gretzky purchased a near-mint version of the card for $450,000, the news made wire services around the planet.

The financial boom in modern-day baseball (with million-dollar-per-season utility infielders) has been more than matched by a similar boom in the baseball collectibles market. Baseball collecting, once the province of children with enough pocket

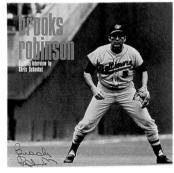

Above and below: Even the most unlikely personalities sometimes become recording artists—like Hall of Fame third baseman Brooks Robinson. Robinson, unlike most players, stayed with Baltimore his entire career, avoiding the need to change addresses each year. Some frequent travelers, like Harry Simpson and Bob Seeds, were even called "Suitcase."

Above: Autographed baseballs, treasured by fans and prized by collectors, have been a critical part of the game's iconography for almost as long as the game itself has existed.

Below: The spikes of Hall of Famer Tom Seaver. Bret Wills's book *Baseball Archaeology* presented baseball memorabilia as the fine art it is.

change for a wax pack or game program, is now the domain of the huckster and card dealer. The irony of the current sports-collecting hobby is that it is just such people that fans were seeking to escape from when they began watching baseball and collecting cards and memorabilia in the first place. Depending on one's view, the baseball-collecting hobby either reached a new high or low when actor Charlie Sheen purchased for over $90,000 the baseball that eluded Bill Buckner at the finish of the crucial sixth game of the 1986 World Series. The press coverage of the auction in which this ball was purchased rivaled the coverage afforded any single game that year.

The first baseball collectibles were items such as scorebooks with hand-tipped photographs of players, like those issued by the Boston Red Stockings in the early 1870s. The first baseball cards would be introduced in 1887 by Goodwin and Company of New York City. Their cards were studio photographs of players hand-tipped onto cardboard and issued under the brand names of Old Judge, Gypsy Queen, and Dog's Head. Players were depicted in staged action poses on these cards and were shown catching balls suspended by strings or "sliding" against a studio carpet.

Both these first cards and subsequent issues were created to help sell products such as tobacco, candy, ice cream, hot dogs, dog food, cookies, potato chips, beer, and bread. Among the most beautiful sets ever issued were the 1911 T-3 Turkey Red cards. Now prized collectors' items, these cards were initially obtained by mailing coupons from Turkey Red, Old Mill, and Fez brand cigarettes. Their large size (5¾" × 8") and gorgeous color lithography make the 125-card set (100 baseball players and 25 boxers) one of the most difficult to complete in the collecting hobby. Other attractive sets include tobacco cards from the pre–World War I era, such as Ramly, Mecca Double Folders, Hassan Triple Folders, and Fatima Team Cards. Later sets such as Diamond Kings, Big League Chewing Gum (Goudey), Play Ball, and Bowman are also among the most colorful and desirable sets for collectors.

The billion-dollar industry of baseball-card collecting has grown tremendously in the past decade. Mark Larson, an associate editor at *Sports Collectors Digest*, a weekly baseball and sports collecting magazine, estimates there are nearly 1.5 million serious baseball-card and memorabilia collectors in America. Baseball card collecting has risen to become the third-most popular hobby in America, behind stamp and coin collecting. Larson estimates the average collector spends well over $300 per year on the hobby.

For the multitude who either entered the hobby too late to obtain the objects they desire or simply don't have the money to invest in baseball items, there is always the Hall of Fame. Baseball cards and a dazzling array of other baseball memorabilia can be seen at the National Baseball Hall of Fame in Cooperstown. Baseball is also a very large part of many other sports museums across the country, such as Baltimore's Babe Ruth Museum, the San Diego Hall of Champions, The Canadian Baseball Hall of Fame, and The Sports Museum of New England. There are even museums located in ballparks, such as Comiskey, Busch, and the Ballpark in Arlington.

Baseball will remain a staple of our popular culture and central to our national identity. In a world that seems to grow smaller and more homogenized every year, the game of baseball remains one American institution, along with rock 'n' roll, that is widely imitated but never duplicated. There is solace in the knowledge that three strikes make an out, 90 feet is the distance between each base, and that until the final out is recorded the game can last literally forever. Our National Pastime is both an art form, artifact, and national treasure. Play Ball!

Hermes Ice Cream had pins manufactured to celebrate the success (and capitalize on) the world champion Pittsburgh Pirates. Promotional giveaways have become a staple of modern baseball.

Brooks Robinson's Orioles jersey, which he wore for 23 seasons.